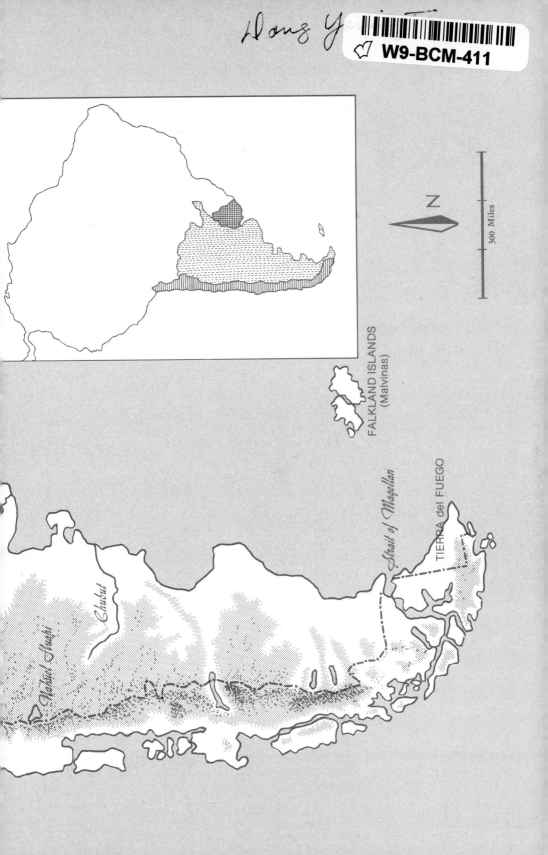

N

300 Miles

FALKLAND ISLANDS
(Malvinas)

Strait of Magellan

TIERRA del FUEGO

Chubut

Nahuel Huapi

The American Foreign Policy Library

Edwin O. Reischauer, Editor

The United States
and the
Southern Cone
Argentina, Chile, and Uruguay

Arthur P. Whitaker

Harvard University Press
Cambridge, Massachusetts, and London, England
1976

Library of Congress Cataloging in Publication Data

Whitaker, Arthur Preston, 1895-
  The United States and the southern cone.
  (The American foreign policy library)
  Bibliography: p.
  Includes index.
  1. South America—Relations (general) with the United
States. 2. United States—Relations (general) with
South America. 3. Argentine Republic—History.
4. Chile—History. 5. Uruguay—History. I. Title.
II. Series.
F2232.2.U6W47   301.29'8'073   76-14400
ISBN 0-674-92841-5

Foreword
by Edwin O. Reischauer

The three southernmost lands of South America — Argentina, Chile, and Uruguay — form a natural grouping in their historical development and relations with the United States. By studying them together, Professor Arthur P. Whitaker has brought more meaning to the study of each. Needing a term that embraces the three together, he has chosen to call them the "Southern Cone," a term that will appeal to anyone with an interest in maps.

The three Southern Cone lands have a climate that is for the most part temperate, in contrast to the tropical or subtropical climates of the rest of Latin America. Their populations are overwhelmingly of pure European stock, in contrast to the heavily Indian, African, and mixed ethnic backgrounds of much of the population in the other lands of Central and South America. They have a more favorable balance between people and land and natural resources than do some Latin American nations. Starting at the end of the nineteenth century, they seemed for a full half century to be leading all of Latin America in economic growth, in progress toward social welfare, and in democracy. But in the past quarter century this bright promise has faded for all three. Their economies have stagnated and even declined. Their social welfare programs have become in part empty promises, unsupported by the necessary economic foundations. Their democracy has been sullied by coups and rampant violence. At times democracy has succumbed entirely to dictatorships. In fact, dictatorship, which once seemed the endemic disease of the rest of Latin America, now shows signs of becoming a recurrent problem for the Southern Cone, just when some of the other lands of Latin America seem to be making progress toward democracy.

The story of the Southern Cone is in one way of very special significance. The other lands of Latin America all have their own fascination, but their distinctive ethnic mixes and historical backgrounds make their national experiences seem somewhat different from those of the lands of Europe and North America. In Argentina, Chile, and Uruguay, on the other hand, we find political, social and economic conditions more like those of North America and Europe, particularly the Latin lands of Western Europe. Their tribulations and failures thus have more relevance for the peoples of North America and Europe and help throw light on the problems of modern times that all these lands face.

Professor Whitaker has devoted the first three parts of his book to careful accounts of three phases in the histories of the Southern Cone nations: the nineteenth century, the half century leading up to World War II, and the period since then. The final fourth part he then devotes to the relations between these three countries and the Unites States, analyzing with clarity the way they have changed over time and have been perceived in different perspectives by the people of these lands and by the citizens of the United States.

This volume is part of The American Foreign Policy Library of the Harvard University Press, which is designed to provide the general reader with perceptive and authoritative accounts of important countries or regions of the world and their relations with the United States. Professor Whitaker has come to his task with the knowledge and wisdom of a lifetime of study of Latin America. This had made it possible for him to combine in this volume a solid mastery of detail with insightful perceptions of general trends. The reader will be rewarded with a sound understanding of how the Southern Cone nations have developed in the past and an informed view of what is going on in these lands today.

Preface

Argentina, Chile, and Uruguay, called the Southern Cone of South America, have important features in common that set them apart from the rest of Latin America, but have never prevailed over the obstacles to their unification as either a political or an economic group. Although some of their common features are older, others of great importance began to take shape a century or so ago as the countries were drawn into the world market economy for the food-stuffs and raw materials they could provide and were further Euro-peanized by immigration. They were rewarded with what then passed for progress and modernization and became in many respects the most advanced of Latin American nations.

Since about 1950, however, all three countries have been beset by economic reverses, social ferment, and political dissension, all of which contributed to the proliferation of guerrilla movements of exceptional strength. A resounding climax in the form of political upheavals was reached in all three countries in the short space of four months from June to September 1973. One result has been to compromise their high standing in Latin America, without solving their basic problems and without bringing them any closer together, even as companions in misery. Another result has been to compli-cate their relations with the outside world, particularly the United States and Western Europe. The capitalist-industrial nations of the Northern Hemisphere, now headed by the United States, had for-merly been regarded in the Southern Cone as promoters of progress; now, they and their growing host of multinational corporations were widely denounced as imperialist exploiters and neocolonialists.

The two concluding chapters discuss the relations of the Southern Cone countries with the United States since independence, with stress on the twentieth century. These relations are examined mainly from the point of view of the United States, partly in conformity with the design of the series to which this book belongs. Another reason is that the role of the United States in the Southern Cone grew from a minor one in most respects until about 1900 to a major one within the next quarter-century. Its role expanded chiefly in the economic and political fields; culturally, Europe was still leading in the Southern Cone. The expansion of the United States' role there in the other fields paralleled and at times anticipated its rise as a world power and superpower. Yet even after its emergence as a superpower, its government's efforts to influence the course of events in the Southern Cone countries succeeded only when strongly supported by key elements among their own people, as illustrated by the contrasting cases of "Nazi-fascist" Juan Perón of Argentina in the 1940s and Marxist Salvador Allende of Chile in the early 1970s.

The intervening chapters between the first and the last two are designed to illuminate the relationship between these countries and the United States by describing their domestic development and sketching selected aspects of their relations with one another and the outside world since independence. Chronologically, the emphasis here, as in the rest of the book, is on the twentieth century. Emphasis is also laid on comparisons of the three countries with one another in a great variety of significant respects: social, economic, cultural, and political. Along with strong resemblances, comparison also reveals sharp contrasts, none more striking than that offered by the upheavals of 1973 referred to above. These produced a thinly veiled military dictatorship in Uruguay and a brazen one in Chile — countries that had for decades been generally acknowledged leaders of Latin America in social welfare and stable democratic systems, free from interference by their armed forces. In Argentina, however, which had been a generation behind the other two in social welfare and a generation ahead of them in political intervention by its armed forces, the upheaval of 1973 ended the seven-year tenure of the last of a long succession of military dictatorships and brought in a government headed by one of the foremost pioneers of populist nationalism, Juan Perón. The sequels to early 1976, in both Southern Cone affairs and U.S. policy, are described with the brevity and tentativeness required by the nature of the limited sources available.

I am much indebted to Mark Falcoff, David C. Jordan, and Fredrick B. Pike for reading various parts of this manuscript and giving me sound advice that I hope I had the good sense to profit by, and to Joseph R. Barager for providing me with information from published sources about the armed forces of the Southern Cone countries. I am also grateful to the Foreign Policy Research Institute, Philadelphia, and particularly to Robert L. Pfaltzgraff, Jr., director of the institute, and Robert C. Herber, managing editor of its journal, *Orbis,* for assistance of various kinds; to the University of Pennsylvania, and especially to Associate Director of Libraries Rudolph Hirsch, for the use of a study room in its main library throughout the preparation of this book; and to Edwin O. Reischauer, editor of the Harvard University Press's American Foreign Policy Library, Aida DiPace Donald, its Social Sciences Editor, and Anita Safran, of its editorial staff, for suggestions that improved the book and for help on its way to publication.

April 1976   Arthur P. Whitaker

Contents

PART THREE
From World War II to the Upheavals of 1973
and Their Aftermath

PART FOUR
United States Relations with the Southern Cone

The United States
and the
Southern Cone

I Introduction:
Unity and Diversity in the Southern Cone

Southern Cone is a convenient group designation for Argentina, Chile, and Uruguay. They occupy the southernmost segment of South America, which, with only a little effort, can be seen to form a cone with a northern base narrowing to a tip just below the stormy Strait of Magellan, in the frigid island perversely named Land of Fire (Tierra del Fuego) by its discoverers. No other designation would be as apt, for these three countries have never formed a separate unit of any kind — political, economic, or cultural — apart from the rest of Spanish America.

Resemblances and Ties

Although the towering Andes separate Argentina and Chile, and the wide estuary of the Plata River and its tributary, the Uruguay River, lie between Uruguay and Argentina, these countries have had much in common ever since Spaniards began to conquer and colonize that part of America in the 1530s. Chile, for instance, provided some of the first settlers in what is now Argentina and included, until the late eighteenth century, one of present-day Argentina's chief provinces, Mendoza. Conversely, Argentina contributed greatly to the liberation of Chile from Spanish rule with General José de San Martín's expeditionary force, whose passage from Mendoza across the snow-capped Andes in 1817 was a feat comparable to Hannibal's crossing the Alps on his way to conquer Rome, with the important difference that San Martín succeeded. Since independence snapped their common bond of Spanish rule, the two countries have often been at odds with each other, but have remained close in many other ways.

On the other side of Argentina, Uruguay has been described as an Argentine province in Brazilian territory. This saying in turn has been called a grim jest. It may be grim, depending on when and how it is spoken, but it is far from being simply a jest. Uruguay is in fact a territorial extension of Brazil, but was governed from Buenos Aires in the colonial period — as part of a viceroyalty, the last half century. While the viceregal tradition of union has lived on in Argentina, to most Uruguayans the thought of their country's being swallowed up by its big neighbor across the Plata is a nightmare. And yet the people of the two countries are very much alike, more alike than those of any other pair of countries in Latin America. For this reason, as well as because of their proximity, each has always been a favorite sanctuary for refugees from oppression in the other.

As former colonies of Spain and Portugal, respectively, Argentina and Brazil inherited conflicting claims to the territory that is now Uruguay. Brazil actually occupied it for a few years after the beginning of the independence movement in Spanish America, but then had to fight a war with Argentina over it (1825-1828). The upshot was that neither got it and, instead, the disputed territory became the independent state of Uruguay. Ever since, Uruguay has been a kind of Belgium of South America, a buffer between two much bigger and stronger neighbors. All the while it has sought to protect itself by playing them off against each other and they have been rivals for influence in it. They have been rivals in other ways as well, for Brazil too extends into the Plata basin, upstream from Argentina and Uruguay, and generally takes an active part in the basin's affairs. The result has been a constant power struggle, with hardly a let-up, between the two South American giants.

This rivalry on the Atlantic side of South America is also of considerable interest to Chile on the Pacific side. Having its own troubles with Argentina, over their common boundary and other problems, Chile has usually sided with noncontiguous Brazil since the latter changed from empire to republic in 1889. In other and more pleasant ways as well, Chile has long had special ties with its fellow dwellers in the Southern Cone. Its liberal Constitution of 1828 was one of the sources of the provisions in Uruguay's first constitution (1830) guaranteeing individual liberties, establishing social equality, and abolishing *mayorazgos* (entailed estates). A little more than a century later Eduardo Frei, soon to become leader of Chile's Christian Democratic Party and president of the republic, returned the compliment by paying public tribute to Uruguay's "perfect democracy." (That was in the 1940s, before Uruguay's economic stagnation and political deterioration had gone far enough to be visible on the other side of the Andes.)

But why segregate these three from the other fifteen Spanish American countries for special treatment? The question may seem as unanswerable as it is obvious, for they do indeed have much in common with the others, beginning with the prevalence of the Spanish language and the Roman Catholic religion, and dependence on foreign trade, capital investment, and business enterprise.

Yet they also have much in common with each other that differentiates them from the rest. To give only one example at this point, they alone lie either very largely (Argentina and Chile) or wholly (Uruguay) in the temperate zone. They do in fact form a group apart, and this fact stands out in studies by Soviet as well as European and American writers. Thus, in two articles published in Moscow in 1964, Argentina, Chile, and Uruguay were the only Spanish American countries included in two key categories of Latin American countries, one comprising those most advanced in industrial development, the other those in which "united and militant trade-union centers have been established and . . . [are] fighting for national liberation."*

At the same time, our three countries differ widely from each other in certain ways, and stress and strain have often marked their relations with one another, though they have never reached the point of war. Argentina, the largest of the three, and the most populous and strongest since the 1890s, has more than once given or offered military aid to the other two. Yet the most persistent themes in its relations with them have been explosive boundary disputes with Chile and the resistance of little Uruguay to Argentine encroachment by land and water.

The Passing of the Belle Epoque

In the present era it is the resemblances of the Cone countries to each other that stand out most prominently, but they do so for reasons that give cold comfort to anyone living there. From the late nineteenth century they led all Latin America for several decades in the achievement of economic growth, cultural advancement, and political stability under comparatively liberal governments. Since about 1950, however, the roles have been reversed and while other Latin American countries prospered, these three lapsed into economic stagnation and social and political discord marked by mounting violence.

The climax came in 1973 with revolutionary upheavals in all three countries. In Argentina former President Juan Perón returned from an eighteen-year exile and regained power unconstitutionally

---

*The other countries in the industrial list were Brazil and Mexico; in the national liberation list, Brazil, Bolivia, and Costa Rica.

but peacefully by outmaneuvering a military dictatorship that, after seven years, was still unable to cope with the country's manifold problems, which by that time included spreading terrorism. In Uruguay terrorism had the opposite effect, for it precipitated not the end but the beginning of a military dictatorship. The event was particularly shocking to democrats because Uruguay was the first welfare state in the Western hemisphere and had been widely regarded for decades past as a kind of American utopia and, to quote Frei again, a perfect democracy. But the most dramatic upheaval of all was the one in Chile, for it came as the crashing finale of a three-year conflict of ever-increasing bitterness between a minority president, Salvador Allende, who, heading a strong Socialist-Communist coalition, was the first freely elected Marxist chief of state in Latin America, and an anti-Marxist majority in both houses of the Chilean Congress. At last the armed forces intervened and in a single day (September 11, 1973) overturned the government and replaced it with a dictatorship of their own making. Allende died that day—by his own hand, we are told.

The armed forces, it will be noted, played a leading part in all three crises, but there is nothing distinctive about that, for in contemporary Latin America military intervention in the political process is the rule rather than the exception. What is distinctive is the situation out of which all three national crises developed simultaneously. These were the only countries in Latin America's more advanced group that had suffered from a prolonged economic stagnation that years of repeated efforts had failed to overcome.

The contrast between their present misery and the *belle époque* to which the upper classes in all three could look back combined with the frustration of the masses' rising expectations to give all the crises a deep psychological dimension. It also profoundly affected their foreign relations by feeding the flames of nationalism and intensifying demands for structural reform or revolution. These effects were obviously of great domestic significance too, but in this instance the foreign and domestic aspects were linked together closely—indissolubly, in the polemical literature of the champions of change. In the sense of widespread acceptance the linkage was something new and involved a sweeping change of opinion and attitude since World War II.

About the turn of the century a nativistic reaction against foreign economic and cultural influence began to gain ground in these countries. This involved, among other things, a gradual decline of the once dominant economic liberalism and a reversal of the formerly friendly attitude towards foreign investments and business enterprise. Simultaneously there was mounting hostility in each country to its traditional political and social order, of which the members of a small upper class or oligarchy were the rulers and chief beneficiaries.

The linkage of these two movements is best represented by the charge, first widely made in these terms in the 1940s, that the human and natural resources of each country were being exploited by a corrupt alliance between its own "country-selling" (*vendepatria*) oligarchy and foreign imperialists. The conclusion drawn from this charge was, not surprisingly, that the hold of the oligarchy could not be broken without breaking that of the foreign imperialists, and vice versa. In a typical formulation of this view, the noted Mexican novelist and essayist Carlos Fuentes wrote in late 1973 that the recent overthrow of Salvador Allende's left-wing government in Chile would be followed there by the imposition of the "sub-imperialist model" of "booming cities, huge foreign investments, and, behind this false facade of prosperity, stagnation in the hinterland, perpetuation of colonial structures, . . . a progress riddled with debt and bereft of autonomy, internal order at the expense of civil freedoms and national sovereignty."

Race, Class, Culture

Underlying the structural resemblances between the Southern Cone countries are others that have to do with the composition and character of their people. Argentina and Uruguay are most alike in these respects. In ethnic composition they are almost identical: nearly 90 percent white, about 10 percent mestizo (mixed Indian and white), and two percent Indian. Argentina, however, started from a very different and typically Latin American non-white base at the beginning of independence in the early nineteenth century, whereas Uruguay was already largely white. Both countries contained substantial numbers of Negroes, but mestizos (the most numerous element in Argentina), and Indians, also still numerous there, were rare in Uruguay.

What transformed both countries ethnically was massive immigration from Europe, principally from Italy and Spain. Beginning in Uruguay, it reached its peak in Argentina in the decade before the outbreak of World War I in 1914 and was renewed on a still large scale from the end of the war until 1930, when the Great Depression brought it to a close except for occasional spurts after World War II. As in the United States, most of the Indians were killed off or (in Argentina) bottled up in reservations. The Negroes disappeared almost completely, in ways and for reasons that are not yet entirely clear. In the epidemics of yellow fever and smallpox that scourged the area their mortality rate was exceptionally high, but gradual absorption through intermarriage seems the most likely explanation. At any rate, both peoples have for decades been not only overwhelmingly white, but also alike in other important respects. They have the highest literacy rates in Latin America (nearly 90 percent) and are very similar in demographic distribution (much more urban than rural and concentrated to an extraordinarily high degree in the capital cities); in economic structure (partly industrial, but still basically agricultural-pastoral); in social structure (a large but fragmented middle class and a large, unionized working class); and in age distribution (in the 1960s, about 28 to 30 percent under 14 years, and 64-65 percent from 15 to 64). For more than half a century both countries have had populations that are homogeneous in many respects and more purely European than the people of the United States.

Chile differs substantially from both Argentina and Uruguay in these and other respects, and yet it resembles them more than it does any other country. Immigration, though never massive as in the other two, was substantial after the 1840s, and the immigrants, who came in considerable numbers from Germany, Great Britain, and France as well as Italy and Spain, contributed greatly to the country's development. Also, Chile has generally stood closer to its two neighbors than to the rest of Latin America in economic development, literacy, and the size and character of its middle class and its organized labor movement.

Of the elements just mentioned, the middle class is the most important. Contrary to a widely held belief, the middle class in all three countries has been a source not of political strength, democracy, and progress but of a pronounced weakness that has had adverse effects in their economic and social life as well. This is the conclusion reached by José Nun in a penetrating analysis of the causes of political instability in Latin America. His predecessor,

Merle Kling, has explained it as a function of the contradiction between the realities of an essentially colonial economy and the political requirements of legal sovereignty. Nun agreed as regards the less developed Latin American countries, but not the small, more advanced group headed by Argentina, Uruguay, and Chile. In his view, the culprit was the middle class, which lacked the homogeneity and cohesion of a true middle class, partly because so many of its members were of foreign origin. These ill-assorted middle-class elements tried to use the masses against the oligarchy, but their chief instrument was the army led by an officer corps drawn largely from the middle class since the turn of the century. Army and middle class are by no means identical, however, in character, interests, and values, and to cap the climax of confusion, both army and middle class have continued to act in the framework of a culture still controlled by the traditional upper class.

In all three countries nationalism is strong but national unity is fragile. This seeming paradox is explained partly by the fact that there are widely different varieties of nationalism, some of them mutually conflicting. The most xenophobic are the most effective, for nothing unites all ranks of society like a call to close ranks against foreigners; it works even when the several segments of society, with their diverse interpretations of nationalism, have responded to the call for quite different reasons. But the spotlight cannot be kept on the wicked foreigner forever, and as soon as it shifts to the domestic scene, unity disintegrates and the rival groups are at each others' throats again.

For the rest, the paradox is explained by a combination of factors. Geography is one of them, though it is more potent in extensive and diversified Argentina and Chile than in much smaller and more compact Uruguay. The latter, on the other hand, has carried institutional fragmentation considerably further than the other two. It has done so by establishing a system of autonomous state institutions which control, among other things, electricity, water, light, fuel, insurance, and banks, and by permitting a similar system to grow up in the private sector of the economy and in the political parties. The result, Aldo Solari pointed out in 1967, has been an increasing atomization of society and an inability to make any but minor changes without a rupture of the system itself.

To mention only one more factor, much of the traditional culture and its values has survived in all three countries. Under this rubric some authorities attribute great weight to the inherited Spanish propensity towards anarchy. The hypothesis is attractive, but it raises the question of whether there is such a thing as national character. Less questionable since it has been documented is the survival of hierarchical and patronal ideas and arrangements that are socially divisive in the modern world. Though perceptible in urban centers, these traditional traits have been most prominent in the rural areas of all three countries — on their farms and ranches, their *haciendas, fundos,* and *estancias.* Even the fiercely independent *gauchos* or cowboys of Argentina and Uruguay and their Chilean counterpart, who rejected all other authority, were obedient to their natural chief, the *patrón.*

The political systems of these countries have always resembled one another in important ways, although all three have changed from time to time and at any given time are much less alike when examined in detail. In main outline they have most of the time been much alike and, while often strongly influenced by other foreign models, have resembled the United States in important respects. All have been based on written constitutions and these have been changed much less frequently than those of most other Latin American countries. They have provided for representative governments which are nominally democratic but have actually been run most of the time by and for the middle and upper classes. Provision has also been made for the separation of executive, legislative, and judicial powers and for the protection of individual rights. All three have operated much of the time under a political party system but with a varying incidence of military dictatorship, which has been highest in Argentina, lowest in Uruguay.

Finally, all of them, at various times since the turn of the century, have made provisions for social welfare. The first to do so, not only of these three but in the hemisphere, was Uruguay, beginning in 1915. Chile's system, started a decade later, was the most comprehensive. Some commentators think that the welfare policies of these countries have been more generous than they could afford and have thus contributed to their economic stagnation. Rejected by others, this proposition has helped to fuel the never-ending controversy over the rival claims of social justice and economic development on the national income.

The question at issue faces all developing countries. In its simplest terms it is whether to save for development or spend for enjoyment.

Authoritarian regimes can easily impose the first alternative, as, for example, the Soviet Union has done since the 1920s and the Franco government of Spain since 1959. In democratic societies, on the other hand, the odds against doing so and surviving are heavy, for the masses are prone to believe that they will have to bear the burden of austerity while its profits will further enrich the upper classes. Once this belief is aroused, it is easily extended to involve the upper classes' foreign associates, thus reinforcing populism with xenophobia.

Populations and Politics

The most obvious of many differences among the Southern Cone countries are those of size in area and population. Argentina, equal in area to the United States east of the Mississippi River, is more than three times the size of Chile, which is nearly five times as large as Uruguay. The gaps in population, though not so great, are nevertheless wide, as they have been throughout the national period. In 1971 Argentina had an estimated population of 23.6 million, Chile 10.0 million, and Uruguay 2.9 million. In the same year there were also substantial differences in birth rate and life expectancy. The excess of births over deaths was only 1.4 per 1,000 population in Argentina and 1.5 in Uruguay, as compared with 2.3 in Chile. On the other hand, in the 1960s life expectancy for males at birth, which was 65.5 years in Uruguay and 63.1 in Argentina, dropped to 58.9 in Chile,* with the result that Chile's population growth did not match its much higher birth rate. The respective population estimates some thirty years earlier had been (in millions): Argentina 13.5 (1941), Chile 5.1 (1942), and Uruguay 2.1 (1940). A comparison of these estimates with those for 1971 shows that Chile's population had gained rather slightly on Argentina's (about 1:2.5 on both occasions) and on Uruguay's only from 2.5:1 to 3:1.

The foregoing figures call for two comments. First, those on life expectancy reflect the fact that, while properly ranked with Argentina and Uruguay among the more advanced Latin American countries, Chile lags somewhat behind the other two in the conditions that make for a long life. Yet shorter life expectancy also makes

---

*In all three countries, add five years for females. In the United States, the corresponding figures were 66.6 and 74.

Chile a younger nation, which has both advantages and disadvantages. In the early 1960s only 4.2 percent of Chile's population was over 65 years of age, as compared with 7.8 percent of Uruguay's and 5.1 percent of Argentina's. On the other hand, Chile was far ahead in the youngest and least productive group, those 14 and under, where the percentages were Chile 40, Argentina 30, and Uruguay 28. In the second place, the figures raise some questions that cannot be answered with certainty. One such is why Chile's population did not gain as rapidly on Argentina's as on Uruguay's despite the fact that Argentina's birth rate was even lower than Uruguay's. An obvious answer would seem to be that Argentina alone of the three received a substantial influx of immigrants in the interval (from about 1940 to 1971). The trouble with that is that most of those immigrants arrived in the late 1940s, which were the Perón regime's sunshine years, and one can only wonder why the economic adversity and political upheavals that plagued Argentina through most of the next twenty years did not have a more adverse effect on its population growth. In Uruguay somewhat similar conditions in a shorter period — the 1960s and early 1970s — led to a population decline.

Differences in development have existed among these countries from the beginning of independence, but Chile has not always lagged behind. In fact, until the close of the nineteenth century it set the pace for all Latin America, thanks to its early achievement of political order and stability and its exploitation and ultimate annexation of provinces rich in nitrates that at first belonged to Bolivia and Peru. About the turn of the century, however, Argentina and Uruguay forged ahead so rapidly that as early as 1910 Chileans were worrying about being left behind. Their country has never caught up. In economic development Argentina has ranked first among the three, followed by Uruguay. One indicator is per capita gross domestic product, which in 1969 was $974 in Argentina, $751 in Uruguay, and $640 in Chile.

Economic development also had a different political and social impact in each country. In Argentina, according to Torcuato Di Tella, nearly all the new industrialists and businessmen were immigrants, who formed a new *burguesía,* or urban upper middle class, and pushed aside the old creole (native) middle class, but could not be bothered to acquire citizenship. As a result, for several decades the country lacked a liberal party capable of offering moderate, legitimized opposition to the entrenched conservatives, whose orientation was rural and upper-class. In more slowly developing Chile, he continues, no such displacement of the old creoles took place. They continued to form the ruling class and Chile continued to be "the Athens of South America as regards democratic evolution," so that from an early stage Chile had the kind of opposition party that Argentina lacked. This may help to explain why, for more than eighty years before 1973, the orderly political process was ruptured only once in Chile, but several times in Argentina and Uruguay. A somewhat similar differentiation between the impact of economic change on Argentina and Uruguay was made in the late 1960s by Aldo Solari.

In social development Uruguay in the 1960s ranked ahead of Argentina by a slender margin, and of Chile by a somewhat wider one. In this case an indicator is enrollment in secondary schools in proportion to population. As Solari points out, limited availability of secondary education serves to perpetuate the elite system of the traditional social order. In secondary enrollment, Uruguay was only one percentage point ahead of Argentina in 1960 (32 and 31, respectively), but was forging ahead rapidly: for the period 1957-1962, its rate of increase was 32 percent to Argentina's 20 percent. Although Chile had the most rapid growth rate (53 percent in that period), it still brought up the rear in 1960, with only 23 percent of the secondary school age group enrolled.

Yet even in Uruguay the ascriptive ties of the traditional order are still strong, the same authority tells us. In both government and the private sector, for instance, whether one gets in and gets on depends on such things as family, club, and political connections (which have been known to count in the United States, too). Standardized examinations are rare, and when they are used they are open only to candidates selected by the criteria just mentioned. Despite such survivals of traditionalism, Solari believes, Uruguay and Argentina are committed to equalitarian ideas to a greater degree than the rest of Latin America. The commitment, primarily expressed in politics and education, is doubtless laudable, but it obviously entails a conflict with the still strong elitism in both countries.

Latent most of the time, this conflict between the old order and the new has occasionally surfaced. It did so conspicuously in Argentina during the first Perón period, 1945-1955, but more strikingly in Chile during Allende's administration, 1970-1973. In Chile, undercommitment to egalitarianism by the ruling classes, and overcommitment to it by the masses, combined to bring on during Allende's term a cold civil war that reached the boiling point in only three years, whereas it took a decade to reach that point in Argentina under Perón.

Politically, the three countries have differed widely in both form and operation, despite the resemblances in these respects suggested above. Social welfare legislation was pioneered by Uruguay three decades, and by Chile two decades, ahead of Argentina. As regards participation in politics, three times as many Argentines as Chileans voted in the national elections of the 1940s and 1950s, although, except that in Chile illiterates could not vote, the basic requirements were substantially the same: manhood suffrage all along, votes for women after the late 1940s, and compulsory voting. As regards political party systems, in the present century Chile has been multiparty, Uruguay bi-party, and Argentina first bi-, then multi-party. Only Chile has had a Marxist government.

A particularly interesting differentiation between Chile's political system and those of the rest of Latin America was made in the 1940s by Alberto Edwards. Rejecting the charge, often made by publicists and historians in other Latin American countries, that Chile had always been a politically backward country, submissive to a monarchical or feudal government and a stain on free, democratic America, he retorted that, on the contrary, the abyss that separated Chile from the rest was by no means one between monarchy or feudalism and democracy, for their systems were simply not democratic; instead, the abyss was between the order and regularity of Chile's society and the anarchy of theirs. To the question why his countrymen had let themselves be governed by a minority for more than a century, he replied that the Chileans, justly called the Englishmen of America, possessed that deference to authority and social discipline which, as Edmund Burke and Walter Bagehot knew, is the necessary basis of free government. Today, Edwards said in conclusion, deference to the oligarchy has been dissipated by the rise of the middle class and the country faces a crisis: a rebellion of the electorate, though not necessarily social dissolution.

A somewhat similar view was taken in 1971 by a North American scholar, W. H. Agor. He describes Chile as a deviant case and compares it favorably with developed political systems in Western Europe. He does not, however, regard Chile as politically unique among Latin American states. Instead, he brackets it with Uruguay and Costa Rica as countries in which the role of the opposition has been substantially legitimized, as shown by the fact that in the past quarter-century opposition parties in each of these countries have won the presidency two or more times and have won more than one-third of the seats in the legislature, and in which there have not been any, or only very brief, periods of unconstitutional rule. Argentina is conspicuously absent from this select group on all counts; at least on the last of them, Chile and Uruguay too will have to be dropped from it in view of the events of 1972 and 1973.

As regards form of government, all three countries have long been centralized republics, though for different periods of time: Uruguay from the beginning of independence, Chile almost as long, and Argentina only since the culmination in the 1930s of a long centralizing process carried out under a nominally federal constitution. A more substantial difference involves the executive power. All three countries have had the presidential system most of the time, but in Uruguay it was twice in this century shelved in favor of a collegial or plural executive somewhat like the Swiss, and Chile around the turn of the century had for more than thirty years a parliamentary system somewhat like the British. Both returned to a form more like that of the United States; Chile in the 1920s, Uruguay (for the second time) in the 1960s. In Chile the powers of the president were still checked by a Congress that has been described as the strongest in Latin America. If anything like that has ever been said of Uruguay's legislature in the present century, it is a minority opinion. In Argentina, presidential preponderance has been maintained from the start and has played an important part in converting Argentina's government from federal to unitary.

Economic Problems and Policies

In all three countries there have been similar developments of the broad outlines of economic policy in the rise and fall of laissez-faire, in the adoption and abandonment of neo-orthodox policy for economic development, and in the expansion of the public sector through government intervention. This expansion, already under way before the Great Depression of the 1930s, received a powerful stimulus from that disaster; and one of the models for it was the Tennessee Valley Authority established in the United States early in that decade. A major purpose of the expansion was to promote economic development, and to that end a new type of government agency, beginning in 1939 with Chile's CORFO, was created.*

Yet, despite these common trends, the economic disparities among the three countries remained wide. In the late 1960s Uruguay had the largest proportion of the labor force working for the government and Argentina the highest concentration of production in companies or agencies under government control. Under Allende, Chile led briefly in both respects, but much of his work was undone after his fall. Per capita income and wages have long been higher in Argentina than in the other two, with the result that over the years it has attracted a considerable number of immigrants from them as well as from its much poorer neighbors, Paraguay and Bolivia.

The agrarian problem, common to all three countries, is believed by many students to be the root cause of their slow economic growth since 1930.† The heart of the problem is generally agreed to be the

---

*For CORFO, see chapter VII. The novelty of this type has been questioned on the ground that some Latin American governments had long since begun trying to promote economic development. There was the important difference, however, that private enterprise was the chosen instrument of the earlier efforts, government action of the CORFO type.

†For a unique feature of Argentina's agrarian problem, see chapter XI.

extremely large proportion of land held by a few owners of great estates, which are often referred to as *latifundios*. Strictly speaking, the term is inappropriate since it connotes the use of servile labor and there are no serfs or slaves in the Southern Cone. There are, however, exploited workers on these estates, and the agrarian problem is social as well as economic. No serious effort at agrarian reform was made in any of the three countries until Chile led the way in the 1960s under President Jorge Alessandri (tentatively) and Eduardo Frei Montalva (in much greater depth). Allende then carried the reform to the stage of revolution, but his extreme measures in this as in other fields were revoked after his overthrow.

Mining has been far more important in the economy and public finance of Chile than of the other two. By comparison, Argentina's mineral production has been very limited and Uruguay's microscopic. In the production of petroleum Argentina has a wide lead, but is not self-sufficient; and Chile is heavily, and Uruguay wholly, dependent on imported oil. In nuclear power, the order is the same: Argentina leading by several lengths, Chile hardly started, and Uruguay left at the gate. Despite several decades of urban and industrial expansion and the handicap of their agrarian problem, all three countries depend heavily on agricultural-pastoral production. Argentina and Uruguay are still large-scale exporters of animal products, as they have been since the late nineteenth century, but no longer of grains. Chile, once an exporter of foodstuffs, has been an importer of them on an increasing scale since mid-century. Chile still has a long lead over the other two as an exporter of wine, much of which goes to the United States, but Argentina has forged far ahead as a producer of wine, ranking among the first five countries of the world in this respect, while Chile ranks fifteenth.

Armed Forces and Nationalism

The interrelation between economics and politics stands out in a comparison of the military in these countries. Since their armed forces took institutional form in the late nineteenth century, they have often played an active and important role in all three, but in different ways and at different times. In none have they possessed monolithic unity more than briefly. As guardians of the constitution, they have most often been defenders of the status quo. In terms of classes, the chief beneficiaries of this defense have been, in chronological order, first upper, then middle class. As their professionalization advanced, the armed forces developed an *esprit de corps* and identity that enabled them to function effectively as a power group.

The widest differences among the military establishments of the three countries in the twentieth century have been with respect to their intervention in politics. In Uruguay there was almost no intervention at all from the end of the civil war of 1904 to 1970, except for a comparatively brief and mild one during the depression of the 1930s. In the late 1960s, however, the Tupamaro guerrillas' protracted campaign of revolutionary violence combined with other problems to bring about a military interference that broadened into a virtual takeover of the government in 1973.

The armed forces of Chile and Argentina were politicized earlier than Uruguay's. Professionalization, well begun by 1900, stimulated increasing recruitment of the officer corps from the middle classes. Paradoxical though it may seem, the lead in politicizing them was taken by liberal parties—by the Radicals in Argentina from about 1900 on, and by the Liberal Alliance in Chile in the 1920s. This was done on the plausible ground that there was no other way to break the hold of an entrenched oligarchy that would not let itself be voted out of power, and the strong middle-class element in both political groups and officer corps must have made it easier for all of them to be satisfied with that justification.

Another factor favoring the armed forces' intervention in politics was the stress laid on the study of national economic and social as well as military problems in war colleges for officers of middle and higher grades. Not unnaturally, such exercises tended to foster among the officer corps a sense of responsibility for the solution of those problems and a belief in their own competence to handle them, especially since there was almost no comparable analysis of national problems in the universities or other civilian institutions. This factor had most weight in Argentina, where matters of this kind received most attention in the higher education of officers. To be sure, in all three countries there was also the contrary pull of a military tradition of nonintervention in politics, and the tradition was reinforced by professionalization, a basic principle of which was that the armed forces must confine themselves to their proper function of guarding national security. But was it to be guarded by military force alone? As the century wore on, the conviction spread that much more was needed. Identifying the need started a process of expansion of military functions paralleling the contemporary one of government intervention in the economic and social welfare fields, and the intervention begun earlier in the field of education.

The expansion of the proper function of the military in public affairs began in the economic field on the very reasonable ground that, under modern conditions, industrial development was indispensable to national defense. Obviously, though, the expansion could not stop there. Industry involved at least labor relations and government policy, and development was a complex social and political as well as economic problem. There remained, of course, the question whether, if the military should take control of the government, they would be able to run it properly, or if it would not be better for them to confine their political action to functioning as one of several power groups, which they had become in all three countries by the second quarter of the century.

Their responses to these questions varied widely. The one in Uruguay has just been noted. The variety has been greatest in Argentina. There the armed forces have played a political role regularly ever since the 1920s in ways ranging from pressure to participation to takeover. In Chile, their first political intervention since the civil war of 1891 began in the mid-1920s and ended in 1933. For the next forty years they adhered to a professional, nonpolitical role until, in the early 1970s, they returned to politics with a vengeance, first joining Allende's extreme left-wing government and then overthrowing and supplanting it.

In all three countries, defense against foreign as well as domestic threats has been a real, not merely a nominal, mission of the armed forces. Assertions to the contrary have often been made on the ground that no foreign threat exists, nor any danger of involvement in a foreign war, except perhaps one between superpowers, in which case these puny military establishments would be useless. Since none of the three has fought a war in almost a hundred years, it may be natural to take such a view, but it is not the view taken by their policy makers, who think the possibility of a foreign war is real, and that is what counts. Their apprehension is not unreasonable, for ever since the turn of the century there have been tensions among them and with other states of the kind that have brought on conflicts elsewhere.

Another common misapprehension about the military is that the countries of the Southern Cone, as of Latin America in general, waste their substance in riotous spending on their armed forces.

This criticism has no merit unless it is assumed that all money spent on the military is wasted. The fact is that, among the countries of the world for which data of this kind were gathered in the 1960s and early 1970s, the Southern Cone countries always ranked in the lowest third, and sometimes near the bottom of that group, in the percentage of the total national budget that was devoted to military purposes.

Nationalism is often associated with the armed forces, and properly so in the Southern Cone. Their attitude towards the different varieties of nationalism, however, has been decidedly mixed. If one may generalize about the attitude of these highly assorted officer corps, it was favorable to the political nationalism of the nineteenth century, neither committed nor hostile to the cultural nationalism that flourished in the early twentieth century, and favorable again to economic nationalism when it was related to national defense, but hostile to it when it became linked with socially revolutionary populism. In this last-named version it was termed the "new nationalism" in the 1960s, but that was inaccurate, for its blend of nationalism with populism had been anticipated in the 1940s by Juan and Eva Perón in their denunciation of Argentina's disloyal vendepatria oligarchy for its "corrupt alliance" with the foreign imperialists who were bleeding their country white.

Economic nationalism was nothing new in the Southern Cone at that time. It had often been voiced in the nineteenth century and was first conspicuously applied in Uruguay early in the twentieth century. It was anti-foreign but not socially revolutionary, and in that form the military could not only tolerate it but cheer it on. The new nationalism, however, combined with xenophobia and Jacobinism to threaten the middle as well as the upper classes and the whole status quo, which it was the traditional role of the armed forces to defend. In all three countries the armed forces accordingly intervened when their leaders deemed it necessary to do so in order to keep the new nationalism from being carried to that extreme. They were most ready to intervene when their monopoly of fire power was threatened by paramilitary organizations, actual or in preparation, of guerrillas, armed workers, or other civilians. This was a major factor in the decision of the Chilean military to overthrow Allende's government, and a perhaps minor but certainly not negligible factor in the setting up of a military dictatorship in Uruguay about the same time. It had already helped to bring about the upheaval of 1955 that wrecked Juan Perón's first regime.

Changing Role of the Church

The role of the Roman Catholic Church in the Southern Cone, as in all Catholic countries, has changed greatly since the mid-twentieth century. In the Southern Cone, from colonial times to early in the present century, almost all the people were members of that church;* though on different terms in each country, it enjoyed a preferential status in all, and the clergy, from prelates to parish priests, was generally conservative. As in Latin America at large, there were church-state conflicts throughout most of the nineteenth century and growing anticlericalism and religious apathy towards its close. Anticlericalism, however, spent itself in the secularization of public education, marriage, and burial and in conflicts over such administrative questions as whether bishops should be chosen by the Vatican or by the respective national governments; and beginning about the turn of the century, apathy gave way to a limited but definite religious revival in some quarters. In other quarters, however, apathy gave way to a revival of anticlericalism, which was fortified by the spread of Marxism from the 1890s on. The result was a sharper polarization of opinion about the Roman Catholic Church than these countries had ever known before and one hardly equaled in the Latin world since the eighteenth-century Enlightenment in the France of Diderot, Holbach, and Voltaire.

An early product of the anticlerical revival was the separation of church and state in Uruguay (1919) and Chile (1924). The diversity of the three countries was thereby increased, for no such change was made in Argentina, where, although there was no complete union of church and state, the national government was required by the Constitution of 1853 to support the Roman Catholic Church. This it has always done and continues to do. The only serious effort to sever the tie was made under Perón in 1955, just before his ouster, to which it contributed.

Yet the greatest diversity that has developed among Catholics in

---

*The chief exceptions were Protestants of various denominations, few but active, in all three countries, and Jews, concentrated mainly in Buenos Aires.

these three countries in the present century is not between one country and another but within the church itself in all of them. To an outsider, the principal rifts seem to be of two kinds. One arises from what we may call ecclesiastical nationalism. This has expressed itself in, for example, the antagonism of some of the local clergy to their many foreign counterparts who have flocked to these countries from Spain, France, the United States, and elsewhere to make good a serious shortage of priests. Another expression of it has been the complaint of "dangerous interference with the work of the national churches" by the Latin American Episcopal Council (CELAM), an organization set up in 1955 to integrate the national churches as a step towards the overall integration of the Latin American countries.

The second and more serious rifts in the Catholic Church are those that have been brought about, mainly since Vatican II in the 1960s, by efforts to make the church a leader in social reform or revolution. Large numbers of the clergy, both high and low, as well as of laymen, are found on both sides of this question, and the controversy over it has led in all three countries to a vertical split which, though probably not permanent, has weakened the church for the time being. The split is least evident in Chile. There the hierarchy had by the 1960s reversed its formerly conservative stand. Its new position, however, was one favoring peaceful reform, not violent revolution, as the firebrands in the Allende regime found to their cost.

One major purpose of the Catholic activists was to strengthen the church by demonstrating to the masses that it had a lively social conscience and was determined to do all in its power to help them escape from economic bondage and enjoy a better life here on earth. Many observers believe that the activists have thereby weakened the church by alienating more supporters than they have gained for it. However that may be, the weakness of the church in Latin America was strongly stressed in an appraisal of its position and prospects published in 1970 and written by one of the clerical leaders of the movement for reform and integration. This was a Jesuit, Renato Poblete, who at the time of writing was a professor of sociology in the Catholic University in Santiago, Chile. He began by rejecting the myth that Latin America is a Catholic continent. In fact, he said, in Latin America the level of lay participation in the church's ritual is "extremely low" and there are fewer priests in proportion to population than in any other continent, including Africa. By the latest count, the average for all Latin America was one priest per 5,700 inhabitants, though the national average varied widely, from (in rounded figures) one priest per 3,000 inhabitants in Chile and Colombia, through 4,000 in Argentina and Uruguay, to 15,000 in Honduras.

Looking ahead, Father Poblete saw only trouble in the two factors that were creating the church's "basic problem" by "shaping the destiny of the continent." One was the demographic explosion, which, he asserted, caught the church with fewer dioceses, parishes, and priests than in the eighteenth century, and a decline in "priestly vocations" (candidacies for the priesthood), which, in recent years, had increased only half as fast as the total population, with resulting dependence on the assistance of foreign clergy. The second factor was the increasing secularization of a pluralistic society. In consequence, as the educational level rose, the proportion of those declaring themselves Catholics declined. In a recent representative case, the decline was from nine-tenths of the adults with only one or two years at grammar school to two-thirds of the adults who had been university students.

In differing degrees the educational systems of all three countries have long been unfavorable to the Catholic Church, which once dominated them. Its share in primary and secondary education is much smaller than that of the public schools. It has one degree-granting university in Argentina, established in 1959 in the face of strong opposition, an older one in Chile, and none in Uruguay. University degrees are needed for the practice of professions and to qualify for government posts, and the great majority of them are granted by the state institutions. In these the atmosphere has been decidedly secular, if not anticlerical, since the University Reform that began in 1918 in Argentina and spread—with changes, of course—to Uruguay and Chile as well as other Latin American countries.

Decidedly secular have also been most other cultural and political manifestations during the present century in all three countries, though again with differences. This is true of the newspapers, magazines, and books published in all their national capitals. Buenos Aires, however, overshadows the other two in this respect. It is, indeed, the largest publishing center in the Hispanic world outside Spain, and is also the seat of *Criterio*, the only Catholic journal in the three countries that combines long life (founded in 1928) with consistently high quality and considerable influence. Though conservative, *Criterio* has been much concerned with secular affairs over the years. Radio, since the 1930s, and television, since the 1960s, have become the principal communications media in all three countries and, despite differences in operation and control, all provide their publics with as mundane a diet of sports, crime, soap operas, news and weather reports and so on, as that offered by the major networks in the United States.

The Outside World

The cone grouping is probably least appropriate in connection with the foreign relations of the three countries comprised in it, for throughout their history they have been least alike and least cohesive in this respect. Like other Latin American countries, they are oriented more towards Europe and the United States than towards one another. Latin American unification movements, regional or general, have had some support among their people, but none has prospered. Besides often quarreling over specific issues, they harbor deep-seated mutual antipathies. A fair sample is provided by a Chilean historian and practitioner of diplomacy, Mario Barros, who, writing in 1970, complained of the disdain that most Argentines had always shown for Chile. Years earlier, a leading Uruguayan statesman and historian, Luis Alberto de Herrera, described Argentina as an even greater threat than Brazil to the security of his country and to "the integrity of our nationalism."

These countries have been pulled apart by various forces: Chile by its location on the Pacific coast, which has given it vital interests of little or no concern to the two fronting on the Atlantic; Uruguay by its felt need to play off Brazil and Argentina against each other in self-defense; and all three, in the present century, by the differences between their respective positions in the Latin American power scale. On this scale Argentina has ranked as one of the great powers, along with Brazil and Mexico, Chile with the middle powers, and Uruguay with the small powers. Even the new common interest in pushing the limit of territorial waters 200 miles or more out to sea for the protection of fishing rights, though it arrayed them against the United States, did not bring them together. The nearest approach to union that has been made in this region was the ABC Pact of 1915-1917, and that was only an *entente cordiale*, not an alliance, and linked great-power Argentina and middle-power Chile not to small-power Uruguay but to Brazil, also a great power. Each of the three power classes, according to Victor Alba, tends to follow a different line. The first, for example, prefers a lone hand to a Latin American concert; the second prefers the concert; and the third looks to the United States for support. Argentina did, in fact, play a lone hand most of the time until the 1940s, priding itself on its wealth, culture, and European connections and character and looking down on mere Latin Americans, a posture for which its foreign minister in the 1930s, supercilious Carlos Saavedra Lamas, was noted. Until the ensuing decade, the three countries had one very important common feature in being under British economic influence, which reached its peak in Argentina, but this failed to unify their foreign policies. Since World War II Britain has been supplanted in this respect by the United States, with the same negative effect. Common traits have not resulted in their making common cause.

Efforts at international cooperation have been made by all three governments, but they have been aimed not at uniting them as a group, but at cooperation on a much larger scale: Latin American, inter-American, or universal (League of Nations, United Nations). In 1920, for example, President Baltasar Brum of Uruguay proposed the formation of an American League of Nations which would have included the United States. More recently the trend has been towards Latin American union without the United States and even as a counterpoise to it or bargaining unit against it — possibilities that were considered from the beginning of independence, but which had been pushed into the background during the full bloom of Pan Americanism. In 1960, at Montevideo, the Latin American Free Trade Association (LAFTA) was set up, with Uruguay, Argentina, and Chile and four other countries as charter members. It did not prosper, however, although in the course of the 1960s Latin American cooperation was given high priority in speeches by leaders in all three countries, especially by Presidents Frondizi of Argentina and Frei of Chile. Both of them at the same time prudently supported the Alliance for Progress, and in return were aided by the United States, both directly and through alliance channels. By the end of the decade both leaders had gone into political eclipse, the alliance was dead, LAFTA moribund, and all three countries were too torn by internal dissension to pursue any set course in foreign affairs effectively.

The climactic upheavals of 1973 in all three countries apparently changed little or nothing in this respect, and tripartite unity or cooperation remained a mirage. The new nationalism's xenophobia — which was largely Yankeephobia — had been curbed in Chile and Uruguay by the military dictatorships set up there. Argentina, however, had moved in the opposite direction, for the restored Perón at once reversed his predecessor's friendly attitude towards the United States.

Relations with states outside Latin America have always been of great importance, for better or worse, to the Southern Cone countries and they have differed widely among themselves in their attitudes towards outsiders. The states that have meant the most to them are, besides the United States, Great Britain for economic reasons and, in the nineteenth century, for its sea power; France, mainly for cultural reasons; Germany, since the late nineteenth century, as military mentor, trading partner, and source of limited but important immigration; and Italy and Spain as sources of far larger and more important immigration. Spain has, of course, had the greatest influence. As their mother country and metropolis during the colonial centuries, it left an enduring imprint that is deeper than any they have received from any other source. It has been fortified in the present century, mainly by cultural means and through both private and governmental channels. All three countries are highly responsive to foreign influence, and no writers since the turn of the century have had a greater impact on them than the two Spanish philosophers and essayists, Miguel de Unamuno and José Ortega y Gasset. At times, Spain's influence has been significant politically, as in the transmission of Falangism, the Spanish brand of fascism, in the 1930s and 1940s. And in seeking to promote its influence of whatever kind — not forgetting its markets — in Latin America, Spain has generally concentrated on these three countries as offering the most fertile field. It has thereby recognized, as Soviet writers, too, are doing, that for all their diversity Argentina, Chile, and Uruguay do possess the unity of a group set apart by its distinctive character.

Part One

Nineteenth-Century Foundations

II Argentina, 1810-1910:
A Modern Miracle

During its three colonial centuries the territory that is now Argentina was one of the least important of Spain's far-flung dominions in America. By 1910, however, it had become a world leader as a source of foodstuffs, as a field for capital investment, and in railway mileage, and among the twenty Latin American nations it had taken first place in almost every respect: political, economic, and cultural. Most of this remarkable change had come about in the last fifty of the nearly four hundred years since Spanish settlement began, and it was on so large a scale and due to such an extraordinary coincidence of domestic and foreign factors as to seem almost a miracle.

A Half-Century of Conflict

Until the 1860s there was little to indicate that Argentina would ever emerge from the rut of near-anarchy and dictatorship, disillusionment and reaction, into which, like the rest of Spanish America, it had fallen even before the wars of independence, begun in 1810, ended in 1825. The census of 1869 showed that Argentina was still like all the rest in having a population made up of a highly assorted ethnic mixture. The components varied from one country to another. Argentina's were mostly Indian and mestizo, with a minority of whites and a very small number of Negroes. The whites were of European, usually Spanish, origin or descent; most of them born in Argentina and called creoles (*criollos*). One more common trait was Argentina's high rate of illiteracy, which was still about 75 percent in the 1860s.

And yet there were a few intimations of better things to come. One was Argentina's ready adaptation to the requirements both of military success in its struggle for independence, and of diplomatic success early in the relationship with Great Britain that was to play so great a part in working the Argentine miracle. Another was the skill and speed with which, from the earliest years of independence, its people developed a new industry, borrowed from Uruguay. This was the *saladero* or meat-salting plant, which was to be the mainstay of the money economy for the next half-century. Still a third was the rapid development of able political and intellectual leaders. It was in the first generation of independence that the formation of the architects of Argentina's future greatness—men such as Juan

Bautista Alberdi, Esteban Echeverría, Bartolomé Mitre, Domingo Faustino Sarmiento—was completed.

The conflicts of Argentina's first half-century were largely domestic. It was the only Spanish American country in which Spanish power was never restored once the struggle for independence had begun, as it did in that country on May 25, 1810.* Its military operations in the war of independence were confined mainly to the remote interior until 1816 and after that to Chile and Peru, where its expeditionary forces under General José de San Martín aided in the liberation of those countries. Argentina fought a war with Brazil from 1825 to 1828, and invaded Uruguay and had brushes with British and French forces in the Plata estuary and with Bolivia on their common border in the 1830s and 1840s. Yet all these were in a real sense as much domestic conflicts as the almost incessant Indian fighting of that period, for they all related in one way or another to Argentina's claim that its boundaries of right included the whole late colonial viceroyalty of Buenos Aires, that is to say, Uruguay, Paraguay, and southern Bolivia, as well as modern Argentina. Almost an obsession then, this viceregal complex was still a factor to be reckoned with in the twentieth century.

In Argentina proper, domestic conflict was constant and universal. It involved the form of government, religion, education, the land system, and economic policy, and arrayed the old against the new, traditionalists against modernizers, nativists against cosmopolitans, conservatives against liberals. In more specific terms, two of the major conflicts arrayed *Unitarios* (centralizers) against Federalists (a term which in Argentina at that time meant decentralizers), and Buenos Aires and such allies as it could get (usually in the Littoral, or Plata-Paraná provinces) against the interior. All the while, Argentina was threatened with disintegration as one effort after another at political consolidation failed and such central authority as did exist was defied by provincial *caudillos* or chiefs, who were a kind of backwoods version of feudal lords.

A necessarily oversimplified bipolar summary of the situation is well represented at one extreme by Bernardino Rivadavia, who in the 1820s led a campaign to modernize the country economically,

---

*This is the conventional date. It will do as well as any other. For reasons that do not need to be gone into here, independence was not formally declared until July 9, 1816. Both May 25 and July 9 are celebrated as national holidays.

socially, and culturally by, among other means, centralizing its government and increasing foreign influence, especially that of France and England; and at the other extreme, by dictator Juan Manuel de Rosas, "Restorer of the Laws," who from 1829 to 1852 headed the self-styled decentralizers and the forces of reaction against modernization. One after the other, both men were ousted and the upshot, politically, was Argentina's new Constitution of 1853.

Free Men and Free Enterprise

The enemies of Rosas, returning from the exile in Uruguay, Chile, and Bolivia into which he had driven them, provided the leadership of the new regime. They resumed the interrupted modernization of Argentina and established a tradition of Argentine history that condemned Rosas and all his works. General Justo José de Urquiza, caudillo of Entre Ríos, a former supporter of Rosas who had headed the force of Argentines, Brazilians, and Uruguayans that overthrew him, called the convention that adopted that constitution. It resembled the constitution of the United States in many respects, including its federal division of power, its separation of powers, its frame of government, and its protection of individual rights and religious freedom.* In addition, in a spirit of economic liberalism it encouraged the free flow of foreign private capital and immigration. With amendments, the Constitution of 1853 still stands, the longest-lived in Latin America.

Some of the new constitution's features, particularly those that bore on rivalry between the *porteños*, or people of Buenos Aires, and the provincials, together with special dislike of Urquiza, led the Buenos Aires authorities to keep that city and province out of the new union for several years. During that time tension mounted until hostilities broke out. When the smoke cleared in 1862, Buenos Aires was the winner and its General Bartolomé Mitre was president for the next six years—the constitutional term.

Mitre and his first two successors, Sarmiento and Nicolás Avellaneda, were exceptionally able and public-spirited presidents and

---

*The constitution provided for government support of the Roman Catholic Church, but also for freedom of public worship by other faiths. English influence had aided in establishing this principle in Argentina in the 1820s, first in Buenos Aires.

all three followed substantially identical policies aimed at consoli-
dating and pacifying the country politically, promoting its development and expanding the area of settlement with the aid of foreign
capital and immigration, and raising the cultural level of the
people. Mitre, soldier, statesman, historian, and founder in 1870 of
a notable newspaper, *La Nación* (one year later than its likewise
notable rival from that day to this, *La Prensa*), dressed, wrote, and
spoke like a European, most of all like his French contemporary,
statesman and historian Guizot. On occasion, though, he acted like
an Argentine caudillo, as when he led his province's revolt against
the central government after his defeat in the election of 1874.
Sarmiento, whose term began just after his return from Washington, where he had been minister to the United States, is best known
as writer and "schoolteacher president." Born and brought up in the
far western province of San Juan, he had a strain of the gaucho in
his makeup. Yet he abhorred gauchos and pilloried them, along
with the caudillos they served, as enemies of civilization in his classic
Facundo, or the Conflict between Civilization and Barbarism
(1845), written in exile in Chile. He borrowed educational ideas
from his friend Horace Mann of Massachusetts and schoolteachers
from New England, and gave his own country the injunction to
"North Americanize" itself. Avellaneda, from Tucumán in the far
north, had been Sarmiento's minister of public instruction and
carried on his two illustrious predecessors' policies. Without waiting
to see what course he would follow after his election, Mitre, whom
he had defeated, took up arms against him and was promptly defeated; but Avellaneda was not Rosas, and no bloodbath followed.

Under these three presidents political consolidation and internal
security were promoted. With the aid of a new weapon, the
Remington rifle, the last few of many revolts by provincial caudillos
were put down despite the distraction of the deservedly unpopular
Paraguayan War, in which it took the Triple Alliance of Argentina,
Brazil, and Uruguay five years (1865-1870) to defeat much smaller
but militarily strong Paraguay. Argentina has never fought a foreign war since then. The decline of the gaucho, speeded by the
spread of the saladero, continued during this period and was
lamented in another Argentine classic, *Martín Fierro*, a dialect
poem sometimes miscalled an epic, which was published in two
parts in 1872 and 1879.

An operation also somewhat misleadingly referred to as the Conquest of the Desert, which was begun and largely completed in 1879, put an end both to Indian attacks on frontier settlements and to the threat from Chile to Argentina's hold on Patagonia, and opened a vast area of fertile pampa land to settlement. It also catapulted its commanding general, Julio A. Roca, into the presidency the following year, which saw the solution of the long-standing and highly explosive Buenos Aires question — the question whether and on what terms Buenos Aires should be made the national capital. It was solved by carving the city out of its province and giving it a status much like that of the District of Columbia, but with the important difference that its citizens had full voting rights in national elections.

Growth and Transfiguration

Between 1880 and 1910 Argentina not only grew at breakneck speed but also underwent a profound economic and social transformation and less sweeping but still significant cultural and political changes. By 1910 it had become one of the world's principal exporters of foodstuffs and a classic example of what came to be denounced as economic colonialism. In this case the term meant that Argentina had become heavily dependent on an agricultural-pastoral economy controlled at key points — finance, shipping, railways, *frigoríficos* (meat-freezing plants) — by foreign (very largely British) investors and businessmen. In the course of these thirty years farming and grain exports caught up with stockraising and meat exports as main sources of national income, and technological developments revolutionized the stockraising industry and aided in shifting the main market for its products from America to Europe. The chief factor in the social transformation was the flood of immigrants, mostly from Italy and Spain, which reached its peak between 1900 and 1914. By the time it began to subside after 1929, Argentina had received since the 1870s more immigrants in proportion to the original population than any other country has ever done, including the United States. As a result, the ethnic composition of the Argentine people had been changed from typically Latin American to overwhelmingly European, and the process was already far advanced by 1910. Other social consequences included the growth of a new middle class and a surge of urbanization. Foremost among the political changes of the period were the rise of the Radical Party (founded in 1892), which seriously challenged the entrenched conservatives, and a nativistic reaction of the old creole stock against the foreign intrusion, as well as against the cosmopolitanism of Argentina's own literary Generation of 1880. One expression of this reaction was the emergence of a nativistic nationalism that was much more dynamic than the liberal nationalism of Mitre's generation.

Already in the 1880s Argentina's headlong economic growth was enriching not only the traditional upper class but also some newcomers to it. The affluent society thus formed reminds one of society in the United States in the Gilded Age of the Grant administration both in its conspicuous consumption and in its hardly less conspicuous corruption. The whole tone of upper-class life changed: in town houses, from austerity to luxury, as Carlos Ibarguren has told us; in the countryside (the "camp," to Anglo-Argentines), from simple ranch house to baronial hall, as we read in Anglo-Argentine W. H. Hudson's *Far Away and Long Ago*.

As Aldo Ferrer sums it up, the rapid growth of the Argentine economy after 1860 was the result of certain given factors, notably a growing world demand and an abundance of new, rich pampa land, and certain other acquired factors, such as railroads, immigration, and national consolidation. A few figures will suggest the scope and rapidity of the growth. The total population of 1.8 million in 1869 more than doubled by 1895 (4.0 million), and doubled again by 1914 (8.0 million). British investments in Argentina grew from $125 million to $850 million in the 1880s and to nearly $1,500 million by 1910. Railway mileage increased from 1434 in 1880 to 9254 in 1890 and 20,805 in 1913, by which time Argentina had one of the seven largest railway networks in the world. Almost all the lines led to Buenos Aires. The area under cultivation increased fourfold between 1872 and 1888; the increase continued in the next two decades, and by 1908 agricultural had left once dominant pastoral production far behind. Pastoral products (mainly beef, mutton, and wool) accounted for 94 percent of all Argentine exports in 1880, but only 30 percent in 1908, while in the same period agricultural products (mainly wheat and corn) rose from 2 percent to 65 percent of total exports.

As Ferrer further notes, the basic institutional feature of the pampa economy was the large production unit with tenant farming. Proceeding on the basis of an analysis too intricate to be examined

here, he reaches the plausible conclusion that an excessive portion
of the national income in this prosperous age went into the pockets
of the great landowners, whose use of it mainly for consumption
rather than production was a main reason why the Argentine economy lost its momentum.

Domestic Strife and Foreign Quarrels

If that dismal prospect occurred to anyone in President Roca's
administration in the 1880s, it was too distant to worry about, but
trouble soon blew up from another quarter. Under the president
who succeeded him in 1886, Miguel Juárez Celman, the Gilded Age
became an era of peculation, wild speculation, and a runaway inflation that was too much even for the dominant agricultural interests,
which had hitherto thrived on inflation and paper money. For the
workers and the rapidly growing middle class, it was ruinous.

In this situation the so-called Revolution of 1890 took place. It
was the work of civilians and some of the military, and the action
that counted was confined to the city of Buenos Aires. The civilians
were creoles, not of immigrant stock, although half the population
of the city was foreign-born. At first the revolt was successful, but
there was friction between its military and civilian sectors and
among the civilians, and the leaders made the fatal mistake of failing to press their advantage. Seizing the opportunity, Vice-President
Carlos Pellegrini and former President Roca, now minister of war,
organized the loyal forces for a counterattack that snuffed out the
uprising in three days. Shortly thereafter, as a sop to the opposition,
President Juárez Celman's colleagues pressured him into resigning,
but that was the only immediate change of consequence. Pellegrini,
a pillar of the ruling elite, moved up a notch to the presidency, the
government went on as before, and so did the oligarchical regime
for another twenty years.

That was hardly a revolution and the episode is important mainly
because of its bearing on Argentine domestic policy and foreign
relations. Juárez Celman's prescription for the economic crisis had
been more inflation and repudiation of foreign debts. If he had
remained in power and had his way, Argentina would have followed
a course like the one that provoked armed intervention in Venezuela
by Great Britain and Germany in 1902. In fact, as H. S. Ferns has
noted, even without that added provocation from the central gov-

ernment, British interests that had suffered severely from the crash
in Argentina demanded intervention there in the early 1890s on the
ground of derelictions by provincial and municipal governments.
Argentina averted that hazard by following Pellegrini's prescription
of maintaining a sound currency and high credit rating and achieved
the all-time peak of its prosperity in the next generation.

The revolt of 1890 is of uncommon interest for two additional
reasons. One is that a rift in the reform organization called Civic
Union, which had played a leading part in the revolt, gave rise to
the organization in 1892 of the middle-class Radical Party (Unión
Cívica Radical). Under the leadership first of Leandro Além and
then of Hipólito Yrigoyen it lived up to its motto of "abstention and
revolution" as a tactic for forcing the adoption of the political reform of 1912, which had the expected result of unseating the conservative regime of the past generation in favor of the Radical Party.

Armaments and Anarchists

The revolt of 1890 is also important because the Pellegrini policy
that emerged in its aftermath strengthened Argentina for the much
more prolonged crisis from the early 1890s to 1902 in its relations
with Chile. Several times in those years the outbreak of war between
them seemed imminent. Chile was cocky over its victory and rich
conquests in the recent War of the Pacific, and Argentina was in
much the same mood because of its spectacular development in the
1880s and because it had caught up with Chile in population and
was forging ahead fast. The long and very largely undetermined
boundary between them provided ample opportunity for disagreement. In their treaty of 1881 Chile, then engaged in the War of the
Pacific, had given up its claim to Patagonia in favor of Argentina,
but other areas from the northern Andes to Tierra del Fuego remained in dispute. In 1891, when Chile became involved in a dangerous dispute with the United States over the the *Baltimore* incident (see chapter XVI), Argentine Foreign Minister Estanislao
Zeballos offered Washington Argentina's aid in the invasion of Chile
in return for the cession of southern Chile to Argentina. The Chilean government got wind of the offer, but chose to lie low. Though
both governments were tempted to use the age-old device of appeasing domestic discontent by stirring up foreign quarrels, neither
country could afford to fight at that time, Chile having just passed

through a civil war and Argentina through the revolt of 1890 and a severe economic depression.

Towards the end of the decade, however, the threat of war became more serious than ever. Argentina was now overtaking Chile in naval strength, too, and the Chilean government had become apprehensive that Argentina would turn the Tierra del Fuego-Strait of Magellan part of any settlement of the now explosive boundary controversy into a pretext for breaking out into the Pacific and challenging the dominant position Chile had won on the west coast of South America. After much war talk on both sides, a settlement was finally arranged with some assistance from the ministers of the United States in both countries, but mainly on the basis of a commitment by Argentina not to meddle in the Pacific. The settlement was embodied in a number of agreements signed in May 1902, and hence known as the *Pactos de Mayo* (May Pacts). They disposed of almost all the familiar questions, and one of them — the first of its kind in modern history, said Secretary of State Henry L. Stimson in 1930 — provided for the limitation of naval armaments. The oft-discussed problem of jurisdiction in the Beagle Channel remained open. It still does. So does the question of the delimitation of the respective Antarctic claims of the two countries, which began negotiations about it in 1905.

In the new spirit of friendliness Argentine Foreign Minister Luis María Drago in December 1902 sought the cooperation of Chile as well as of Brazil in proposing the Drago Doctrine to the United States (see chapter XVI), and Argentina and Chile erected a statue of the Prince of Peace, called the Christ of the Andes, on their frontier as a pledge of perpetual peace. Hardly had the monument been dedicated, however, when the era of good feeling so hopefully symbolized by it was brought to an abrupt end by Brazil's precipitation of a naval arms race, whereupon Argentina and Chile canceled their naval limitation pact of 1902.

Argentina now resumed the strengthening of its land and sea forces that it had carried on vigorously while the protracted crisis with Chile was at its height from 1898 to 1902. Appropriately enough, General Roca, who had done much to improve them in his first administration, was president again during these years. Among other things, he now promoted professionalization of the officer corps by founding a school for the advanced training of higher officers and basing promotion on seniority and technical proficiency, establishing universal conscription, and beginning the practice of sending Argentine officers to Germany for further training (Robert Potash tells us that between 150 and 175 officers had been sent there for this purpose by 1914), as well as bringing German officers to Argentina as instructors. General Pablo R. Riccheri was Roca's right-hand man in this program and carried on effectively after the end of Roca's administration in 1904.

The Argentine navy was receiving similar attention. Its rapid growth in fighting ships was its most striking development, as it was also the most graphic illustration of the shifting balance of power between Argentina and Chile. In this respect, by 1910 Argentina had forged ahead of Brazil and far outstripped Chile. Pained recognition was accorded this fact by Chile's leading newspaper, *El Mercurio*, on May 15, 1910. In an article of two and a half columns, captioned "Naval Power in South America. The balance of the last twenty years, 1890-1910," and signed "J. G.," the writer began by saying that among the "transcendental changes" during this period, the most striking was one which Chileans could only deplore, namely, the rapid rise of Brazil and Argentina. The following statistics of naval tonnage, which he proceeded to give, explain his discomfort:

	1890	1901	1910
Brazil	33,785	27,500	57,324
Chile	23,000	44,300	20,850
Argentina	14,000	39,564	81,347

The great strengthening of Argentina's armed forces was, in fact, at first aimed at dynamic Chile rather than Brazil, and all along it was probably designed to meet potential foreign rather than domestic threats — the navy would be of limited use at home and had apparently been of no use in the revolt of 1890. And yet, as the years passed after 1890, it seemed increasingly likely that the military — army, rather than navy — might have to be used extensively for the preservation of domestic order and security. This was because among the horde of immigrants pouring into Argentina were enough revolutionaries, especially anarchists from such European hotbeds as Barcelona, to cause grave concern among the governing classes. Foreign anarchists controlled a large part of the new organized labor movement, and socialists most of the rest. At best, the foreign-born, who made up one-fourth of the whole country's population and half of the national capital's, took so little interest in public affairs and had so little sense of responsibility for the state of the nation that 99 percent of them did not even bother to become naturalized, much less take an active part in the political process. Even Sarmiento, once an ardent advocate of massive immigration, was dismayed by its consequences as far back as the mid-1880s. Accordingly, in November 1902, the government adopted a Law of Residence which permitted the deportation of any foreigner who in any way "compromised the national security or disturbed the public order." Under the terms of this act, merely taking part in a strike was such an offence. As Samuel Baily aptly observes, although "organized labor had clearly emerged in Argentina" by 1910, it was still "outside the institutional structure of the country."

Foreign Influences, Nationalism, and the Centennial

Immigration, which reached its peak at this time, was even more important to some other sectors of Argentine society than to the working class. Half the immigrants were seasonal workers (*golondrinas*, swallows), who came only for the harvest season and then returned home (Italy or Spain, in most cases) for the harvest season there. Even so, the half who remained in Argentina were so numerous that by 1914, 30.3 percent of the total population were foreign-born, which was more than twice as large a proportion as the largest ever reached in the United States. They made up 39 percent of Argentina's working population in 1895 and 47 percent in 1914, but they bulked even larger in some middle-class occupational groups: from two thirds to four fifths of the entrepreneurs, about half the doctors and lawyers, and somewhat more than half the commercial office workers. In other groups, however, they were much less numerous, providing only one-third of the government office workers, ten percent of the landowners, and one-third of the domestic servants. Down to the end of this period, even the sons of immigrants hardly ever rose to high political office. The outstanding exception was Carlos Pellegrini, son of an Italian father and an English mother, and yet a founder of the exclusive Jockey Club of Buenos Aires and president of the republic. To be sure, his father was no ordinary immigrant, but an artist as well as an engineer.

On the other hand, immigrants and their sons often took a prominent part in the intellectual, literary, and artistic life of the period,
almost always in Buenos Aires, in which the cultural activities of
Argentina were now concentrated to an even higher degree than
were those of France in Paris, or of Great Britain in London. Three
examples, all intellectual or literary leaders (the terms were not
always mutually exclusive), were Alejandro Korn, born in Argentina of German parents; José Ingenieros, born in Italy but educated
largely in Argentina; and Paul Groussac, born and brought up in
France.

Argentina's own Generation of 1880 had been an outstanding
propagator of the great influence of France in literature. That influence was felt in other ways as well. One of the most salient was the
reconstruction of much of Buenos Aires to turn it physically—as it
was already claiming to be spiritually—into the Paris of South
America. To this end the government wrecked and then rebuilt,
much of it on French models, block after block of the old city, or
"big country town" (*gran aldea*), as it was affectionately called by
the nostalgic, derisively by modernizers. The operation was reminiscent of the one Baron Haussmann performed a generation earlier
on Paris itself, under Napoleon III.

The deference shown to France in cultural matters and to England in business and finance was beginning to provoke a strong reaction among patriotic Argentines by the first decade of the century.
As the Generation of 1880 began to lose its drive and its grip, creole
nativism, earlier crudely expressed in *Martín Fierro* and gaucho
tales and plays, found much more sophisticated expression in the
new nationalism of the Generation of 1910. As that development
took place very largely after 1910, it will be discussed in a later
chapter.

Along with the change in the intellectual-literary climate came
one in the political climate as well. The latter change was signalized
by the spread of a fatalistic belief in the inevitability of the oligarchy's surrender to the growing clamor of the Radical Party and the
slightly younger and much smaller Socialist Party for a sweeping
electoral reform that would democratize the government. Perhaps
the best illustration of the change is the reversal of the attitude of
that former Horatio at the upper-class gate, Carlos Pellegrini, towards the reform in question. In his last speech to the Senate, delivered shortly before his death in 1906, he warned that the only way

out of the vicious circle of alternating rebellion and amnesty into which Argentina had fallen was to "open the floodgates to the people."

Pellegrini's like-minded contemporary and close associate since the 1880s, patrician Roque Sáenz Peña, took up the torch and procured the passage in 1912 by a reluctant conservative Congress of the epoch-making electoral reform law that bears his name (see chapter V). In the campaign preceding his election to the presidency in 1910, Sáenz Peña underlined two urgent needs, one for electoral reform as the only cure for the current malaise in Argentina, and the other for economic diversification to reactivate an economy already growing sluggish, to give it better balance, and to diminish Argentina's dependence on foreign capital investments by diverting domestic capital from conspicuous consumption to productive enterprises. In both respects his program was in harmony with the spirit of the centennial year, for the country was celebrating the historic beginning of independence on May 25, 1810. Campaigning as a nonpartisan candidate, he received all but one of the votes in the Electoral College, as James Monroe had done in the United States in the election of 1820 during the "Era of Good Feeling."

Argentina's centenary of independence was celebrated with so much pomp and circumstance that it completely overshadowed the Pan American conference held in Buenos Aires during its course. Because Sáenz Peña perceived strong implications of anti-Europeanism and United States hegemony in Pan Americanism, he was from the start in the vanguard of its critics. In the very first conference of the Pan American series, he delivered a philippic against Secretary of State Blaine's plan for an American customs union. By 1910, however, the movement had been purged of its bias against Europe and reduced to little more than a series of infrequent goodwill conferences, and Argentina's Anglophil-Francophil governing class had become reconciled to it to the extent of hosting the fourth conference.

The bias of this governing class in favor of far-off Europe was curiously combined with a nationalism that was part conservative, part nostalgic, and part expansionist. The expansionist strain stood out prominently in a book published in 1910 by the prestigious newspaper *La Nación* in the year of the conference but in honor of the centenary. The book was a collection of essays by various writers, including some of the nation's very best, like Joaquín González and Ricardo Rojas. The contributors were far from unanimous on most questions, but not one of them failed to endorse the idea of reconstituting the colonial viceroyalty of Buenos Aires as something not only desirable but bound to take place. In plain words, that meant reincorporating Uruguay, Paraguay, and much of Bolivia — all three independent for close to a century — in Argentina. The idea, old as the beginning of the independence movement and the breakup of the viceroyalty, had never died out. Even Sarmiento had supported it to the extent of advocating the reunion of Argentina and Uruguay, with a common capital on the island of Martín García, which lies between them in the Plata estuary and was then claimed by both governments. Most Uruguayans, however, rejected the idea out of hand. This may be why González, in his contribution to the volume, characterized Uruguayan nationalism as "ferocious and aggressive."

James Bryce, on his visit to Argentina in 1910, noted even in the "average" Argentine "that jubilant patriotism and that exuberant confidence in his country which marked the North American of 1830-1860." Looking back to this time many years later, Argentine historian José Luis Romero observed that two of its features were the definitive stamp of approval that its opinion-makers put on the themes of national greatness, enviable destiny, and innate virtues, and the wave of xenophobia set in motion by their official rhetoric. All in all, surface appearances in the centennial year warranted the self-assurance, tinged with dreams of glory, with which Argentines of the upper and middle crusts peered ahead. They could not foresee that in just twenty years their vaunted economy would be facing ruin and another long cycle of violence and upheaval would begin which would expose the pathetic fallacy of their best leaders' faith in "opening the floodgates" to the people as a political panacea.

III Uruguay, 1810-1900:
From Artigas to *Ariel*

Though six times as large as Belgium, Uruguay has throughout its history occupied a no less precarious position between two far larger and stronger states, both of which are great powers on the Latin American scale. James Bryce took little note of such hazards when he set down his generally perspicacious "observations and impressions" after a visit to Uruguay in November 1910, as part of his four-months visit to South America. His only comment on that country's intermediate position described it as "a garden plot between two vast estates." What is more, he paid Uruguay the highest compliment in a European observer's power by declaring that in "no part of South America, except perhaps southern Chile, would a European feel more disposed to settle down for life" than in Uruguay. It was, he further noted, one of those countries that, as history shows, thrive on war, while others are ruined by it. According to him, Uruguay saw more incessant fighting from 1810 to 1876 than any other part of the world had seen in the last hundred years, and there had been frequent conflicts since 1876; and yet the country had continued to grow in wealth and population, the flow of capital had been free and (capping the climax) Uruguay's bonds averaged about par on the London stock exchange.

Artigas and Independence

Uruguay's start had been far from promising. It was not settled by Spaniards until the 1720s and in the next half-century it was handicapped by several retarding factors: Spanish commercial policy, which kept the Plata closed to regular overseas trade until 1778; the hostility of Portugal, which claimed this territory as part of contiguous Brazil and fought for and in it; and the opposition of Spanish Americans on the Buenos Aires side of the river to its settlement by anyone, since that would interfere with the profitable business in hides and horns that they had built up in frequent roundups of the country's enormous herds of wild cattle. The territory did not even have a name of its own and was called simply the Banda Oriental (Eastern Shore).

In the late 1770s Portugal gave up its claim and Spain opened the Plata to overseas trade. After that, Montevideo enjoyed a rapid growth, thanks to its location at the mouth of the river, its superior harbor, and its important share in the importation of African slaves, in which ships from the United States took an active part. It was closely connected with Buenos Aires in many ways, but from the beginning there was rivalry between the two cities, and it was sharpened by developments in the early nineteenth century. Although Uruguayan forces aided the porteños in expelling British invaders of Buenos Aires in 1806, the second invasion a year later, likewise driven back from Buenos Aires, overwhelmed Montevideo. The British continued to hold it for nearly a year, to its profit, mainly through increased trade and expenditures by the occupiers. After they left and the struggle for independence began, the concentration of Spanish royalist forces in Montevideo made it the chief focus of resistance to the liberation movement in the Plata area, while Buenos Aires was the focus of the movement itself.

Outside Montevideo the cause of independence had strong support, which was personified by 47-year-old José Artigas. Born in Montevideo, he was a grandson of one of its 34 original settlers. At his father's estancia he soon took to country life, much as did his younger Argentine contemporary Juan Manuel de Rosas, and before long established himself as a natural leader in the new and turbulent society of the Banda Oriental. He was not, however, the typical caudillo, hostile to all organized government, as Sarmiento later pictured him. Nor, at the other extreme, was he an Uruguayan nationalist. Instead, he was an Argentine federalist, who fought for a federal system in the Plata area modeled on that of the United States.

For a time he won many followers on both sides of the river, but ultimately he was crushed between the implacable centralizers in Buenos Aires and the Portuguese in Brazil, who revived their claim to the Banda Oriental and invaded it in 1816. Artigas managed to keep fighting until 1820, when he was forced to flee first to the Argentine province of Corrientes and thence to neighboring Paraguay. There, on a farm in the *maté* country, he eked out a living until his lonely death in 1850 at the age of 86. Not until long after was he rehabilitated and transfigured into a national hero.

After the flight of Artigas the Uruguayan independence movement did not revive until 1824, when Brazil, now itself independent, undertook to annex the Banda Oriental permanently. In 1825 Argentina joined in the fray and its war with Brazil lasted until 1828. Both sides lost, in the sense that neither got the disputed territory.

Instead, under British influence, which was strong in Rio de Janeiro and Buenos Aires as well as Montevideo, the treaty of peace provided for the immediate and complete independence of Uruguay.

If the Uruguayans were as ill prepared for independence as has been charged, they at least had the good sense to draw on the experience of older neighbors in framing their constitution and not to proscribe those of their fellow countrymen who had taken the wrong side in the kaleidoscopic struggle for independence since 1810. In drawing up the country's first constitution, that of 1830, the predominant foreign influence was that of Argentina and Chile. Their influence was largely personal, although Chile's constitution of 1828 was one of the principal sources considered by the constituent assembly. Like its Chilean model, Uruguay's constitution was comparatively liberal, but it long outlasted Chile's, mainly, it would seem, because it was more flexible and did not go to extremes in controversial matters that counted most in that era, such as liberalism versus conservatism, and federalism versus centralization.

Liberalism also inspired the land system adopted in 1833, but its results were hardly less disappointing than those of the similar and somewhat older one in Argentina. The chief beneficiaries were not the intended ones, the small farmers, but the large, stock-raising landowners, whose new acquisitions were used for pasture rather than crops. The result was to strengthen the pastoral, hierarchical type of society inherited from the colonial period, when Uruguay was even more decidedly a cattle country than its neighbor across the Plata. It had started out as a gigantic corral packed with enormous droves of wild cattle and hemmed in on three sides by water. It had continued that pattern by anticipating Argentina in the introduction of the saladero and by being closer, by both land and sea, to one of the best markets for saladero products, Brazil. Except for Montevideo, with its merchants and a small, incipient middle class, it was a two-class society: at the top, the landowner and the caudillo (often combined in one person), and at the bottom, the gauchos who, as in Argentina, were being reduced to the status of hired hands.

The Great War, 1839-1851

There were striking similarities as well as differences between the two principal caudillos, Rosas of Argentina and Fructuoso Rivera of

Uruguay. Rivera had given decisive support to the "Thirty-Three," the little band of heroes of the independence movement in its final phase, whereas Rosas had left it to others to free Argentina. Many other comparisons of the two have been made. One of the most interesting, though it is biased in Rivera's favor,* was written by the French consul in Montevideo in July 1939, when both men were second-term presidents of their respective countries. They both, wrote the consul, favor the triumph of the *campesinos* (rural people) over the cities, of the semi-savage, *sansculotte* gaucho over enlightened social man — in a word, the triumph of "barbarism over civilization."† But he went on to point out abysmal differences between the two men, saying, for instance, that Rosas used public power to exterminate his political enemies, and public funds to gratify his avarice, whereas Rivera was magnanimous in clemency to his enemies and used public funds only to serve his inclination to prodigality and "princely generosity." The two were so incompatible, he concluded, that proximity made it impossible for them to coexist in peace. Rosas had sworn war to the death on Rivera, and Rivera had returned the compliment.

In fact, Rivera declared war first and his reasons were more complicated than incompatibility. The civil war aspect of the Great War was a continuation of a conflict already under way between Rivera and another caudillo, Manuel Oribe. In 1836 the power struggle gave name to what have been the country's two main political parties ever since: Blanco (white) and Colorado (red). One day in August of that year, it seems, Oribe instructed his troops to display a white emblem bearing the inscription "Defender of the Laws" (reminiscent of his friend and ally-to-be Rosas's title, "Restorer of the Laws"). Rivera's followers retorted with a device of their own. It was at first blue, but when that soon faded, they changed to red, not as an assertion of radicalism (they were no more radical than the Blancos), but simply because red was a more durable color and was commonly used to dye the cloth for making ponchos and *chiripás* (blankets) that everybody wore, so that it was easy to obtain.

Rivera's declaration of war on Rosas was made in February 1839

---

*The bias arose from the fact that France was at war with the government of Rosas and allied with that of Rivera.

†Compare Sarmiento's use, six years later, of "civilization and barbarism" in the full title of his *Facundo*, which likewise identifies caudillos and gauchos with barbarism.

under pressure from his allies. One of them was the French consul's government, already embroiled with Rosas. His other allies were the Argentine province of Corrientes and the southernmost state of Brazil, Rio Grande do Sul, where secessionists were in control. Pressure in the same direction came from the Argentine exiles in Montevideo, who had already begun their own paper war of propaganda against Rosas. Finally, the Blanco leader Oribe was receiving aid from Rosas.

A census taken four years before the war began showed that Uruguay had a population of just over 128,000, of whom 3,500 were Negroes (most of them slaves), 800 mulattoes, 580 Indians, and the remaining 123,000 white. Among the whites, 25,000 were Europeans, 4,000 Brazilians, 3,300 from other Spanish American countries, and all the rest creoles. The absence of mestizos from the list has been explained on the ground that there had been no mating of Spaniards or other whites with the Banda Oriental's Indians, the exceptionally warlike and primitive Charrúas. After 1835 the European element increased rapidly, undeterred by the war. From 1835 to 1848, 48,118 foreign immigrants entered the country, more than one-third of whom were French, nearly one-fourth Italian, and the rest, in descending order, Canary Islanders, *africanos,** and Spaniards. In 1843, the fifth year of the war and the first of the long siege of Montevideo, the city had a population of just over 31,000, more than 60 percent of whom were foreigners, nearly half of them French and Italians and the rest Spaniards, Argentines, and Negroes, in that order. A count the preceding year showed that the city had only one bookstore, but 1,740 industrial establishments of all kinds, including 37 saladeros, 70 pastry shops, 249 general stores, and 488 bars and taverns. The exports consisted mainly of salt beef, hides, tallow, and wool, which were shipped to England, France, Brazil, Spain, and Cuba, in that order. To Argentine Sarmiento, the Buenos Aires of these years seemed all Spanish, Montevideo cosmopolitan.

The war lasted a dozen years. That fact alone might be enough to justify Uruguayan writers in calling it *la Guerra Grande*, the Great War, but there are even better reasons. It was a foreign as well as a civil war. France and Britain intervened in it forcibly for several

---

*Presumably Negroes from Brazil or Argentina, and not slaves directly from Africa, since the slave trade had been abolished.

years in support of their commercial interests, and with their aid
Montevideo withstood its nine years' siege. At one time they had as
many as 50 warships with a complement of 6,000 men in the Plata
estuary, and these prevented Rosas from either blockading the port
or making simultaneous assaults on the city by land and sea. At one
point, when Montevideo's ground forces numbered 2,810, more
than half of them were foreigners: 1,000 French, 400 Italians, and
220 of other nationalities. In addition, one of the two principal military engineers was the captain of the French legion, and one of Argentina's best generals, anti-Rosista José María Paz, was in overall
command of the city's defenses. The Italian Giuseppe Garibaldi,
who had already had experience as a freedom fighter on the side of
the rebellious Brazilian state of Rio Grande do Sul, an ally of the
Rivera government, passed into the service of the latter in 1842. His
most notable service to it was in reopening, in 1845, the navigation
of the Uruguay River, which Rosas had closed. The historian Carlos
Rama credits Garibaldi also with stimulating the growth of a vigorous Italian community in Uruguay.

With each contestant invading the other's territory, the war
spread. So did discontent in Argentina, where in 1842 Corrientes
joined with two other provinces, Santa Fe and Entre Ríos, in a
league with Uruguay against Rosas. After the war had dragged on
for nearly a decade with no end in sight, Great Britain, never so
deeply involved as France, decided to withdraw, and France, shaken
by its own revolution, followed suit. They not only terminated their
aid to Montevideo, but entered into treaties with Argentina in 1849
and 1850, respectively, which gave Rosas a diplomatic victory. Both
powers accepted his contention that the navigation of the Paraná
River was subject to Argentine laws and regulations. Their capitulation seemed certain to prove fatal to the Montevideo government,
and perhaps even to Uruguayan independence. In a sudden reversal, however, Rosas was overthrown in early 1852 by the Triple Alliance of Montevideo, Entre Ríos, and Brazil—an alliance formed
against him less than a year after the treaty embodying France's
capitulation to him was signed.

Unhappily, the very treaty of 1851 by which Brazil's aid had been
obtained put that country's imperial government in a stronger position than ever to intervene in its small neighbor's affairs. It did so by
committing Brazil to defend "the legal order" in Uruguay. With
some plausibility the Brazilian government interpreted the clause as

establishing its right as well as its duty to interfere. The Argentine successors of Rosas had no such warrant, but they found one in Brazil's actions. Uruguay's economy, too, was a source of anxiety to its leaders. Although the commerce of Montevideo had benefited from Anglo-French naval protection, the war losses of the rest of the country were heavy. A three-month investigation at the end of 1852 showed, for example, that the number of cattle had dwindled from 15 million head in 1843 to 8 million nine years later.

Foreign Penetration and Economic Growth

Heavy though the countryside's losses had been, they were not crippling, probably because the fighting had been largely confined to Montevideo and its environs and because the economy was simple, largely self-sufficient, and hence not highly vulnerable. At any rate, in the next sixty years the population increased rapidly with the aid of a flood of immigrants, while the economy expanded greatly under the impulse of an expanding European market and foreign capital, technology, and business enterprise. In short, the changes resembled those that were taking place in Argentina on a much larger scale during the same period. There were, however, two substantial differences. Ethnically, the only major change in the makeup of Uruguay's population, already overwhelmingly white in the 1830s, was the addition of a single national element that was both new and large, the Italian, and even in that respect a start had been made during the Great War. In beginning early in the national period, Uruguay's experience was more like Chile's than Argentina's, though Chile's volume of immigration was proportionately much smaller and more of its immigrants came from non-Latin countries. In the second place, economic change was much less far-reaching in Uruguay than in Argentina and Chile. It consisted mainly in intensifying Uruguay's specialty, livestock-raising, and in stimulating a closely related and quite modest industrialization, chiefly in food processing, with ancillary improvements in transportation, communications, and banking facilities. Uruguay did not become a great wheat producer, as Argentina did, partly because of differences in soil. Nor, lacking mineral resources, did it carry industrialization as far as the other two. Foreign economic control and cultural domination had been established in all three countries by the turn of the century, but one gets the impression that both processes had been carried furthest in little Uruguay, which may be why the reaction prevailed first there.

The Great War was hardly over when the rapid increase of Uruguay's population began. The first census, 1852, showed a population of 132,000; the second, in 1860, 229,000; an estimate in 1873 was 450,000; and in 1908 the third census gave the total as 1,042,000 (all rounded figures). The rate of increase for 1852-1860 was more than 70 percent, and for the whole period 1852-1908, 700 percent. The growth was most rapid in Montevideo. It received an early stimulus from the Paraguayan War, 1865-1870, during which it served as a supply center for the Brazilian forces and its merchants are said to have reaped enormous profits. During this half-century, the city's population leaped up from 34,000 in 1852 to 215,000 in 1889 and on to 309,000 in 1908, and, as noted, its share of the total population increased from 25 percent to 30 percent. As in Argentina, migrants from the interior came to the city because the enclosure of fields with barbed wire threw them out of jobs; and even if immigrants did not prefer urban to rural life, as most did, they soon learned that it was hard for them to obtain land or employment in the countryside.

Farming did not prosper, but stock-raising did. Cattle and sheep multiplied and early in the next century frigoríficos were established. The economy became more unbalanced, vulnerable, dependent on the world market, and under foreign control. The government itself pointed the way and set the pace: by 1900 its external debt, $100 million, was the largest per capita in all Latin America. Foreigners had by now acquired the majority of rural properties and owned most of the railroads. The construction of the latter was the most novel economic development of this half-century. As in Argentina, most of the lines fanned out from the national capital and chief seaport. The first line was built in 1869 and by the end of the century Montevideo had been linked with towns in most parts of the country, including Rivera at the other extreme, on the Brazilian frontier. Stock-raising dominated the country more than ever, and cattle came first among the livestock. A census taken in 1900 showed more than 26 million head of cattle, a more than three-fold increase since the end of the Great War; of these, nearly half belonged to foreigners, most of them Brazilians. Again as in Argentina, there was a rural society, the Asociación Rural, founded in 1871. A dozen years later the owners of the saladeros, too, founded a society in a concerted effort to reverse the decline of salt-meat exports, but the effort failed as public preference caused a swing to other methods of preserving meat that yielded a more palatable product. The largest plant using them was Liebig's, at Fray Bentos near the port of Montevideo; it adopted canning and developed an extract that became popular in Europe and the United States. Wool was an increasingly important export item as a result of improvement in the breeds of sheep. Other exports included cattle on the hoof, hides, some wheat and corn, and an exotic item, ostrich feathers.

Foreign economic penetration was facilitated by the conversion of the country's leaders to economic liberalism, which grew to its height in Uruguay in the last third of the century. As in Argentina and Chile, it signified advocacy of free enterprise and opposition to government intervention in the economy except to promote its growth by helping private enterprise. By the 1890s its consequences were beginning to provoke a reaction in favor of government intervention, but this had only limited effect for another ten or fifteen years.

As noted by Juan Pivel Devoto, at the same time that the government's role in economic affairs was being narrowly restricted, it was expanding its social functions by taking over several that had traditionally been performed by the Roman Catholic Church. Among such measures were those secularizing cemeteries, exempting children in public schools from religious instruction at their parents' request, making civil marriage compulsory, limiting the number of religious houses, and subjecting them to government inspection. Most of these measures were adopted between 1861 and 1885. They accompanied, and in some respects anticipated, similar secularization movements in Argentina and Chile. In the development of public education, on the other hand, Uruguay lagged somewhat behind Argentina. Education, too, was a function once performed primarily by the church. In theory, the latter had been supplanted in Uruguay by the state, but nothing effective was done about it until the passage in 1877 of a law establishing free and compulsory primary education. It was largely the work of José Pedro Varela, the Uruguayan counterpart in public education of the Argentine Sarmiento, but a generation younger. Many of his ideas had come from Horace Mann, as had Sarmiento's, and from a French economist and educator, Courcelle Seneuil, on whom, as we shall see, Chilean policy makers also leaned heavily. Valera deserves much credit for the fact that within another generation Uruguay was leading Latin America in literacy and, as he had prayed it would, was producing more thinkers and fewer gauchos.

Party Strife and Assorted Dictatorships

The end of the Great War did not bring peace to Uruguay. It only stopped the foreign phase of the war, whose domestic phase, the conflict between Blancos and Colorados, continued in one form or another, military or political, through the second half of the century and beyond. The Colorados, some writers say, were primarily an urban party, the Blancos mainly rural. In fact, Blanco strength in the only large urban center, Montevideo, was considerable, especially among the politically active upper class, while the Colorados were about as much a rural party as the Blancos, and the greatest of all the caudillos, Fructuoso Rivera, was a Colorado.

The turbulent situation in Uruguay, resembling the one in Argentina in the 1820s out of which dictator Rosas emerged, led an enlightened minority to repudiate both parties and launch the *principista* movement, which reached its height in the 1870s. Its followers adopted the label "National Party," but others called them slightly disguised Blancos. Though the movement failed in the short run, it has been credited by leading historians Edmundo Narancio and Jacinto Oddone with having made the survival of militarism impossible, and the development of democracy possible, in Uruguay. What is more, Narancio describes the movement's liberal and constructive "civilian creed" as the backbone of the history of not only Uruguay but the whole Plata area, and as a major theme in the history of Chile and other Latin American countries. Among its chief exponents he includes Andrés Lamas of Uruguay, Sarmiento, Echeverría, and Mitre of Argentina, and José Victorino Lastarria of Chile.

A less flattering appraisal of the principistas is given by Alberto Zum Felde. He begins by treating them as spokesmen of the reaction of urban Montevideo against the gaucho influence of rural Uruguay. He notes a striking similarity, "making due allowance for the differences of environment and of the factors involved," between this moment in Uruguayan history and the one in Argentina preceding the rise of Rosas. As he sees it, the principistas' short-lived government suffered from the same fatal defect as the modernizing porteño government of Rivadavia a half-century earlier. Both governments seemed to think they were the whole country, and the principistas fancied that, by excluding the caudillos from office, they had suppressed caudillism and, along with it, the gauchos and traditionalism.

Neither country escaped dictatorship. Argentina had only one dictator, Rosas, but if we count from 1835, he lasted seventeen years. Uruguay had three, all in rapid succession from 1876 to 1890. Two of them were thoroughgoing, the third and last transitional to civilian rule. Although all were military, even the first two were comparatively mild. During the transitional dictatorship, 1886-1890, the political climate was one of peace and reconciliation, and the expanding European market's demand for Uruguay's products, along with European capital and enterprise, mainly English, helped to make the economic climate one of buoyant optimism. Corporations and banks were established, railroad and streetcar lines started, residential districts built, and electric lighting introduced. For Montevideo as well as for Buenos Aires, this was a Gilded Age.

Perhaps the most striking figure of this Uruguayan boom period was a Spaniard, Dr. Emilio Reus, called "the modern conquistador." Promoter and publicist, he was also a lawyer and a dramatist. After starting his American operations in Buenos Aires, he transferred them in 1887 to Montevideo. There he founded a bank and a construction company, built houses, parks, beach resorts, and a Grand Hotel to house an expected host of summer visitors from Argentina, and became the arbiter of finance and politics, a prodigal dispenser of favors, the lion of clubs, and the darling of salons. At his grandest, his I.O.U. for 3.7 million gold pesos, said to have been the largest ever signed, was accepted without demur. All his projects, however, were wrecked by the economic crisis of 1890, which was severe in Montevideo as well as in Buenos Aires; the hotel project suffered the added misery of competition from a new and elegant resort at Mar del Plata, Argentina. Dr. Reus died bankrupt in 1891. His Grand Hotel remained vacant for several years until it was taken over by the University of Montevideo.

The Decade of Rodó's Ariel

As the population of Montevideo multiplied six-fold between 1852 and 1889, the proportion of foreign-born among its inhabitants fell from 48 to 30 percent. Most of the foreigners were Europeans, and yet their relative decline in numbers was offset by an increase in the influence of Europe, especially of France in the cultural sphere and England in the economic. As a result, the gap widened between the capital and the interior, where the traditional Hispanic American way of life remained largely untouched by these novelties. In the course of the 1890s, a further extension of the railroads did something to bring the two closer together, as did the paean to tradition which was Montevidean José Enrique Rodó's never-to-be-forgotten *Ariel*, published at the end of the decade. Yet the gap was still wide when the new century began, bringing with it still newer and more forward-looking ideas, particularly about the social and political order in Uruguay.

Even during the economic crisis of 1890, the relative well-being and cosmopolitanism of Montevideo impressed visiting North American journalist Theodore Child, who had already visited Buenos Aires. In both cities, everything literary seemed to him to have been borrowed from France. Montevideo, which had had only one bookstore in 1842, now had several, and all their windows were crowded with books imported from Paris as soon as they were published. Among the most favored authors, all but Tolstoy were French: Guy de Maupassant, the Goncourt brothers, Coppée, and "the ever-present" (but now forgotten) Georges Ohnet. Inside the stores were Spanish translations of the same authors and also of Jules Verne and Paul de Koch. The Spanish classics, on the other hand, even *Don Quijote*, were hard to find, and for some of them, including the works of Lope de Vega, Calderón, and Quevedo, our informant looked in vain. As for the city's own literary activity, he found none at all, except that of political leaders and writers on finance. There were also big music stores and assorted shops well stocked with luxury articles, such as precious stones, silver, furniture, *objets d'art,* crystal, and women's clothing and accessories, brought from all over the world — Paris, Vienna, Milan, Yokohama, the Orient.

On the other hand, the only building Child found worthy of note was the old colonial Government House. In front of this, though, was a long bench on which, all day long, sat soldiers of the presidential guard, most of them "Negroes or colored men," with cigarettes in their mouths. As for society, he said, these people, like other Hispanic Americans, still had a closed family life and were hard to get to know; as in Buenos Aires and Santiago, there was no social animation except when a millionaire gave a party or the aristocratic club a ball for the cream of the creole families, or when there was an opera. The horse races, which the public was permitted to attend, were marked by an elegance and good manners that contrasted sharply with the porteño races, where he found the people ill-dressed and tasteless. However, concluded Child with evenhanded justice, Montevideo had no park that could compare with beautiful Palermo in Buenos Aires.

After a quick recovery from the crisis of 1890, economic growth was substantial until 1897, when it was interrupted by another civil war, fortunately brief. Montevideo gained from the extension of the westward railroad line upstream to Colonia, and from the construction of modern port facilities to match those already built at Buenos Aires. Both operations were financed through Baring Brothers of London, whose long-standing financial ties with Buenos Aires were no bar to the firm's serving the rival port of Montevideo with equal alacrity. The decade was also marked by a slight but significant change in economic policy in the direction of state control through the nationalization by purchase of the electric light company and the establishment, which had been long resisted, of a state bank, the Banco de la República. The new policy line was to be carried much further away from laissez-faire in the next quarter-century and to differentiate Uruguay clearly from its fellow members of the Southern Cone.

The two economic developments just mentioned involved political decisions and were harbingers of new issues that shaped new alignments under the old party labels. In 1890, civilians had supplanted the military in control of the government and for several decades thereafter the military were not to re-establish themselves except for brief interventions. Political problems remained in the forefront, but the new issues were increasingly those subsumed under the umbrella term, "the social question."

As described by Arturo Ardao, the social question was introduced into Uruguayan public life for the first time in 1893 by the Liberal Club of Montevideo, which campaigned for reforms including the creation of a "political-social" municipal government, the protection of women and children, and the relief of poverty. Thus introduced, the social question was superimposed upon the religious question, which had simmered or boiled from the 1860s to the 1880s. The liberal movement, once mainly anticlerical, now became the ground in which the first social agitations germinated.

One consequence was the cooling-off of many liberals, whose liberalism was political and anticlerical, and who were conservative on social questions.

Originally named the Francisco Bilbao Liberal Club in honor of the noted Chilean writer and reformer, the club dropped his name in 1900 because, to them, it no longer stood for the things the club now valued most. By this time they had moved well beyond the anticlericalism with which they identified Bilbao, and even this was no longer based on the same grounds. As one of his compatriots wrote to a friend in Montevideo as far back as 1894, "poor Bilbao is antiquated," for, as he explained, Chilean anticlericals now attacked the Catholic Church not as the citadel of despotism and in the name of liberty, but as the refuge of ignorance and in the name of science.

Several years were to pass before the social question would become a major concern of national policy. In the meanwhile, it was politics as usual, except that the old familiar "Wars of the Roses" between Colorados and Blancos, which had been reduced to occasional skirmishes for two decades, erupted in 1897 into the first full-fledged civil war since 1876. It was started by the Blancos, who had been excluded from national office all that time. It ended that same year on terms that improved their position somewhat. The Colorados were left in control of the central government, but the Blancos were given six departments and (an odd touch) $200,000 towards the expenses of their revolt.

This arrangement kept the country in a state of unstable equilibrium until 1903. Under it Uruguay had, in effect, two governments: a Colorado government headquartered in Montevideo, and a Blanco government headed by the last of Uruguay's great caudillos, Aparicio Saravia, whose capital was his country estate in the interior. At the turn of the century the Montevideo government, with Juan L. Cuestas at the helm until 1903, gave the policy of statism modest momentum. It set up economic commissions, initiated some public works, and completed others, among them the modern port facilities at Montevideo.

Culturally, too, the 1890s were a germinal decade. Foreign traveler Child's dictum that Montevideo had no writers except on political and financial matters had little justification when he made it in 1890, and none at all ten years later. Already in 1890, two Montevideans, Eduardo Acevedo Díaz (born in 1851) and poet Juan Zorrilla de San Martín (born in 1855), were writers of distinction. Even more distinguished was José Enrique Rodó, whose long essay *Ariel*, published in 1900, quickly won him an enthusiastic following and enduring fame through Spanish America. Later, it even achieved a measure of renown in the United States, though for the wrong reasons.

Oddly enough, most of these New World writers were saturated with the Old World's *fin de siècle* pessimism. Carlos Reyles, for instance, wrote about tortured souls in Uruguay, and had to cross the Atlantic to find enchantment, as he did in Seville, where he wrote about it in *El embrujo de Sevilla*, to the delight of a whole generation of readers. Even Rodó at times succumbed to the anguish fashionable in his day, and young philosopher Vaz Ferreira's public profession of faith in "the moral progress of the human spirit" made him a lonely figure amidst the surrounding intellectual gloom.

Rodó, also young (born in 1871, a year before Vaz Ferreira), saw a ray of hope. It illuminates his *Ariel*. This essay is one of those works that everybody talks about and few read. As a result, it has been persistently misinterpreted in the United States, where it is often cited as if it were only an attack on this country and a prime specimen of Yankeephobia. To be sure, Rodó does picture the United States to his readers as a leading exponent of the Caliban-like materialism against whose lures he warns them, and he does say of the United States, "I admire it, but I do not love it." But not loving it hardly makes him a Yankeephobe, and his warning against Calibanism is addressed first and foremost to his fellow Spanish Americans, whose own propensity towards materialism had been strikingly exhibited in Uruguay and Argentina in the quarter-century ending in 1900.

Ariel is not only a warning but an appeal — an appeal to Spanish Americans to hold fast to the Ariel spirit of the Hispanic race's glorious humanist tradition, which Rodó traces back lovingly to classical antiquity. His traditionalism marks him a conservative, and yet, as Arturo Ardao points out, he described himself as a liberal and a freethinker, which only goes to show how relative such terms are. His freethinking, shaped by the influence of Ernest Renan and his *Vie de Jésus,* was that of an agnostic full of admiration for Jesus and primitive Christianity. As the noted Mexican intellectual Samuel Ramos said, *Ariel* is a work of Christian as well as Hellenic humanism. Obviously, Rodó the humanist could not go along with the positivism and new scientism of his contemporaries and his traditionalism was out of phase with the increasingly forward-looking spirit of the times and the determination not to preserve things but to make them over. Only thirteen years after Rodó's death at the early age of 45, his fellow countryman Juan Zorrilla de San Martín could write with approval that, in the opinion of not a few Spanish Americans, it was high time to get rid of Ariel, "the cause of our inertia," and to acclimate Caliban, "forger of Anglo-American progress." Yet, as will appear later, traditionalism was only temporarily submerged and did not sink but still remained a vital force in all the Southern Cone countries in the third quarter of the twentieth century.

IV Chile, 1810-1910:
From Liberation to Dependency

Unique among all nations in its geography, Chile became in the nineteenth century unique among Latin American states in two other respects. It achieved political stability in the 1830s, two or more decades ahead of all the other states. Then, victory in the War of the Pacific (1879-1884) gave it a monopoly of a natural resource in great and increasing demand in Europe and the United States: the world's only large deposits of nitrates, which were widely used for purposes both of peace (fertilizers) and of war (in explosives). Ironically, however, these unique features, by making Chile exceptionally attractive to foreign investors and entrepreneurs, helped to assimilate it soon to the common Latin American type of "neocolonial" dependency on foreign corporations and the world market. The only large sector of the Chilean economy that remained under firm control by its own people at the close of the 1920s was the agricultural. This was dominated by great estates, most of whose owners were Chileans. They belonged either to its traditional aristocracy or, increasingly from the late nineteenth century, to its new plutocracy of industry and finance, who bought land more for its social prestige than for its economic value and in many cases were closely linked with foreign interests.

The process of neocolonization had already gone far enough by 1910 to provoke the beginning of a nationalist reaction among Chileans that reached its culmination in the early 1970s. The present chapter will stop with the foreign economic penetration that provoked it and the centennial celebration of political independence that gave it further impetus.

Independence and Chaos

In Chile, as in Argentina, the beginning of the struggle for independence dates from 1810. Unlike Argentina, Chile was reconquered for a time. When its liberation was finally achieved, in 1817-1818, it was with the indispensable assistance of General José de San Martín's expeditionary force from Argentina and of a navy which, though Chilean, consisted largely of surplus warships bought from the English East India Company. It was commanded by a cashiered (but later exonerated) British admiral, Lord Cochrane. British influence in Chile, apparent from the beginning of its independence, grew until the end of the century.

The new republic's first government was a military dictatorship. Its leadership was first offered to San Martín, but he prudently declined it in favor of Bernardo O'Higgins, commander of Chile's patriot forces during the war. O'Higgins, who on a long visit to Europe had acquired some ideas of the Enlightenment, now decreed a number of enlightened measures, including the abolition of entailed estates (mayorazgos). These brought him into frustrating collision with the country's semi-feudal aristocracy, headed by a titled nobility, in comparison with which the upper class of Buenos Aires seemed democratic. Chile's foremost revolutionary propagandist, the priest Camilo Henríquez, held up as a model for Chile the enlightened government of Buenos Aires, the patriotism of its people, and the democratic tendency of its institutions. The porteño government could not have agreed more. Its instructions to General San Martín declared that the colonial system in Chile "has always differed greatly from the other southern provinces [of Spanish America], for feudalism has prevailed there in almost its full strength and the lowest class of people has had to bear the weight of a conceited nobility and of a concentration of wealth in this small class." San Martín was then given the delicate task of lightening the burden of the lower class without alarming the aristocracy by a "violent transition" at the expense of their "rights and status." It is hardly surprising that he declined the dictatorship and this responsibility with it.

The struggle against aristocratic privilege was one of the factors that made the whole decade of the 1820s a time of turmoil in Chile. Another was the racial diversity of its people and the privileged status of all whites as compared with the other groups. Of a total population of some 500,000 in 1808, only 150,000 were whites (creoles). There were about 200,000 mestizos, 15,000 Peninsular Spaniards (most of whom were soon to be eliminated in one way or another), a handful of foreigners (79 in 1809), a few thousand Negroes (mostly slaves, of whom about 4,000 were freed by the abolition of slavery in 1823), and some 100,000 Araucanian Indians. Unrest among the non-white groups continued until the early 1830s, when a conservative regime was set up that again governed the country with a strong hand. Frontier clashes with the Indians were frequent until they were finally subdued in the early 1880s, a few years later than the Indians in Argentina.

O'Higgins was forced to go into exile in Peru in 1823. In the next few years confusion in Chile became chaos which turned into a civil war (1829-1830). As in Argentina, one cause of the conflict was a controversy over federalism versus centralism, but there was a division on broader issues between liberals and conservatives. In 1828 the liberals got the upper hand and proclaimed a constitution drafted for them by a learned but doctrinaire liberal exile from Spain, José Mora. Appropriately called an ideologist (*ideólogo* in Spanish, but a term that had recently come into use in most countries on both sides of the Atlantic), Mora produced a constitution that was written in beautiful Spanish but did not fit the situation in Chile. Much less did it suit the conservatives, who scrapped it after starting and winning the civil war.

This short-lived constitution was, as we have seen, an important source of Uruguay's Constitution of 1830, which lasted nearly a century. The explanation of the difference in longevity seems to lie mainly in two social differences between the two countries. First, Uruguay's aristocracy was not nearly so powerful as Chile's, being much newer and less firmly rooted, and also being more narrowly based on land-owning, whereas Chile's was mercantile as well, and so had many more dependents and clients. A bourgeois aristocracy, Alberto Edwards called Chile's in his book on the "aristocratic Fronde" (*La Fronda aristocrática*), one of the classics of Chilean historical writing. The Chilean elite were almost alone in the Hispanic world in regarding trade as compatible with aristocracy. Their attitude has been attributed to the strong Basque element among the leading families of Chile from early colonial times. These no-nonsense Basques differed from other Spaniards, notes Jaime Eyzaguirre, and agreed with the elites of old Venice and the Hanseatic League in looking on "merchant prince" as being not a contradiction in terms but an accurate designation for society's foremost members.

In the second place, by the 1830s foreigners were proportionately much more numerous in Uruguay than in Chile; many of those in Uruguay were liberals, and those who were not had no interest in upsetting the Constitution of 1830 for the benefit of the landowning aristocracy. In Chile, on the other hand, the microscopic foreign element of 79 persons in 1809 remained minuscule for half a century to come. Some of them took an important part in Chilean affairs, especially economic affairs—a fact reflected in the high incidence of non-Spanish names, mainly English, French, German, and

Italian, among the country's men and women of prominence. Besides being few in number until after mid-century, they seem to have fitted easily into a society dominated by a "bourgeois aristocracy" whose economic interests were broad enough to accommodate theirs quite comfortably.

Portales and the New Regime

The leader in fashioning an oligarchical regime out of materials of this kind was Diego Portales, a native of Chile, who in his own person represented the ruling class's fusion of aristocracy with trade. Like Rosas of Argentina, he was born in 1793, came from an upper-class family, reached manhood during the first phase of the struggle for independence, and took no part in it. Instead, he went into trade, which occupied him profitably and, until 1826, fully. In that year he entered politics for the first time, for business reasons, and as the head of a business group which soon formed a coalition with the aristocracy. Their aim was to stop what they regarded as a drift towards anarchy and to restore law and order for the first time since 1810. The upshot was the civil war of 1829-1830. The coalition won it, ousted the liberal regime, and scrapped the Constitution of 1828.

After the conservative victory, Portales proved himself, in Alberto Edwards's words, "a Julius Caesar on a small stage." The analogy is not perfect, if only because Portales had someone else appointed chief of state and operated behind the scenes much of the time. In or out of government, he took the lead in creating a stable, professional government that was nonpersonalist. He pushed Chile into a preventive war (1836-1839) with Peru and Bolivia, the success of which helped to consolidate the new regime and laid the foundations of Chile's foreign policy. (Portales was assassinated in the midst of war, in 1837.) Among the foundation stones he provided were nationalism and opposition both to continental Spanish American union and to the Monroe Doctrine. The United States, he said, planned to conquer all America, if not at once, then surely some day, and not by force of arms, but by influence in every sphere.

Chile's epoch-marking Constitution of 1833 institutionalized the regime that Portales was largely instrumental in establishing, but he took no part in the convention that adopted it. Although he wanted a constitution, since, given the climate of the times, one was needed to legitimize his regime, he had little interest in general principles and less in drafting constitutions. If, however, this one had not provided the kind of government he thought the country ought to have, he would no doubt have fought it to a finish.

The Constitution of 1833, like its predecessor of 1828, was drafted by a single person, but this time the author, Mariano Egaña, son of a patriot leader, was admirably equipped for the task. After long residence in London as Chile's envoy in the 1820s, he returned home convinced that the British system of king, lords, and commons provided just the right kind of balance his country so urgently needed. Also convinced, however, that it was high time for the leaders of the new Spanish American states to have done with their indiscriminate borrowing of foreign ideas and institutions, he made it his first principle that the British system must be adapted to the particular needs and capabilities of the Chilean people. The constitution that he drew up and the convention adopted provided for a strong president and a bicameral legislature consisting of a senate and a chamber of deputies and vested with the power of the purse and a veto on cabinet appointments. The members of both houses were to be chosen by indirect elections based on a restricted suffrage; the literacy requirement alone must have excluded fully three-fourths of Chile's adult males at that time. All women, of course, were excluded. A hierarchy of national courts was created. As in England, there was an established church; in Chile it was naturally Roman Catholic. The only feature of the constitution to which Portales objected seriously was its guarantee of individual rights. The proposition that the government must wait ("with folded arms," scoffed Portales) until a criminal was caught in the commission of a crime was to him incomprehensible. "In Chile," he wrote to a friend, "the law serves no purpose but to produce anarchy. Damn the law, if it doesn't let the government act freely at the right moment! This respect for the criminal, or the presumed criminal, will soon be the finish of this country."

Interpretations of this constitution have varied widely, particularly as regards the presidency. Ricardo Donoso, a leading Chilean authority, describes the president in one passage as a monarch in republican garb, and in another passage as a dictator. North American Richard Morse, on the other hand, sees in the countervailing powers vested by the constitution in Congress and the courts a recreation of the ancient "Spanish patrimonial state" with its safeguards against tyranny.

The regime Portales did so much to construct remained intact for many years, whereas those of other dictators, such as Rosas of Argentina and Díaz of Mexico, ended with their hold on power. The historian Eyzaguirre suggests that this was because theirs were more personalist than his, and less congruent with the psychology of their people. That is probably right as far as it goes, but more remains to be said in explanation of the remarkable stability of the Chilean political and social system for the next hundred years. Nor, as Maurice Zeitlin observes, can we be satisfied with other common explanations, such as the tradition of political democracy in Chile, the readiness with which its political parties formed coalitions, and the comparatively high level of Chile's economic development. His own comprehensive explanation, based on Seymour M. Lipset's "conflict theory" of politics, takes the form of seven interesting hypotheses. According to the most attractive of these, the capacity of Chile's ruling classes to govern effectively in the national interest was demonstrated, and their confidence bolstered, by the breadth and pace of the country's early economic development.

Growth and Territorial Expansion

Looking at the history of Chile since 1830 from the point of view of the political and social circles of Santiago — an appropriate vantage point, given the crucial importance of those circles in the national scheme of things — Alberto Edwards divides the first ninety years into three equal periods: 1830-1860, presidential domination and a government above parties, which were rudimentary, if they existed at all; 1860-1890, a government with parties, which now took shape, and an unstable equilibrium between president and Congress, a period that ended with the civil war of 1891; and 1891-1920, the classic period of presidential eclipse and parliamentary government under an ultraconservative oligarchy.

By 1850, Chile's half-million population at the beginning of independence had grown to 1.3 million, from which it went on up to 2.9 million in 1900 and 3.2 million in 1907, the last census before 1920; a substantial increase, but slow by comparison with Argentina and Uruguay. As population increased, so did urbanization. By the very broad definition of urban as including towns of as few as 1,000 inhabitants, the urban percentage of Chile's population increased from 27 in 1875 to 43 in 1907. By the more realistic definition that raises the floor from 1,000 to 10,000, the urban percentage in 1900 was only 21.8. As in Argentina and Uruguay, the national capital was by far the largest city and was growing most rapidly, but the discrepancy was not nearly so great in Chile. In 1895, for instance, Santiago contained about one-tenth of the nation's population, as compared with one-sixth in the case of Buenos Aires and almost three-tenths of the total in Montevideo five years later. In the same years Santiago was less than twice the size of the country's second city, Valparaíso, whereas Buenos Aires was several times larger than Argentina's second and third cities (Rosario and Córdoba) combined, and Montevideo led in Uruguay by an even wider margin. Thereafter, however, the concentration in Santiago increased so rapidly that by 1930 its population was nearly 30 percent of the national total.

The chief differential factor in Chile's slower rate of growth from mid-century to the 1920s — Argentina's rate was more than twice as fast, Uruguay's more than three times — was immigration, which Chile was far less successful in attracting than the other two. A promising beginning seemed to have been made when in the 1850s a substantial number of Germans settled in the south, in the Valdivia-Osorno area. The early promise was not fulfilled. In 1907, when immigrants had been flooding into the other two countries for a quarter-century and the flood was nearing its peak, the proportion of foreign-born in their populations was about 25 percent in Uruguay and close to 30 percent in Argentina, whereas in Chile it was just under 5 percent, a figure it never exceeded.

Despite its much smaller volume in Chile, immigration provoked a nationalist reaction in the early 1900s there as well as in Argentina, but with the difference that in Argentina the brand of nationalism provoked by it was upper-class and nostalgic, whereas in Chile it was middle-class and economic. The intellectual exponents of this resentment, Carl Solberg tells us, attacked foreign capitalist penetration as well as immigration. As early as the first decade of the century, writers such as Nicolás Palacios and Francisco Encina (author in later years of a best-selling history of Chile) were demanding that the government take action to prevent a foreign economic conquest of Chile.

That Chile fell so far behind in attracting immigrants was not for lack of trying. Rather, as Nicolás Sánchez Albornoz points out, Chile did not fulfill either of the two basic requirements for attracting a large volume of immigration, which were, first, the ability to produce the commodities demanded in Europe, and second, the existence of a serious labor shortage. To this it might be added that Chile was remote from the source of the immigration it wanted to tap, Europe.

In spite of these handicaps, Chile early developed an active sea-borne trade, principally in colonial times with Peru. From the 1790s onward, ships from the United States frequented Chilean ports; they came from various parts of the country, but the Chileans lumped them all together as *bostoneses* (Bostonians). Although the volume of trade with the United States was never large until the twentieth century, it took lively spurts at times, notably in the shipment of foodstuffs to California for several years after the beginning of the gold rush there. Thousands of Chileans took part in the rush. About the same time, Chile developed a modest but substantial trans-Pacific trade, mainly with Australia. The increase of Chile's overseas contacts was stimulated by the introduction in the 1840s of steam navigation by an entrepreneur from the United States, William Wheelwright. Another like him, Henry Meiggs, became a pioneer in railroad construction in Chile, which began in 1852.

Improvements in transportation strengthened Chile's agrarian system, which was one of the chief supports of its stability under upper-class rule. Dominating the system were the great landowners, whose estates contained nearly all the best land in central Chile. The rural labor force, whose support underlay their power in national politics, was made up mainly of two groups: the *inquilinos* or servant tenants, "the cream of the labor force," and the peons, who were "a miserable and vagrant sort," in other words, migrant workers. As Arnold Bauer has demonstrated, after the mid-nineteenth century the increasing demand for Chilean foodstuffs produced a corresponding increase in pressure on the labor force. Other countries' solutions for problems of this kind were either to import labor or to use farm machinery, or, as in the case of Argentina, to do both. Chile did neither. Its labor supply, according to Bauer, was abundant throughout the century, and its landlords' solution was to make more demands on that labor force. Any worker who was unwilling to stay on their terms had no choice but to move to a city, probably Santiago, or to the mining region of the north, or to emigrate, as many did. Some, for example, emigrated to Argentina, where wages were eight or ten times higher. Emigration, however, only drained off the surplus population, and enough workers remained to maintain the system virtually intact until the 1960s.

The improvements in transportation and communications also stimulated Chile's export trade. Copper was its chief export item in the middle third of the nineteenth century, and from 1850 to 1880 Chile held first place in world production, accounting for from one-third to one-half of the total. Most of Chile's copper went to England, but the mining and smelting of it, which had been carried on in Chile in pre-Columbian and colonial times, remained in Chilean hands. Production methods, however, were primitive and after 1880 competition from the United States and Spain brought about a rapid decline of the industry in Chile, which did not begin to recover until after 1900.

Second in time, the nitrate industry grew rapidly in the 1870s and 1880s in the Chilean economy as well as in world production, thus compensating for the decline of the copper industry after 1880. When the Chileans began to exploit nitrates on a large scale in the 1860s, the principal deposits lay in two foreign provinces, Bolivian Antofagasta and Peruvian Tarapacá, both in the Desert of Atacama. The penetration of these provinces by Chile reminds one of the penetration of Mexican Texas by settlers from the United States some forty years earlier; so does the sequel. Controversies boiled up between Chile and each of the other two governments; they formed a secret alliance, and Peru started to nationalize what was by then the largely Chilean-owned nitrate industry in its province of Tarapacá. The War of the Pacific broke out in 1879. It was a replay of the war of 1836-1839 in the sense that Chile was again outnumbered by the other two, and again Chile won. This time, however, it made territorial acquisitions. From Peru, under the Treaty of Ancón (1883), dictated to the loser on its own soil, Chile received Tarapacá and the right to occupy the adjoining provinces of Tacna and Arica for ten years, after which a plebiscite would determine whether they should revert to Peru or be ceded to Chile. From Bolivia, under a truce (1884), Chile took the whole province of Antofagasta, turning the defeated into a landlocked country.

The war and its outcome left a heritage of bitter resentment in the two defeated and despoiled countries. It also gave rise to thorny questions that were not settled for years to come, if ever. Another consequence of the war was the Chilean government's opposition for many years thereafter to any inter-American or other international

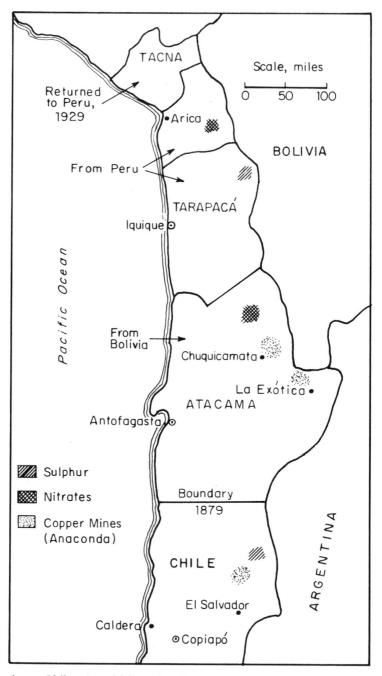

Northern Chile: Acquisitions in the War of the Pacific, 1879-1883,
Showing Copper Mines and Other Minerals

arrangement under which its right to the conquered territories might be called into question. On the other hand, Chile's war booty was a bonanza. This was what gave it a virtual nitrate monopoly until the end of World War I in 1918. In addition, Antofagasta and Tarapacá contained most of the ores that were to make possible a revival of the copper industry in the early twentieth century on a much greater scale than before. The exports of nitrates and copper enabled Chile to maintain its international balance of payments, and the export taxes on them provided the great bulk of the government's revenues for many years to come.

Laissez-Faire, Social Reform, and Anticlericalism

Foreigners soon gained control first of the nitrate and then of the copper industry in Chile, both of which had been in Chilean hands. That they were permitted to do so was in conformity with the prevailing doctrine of laissez-faire or free enterprise. That doctrine had begun to prevail in Chile in the late 1850s, partly through the missionary labors of Jean Gustave Courcelle-Seneuil, whom we have already met in Uruguay and who for eight years served as adviser to Chile's ministry of treasury. The conversion of the Chileans lasted more than half a century. The first major political group to backslide was the Radical Party, which officially renounced laissez-faire at its convention in 1906.

The issue of social reform was a chief factor in undermining faith in that doctrine. It was also an important factor in the controversy over church-state relations. That went on throughout the rise, reign, and fall of laissez-faire, from the mid-nineteenth century to the 1920s, when both issues were settled, after a fashion. A major personality involved in the controversy was Francisco Bilbao, who in his short life (1823-1865) achieved international renown as a writer and was the first native-born Chilean to do so. He drew inspiration from his senior by a generation, the French poet, publicist, and Catholic reformer H. F. R. de Lamennais. Though a devout Roman Catholic and a member of the upper class, Lamennais deplored the church's ties with that class and the state in the maintenance of an unjust social system. His books made a great impact on Argentine exiles of the Rosas period, particularly Alberdi and Echeverría, and the exiles helped make them well known in Chile and Uruguay.

The mood in Chilean intellectual circles in that period was ani-

mated and hospitable to new ideas and foreigners, among whom
were Sarmiento and the illustrious and versatile Venezuelan, Andrés
Bello. Francisco Bilbao grew up in this stimulating atmosphere. He
rushed into politics on the left wing and propagated Lamennais'
ideas and his own in books, articles, and speeches that won him the
admiration of liberals throughout Latin America. A generation
after his death he was still so greatly respected in Uruguay that, as
we have seen, the Liberal Club of Montevideo named itself for him.

Bilbao was one of the United States' most merciless critics—
though not for its economic penetration, which had hardly begun—
until the 1860s, when it took a stand against the French invasion of
Mexico and began to abolish slavery. Bilbao thereupon reversed his
stand and in 1864 even called on Latin America to ally itself with
the United States. Although there was reason for his reversal, by the
end of the century it had made his brand of liberalism seem anachronistic to Latin American liberals, especially in Uruguay and his
own Chile.

José Victorino Lastarria, politician and publicist, lawyer and professor of law, was a leader in the continuing effort to make Chilean
society more secular as well as more liberal. His efforts were directed
mainly toward the latter aspect, but succeeded better in the former,
in spite of the strong hold of traditional religious practices and beliefs on both the upper and lower classes of society. Even in relatively
cosmopolitan and modern Santiago, the streets were kept clear for
religious processions from Thursday to Saturday of Holy Week by
prohibiting all traffic except pedestrians and physicians on horse-
back. Places of business were permitted to be open only from dawn
until 8 A.M., and hawkers of bread and water to circulate only until
11 A.M.

The abandonment of such regulations in the 1870s illustrates the
increasing secularization of Chilean society. In that decade and the
next, anticlericalism made rapid progress in Chile, as it was doing in
Argentina and had begun to do in the 1860s in Uruguay. In Chile,
the requirement of religious instruction in public secondary schools
and the university was abolished; a dispute between the government
and the cathedral chapter of Santiago led to the expulsion of the
papal nuncio and a severance of relations with the Vatican (shortly
before a similar breach between Argentina and the Vatican); and
Congress secularized cemeteries and legalized civil marriages. These
measures were hailed by liberals as promoting religious liberty. In

the political field they were matched by an electoral reform law adopted in 1884, but that was flagrantly violated the very next year by the same administration that had procured its passage.

From Presidential to Congressional Government

Another reform urged with special zeal by Lastarria was the curbing of presidential power. This issue was resolved during the administration of President José Manuel Balmaceda at the close of the agitated decade of the 1880s; it came to a head under greatly increased pressure from what historian Julio Heise González calls "creole parliamentarism," which was as old as the constitution itself. Ironically, as Alberto Edwards pointed out, Balmaceda himself had once been "an apostle and precursor" of the parliamentarism that was to be his undoing in 1891.

There is now general agreement among historians that the clash between Balmaceda and Congress was not merely one of personalities or constitutional interpretation, but there is still considerable disagreement as to what else was involved. Julio César Jobet declares that nitrates are the key to the "revolution" against Balmaceda. He attributes it to the opposition of "the landholding and plutocratic class and the imperialist consortiums" headed by Thomas North, "nitrate king" and representative in Chile of English capitalism, to the president's "great economic and social plans" to nationalize the nitrate industry, socialize banks and loan institutions, diffuse technical and professional training more widely, and carry out an ambitious program of public works. A different view is taken by Eduardo Frei Montalva in a history of his country's political parties written before he became president of the republic. Frei attributes the clash only partly to Thomas North and Chilean and foreign bankers and maintains that it was due also to the resentment of conservatives over Balmaceda's support of anticlerical measures and to that of their "patrician" inner core to his incitement of lower-class belligerency. Heise González, on the other hand, insists that the conflict was between two sectors of the "bourgeoisie" and that the "popular masses" (a term he uses interchangeably with "lower classes") were completely out of the fray—below rather than above it.

Six months after the short-lived "revolution" of 1890 in Argentina, and near the end of Balmaceda's five-year term, his conflict with Congress was brought to a head by a dispute over cabinet appointments. When Congress tried to force him to give in by refusing to pass an appropriation bill, Balmaceda declared the preceding year's revenue act still in effect—a clearly unconstitutional action by which he lost legitimacy in the eyes of most of the ruling class. Both sides appealed to the armed forces and they responded by bifurcating along service lines. Most of the army sided with Balmaceda, the navy with Congress, because, we are told, the traditionalist, German-trained army automatically obeyed its commander-in-chief, the president, whereas the navy had been shaped by the influence of its British mentors in a spirit of bourgeois constitutionalism.

The eight months of fighting began and ended in 1891. It cost 10,000 lives. Congress won, thanks to the navy's control of the high seas, which gave Congress quickest access to the northern mining area, the source of two-thirds of the government's revenues, and also to essential foreign sources of arms and ammunition. Balmaceda took refuge in the friendly American legation and, when he saw all was lost, committed suicide.

Continuity and Change in the Parliamentary Period

As Jay Kinsbruner says, the civil war of 1891 was a watershed in the history of Chile. The pace of the ensuing change was, however, slower and much less marked than we usually associate with the term watershed. Most of the factors that stand out in the next generation were already there in the preceding one. These include not only elements of the infrastructure that necessarily change slowly, such as the mining and agricultural systems and the ethnic composition of the people, but also political, social, and cultural elements of the superstructure. By 1890, labor unions and labor violence were already familiar in Chile, and all but one of the political parties of any significance in the next two decades had taken shape. Foreign investment and foreign business enterprise had become a major factor in the Chilean economy in the 1880s, and the United States and Germany were beginning to offer Great Britain a competition in this field that was to become much sharper after 1890. Newspapers long antedated 1890 and merely continued thereafter to play their role as an unrivaled means of mass communication until radios first came into widespread use in the 1930s. The armed forces, which played a decisive part in the political conflict in 1891 and were to repeat the operation more than once in the 1920s, were descended in a direct line from the armed forces of the war of independence, and the factors that modernized them were in operation before 1890. These factors included service academies, technological improvements, and training by foreign experts, as indicated above: German for the army, British for the navy.

Finally, there was continuity in the field of education. An apt illustration is the controversy over the *estado docente*, or "teaching state," a term that signified a state-controlled system of public instruction. This was attacked by the clerical-conservative sector with equal bitterness before and after 1890. Among the leading champions of state education were, before that date, one of Chile's and South America's great historians, Diego Barros Arana, and after it, his former student Valentín Letelier, one of Chile's and South America's leading educators. In the end, the "teaching state" won out. To Letelier and to many of his contemporaries in Chile, it seemed logical to extend the rationale of state intervention from the field of education to that of the economy. Accordingly, Letelier played an important part in bringing about the Radical Party's renunciation of laissez-faire in 1906.

If so much of what was thought and done after 1890 had been anticipated years before, then what was new? Much was new in detail, of course, but the most striking changes, such as those in personnel, parties, corporations, technology, and international ties were changes in degree and not in kind. There were two major exceptions to this generalization. One, already referred to, was the beginning of a slow but massive change, first in public opinion and then in public policy, from laissez-faire to state intervention in the economy; the other, the appearance of Marxism as a political force. Otherwise, the principal impression one gets from scanning the post-1890 scene is of seeing old faces in new garb.

The greatest degree of change in this period took place in the character of the government itself. Without bothering to adopt a new constitution, the oligarchical Congress pushed the president into the background and turned the game of politics into a pleasant pastime for opulent magnates. As upper-class Edwards describes it, though this oligarchy still boasted an aristocratic background, it was increasingly plutocratic, a seat in either chamber was regarded as equivalent to a title of nobility, and seats, openly purchased, sometimes cost as much as a million pesos (a peso being about equal to a dollar). The oligarchy divided into factions and one government succeeded another so rapidly and with so little difference from one to the next that this game of musical chairs made a mockery of Chile's so-called parliamentary system. This farce combined with the still dominant doctrine of free enterprise to deprive Chile of effective government where economic and financial problems were concerned. To the ruling class, such problems seemed hardly to exist. Most government expenses were covered by revenue from nitrate exports, and most of the rest by emissions of paper money. Although the resulting inflation was apparently not planned by the oligarchs, they profited from it while the poor, including the relatively poor middle class, suffered.

Yet at the same time control of key sectors of the national economy was passing from the oligarchs and other Chileans to foreigners. Chief among the latter were British interests, which, until 1890, dominated commerce as well as nitrates. After that, primacy gradually shifted to Germany and the United States, as related by Chilean historian Hernán Ramírez Necochea. Through the Hamburg Amerika and Kosmos shipping lines and branches of its principal banks and industrial firms, Germany moved in slowly in the 1870s, accelerated greatly during Balmaceda's anti-English administration, and increased German trade with Chile tenfold between 1895 and 1913. By the latter date Germany had taken first place as a source of Chile's imports and second place in its total trade. Until 1900 United States interests were represented mainly by W. R. Grace & Company, which was active in the nitrate trade as well as shipping. A branch of the New York Life Insurance Company was established in Santiago in 1900 and four years later William Braden began the phoenix-like revival of the copper industry. Something like a stampede followed. American investments in Chile soared from $5 million in 1900 to $200 million in 1920, and commerce rose from $13.7 million in 1890 to $104.4 million in 1913. The United States' share of Chile's total trade rose from 5 percent in 1880 to 19 percent in 1913.

For some Chileans, too, business was now booming, but by 1910 uneasiness over the foreign penetration was beginning to spread. So also was the realization that their country was falling behind its Argentine rival across the Andes in population, wealth, and power. It is hardly surprising that Chile's centenary of independence in that year was celebrated with a great deal less éclat than Argentina's.

Part Two

From Development to Depression

V Argentina:
Fall from Euphoria, 1910-1940

Mar del Plata is Argentina's best known seashore resort and the equivalent of Uruguay's Punta del Este and Chile's Viña del Mar. It fronts on the Atlantic Ocean some 250 miles southeast of Buenos Aires. Its history as a porteño pleasure dome, told in gaudy detail by Juan José Sebreli, dates from 1886, when the first wave of tourists arrived by the just-completed railroad line linking it with the capital. These were no ordinary tourists, for among them were Carlos Pellegrini and Paul Groussac, who moved in select political, social, and intellectual circles. Two years later, Pellegrini presided, and the future Tsar Nicholas II of Russia was a guest, at the banquet inaugurating the luxurious Bristol Hotel, around which the high life at Mar del Plata revolved for the next half century. Its *belle époque* as a playground for the upper crust lasted almost as long. In 1934, however, the middle class began to take over, only to be jostled in turn, only a dozen years later, by the vanguard of a working class invasion.

The middle class suffered from this kind of squeeze in other ways as well. Two examples will suffice. The electoral reform of 1912 seemed to augur a long period of middle-class domination under a representative system of government, and in the election of 1916 the middle-class Radical Party did indeed wrest control from the oligarchy. Yet only fourteen years later the Radicals were defenestrated by a military dictator, from whom control soon passed back to the oligarchy for a dozen years and then on to another military dictatorship and the Perón regime. The other example is the essentially middle-class University Reform movement, which in 1918 began to revolutionize the country's upper-class system of higher education, only to languish in the 1920s and, when revived in the following decade, to be identified with social reform in the interest of the lower classes.

The rise and frustration of the middle class therefore seems a suitable theme about which to group the major developments from the centenary of 1910 to Hitler's conquest of Western Europe in 1940, which was an event of the first magnitude even for far-off Argentina. The period was marked by important developments in almost every aspect of the nation's life. It began in euphoria and ended in a double depression, psychological as well as economic. After an overview of the whole period, key developments of the pregnant 1930s will be examined, with special attention to those that point towards the emergence of Juan Perón and his regime in the mid-1940s.

Revolution by Consent

President Roque Sáenz Peña could have been called, with as good reason as Franklin Roosevelt, a traitor to his class. He came of a patrician family of Buenos Aires, and yet he played a major role in the enactment of the electoral reform of 1912 that made it possible for the Radical Party to break the conservatives' monopoly of power in 1916 by electing its own candidate for the presidency, Hipólito Yrigoyen. For the next fourteen years the Radicals held control and seemed to be strengthening their hold on it until just before the end. Their greatest victory came in 1928, when Yrigoyen won a second term by a landslide.

The oligarchs' acquiescence in their defeat and protracted exclusion from a government they had managed with mounting success for half a century constituted a revolution by consent that contrasts sharply with the intransigence of the Mexican oligarchy and the bloody revolution of these same years which ousted it along with its presiding genius, Porfirio Díaz. The contrast is almost as sharp with the stubborn, if not intransigent, resistance of this same Argentine oligarchy after its restoration in 1930 to all the mounting pressures for change to which it was subjected from various directions. As a result, it was again sent packing in 1943, this time not by ballots but by the armed forces and without a return ticket.

Sáenz Peña was admirably equipped for the task of inducing a refractory conservative Congress to pass the electoral reform laws. Besides being a member of what conservatives still thought of as the natural ruling class, he had a long and distinguished record of public service, most of it diplomatic. Born in 1851, he was president of the provincial Chamber of Deputies when only 26 and then had a Byronic interlude of military service with Peru in its war with Chile, followed by several sober years of law practice. Beginning in 1888, he devoted some twenty years to diplomacy. During that time he was, among other appointments, ambassador to Uruguay, Spain, and Italy, and a delegate to international conferences in Montevideo, Washington (1889-1890), where he made his famous "America for humankind" speech, and the Hague Peace Conference of 1907, where he headed his government's delegation.

The celebrated electoral reform laws of 1912, generally referred to collectively as the Sáenz Peña Law, made four major changes in the existing law. They provided for: (1) the secret ballot, to replace voice voting and thereby curb intimidation of voters, as, for exam-

ple, of employees and tenants by employers and landlords; (2) a new
registration of voters, to replace an outdated one containing too
many names of men now dead if they ever lived; (3) compulsory
voting; and (4) the "incomplete list" of candidates, a provision intended to ensure minority representation and to foster the development of a two-party system by allocating two thirds of the seats in
each constituency to the party receiving the largest number of votes,
and the remaining third to the party with the next highest number.
Manhood suffrage had been nominally in effect since 1853.

In force for most of the next half century, these provisions varied
widely in effectiveness from time to time and from place to place.
Generally speaking, the secret ballot worked much better in urban
than in rural areas and was long a dead letter in isolated places. The
new registration was duly conducted but soon became outdated.
The two-party system was never established (it flourished in Uruguay), but at least there were usually fewer parties than in Chile and
minorities did have representation. Compulsory voting too remained a dead letter for many years, but there was a large and
steady increase from this time on in the proportion of voters to the
number eligible to vote. It rose from 9 percent in 1910 to 30 percent
in 1916, 40 in 1928, 48 in 1937, 56 in 1946 (Perón's first election),
84 in 1963, and nearly 90 percent in 1973 (Perón's third presidential
election).

In estimating the importance of the Sáenz Peña Law, we should
remember that some of the major factors adversely affecting the
electoral system lay outside its scope. Among these were its perversion by bribery, corruption, and stuffing the ballot box, and the
cancellation of it by force. Unhappily, perversion and cancellation
were to prevail during most of the law's half century of life. The
national elections of the period of Radical control, 1916-1930, appear to have been largely free from both. Yet even then the system
was distorted by the Radicals' lavish use of the power of federal intervention in the provinces to eject unfriendly provincial governments, thereby shifting votes to the Radical Party in both houses of
Congress and the Electoral College.*

The first national election held under the Sáenz Peña Law was

---

*Such interventions have been frequent in Argentina. The constitution authorizes them for
(among other purposes) the maintenance of a republican form of government. The Constitution of the United States, from which the provision was borrowed, contains a similar stipula-
tion, but, in sharp contrast to Argentine practice, it has rarely been invoked except during
the post-Civil War period of Reconstruction.

that of 1916. By that time Sáenz Peña was dead, but the vice-president who replaced him executed the law faithfully. The Radical Party's presidential candidate was its peerless leader for the last twenty years, Hipólito Yrigoyen.* He won by the narrowest of margins. Even that was provided by a one-time fellow Radical, who had left the party and frankly detested its candidate. This was Lisandro de la Torre, one of the most attractive figures in Argentine public life during this period, and the leader of the small Progressive Democrat Party, which dominated his own province of Santa Fe but had little strength elsewhere. Yrigoyen led in the popular vote but fell just short of a majority in the Electoral College. Since the only alternative was the continuation of the oligarchical regime, which seemed to de la Torre even worse, he reluctantly came to the rescue and Yrigoyen was elected with not a vote to spare.

Middle-Class Radicalism

Hipólito Yrigoyen was described by a contemporary, Carlos Ibarguren, as looking like an enigmatic Buddha. There was certainly much that was enigmatic in his career. Other Argentines who were comparable in character and ability to Lisandro de la Torre, such as Juan B. Justo and José Ingenieros, and who knew Yrigoyen well, likewise broke with him early and had a lasting aversion for him. Yet, in his third of a century as leader of his party, he won the enduring devotion of many of its members. He suppressed a general strike in the "Tragic Week" of 1919 with a heavy hand, and the benefits labor received from him during his eight years as president were scanty, especially in comparison with those conferred on labor in Uruguay by his contemporary José Batlle y Ordóñez. And yet he won renown as the champion and benefactor of labor and the common man in general. The mass enthusiasm he aroused almost to the end is particularly hard to understand in view of the fact that he had none of the charismatic qualities usually associated with mass leadership. He disliked public appearances, was a poor public speaker, and not much better as a writer. He was deficient in machismo, being neither a military hero of the Roca type, nor a flamboyant gaucho like Rosas, nor (though he had mistresses) a lover of great renown. Instead, he was a rather obscure schoolteacher who moon-

---

*His own spelling. The name is usually written Irigoyen.

lighted as a ganadero or cattleman on rented property, so that he had neither the prestige of an estanciero nor the popular appeal of a gaucho.

In fact, Yrigoyen was neither rich nor poor, neither outstanding nor insignificant, but somewhere in between; and perhaps that partly explains his success as a party leader. For his was a middle-class party, and in Argentina what is described for convenience as the middle class was in his day simply a heterogeneous aggregation of in-between fragments of society. Its Argentine students tell us that it was the largest middle class in Latin America at that time and was still growing, and that it comprised perhaps 30 percent of the population in 1914 and 40 percent in 1940. But they also tell us convincingly that it lacked unity and esprit de corps. The shopkeepers, office workers, and skilled artisans on its lower edge had nothing more in common with members of its upper fringe than their common dread of organized workingmen, by whom they felt threatened. As for the upper middle class, its members liked to identify themselves with the class just above, whose manners they copied and whose values they accepted. As we have noted elsewhere, the new industrial middle class, which had begun to emerge in the 1890s, and which might have provided the whole class with effective leadership, was made up largely of men of immigrant stock who took no part in public affairs and did not even become naturalized.

Originally, therefore, the Radical Party was for the most part a native Spanish American, creole party, and that gave it some semblance of unity. After its success in 1916, however, the operation of the bandwagon syndrome attracted an assortment of recruits that increased its heterogeneity. It did not even have a definite program or vision to hold it together after reaching its original goal of electoral reform. Yrigoyen did leave a considerable heritage of slogans and pseudopolicies, but the most important of the latter, economic nationalism, was never clarified and his application of it was inconsistent and narrowly limited. When his party's opponents challenged it to produce a platform, he denounced them as impertinent. He even asserted that the UCR (Unión Cívica Radical) was not a party at all "in the militant sense," but was instead a "conjunction of forces emerging from the opinion of the nation."

In fact during Yrigoyen's lifetime the UCR was a party, though perhaps not a very well organized one, and it was a prime illustration of personalism in politics—as its secessionist faction in 1924 alleged, calling their new party Antipersonalist. The original party rose with him, fell with him, and did his bidding, and its creole bond of unity was sealed by his leadership. But how did he do it, lacking most of the usual attributes of leadership? The question has puzzled posterity, as it did in those days all but his devotees.

No generally satisfactory explanation has been offered, but perhaps a clue to one is provided by Yrigoyen's extraordinary blend of mysticism and sanctity with plain political horse sense. His discourse about the Radicals' and his own role was larded with such words as cause, creed, and apostolate. His obscure style shrouded these words in an otherworldly haze, the effect of which was heightened by his addiction to Krausism. Kraus was a German philosopher of little note elsewhere in Europe whose writings had a great vogue among Spanish liberals at this time. In the words of Fredrick Pike, Krausism "was in keeping with the Spanish temperament because it accepted the importance of intuitive and even mystical experience in arriving first at morality and then at religion." To which it should be added that Yrigoyen had a strong strain of the Spanish temperament and stressed Argentina's ties, past and present, with Spain, as when he officially dubbed Columbus Day *Día de la Raza*, meaning "Day of the [Spanish] Race." Intentionally or not, his air of enigmatic Buddha intensified the mystical effect still further. Yet, along with all this, he kept a sharp eye on the practicalities of politics and showed a fine sense of timing. In his two presidential campaigns he played the unwilling candidate until the party almost literally dragged him into the arena.

During the period of Radical domination from 1916 to 1930 there were three quite different administrations by two utterly different men: Hipólito Yrigoyen (1916-1922), Marcelo T. de Alvear (1922-1928), and Yrigoyen again (1928-1930). Much as the three administrations differed from each other and from the preceding conservative governments, when the Radicals' term was over, they had made no fundamental change in either the government or the economy. One in higher education that might perhaps qualify as fundamental, the University Reform, was begun (1918) and largely carried out independently of the Radical Party. That reform was nevertheless one of the highlights of Yrigoyen's first six years in the Casa Rosada. Others were his resolute adherence to neutrality throughout World War I, which ranged him with Chile and against the United States after the latter entered the war in April 1917; his suppression of the general strike in 1919; his taking Argentina into the League of Nations and then quickly out again in a huff over a fancied slight; and, at the close, the founding of the government petroleum agency YPF (Yacimientos Petrolíferos Fiscales).

Alvear, his handpicked successor, was a member of an old patrician family and the leader of the Radical Party's conservative wing. In 1924 he broke with Yrigoyen over the latter's meddling in his administration and formed a separate party. It kept the Radical label but added Antipersonalist. Alvear gave YPF its first director and strong encouragement, and in general his administration differed more in tone and personnel than in policy from Yrigoyen's.

In 1928 the Antipersonalist presidential candidate suffered a crushing defeat at the hands of Yrigoyen, an eleventh-hour entry in the race. His second administration, cut short by the coup of 1930, was hardly a year old when the Great Depression that began in 1929 struck Argentina's vulnerable export economy early and hard. His failure to cope with the problems it spawned was complete. By mid-1930 he was 78 and seemingly senile, and he neither acted nor let others act for him. In addition, his administration had become as flagrantly corrupt as any under the oligarchy; and, in the words of Ricardo Rojas, himself a Radical, the government had violated the Sáenz Peña Law by its interventions in the provinces, had nullified the collaboration of cabinet and Congress, and had deserted the Radical Party's own principles and democratic ideals.

Through all three administrations there had been a rising tide of fascist and other antidemocratic and authoritarian sentiment in postwar Europe. The current converged on mimetic Argentina from various sources, principally the France of Charles Maurras, the Spain of dictator Primo de Rivera, and the Italy of Benito Mussolini. One feature of the new authoritarianism was the belief—not confined to the armed forces themselves—that it was their mission to save the nation from disaster at the hands of corrupt and bungling politicians. Examples provided by Argentina's near neighbors were, in Chile, the establishment of the military dictatorship of 1927-1932 under Colonel (later general) Carlos Ibáñez, and, in Brazil, the decisive role of the military in the revolution of October 1930 that ousted the constitutional government and brought Getulio Vargas to power.

In Argentina, the antidemocratic current toppled Yrigoyen's government on September 6, 1930, in what is called a revolution. Yet, though it was a deadly serious affair and marked a turning point in Argentine history, the operation was carried out in a way that would have been comical if there had been no bloodshed — and, in fact, there was very little. The government was overthrown by a tiny fraction of the armed forces that represented their two extreme age groups and almost nothing in between.* Old General José F. Uriburu, one of the army's two most prestigious officers, led the revolutionary band, and a battalion of cadets from the military academy made up the great bulk of it.

It was not apparent at the time that this was no laughing matter. Applauded by crowds happy that something was at last going to be done about the depression and as enthusiastic over Yrigoyen's easy expulsion as they had been only two years earlier over his landslide re-election, Uriburu's musical comedy force met with little resistance as it proceeded with its takeover. That was ostensibly designed to be only a brief prelude to the restoration of constitutional government purged of Yrigoyenist iniquity. Among the amused spectators of the Radical government's fall, says Torcuato Di Tella, were the great bulk of the bourgeoisie, the intellectuals, and organized labor, all of them critical of the regime, often for opposite reasons.

The applause died down when, a month later, General Uriburu unveiled his real plan. This was not to protract his military dictatorship, but something much more serious and more alien to Argentine ways and traditions: to change its governmental system to a corporative one that looked like a cross between the fascist system of Italy and that of Spain. His proposal represented the thinking of the self-styled Nacionalistas, a new right-wing group that remained small but influential into the Perón period. Most Argentines were nationalists of one kind or another, but the Nacionalistas' variety was elitist and fervently clerical and rejected not only political but also economic liberalism, including laissez-faire. This was too much even for many of the oligarchy and the armed forces, among them the army's other most prestigious officer, General Agustín P. Justo. Although Uriburu twisted and turned, he was too maladroit a politician to cope with their pressure, which combined with his own ill health to extort his consent to the re-establishment of constitutional government.

---

*It has been charged that American oil interests promoted the revolution. They may have been quite capable of doing so, but the charge has never been documented and, as an explanation, it is superfluous.

Conservative Restoration

Accordingly, a national election was held in November 1931. The Radicals nominated Alvear, whom the crisis had brought back into the original party. He was disqualified by the government, however, on the valid ground that the constitution prohibited re-election of a president until another term (six years) had elapsed since the end of his own; and only three years had passed since the end of Alvear's. The Radical Party became enraged and refused to nominate anyone in his place though it was free to do so. It sulked for the next four years, returning to its pristine policy of "abstention and revolution." Many members of the party, however, joined Democrat Progressives and Socialists in forming a coalition, the Alianza Civil, with Lisandro de la Torre as its candidate. It remained the chief opposition party until the Radical Party resumed normal political activity in 1935.

The conservative party, now calling itself National Democrat, chose General Justo as its candidate for the presidency. In addition to a distinguished service record and great influence with his fellow officers, Justo had served in Alvear's cabinet in the 1920s and bore the Antipersonalist Radical label, which had more drawing power than National Democrat. The second place on the ticket went to National Democrat Julio A. Roca, Jr., son of the former president. In what the opposition denounced as a thoroughly dishonest election, Justo won by a wide margin and was inaugurated in February 1932. Uriburu took part in the ceremony, then left for Paris, and died there of cancer a few months later. Yrigoyen, after imprisonment for a time on Martín García Island, died in Buenos Aires the next year. His death was followed by another reversal of public sentiment, this time a powerful one in his favor. It was probably due in large part to disillusionment over the sequel to his loudly acclaimed overthrow. Whatever the explanation, he passed straight from life into the national mythology as his country's pre-eminent friend of the people. Henceforth, politicians with any pretension to popular leadership fought for his mantle. Chief among the claimants in the next decade was Juan Perón.

For the next eleven years the country was governed by the restored oligarchy through the Concordancia, which was a coalition of the National Democrats, the Antipersonalists (now deprived of Alvear's leadership), and, in the early years, Independent Socialists. Reflecting the lively controversy over its history, the period has been labeled in widely different ways. Hostile critics call it the "Infamous Decade," which considerably exaggerates its iniquity, bad though it was in a number of ways. Perhaps the thing about it that was most harshly and at the same time most justifiably criticized was that, while making a pretence of governing constitutionally, the Concordancia made systematic use of fraud to maintain its monopoly of power year after year in the face of an opposition that claimed to, and probably did, represent a majority of the people. Without convincing anybody, the regime's apologists came up with a label for the period that transmuted vice into virtue: according to them it was a period of "patriotic fraud," which considerably exaggerates the Concordancia's disinterestedness.

The label used here is "Conservative Restoration," with the caveat that, although the beef barons of the estancias were again in the saddle, there were wide differences between the conservative regime of the period before the reform of 1912 and the one restored in the 1930s. One of the two greatest differences between them was that the conservatives of the Restoration took long strides away from the comparative liberalism of their predecessors' principles of free enterprise and free speech. In violation of these they imposed government controls on both the economy and the press that foreshadowed salient features of the Perón regime. The other major difference was the Restoration's lack of the flexibility demonstrated by its predecessor on more than one occasion, most conspicuously when it enacted the electoral reform of 1912. By contrast, the Restoration made no significant concession to the mounting pressures from the middle class and the rapidly growing industrial labor force; and it was equally unresponsive to the demands of an international situation that changed with dizzying rapidity in the course of the 1930s.

The end of that decade is as far as we shall follow the Restoration in this chapter, for in 1940 World War II began in earnest with German conquests from Norway to the Pyrenees that vitally affected Argentina's internal situation as well as its foreign relations. The presidential pattern is still useful for the history of these eight years, and it is quite simple: Agustín F. Justo from 1932 to 1938, and Roberto Ortiz for the rest of the decade.

In its early years Justo's administration was mainly concerned with two problems: economic recovery and internal security. With luck, it handled both successfully. Its major economic policies were to tighten bonds with Argentina's chief trading partner and banker, Great Britain, as was done by the controversial Roca-Runciman Pact of May 1933,* and to impose greater order, efficiency, and stimulation. This was done by establishing exchange and production controls, and by other measures such as the centralization of the banking system and internal taxes, an extensive road building program, and the imposition of the country's first income tax (for fiscal rather than social purposes). As intended, the chief beneficiaries were the agricultural interests, above all the beef barons, but incidentally industry too was stimulated and in the mid-1930s began a rapid, steady growth that by 1940 had put it on a par with the agricultural-pastoral sector as a source of national income.

The problem of internal security was mainly one of suppressing several uprisings from 1932 to 1935 by ousted Radicals. They succeeded in gaining the support of a small fraction of the military, but the great majority of the latter remained loyal to the government and formed its Pretorian guard. Subversive efforts ceased almost entirely after Alvear in 1935 persuaded the Radical Party to renew its participation in politics. His action was denounced as a sellout by its hardliners, but they were a small minority, divided among themselves,† and after 1935 something like peace was restored on the home front, where prosperity, too, was beginning to return.

As a result of these favorable developments, President Justo was able to devote the closing years of his administration mainly to foreign affairs and preparations for the election of 1937, in which his successor was to be chosen. His foreign minister, Carlos Saavedra Lamas, was a son-in-law of Roque Sáenz Peña but certainly not his spiritual heir, and a diplomat of considerable ability but little imagination, who would have been brilliantly successful in quieter times. Foreign relations had been important from the beginning of the administration—witness the Roca-Runciman Pact—but bulked even larger in its later years as the international tension increased.

---

*The Roca-Runciman Pact protected Argentina's vitally important share of the British meat market, which had been endangered by the imperial preference plan adopted at the recent Ottawa conference. In return, Argentina gave preferential treatment to British frigorificos, imported goods, and investments in public service and "other enterprises." The pact was bitterly denounced as a sacrifice of Argentina's national interests for the benefit of the big estancieros and their British allies.

†The principal minority group was the left-wing nationalist one called FORJA, most of whose members went over to the Peronist movement in late 1945.

The Chaco controversy, which had just led to a three-year war between Bolivia and Paraguay, was settled at a three-year Inter-American conference in Buenos Aires (1935-1938), with Saavedra Lamas presiding; the United States, represented most of the time by Spruille Braden, played an important part in it. In 1936 Saavedra Lamas was elected president of the League of Nations Assembly, and, as the author of a largely superfluous peace pact, was awarded the Nobel Prize for Peace. In December of the same year another Inter-American conference, this time on defense of the Western hemisphere, met in Buenos Aires, and President Franklin Roosevelt journeyed 6,000 miles by ship to that city for the occasion—a courtesy which did not deter Saavedra Lamas from opposing, with almost complete success, the efforts of the United States to lay the foundations for an Inter-American security system at this conference. Like many of his fellow countrymen, he took his country's hegemony in Latin America for granted; the pessimism of the decade had not diminished his confidence in it, but he saw a threat to it in Roosevelt's vigorous courtship of Latin America, and acted accordingly. His attitude is understandable, but in this as in other matters his diplomacy was negative and shortsighted and left nothing for his successors to build on. In Western hemisphere affairs he offered no meaningful alternative to the United States' regional plan, though the latter left ample room for alternatives. In world affairs he could think of nothing better than to cling to the already discredited and disintegrating League of Nations, and to Argentina's "special relationship" with Great Britain, when that country seemed to be drifting rudderless towards the approaching cataclysm.

On the other hand, just because of its long-standing economic pre-eminence in Argentina, Britain was the favorite target of the country's increasing tribe of anti-imperialist snipers in the 1930s. Although the United States had narrowed the gap in both respects, especially as a target for anti-imperialists, it still lagged far behind Britain. As an investor it had been a late starter. General Electric began to do business in Argentina in 1899 and was followed by the United Shoe Machinery Company in 1903 and the Singer Sewing Machine Company in 1905, but the first large investment—the purchase of one of the principal frigoríficos by Swift and Company—was not made until 1907. A much-needed facility was provided by the establishment of branches of United States banks in Buenos Aires, which was made possible by the Federal Reserve Act of 1914.

In November of that year the National City Bank of New York led the way, to be followed soon by the First National Bank of Boston.

In the next fifteen years American investments and business enterprise continued to grow at a rate rapid enough to make the United States by the mid-1920s a close rival to Britain as a whipping-boy for anti-imperialists such as Manuel Ugarte, José Ingenieros, and Ricardo Rojas. The growth of economic relations, however, was hampered by the fact that the economics of the two countries were not complementary but competitive. This fact was brought out in high relief by the exclusion of Argentine beef from the United States after 1927 under a sanitary regulation which, though justified on the ground of the existence of the foot and mouth disease in Argentina, actually protected cattlemen in the United States against formidable competition. The offense given by this measure to powerful interests in Argentina, together with the fact that the United States always bought far less from Argentina than it sold to that country, assured the British of continuing to enjoy preferential treatment of their trade and investments so long as the conservatives remained in power. When World War II broke out, the United States still lagged behind Britain in total trade with Argentina, and its investments there, amounting to $320 million, were only one fourth as large as Britain's.

For the election of 1937 the Concordancia again nominated for the presidency an Antipersonalist, Roberto M. Ortiz, and for the vice-presidency a National Democrat, Ramón S. Castillo. Ortiz, a successful porteño lawyer and counsel for British firms, was noted for his integrity and comparative liberalism. Castillo, a large landowner from the north, was a rock-ribbed conservative and, although moderately pro-British, he favored strict adherence to the neutrality policy that his party had maintained while in power during the first half of World War I. The Concordancia's choice of candidates was as good as could have been expected, but its methods during the campaign and election were even worse than usual, and "patriotic fraud" outdid itself in routing the Radical Party's ticket headed by Alvear.

President Ortiz held office only from February 1938 to June 1940. Suffering from diabetes, he then let Vice-President Castillo take over as acting president, while he himself took leave of absence, from which he returned only briefly before resigning in July 1942. He died the following month. He had been expected to make amends for the scandalous method of his election by instituting reforms. Although he wanted to do so, the expectation that he could bring about a thorough reform was unrealistic, given the shortness of the time at his disposal, the intractability of the problem, and the heavy pressure of other problems, both domestic and foreign. The international crisis worsened every year. Argentina had important ties of all kinds with Europe, and in 1938 came Munich, in 1939 the outbreak of the war, and in the first half of 1940 Hitler's lightning conquest of Western Europe and his submarine blockade of Britain and threat to invade it. The resulting shock to Argentina created problems, both political and economic, which were extraordinarily difficult to handle because the country at large and the Concordancia itself were deeply divided over them. One question was whether Argentina should join in the movement for closer inter-American cooperation for defense, which Saavedra Lamas had checked but not stopped. Ortiz was conditionally favorable to it, Castillo unconditionally opposed, and it was just as the question was given urgency by Hitler's conquest of Western Europe that illness forced Ortiz to retire for the first time in favor of Castillo. These two events together marked the end of the Conservative Restoration as originally constituted. Up to this point it had been characterized by the preponderance of Justo's and Ortiz's Antipersonalists and of domestic over foreign affairs. In the three remaining years of the Restoration, the preponderance shifted to Castillo's National Democrats and foreign relations.

By no means all the blame for Argentina's political ills under the Restoration should be assigned to the Concordancia. In the only opposition parties of any consequence after 1935, Radical and Socialist, the leadership was old and tired and the younger members, such as those in the Radical offshoot FORJA, were sharply critical of it on many grounds. Still worse, the public had lost faith in all political parties. If we may believe Alberto Ciria, they had good reason for distrusting the only large opposition party, the Radicals. According to him, the opposition they offered in Congress was not even honest. In one instance of improper collaboration with the ruling party cited by him, the Radical members whitewashed a corrupt government deal involving electric power concessions; in another, they tolerated without protest the seating of delegates known to have been irregularly elected.

In addition, except for the shortlived Alianza Civil of 1931-1935, the fragmented opposition could never get together even for the purpose of defeating the government. The Popular Front tactic, inspired by Moscow, which succeeded in Chile in 1938, never got off the ground in Argentina. The Socialists did not trust the Communists, and the Radicals did not trust anybody; besides which, the latter fancied themselves the true majority party and refused on principle to enter into alliances. This political fragmentation may have been due in some measure to the enduring Spanish trait of intolerance, which Argentina's own writers have noted in their fellow countrymen as well as in Spaniards. Interestingly enough, in his recent account of this period Alberto Ciria unconsciously illustrates the persistence of the trait by describing the opposition parties as having been "co-opted by the system [meaning the Concordancia]" merely because they "co-participated in Congress" by taking part in congressional elections and the normal proceedings of Congress. Obviously, where there is intolerance of the minority for the majority, as well as of the majority for the minority, not only will there be political fragmentation, but representative government itself becomes unworkable.

A relatively new but insistent problem, that of women's rights, was vigorously debated during the interwar years only to remain unsolved until the Perón era. According to Argentine historian Y. G. Anzoátegui, the feminist movement in that country dates back to 1854; in 1890 one of its leaders was a speaker at the first anniversary celebration of the founding of the Civic Union; and in the national centennial year, 1910, the First International Women's Congress met in Buenos Aires at the call of the Argentine University Women's Association. The congress drew up a rather ambitious legislative program regarding women's civil and political rights, legitimate and illegitimate children, divorce, alcoholism, gambling and prostitution, but not until after World War I does the demand for votes for women seem to have been pressed with determination.

In 1918 a Nationalist Feminist Union was founded under the presidency of Dr. Alicia Moreau de Justo, wife of the Argentine Socialist leader J. B. Justo and herself a prominent member of the party. As part of a publicity campaign, a book was published in 1921 quoting statements in favor of women's rights by men of distinction such as former foreign minister Luis María Drago and future foreign minister Carlos Saavedra Lamas. Time and again in the interwar decades bills giving women the vote were introduced into Congress, but all failed to pass. Indeed, the movement lost ground. In San Juan province, women had had the right to vote in municipal elections ever since the time of Sarmiento, the province's most illustrious son, and they were given it in provincial elections in 1927. Only three years later, however, San Juan was "intervened," as were most of the other provinces, and the interventor deprived them of the vote. His reasoning was that since the federal constitution guaranteed equal rights to all Argentine citizens, and since women did not have the right to vote in the other provinces, they could not have it in San Juan alone. There matters rested, we are told, until the revolution of 1943 brought to power new men with modern, revolutionary ideas.

Literary Nationalism and Pessimism

In 1968 Jorge Luis Borges wrote that, while it was impossible to fix the date precisely, Argentina's gradual decline certainly began with "the acts that gave the government to the Radicals," that is, about 1912-1916. Whether or not he was right, no one in the literary circles in which Borges was beginning to make a name for himself in the 1920s seemed to think that anything like a national decline was under way at that time. Many were to think so, and say so again and again, in the next decade, but no change that took place in Argentina between 1910 and 1940 is more striking than the sudden change of mood from the optimism of the centenary of 1910 and the next twenty years into the pessimism of the depression decade. For rapidity, the decline was comparable to the Wall Street crash of 1929 that helped to bring it on. It was accompanied by a related but less abrupt change: the decline of the liberal nationalism that had prevailed from the post-Rosas generation of Mitre and Sarmiento on through the centenary to the 1920s, and the rise of competing varieties of nationalism, both left and right-wing. One is tempted to attribute these changes largely to the shock of the economic depression, but, while it was a contributory factor, both changes had begun before it was felt, and that means that both had other origins. At least one development — the reaction of creole nativism against the immigrant deluge — was a source of both the pessimism of the 1930s and the diversity of its forms of nationalism.

The tradition of a nationalism that was liberal and optimistic — perhaps liberal because it was optimistic — was carried on by Ricardo Rojas, a leader of the literary Generation of 1910, in *La restauración nacionalista* (The Nationalist Restoration), *La Argentinidad* (Argentinity), and other works. There was more than a touch of nostalgia in his kind of nationalism, in the sense of pride in his country's past, but he was no chauvinist. Evidences of xenophobia might be found in his attack on cosmopolitanism and his concern over the watering down of traditional Argentine values by the immigrant flood — a concern that the Uruguayan José Enrique Rodó had already expressed regarding his own country in his masterpiece, *Ariel*. However, Rojas was never exclusivist or parochial in his writing and he only wanted to keep foreign influence, whether cultural, economic, or demographic, at a level compatible with the independence of Argentina and the integrity of what he conceived to be its national character. In his last major work, a biography of Sarmiento entitled *El profeta de la pampa* (The Prophet of the Pampa), he still took the same stand, maintaining, even in opposition to his revered Sarmiento, that Argentina's major problem was not the internal conflict between civilization and barbarism, but the defense of its independence in all respects against foreign domination.

Nationalism coupled with optimism continued to characterize the main stream of Argentine literary production through the 1920s. The prolific and widely read José Ingenieros, rejoicing that the Argentine people had now become a white race, called upon the nation to fulfill its obvious destiny by playing a leading role in South America, but he insisted that this "imperialism," as he frankly called it, must be pacific. In 1929 José Ortega y Gasset, just back in Spain after another visit to Argentina, wrote: "To belong to this people is a source of pride that animates every Argentine. He is born with a blind faith in its glorious destiny." Even after the Great Depression had shattered this faith in many others, the "grand old man" of Argentine Socialism, Alfredo Palacios, was still declaiming in 1934, with vintage 1910 optimism, that every person in "this generous land" should be proud of his nationality, for Argentina's "pure, idealistic tradition . . . represents the highest and most advanced tendency in the world today."

The most lurid illustration of the fall from this exalted plane into pessimism is Ezequiel Martínez Estrada's *Radiografía de la pampa* (X-Ray of the Pampa), published in 1933. The book also illustrates the defection from liberal (or as the author was later to call it, "canonical") nationalism. Highly praised as "a landmark" and "epoch-making," and described by the noted literary historian Enrique Anderson Imbert as equal in profundity to Sarmiento's *Facundo, Radiografía* has also been mercilessly pilloried as murky though shallow, and pretentious but derivative. Despite its title, it is an "X-ray" examination of the whole of Argentina and not merely of the pampa, and it examines country and people in a historical perspective reaching far back into pre-Columbian times. In its conclusion, nothing was right in Argentina; but the country's fundamental defect was that it was the product of the implantation of an alien European social and cultural structure which, besides being fatally defective in itself, was totally out of harmony with the "spirit of the soil," the ancient and unchanging "telluric" forces at work in Argentina; and it was much too late now to do anything about it. This was a counsel of despair, and yet the book's underlying assumption that Argentina's telluric forces had made it a great place until it was corrupted by Europeans appealed to the rising tide of xenophobe nationalism and social unrest in Argentina at this time. In addition, the book is written in a style highly praised even by otherwise hostile critics, and in the post-World War II decade, when "alienation" and "intellectual" were virtually synonymous, *Radiografía* was the Bible of the young intellectuals. Its great vogue and influence have subsequently diminished. Marxist writers have been especially critical of Martínez Estrada's "irrational pessimism" and romantic anarchism and of his going on at great length about cosmic forces while remaining silent about the real roots of Argentina's troubles, such as the oligarchy.

Radiografía has attracted singularly little notice outside Argentina for a book bracketed with *Facundo*, which has long enjoyed international readership as well as fame. Like the author's other principal books,* *Radiografía* deals exclusively with Argentina, but so does *Facundo*. A partial explanation may be that he belittled Europe and European thought, and yet identified himself with a passing European intellectual fad. Several other leading Argentine writers also followed it at that time, which is one of the main reasons why the matter is worth mentioning here.

The fad in question was a manifestation of the widespread irra-

---

*These include *La cabeza de Goliat* and *Muerte y transfiguración de Martín Fierro*, both of which are much preferred by some readers, including Peter Earle, who explains why in his recent notable study of Martínez Estrada's writings.

tionalism of the period. Specifically, it was the pseudo-mystical notion of a "spirit of the soil," a telluric force that shapes human destinies and breaks those who defy or try to alter it. The list of Argentine writers beguiled by the notion included even Raúl Scala-brini Ortiz. He is best remembered for his Anglophobe history of Argentine railroads (1940), but years earlier he had made much of the "spirit of the soil" in his otherwise fascinating interpretation of porteño character, *El hombre que está solo y espera* (The Man Who Is Alone and Waits, 1931). There can be little doubt that he borrowed the thought from some European writer or writers. Of the three, all pessimists, who most powerfully influenced Argentina's intellectuals in the 1920s and 1930s—José Ortega y Gasset, Oswald Spengler, and Count Keyserling—the last two related their pessi-mism specifically to the idea of telluric forces.

The influence of Ortega and Spengler long outlasted the 1930s and was apparent in other ways as well, but early in that decade Keyserling outshone even them. His vogue seems to have been due to a well-timed personal appearance in Buenos Aires during which he reinforced a ready-made reputation for mysticism with a masterly performance as a kind of occidental guru. Subsequently, a book reflecting upon his visit, entitled *South American Meditations* (Spanish edition 1932), weakened his hold on the Argentines. This is hardly surprising, for his book lumped them together with all other South Americans, to whom they felt far superior, and generalized about them unflatteringly. Fair samples are "the frenetic and reptil-ian sexuality of the South American" and the explanation of his "profound melancholy" by the old adage, "post coitum animal triste." Yet even at the end of the decade one of Argentina's out-standing intellectuals, the novelist and essayist Eduardo Mallea, while branding Keyserling's "theorizing about Hispanic America" superficial and unjust, paid tribute to his skill in handling "the most exalted human questions."

Mallea himself was an eloquent exponent of the pessimism pre-vailing in Argentina in the 1930s. His case is especially important because he had intellectual ballast and was well connected, being a member, as was Jorge Luis Borges, of the select group formed around the literary magazine *Sur,* founded in 1931 and edited by Victoria Ocampo, a combined Madame de Staël and Gertrude Stein. Also, Mallea had made his reputation by the middle of the decade, so that his pessimism can hardly be attributed to personal frustration. Born in Bahía Blanca in 1903, he was descended from a San Juan family closely related to Sarmiento's, and his father, a successful physician, gave him a good education, first in Bahía Blanca and then at the University of Buenos Aires. He early developed a deep devotion to English literature; of the many evidences of it, one of special interest in the present context is his use, as a motto for his *Historia de una pasión argentina* (History of an Argentine Passion, 1937), of two lines from Milton's *Paradise Lost*: "Millions of spiritual creatures walk the earth / Unseen, both when we wake and when we sleep."

The title of his book, and the fact that Mallea was primarily a novelist, might seem to mark it as a bedroom romance, but in fact it is a long essay in search of the essence of Argentinity, the "real Argentina." As such, the distinguished Argentine philosopher Francisco Romero, in a prologue to the second edition, compared it to Descartes's *Discourse on Method* in its search for "total reality." Although Mallea's book is pessimistic, it is not, as was the recently published *X-Ray of the Pampa,* a counsel of despair. Instead, it insists that present-day, "visible" Argentina, bad as it is, is the result of the desertion, since the turn of the century, of the high standards of the now "invisible" Argentina of our forefathers. There is no need to despair, it concludes, if only the people will return to those standards. Lest the point be missed, the book compares Argentina to the Prodigal Son.

As the foregoing suggests, a nostalgic nationalism like that of Ricardo Rojas a quarter-century earlier was one of this book's messages. First among the old virtues it sought to revive was "the now lost sense of Argentinity" — a sense our forefathers expressed with almost religious zeal, as in Avellaneda's unforgettable oration over the repatriated remains of Liberator San Martín. Mallea exaggerated somewhat in saying that this particular variety of nationalism had been forgotten, but it was in fact overshadowed in the 1930s by more militant brands. Chief among these were, at one extreme, the popular nationalism represented by FORJA, which has already been mentioned, and, at the other extreme, a dynamic right-wing nationalism. The latter, though represented in politics by the Nationalists, was more comprehensive and less homogeneous than that rather restricted group's version of it. It comprised a number of different strands; clerical, economic, aristocratic, elitist, authoritarian, and military, derived from France, Italy, Germany, Spain, and of course Argentina itself. What distinguishes it most clearly from the likewise elitist but nostalgic nationalism of Mallea is its urge to corrective action, with a view to reversing deterioration at home and putting an end to domination from abroad. Leopoldo Lugones, poet turned pamphleteer and anarchist turned militarist, expressed one of its many facets with his "hour of the sword" call for renewal. His *La grande Argentina* (1930) is described by Dardo Cúneo as "one of the most profound analyses ever made of Argentine reality," which is high praise from the sympathetic biographer of Socialist leader J. B. Justo. In this and his *Política revolucionaria* the following year, Lugones called for a complete change in the country's political system; not out of hostility to democracy or the republic, both of which he declared must be preserved as inseparable from the concept of nationality and independence, but in order to replace the present national constitution of "Anglo-Saxon" mold with one of native Argentine mold.

Father Meinvielle represented another facet with his antidemocratic "cross and sword" fusion of clericalism with militarism. Still another, the economic, found expression in works on British economic exploitation of Argentina, chief among them one on Argentina and British imperialism by Rodolfo and Julio Irazusta and, at the very end of the decade, the railroad history by Raúl Scalabrini Ortiz, who was an adviser to Perón after 1944 and the first to approach him about nationalizing the British-owned railroads. Implicit when not explicit in all these facets of nationalism was aggrandizement of the role of the national government in the solution of all national problems, domestic as well as foreign.

Arms, Oil, and Industry

For a decade after General Uriburu's brief dictatorship there seemed little disposition on the part of the military to accept conservative Catholics' invitations to join "the cross" (the church) in any political crusade. What little willingness any of them showed to intervene in politics in any way came in response to urgings from liberals to help reinstate the ousted Radicals in the early years of the Conservative Restoration. Most of the military, however, sided with the government and quickly suppressed the three Radical uprisings, all minor, between 1932 and 1935.

The prevailing noninterventionist attitude of the military during this decade was clearly stated in a speech delivered in Buenos Aires on July 10, 1931, by the head of the influential army officers' club, Círculo Militar. He repeated almost verbatim the injunction given in this same place five years earlier by his predecessor, Enrique Mosconi, to adhere to the tradition of a nonpolitical army, a tradition said to have been instituted by the Liberator, General San Martín. Without mincing words, he told his fellow officers that "the army is not a political force . . . but a child of the people . . . at the service of the nation . . . [and] is guided by the old spirit of the Army of the Andes," meaning, of course, the army commanded by General San Martín. The timing of the speech and its title, "the Mission of the Army," made it sound very much like a rebuke to General Uriburu, whose dictatorship still had several months to run. Early the following year, the officer who delivered it was made minister of war by President Justo — a fact which indicates that he had indeed voiced the preponderant opinion of the officer corps at that time regarding the mission of the army.

During the rest of the decade the armed forces, while discharging their obligation to serve and support the government, had no hand in it except that, in accordance with long-standing practice, the cabinet ministers of war and marine (navy) were officers in the respective services. With that exception the armed forces stuck closely to their professional tasks and remained an instrument of the civil government, in accordance with the constitutional provision, identical with one in the Constitution of the United States, that the president of the republic is also commander-in-chief of its armed forces.

This relationship was maintained intact when in 1938 the presidency passed from General Justo to a civilian, lawyer Roberto Ortiz. Proof of its integrity came at the very end of the decade when the army carried out a delicate and dangerous political intervention in the province of Buenos Aires on the president's initiative and in ways of his choosing. This was part of a nationwide effort he made to put an end to the conservatives' systematic use of fraud and force, by which he himself had been elected. For this purpose he invoked the constitutional power of the federal government — a power frequently used by his predecessors — to intervene in the provinces.

As Robert Potash describes the intervention in Buenos Aires province, President Ortiz prepared the way by intervening in February 1940 in his own Vice-President Castillo's home province, Catamarca, to upset an electoral victory that Castillo's party had won by notorious fraud; the interventor in this case was a retired army general. In the far more difficult Buenos Aires case, Ortiz employed as interventor one of the highest-ranking active generals and a considerable body of troops in what amounted to a military operation. It was completely successful and, as Potash comments, the army had shown that it would "support a government committed to the restoration of democratic practices." Only four months later, however, ill health forced Ortiz to delegate his powers to Castillo. In the interval between these two interventions, the newspaper *La Prensa* had warned against such involvement of the armed forces in politics, and interestingly enough, the warning was sounded not on the ground that it would give the military a hankering for political power, but, on the contrary, that it might lead to attacks by politicians on the military.

It was into the economic sphere rather than the political that military activities and aspirations seemed to be moving in the two interwar decades. Careful consideration of the nation's economic needs, however, showed that they could not be divorced from political decisions on both domestic and foreign policy. The career of Colonel (later general) Enrique Mosconi, first director (1922-1930) of the government petroleum agency YPF, is a case in point.

Twenty years before Mosconi's appointment to that post, an act of Congress (Law No. 4,167) prohibiting the alienation of mineral and certain other lands used the word petroleum (*petróleo*) for the first time in the history of Argentine land legislation. Five years after that, the first discovery of an oil field in Argentina was made by accident while government agents were prospecting for fresh water near the port of Comodoro Rivadavia on the coast of Patogonia. Immediately part of the area was reserved to the government and the rest opened up to exploitation by private enterprise under a kind of licensing system. For the next six years, however, government action was blocked in the name of laissez-faire and private enterprise was hampered by British coal interests, which were supplying a large part of Argentina's fuel requirements and did not relish competition. Action came at last in 1913 as a result of an oil expert's sensational speech in Congress on the potential wealth of Argentina's oil resources and on their scandalous mismanagement and neglect by the government. President Sáenz Peña promptly took remedial measures, but after his death a short time later they were largely nullified in favor of private oil companies, among which were Royal Dutch, Anglo-Persian, and Standard Oil of New Jersey.

When in 1918 another oil field was discovered, this time at Huincal in Neuquén, a south central province abutting the Andes, President Yrigoyen still followed what an unfriendly critic called a give-away policy that brought foreign monopoly of Argentine oil production to its zenith. In the closing months of his administration he established YPF, but with a small budget and no director. His successor, President Alvear, lost no time in filling the post by the appointment of Colonel Enrique Mosconi (October 19, 1922). Before World War War I Mosconi had been one of the army officers sent to Europe for advanced study and training, and he was a specialist in engineering. As director of the army's air service at the time of his YPF appointment, he had just completed the construction of the airport at El Palomar, near Buenos Aires, in a very short time and with a very limited budget. Years later he said he thought he was chosen to head YPF because this achievement came to President Alvear's attention through a reference to it in an interview published in *La Nación* early in October.

Another reason for his appointment may well have been that, as director of the army's air service, he had acquired some familiarity with petroleum supply problems. One incident especially stimulated his economic nationalism and focused it on the oil business. One day in August 1922 he was organizing a series of extensive flights and sent an officer to the city to arrange for the necessary supply of aviation gasoline with the West India Oil Company, a subsidiary of Standard Oil of New Jersey, only to have the officer return with word that cash on the barrel head was required. Mosconi himself then went to see the manager of the company, found him smoking a fine cigar of "extraordinary dimensions," and got the same answer: no cash, no gas. "I told him," records Mosconi, "that this was impertinent and unacceptable, but out of courtesy I did not tell him of the oath I took then and there to do all in my power to break the trusts."

A strain of nationalism tied to technology could already be detected as early as 1918 in a speech Mosconi delivered on the battlefield of Maipo (Maipu) at a celebration of the centenary of that decisive battle in the Chilean war for independence. Recalling how in 1816 General San Martín (who was then preparing his expedition to Chile) said that it was easier to declare independence than to find a single American who knew how to make a bottle, Mosconi told his audience: "Our forefathers could not make bottles, but they did make gunpowder and cannon, but today you [Chileans] and we [Argentines] make bottles but not gunpowder or cannon. We both must bestir ourselves, for only strong peoples can defend their freedom and sovereignty."

Mosconi's conception of the armed forces' role was broad, but it never included meddling in politics. On July 8, 1926, as president of the Círculo Militar, he delivered a speech at a joint army-navy dinner on "The Mission of the Armed Forces," in which he declared that under the constitution it was the officers' duty to stick to their "military profession" and never to intervene in, or even be alarmed by, domestic political conflicts, for these showed the aptitude of a people for exercising their rights as citizens. So long as we observe these rules, he declared, the nation's traditions will be safe and it may go quietly about "expanding its creative forces."

Two months later, at a dinner honoring him for his promotion to general, Mosconi spoke on "The Economy and the Military Profession." Not surprisingly, his central theme was oil, which he described as "that preponderant element in the life of modern nations, in peace as well as in war, which is of transcendent importance for our country." Replying to the charge that state enterprises in general were inefficient, he said that depended on whether the government drew up and enforced proper guidelines. President Alvear had done so for YPF, he continued, and since its first year that agency had already doubled production and almost doubled its revenues and would have done even better if Congress had passed a petroleum law urged upon it by the president.

Economic nationalism, the integration of Latin America as a counterpoise to the United States and Europe, and a warning against excessive expenditures on arms, coupled with a plea for the construction of Argentine industries capable of producing the necessary arms—these were the main features of Mosconi's address in Buenos Aires on April 19, 1929, to an anti-imperialist group of university students. He reaffirmed "Argentine optimism" unreservedly, but coupled it with an admonition to watch the international horizon closely and build up the nation's strength. By developing industry and the whole economy, he concluded, Argentines will succeed in forming a "sure awareness of our strength," in taking complete control of the country, and in carrying to the farthest limit "the vibration of the national soul."

General Mosconi had stayed on as director of YPF when Yrigoyen succeeded his Antipersonalist rival Alvear in 1928. This was in perfect accordance with his nonpolitical prescription for the military, but just the same he was out of office within six hours after Yrigoyen's fall on September 6, 1930. Where Mosconi had stood in relation to the more radical trend of the deposed president's petroleum policy during his truncated second term is a question that needs further study. At any rate, his expert services never found employment again in the remaining ten years of his life. This did not prevent him from continuing to propagate his ideas actively. They were increasingly marked by economic nationalism coupled with Latin Americanism. In 1936, for example, he devoted the epilogue of his book on Argentine oil (*El petróleo argentino*) to supporting the proposition that, having made a "handsome profit" from YPF,* Argentina could count on gaining greatly by applying the same kind of economic nationalism to other sectors of its economy, and its example would be followed by other Latin American countries. Sectors especially recommended by him were telephone services, light and power, and insurance, the last-named to be provided either by a special bank, as in Uruguay, or by enlarging the functions of Argentina's Banco de la Nación. Beyond this, he continued, YPF's "nationalist spirit . . . points the way to our economic liberation, to our industrial development undertaken by ourselves with our own will, effort, and capital . . . without previous commitment to either free trade or protection, and choosing between them on the merits of each case." YPF, he concluded, has proved that *"our country has reached the technical and administrative maturity necessary to conduct the most difficult undertakings that characterize the complex economic structure of modern nations."* The italics are his.

Mosconi died on June 4, 1940, just as Hitler's Germany was completing its conquest of Western Europe, and in the turmoil of the next half-dozen years he seemed almost forgotten. In 1947, however, a commission for a monument to him was set up and we are told that the publicity campaign carried on by it among legislators, government officials, labor unions, and others prevented Perón's

---

*Mosconi specified that YPF had cost the government only 8.7 million pesos and in return had "produced an increase in the nation's wealth" of 582.6 million pesos by 1935, with more to come every year thereafter.

minister of industry, Miguel Miranda, from carrying out his plan to convert YPF into a mixed government-private corporation, a change which would have played into the hands of the "ever-watchful" Standard Oil Company of New Jersey.

Industrialization and diversification was also the message of Alejandro E. Bunge, Argentina's foremost writer on economic questions in the interwar decades. In a book published a year before the beginning of the Great Depression, he warned that Argentina's existing economy had reached the limit of its growth, and besides being one-sided and dominated by foreigners, was highly vulnerable to disturbances in the world market. Disaster lay not far ahead, he insisted, unless Argentina industrialized, and the government should intervene in the process in order to make certain that the country got the right kinds of industries and kept them from falling under foreign control.

Industrialization did in fact proceed in Argentina at an accelerated pace in the 1930s, especially after 1935, though without the direct government intervention urged by Bunge. By 1940 the value of manufactures had caught up for the first time with that of agricultural and pastoral products. In number of workers employed, industry increased from 1.25 million in 1914 to 2.77 million in 1940, or 122 percent, whereas the agricultural-pastoral sector's increase in the same period was only 19 percent (from .88 million to 1.05 million). The increase in the number of industrial workers was most rapid in the 1930s: the annual average rose from some 47,000 in the period 1914-1933 to 85,000 in the next seven years. Similarly, the number of industrial establishments increased by about 40 percent between 1935 and 1940 (from 40,600 to 57,200).

While the vast majority of these establishments were very small, employing not more than five workers, the number of large plants was considerable. In 1935, for example, 93 plants employed 90,000 workers. The big factories, however, were not producing the kinds of goods that Mosconi and other military leaders wanted. Instead, as Alberto J. Pla points out, they were typically frigoríficos, sugar and flour mills, paper and textile mills, and oil refineries. Thirty percent of all the industrial establishments and 50 percent of their workers were concentrated in Greater Buenos Aires, which now contained nearly one third of the country's total population.

To be sure, civilians, including industrial leaders, gave lip service to the wishes of the military. Thus, in October 1932, as reported by

the newspaper *La razón*, Luis Colombo, director of the manufacturers' association Unión Industrial, said in a speech that a "great,
diversified, and progressive industry" was indispensable to the
armed forces, but his organization did nothing to develop it. In fact,
says Dardo Cúneo, the Unión Industrial was handmaiden to the
import-export trade with Great Britain and never aimed to go
beyond an industrial development complementary to it. It sought
tariff protection only for manufactures of this kind, and competition with imported British goods was out of the question. In short,
the Unión Industrial was subservient to the circle that dominated
this trade (and the Conservative Restoration, for that matter),
which was a combination of the agricultural and pastoral magnates,
best represented by the Rural Society of Buenos Aires, and the principal merchants, brokers, and bankers engaged in foreign trade.

Rifts were beginning to appear in this imposing phalanx, however. The depression, says Adolfo Dorfman, finally snapped the tie
that had held farm and factory together during the happy decades
before 1930. When in 1939 the Rural Society and its Rosario counterpart demanded the repeal of a protective duty on finished goods,
the once supine Unión Industrial retorted sharply, and their beautiful friendship was never quite the same again. Another example is
the same society's propaganda campaign early in that decade in
defense of the Argentine horse against motorized agricultural
machinery. The tractors, it was pointed out, had to be imported, so
that buying them enriched the foreigners, while using the traditional horse would keep the money in Argentina and provide a
market for many Argentine products, from alfalfa to saddles. But
there was also dissension within each sector. In 1935 a breach, first
opened in the 1920s and then temporarily healed, was reopened
between the Rural Society of the capital and the smaller rural societies of the interior. This arrayed the big estancias, closely tied to
Britain and the foreign-controlled frigoríficos, which favored government controls and were favored by the government, against the
smaller producers. They stood for economic independence, urged
that cattlemen break the foreign hold by going into the frigorífico
and marketing business themselves, and denounced the Roca-
Runciman Pact as a sellout to Britain for the benefit of Argentina's
beef barons at the expense of the rest of the country.

A similar schism developed somewhat later among the industrialists. It may have been partly due to the fact that the rapid growth of

industry in the 1930s spurred the development of what Alberto Pla calls an "entrepreneurial mentality," by which he means primarily a group mentality in contrast to the individualistic mentality of the preceding generation of manufacturers. Certainly the new industrialists resented the Unión Industrial's subservience to the ruling agricultural-commercial clique as a bar to the more thoroughgoing industrialization they were eager to begin. This would involve competition with foreign, including British, imports and would also serve the interests of the armed forces. On both counts the new industrial group was qualified to become, as Pla puts it, "the protagonist of important changes in the near future"—meaning under the Perón regime.

VI Uruguay, the First Welfare State, 1903-1942

On March 1, 1903, a change in presidential administration resulted in a gradual but massive shift in public policy that turned Uruguay into a welfare state, thereby further differentiating it from Argentina and the rest of Latin America. On that day a worthy but rather mediocre chief executive was succeeded by a talented and energetic trail-blazer, José Batlle y Ordóñez. Batlle invigorated the presidency for eight of the next twelve years and continued to dominate his party and the country at large until his death in 1929 at the age of 73. By that time he and his fellow Colorados had made of Uruguay what seemed in the ensuing depression decade a utopia of social justice, in sharp contrast with Argentina under the restored oligarchy, and with Chile, which had begun to tread the welfare path only in the mid-1920s.

The welfare state was not Batlle's only innovation. He also brought about the separation of church and state and pioneered in economic nationalism and in the shift from a single to a collegiate or plural executive as an insurance against dictatorship. His own lavish use of executive power seemed to some the best proof that such an insurance policty ought to be taken out.

Batlle Begins Political and Social Reform

Not a Marxist but a social democrat, José Batlle had no ready-made plan for sweeping social reform when he first took office. What he accomplished was a series of piecemeal reforms, most of which were adopted during and after his second term, which ran from 1911 to 1915. In his first term, 1903-1907, his interests and achievements were mainly political. "I am convinced," he said shortly before his first election, "that the remedy for all our ills lies in electoral freedom, in honest elections." In this respect he resembled his Argentine contemporary Hipólito Yrigoyen.

Considering Batlle's background, his involvement with politics was only natural. The son of President Lorenzo Batlle (1868-1872), he was born in 1856 into a society which, as Simon Hanson puts it, was completely preoccupied with politics until early in the next century. He was given a conventional education in Montevideo and the trip to Europe (1880) that was usual for sons of upper-class families, and there was nothing out of the ordinary about his devoting himself thereafter to politics and political journalism. The newspaper he founded in 1886, *El Día* (The Day), was exceptionally successful, influential, and long-lived; it is still very much alive today. Sold for two cents a copy, it was Uruguay's first newspaper aimed at mass circulation, and it was on target from the start. In fact, until the beginning of Batlle's second term, there was nothing remarkable about his career except its success. He thought and acted conventionally and lived well. Since his large frame inclined to corpulence, there was a play on words as well as a touch of malice in the nickname "Pepe Botella" (Joe Bottle) used by his opponents to suggest that he was a heavy drinker.

Besides politics and journalism, Batlle was deeply interested in philosophy, especially in Krausism, which, according to Milton Vanger, was a strong influence throughout his life; this is another trait that he shared with his Argentine counterpart Yrigoyen. Several features of Krausism explain its special attraction for Batlle. Thanks to its Spanish interpreters, it was well established as a philosophy for Hispanic liberals. It aimed at the creation of a church based not on revealed religion, as was Roman Catholicism, but on "natural virtue and social religion." It spoke out strongly for the lower classes' right to social justice but just as strongly for the maintenance of a hierarchical social structure. And it advocated a kind of cellular organization of society into associations somewhat like the "autonomous entities" that, from about 1900, were set up in increasing numbers by the Uruguayan government under Batlle and his co-religionists.

Batlle's first term teemed with military, educational, and economic problems, but all of them were basically political. He had hardly taken office when caudillo Saravia and a formidable force of Blancos flew to arms over alleged intrusion into their bailiwick by the central government. Outgunned, Batlle temporized until he had built up the national army sufficiently. Then, in 1904, he challenged a showdown by intervening in a Blanco department, and the war was on. It was short but bloody. Not only were the Blancos badly beaten, but Saravia and many of their other leaders were killed. Batlle promptly canceled the coparticipation agreement of 1897 with them, thereby extending the supremacy of his government and party over the whole country. Despite internal rifts, the Colorado Party remained in power until 1932.

During the civil war, Argentine meddling in Uruguayan affairs began again. Apparently with the consent of President Roca's government, if not at its orders, arms were shipped to Saravia; among them was a battery of Krupp guns, for the Argentine army was now getting arms as well as military training from Germany. When Batlle's government learned that another big shipment of Argentine weapons was about to be made to Saravia, it urgently requested that the United States interpose and put a stop to the practice, asserting that, but for the arms Saravia had received from "neighboring republics," the rebellion would not have lasted two months. What Batlle asked for was not forcible intervention, but only that the United States make a naval demonstration in the Plata River and diplomatic representations in Buenos Aires. Made and repeated in August 1904, the request was turned down by Secretary of State John Hay "for cause," one cause being that at that time the navy had no ship closer than the Cape of Good Hope. "But," mused Hay, "if a ship could look in there some time, it might do no harm." As it turned out, the United States' interposition was not needed.

Much of the remainder of Batlle's first term was devoted to recovery from the civil war. Some time was found for reforms in education, mainly with a view to improving the quality of the electorate (the illiteracy rate was still a high 45 percent) and for a defense of the nation's economy against foreign domination; but more was done about both problems during Batlle's second administration and they will be discussed in that connection. There was also concern over the high rate of illegitimacy, which was said to be about 25 percent of all births. That problem, however, did not seem amenable to solution through secular channels, and reliance on church channels was out of the question for a government headed by José Batlle. His anticlericalism, though somewhat tempered in recent years, was still implacable.

Although he was an economic nationalist, Batlle was so far from being a fanatical xenophobe that he welcomed foreign capital investments, companies, and experts so long as they were useful to Uruguay and did not dominate or exploit it. In this favorable atmosphere — rendered more so by good world market prices for its products — the country's economic growth was rapid. Frigoríficos and roads were built, and between 1902 and 1907 the number of pedigreed cattle increased six-fold and of pedigreed sheep more than thirty-fold. To stimulate orderly growth, Batlle appointed a minister of *fomento* (development), 35-year-old José Serrato, an engineer and grandson of a French volunteer in the defense of

Montevideo in the 1840s. Serrato and Batlle, Vanger tells us, were among the first economic planners and they learned early the difficulty of economic planning in an underdeveloped country.

Until 1905 Batlle followed a policy of benevolent neutrality in industrial disputes. In that year one of the country's biggest industries, its port, was crippled by a strike of stevedores and port construction workers involving 11,000 men. Describing their union as a construct of anarchism, the employers were able to break the strike and shatter the union by bringing in gauchos as strikebreakers. Throughout the strike Batlle adhered to his hands-off policy, except for appointing an official fact-finder. The incident led, however, to a shift in his thinking and its concentration on social problems. "In countries like ours," he said, "where the problem of liberty is already resolved, it is necessary to begin to resolve social problems." His first step in that direction was a labor reform project calling for an eight-hour day, a weekly day of rest, and shorter hours for women and children. It was not until December 1906, after an election had given liberals firm control of the Senate as well as the lower house, that he submitted his reform project to Congress.

By that time, less than three weeks of his term remained. He picked as his successor Claudio Williman, a member of his cabinet. Vanger calls this the "greatest single stroke in assuring his re-election" in 1911. Williman, attorney for the British railroads, was conservative enough to mollify the Blancos, who, under a successor as radical as Batlle himself, might have started another civil war that could have closed the door to his re-election. On the other hand, Williman supported enough of Batlle's measures to be acceptable to their party, kept quiet about the rest, and was completely loyal to his chief. During his term he concentrated on generally popular measures such as the concentration of public works and the improvement of the schools and the administration. There was trouble with organized labor and he broke a railroad strike, but that did not make him or the Colorado Party unpopular. In Uruguay, as in Argentina at that time, anarchists were strong in the labor unions and they enjoyed little public favor.

Socialism Without Marx

In 1911 Batlle was re-elected as he had planned. Vanger, combating the middle-class stereotype, argues convincingly that in this case the political division did not follow class lines. Instead, "political control worked on class." The Colorado Party cut across class lines, it won a resounding victory, and Batlle was in a strong position to go ahead with his program of reform.

In sharp contrast to his first administration, when he was a liberal democrat, Batlle in his second "crossed the limits into socialism." So says Alberto Zum Felde, and he quotes the great man's "most loyal disciple," Domingo Arena, as saying that Batlle and his followers took over "all that is reasonable, humane, and practical in the socialist program." But Batlle was not a Marxist and Hanson is right in holding that his expansion of the state's domain was not systematic and followed no theoretical plan.

The wide difference between Batlle's first and second administrations has been explained as a result of his protracted visit to Europe between the two. That was no doubt an important factor, but the decisive effect of the visit seems much less clear in his social measures than in his proposal of a collegiate executive, to which we shall return later. Another factor, probably important though impossible to weigh, was the political climate in the Atlantic world. Uruguayans as well as Argentines were highly responsive to it, and he had no need to visit Europe to be affected by it. Whether under the label of the Progressive Party in the United States, or of the Liberal Party of Lloyd George in Britain, or of the Radical parties of Clemenceau in France and Yrigoyen in Argentina, or of revolution in the Mexico of Madero, sweeping change for the benefit of the common people was in the air on both sides of the Atlantic. In each country the general trend took a particular form according to local circumstances. In Mexico, where the entrenched oligarchy was unyielding, there was slaughter and destruction for a decade beginning in 1910. Argentina, too, had an entrenched oligarchy, whose position was fortified by the prestige of success, but, in a process likewise begun in 1910 but concluded only two years later, it was flexible enough to concede an electoral reform that constituted a peaceful revolution.

The Uruguay of the early 1900s presented still another kind of situation and process. There the oligarchy was not nearly so firmly rooted as the Argentine, much less the Mexican. The same was true of the whole traditional order in Uruguay. Though still strong in the cultural sphere — witness Rodó's *Ariel* — and in the family system and social customs, it was weak in the country's social and economic structure. This was not of the quasi-feudal type so common in other Spanish American countries. To an even greater degree than Argentina's, its society had been shaped by the cattle industry, so that it was made up for the most part of gauchos and caudillos, with only a few townsmen, fewer peasants, and no serfs. Tradition lived on in a hierarchical spirit that not even nineteenth-century commercialization and urbanization extinguished, though they did increase the openness of society to innovation. Another prop of the traditional order, the Roman Catholic Church, had always been weaker than in most other Spanish American countries, and at the beginning of Batlle's second term its disestablishment was near at hand.

In short, the obstacles to change were fewer in Uruguay than in Argentina and Chile; but what direction should change take? Electoral reform of the kind adopted by Argentina in 1910-1912 was not urgently needed. There was already an approximation to manhood suffrage in practice; the majority party was already commited to democratizing its own procedures, and women were not yet clamoring for the vote. In this situation Batlle had some excuse for making the claim, quoted above, that Uruguay had already resolved the problem of liberty, especially since he went on at once to say that it must now begin to resolve social problems. This injunction, it will be noted, was issued before he began his long visit to Europe in 1907.

In order to understand why Batlle took the course he did in his second administration, we must also take into account the kind of human materials he had to work with in the Colorado Party. He surely took it into account, for he was a very practical politician; it was, for example, by making a deal with a squad of Nationalists (Blancos) that he squeaked through in the presidential election of 1903. His party was no more homogeneous than Yrigoyen's Radical Party, and, as he could not have failed to foresee, his social program met with strong opposition from its right-wing members. Called Riveristas, they were the counterpart of the schismatic Antipersonalist Radicals in Argentina.* The result was to heighten his dependence on his party's left wing, with which he had always been identified.

---

*With the difference that, while the Antipersonalists formed an entirely separate party, the Riveristas remained within the Colorado Party as an autonomous group, as was permitted by the electoral law of Uruguay.

The specific character of the Colorado left wing at this time was determined by two factors. One was a product of Uruguay's wide-open-door immigration policy, which, as Hanson notes, made it a dumping ground for aliens rejected or deported by neighboring states; Uruguay had no equivalent of Argentina's tough Residence Law. Some of these immigrants became leaders of the labor movement, which Batlle fostered with loving care. The second factor also involves Uruguay's immigrants—mostly Italians and Spaniards, it will be recalled—who, unlike similar elements in Argentina, took an active part in politics early and on a large scale. The party for them was the Colorado. We have it on the authority of Carlos Real de Azúa that the party's core, *batllismo* (Batlle-ism), was broadly based on middle sectors of recent immigrant origin and that the members of these sectors were endowed with a universalist ideology of the European radical-socialist kind.

This explains, according to Real de Azúa, why Batlle was not really a nationalist "in the full sense of the term," despite the nationalizations that both of his administrations fostered. He had the mistaken belief, the argument runs, that it is ideas that unite nations, classes, and peoples—hence his party's strong pro-United States stand in World War I—and failed to see that ideologies are merely decorative masks concealing the "umbilical alliance" of large-scale investment and export capital with "the Western governments" (meaning those of the United States, Britain, France, and Germany).

The truth that Batlle failed to see, he continues, is today a commonplace in the world's "marginal" countries, by which he means the peripheral or developing countries, the Third World. That may be so, but it is hardly helpful to judge Batlle by a commonplace of today that was unknown to him and his contemporaries. As for the assumption that there is only one true nationalism, no such thing exists. Instead, nationalism takes many different forms, and these have been described in detail by specialists. Here it is enough to describe Batlle as a moderate economic nationalist and a pioneer of this kind of nationalism in dealing with problems created by a phenomenon new to Latin America: the great wave of foreign capital investment, business enterprise, and technology that had been sweeping over the area since the 1860s. His kind of nationalism, however, differed from the common political variety in disparaging the rituals of patriotism, as when in 1920 his newpaper *El Día* published a letter defending people who refuse to take their hats off for the national anthem on the ground that their heads might get cold.

Although Batlle followed no theoretical plan, it is obvious that his economic nationalism was interrelated with his social welfare policy. " . . . A wasteful administration by the State is always preferable to the efficient management of an industry by foreign enterprise," he asserted at the beginning of his second term in 1911, and, as if to forestall complaints from the free enterprise sector, he observed that "the sphere of state intervention is expanding in every civilized country." Appropriate measures followed. In 1911 the government entered the insurance field, in which United States companies had been prominent. The next year it nationalized the light and power business. In 1915 it began to purchase the British-owned railroads; more than thirty years then passed before Argentina followed this example. Later measures included the establishment of a state mortage bank, the construction of state railroads, and the establishment of a chemical institute.

To operate the nationalized enterprises, increasing use was made of autonomous agencies (*entes autónomos*). This was an institution that had first come into use at the turn of the century. Legal warrant for it had been found at that time by a loose construction of the constitution, but Batlle justified it by the requirements of social justice. The great gap now separating rich and poor, he argued, must be lessened, but it was not opened up deliberately by the more fortunate, "nor is there any reason for class hatred for we all covet riches" (this was the Krausist speaking). The real source of economic inequality, he continued, is the difficulty of bringing about a just distribution of wealth, and this is where the state comes in: it must intervene to reduce the inequality. One instrument employed for this purpose by him and his successors was the autonomous agency. They set up so many agencies of this type that by the late 1920s it had become one of the most distinctive features of Uruguayan public life. For a time these agencies worked well, but by the 1950s they were coming under fire for a number of reasons that will be examined in a later chapter.

Other instruments employed by Batlle and his successors in their effort to lessen the gap between rich and poor were organized labor and social welfare measures. Labor legislation began with the eight-hour day and six-day week and the regulation of working conditions, and went on after the end of his term in 1915 to workmen's compensation, minimum wages, separation allowances, and old-age pensions. Organized labor was also protected in the right to strike, aided by government intervention in industrial disputes, and given moral support, both official and semi-official. An instance of the latter is the proposition advanced in 1908 by Batlle's *El Día*: "Every strike is justified and it would be ideal if all could be successful." One reason for *El Día's* enthusiasm for strikes at that time was the national benefit: the pay raise won by a tramway workers' strike would go into the pockets of Uruguayans instead of flowing out of the country in profits to the lines' British and German shareholders. When, as in this case, strikes were "soak the gringo" operations, they continued to enjoy public sympathy, but this dwindled as nationalization proceeded and foreigners were supplanted by the government and private enterprise of Uruguay itself in most industrial and commercial activities.

Agrarian reform was not attempted by Batlle or his successors. He even asserted in the campaign of 1910 that there was "no pressing agrarian problem requiring the attention of the government." His attitude may have been due in part to unwillingness to challenge the great landowners at a time when the threat of another civil war was already imminent. It seems, however, rather to reflect the nineteenth-century quality of his mind, which combined a gross overvaluation of political processes with an ignorance of economics. However common and understandable, this combination had particularly regrettable consequences for Uruguay.

It was not that Batlle and his party did nothing for the rural sector. On the contrary, the improvement of livestock breeds was encouraged, with the favorable results already mentioned; small farmers were aided by the extension of rural credit and otherwise, and even the forgotten man of the countryside, the rural worker, was remembered long enough to provide him with a minimum wage law, though not necessarily with the minimum wage. But Batlle stopped with half-way measures of this kind, apparently in the sincere belief that "natural forces" would bring about the breakup of great estates, a more equitable distribution of land ownership, and more effective use of the land. He showed no such faith in the beneficent operation of natural forces where urban problems were concerned, but here he had quite as much faith that problems would be solved if only the right laws were enacted. The laws on labor, for instance, would render a redistribution of wealth unnecessary by raising the standard of living. While he brought about the adoption of many measures of an economic character, he never outgrew his old conviction that "the remedy for all our ills lies in electoral freedom, in honest elections." Perhaps this was why he denied the existence of a "pressing agrarian problem." Whatever his reason for taking that view, his enormous prestige helped it prevail then and later, so that subsequent governments for a generation to come left virtually untouched an agrarian situation that is now generally regarded as a major source of Uruguay's many woes.

Strengthening the economy by diversification was one of the methods by which Batlle hoped to establish Uruguay's economic independence. Between his first inauguration and his death in 1929 the economy expanded greatly, but instead of diversifying, it became more and more dependent on cattle and sheep, and instead of diminishing, foreign capital and foreign business enterprise gained control of the new key industry, meat-processing in frigoríficos. The country's first plant of this kind, La Frigorífica Uruguaya, was founded in 1902 by a group of nationals, financiers and stockmen, and began production in 1905. For a few years thereafter it lost money, and although by 1910 it was paying a tidy dividend of 12 percent, its owners were happy to sell out to an Argentine company in 1911. In the same year Swift and Company, already in business in Argentina since 1907, opened a plant in Uruguay. This was followed in 1915 by Armour's Artigas plant, named—presumably without intentional irony—for the hero of Uruguay's independence.

Such investments were encouraged by the local climate, which had been favorable since the mid-nineteenth century and remained so until well into the twentieth. In the twenty years ending in 1903, for example, Liebig's meat extract company paid an average annual dividend of 19 percent plus stock dividends, and then got the export tax on its products reduced by threatening to move to Argentina. Two Colorado deputies tried to block the reduction by arguing that the company obviously needed no tax relief and that all foreign companies were "inspired by cold and calculating egoism" and exported most of their profits as well as their products. Their party, however, had taken no position on the question, whereas the Blancos favored the concession, and so the effort failed. Further encouragement to investments came from the Underwood tariff of 1913, which removed the duties on beef imported into the United States. The latter's trade and investments in the whole Plata area also benefited from the establishment of branches of national banks of the United States, which began in Buenos Aires in 1914.

Though not alone in promoting Uruguay's animal products boom —British as well as Argentine interests also had a hand in it—the United States led the field. The Swift plant, for example, in its first year of operation, 1913, accounted for more than one-half each of all the cattle and sheep "sacrificed" (slaughtered) by the country's frigoríficos that year. Its feat was attributed to superior equipment and procedures. Under the added stimulus of World War I, the total value of trade between Uruguay and the United States almost doubled in two years, jumping from $13.4 million in 1914 to $24.7 in 1916. The increase was based mainly on the rapidly growing herds of cattle and sheep in Uruguay's farm-to-frigorífico complex.

However good the animal products boom was for business, it was not diversification, and instead of being strengthened, the economy of Uruguay was becoming more dependent on the world market and vulnerable to disturbances in it. After their brief experiment with a processing plant of their own in the first decade of the century, stockmen were happy to leave that prosaic activity to foreigners while they themselves returned to the wide open spaces and their herds. Since the grasses in Uruguay are less rich than those in the Argentine pampa and the soil is not suitable for alfalfa, they were at a competitive disadvantage in this respect, but they made up for it by importing smaller but sturdier breeds of cattle. The boom continued into the 1920s.

The tourist trade was another enterprise fostered by the authorities. More fortunate than promoter Reus's big tourist hotel completed just in time to have its business ruined by the crisis of 1890, three hotels built subsequently for the same purpose fulfilled their destiny. Their success was attributed to their gambling casinos, which attracted heavy Argentine patronage. In 1915, in accordance with the trend of the times, the city of Montevideo bought all three. But once the city had them, it could not make up its mind what to do with them until, after trying other formulas, it returned them to private management on a fixed rental basis.

Plural Executive and Disestablishment
Under the Constitution of 1919

In the second edition of his excellent little introduction to Uruguay and its modern history, George Pendle makes the arresting statement that since 1911, constitutional reform has been the main issue in that country's politics. His statement would be arresting in any context but is all the more so because it occurs at the beginning of a chapter that bears the title "The Evolution of the Welfare State." From this title, one might expect that the focus of the chapter would be on welfare and the politics of welfare. Instead, faithful to the promise of its opening sentence, Pendle keeps its focus on constitutional reform and the chapter's high point is its discussion of the new Constitution of 1919, the country's first since 1830. Moreover, in the new constitution and the discussion and debates about it, the two reforms that stand out most prominently are the change from a single to a plural executive and the separation of church and state, neither of which innovations had any direct connection with the welfare state. And yet, as we shall see, both of them did have an important, though not very obvious, bearing on it.

Long before 1911, constitutional reform was, if not the main issue, still a most persistent one in Uruguayan politics. Constant agitation in favor of it began at least as early as 1854. It accomplished nothing, however, and by 1905 the advocates of reform had become so frustrated that one of them, Luis Melián Lafinur, though a leading authority on constitutional law, branded as humiliating, absurd, and a violation of the rights of the sovereign people of Uruguay the contention that the present constitution could be amended only in accordance with the procedures stipulated in it. Those procedures made amendment of it depend on congressional action, and Congress was never willing to open the door to amendment for fear that the constitution would be altered to permit the president's re-election and perpetuation in power. This was identified by Lafinur as one of the two main causes of the insufferable delay. The other was the fear of Catholic leaders that constitutional reform would lead to the establishment of the most complete religious freedom. A third reason for the delay was the great respect many people felt for the existing constitution; excessive veneration, some thought it. One such was José Enrique Rodó, who, in a speech in 1904 supporting the demand for immediate constitutional reform, said: "For three quarters of a century, we alone in America have remained immovable and static, not in the truth about the constitution, but in the Platonic cult of a constitution."

Since Congress still remained "immovable and static" a year later, Lafinur then proposed that it be bypassed by the sovereign people's election of a constitutional convention. In the end, a convention was held, but not until another twelve years had elapsed, and Congress was not bypassed. Batlle was partly responsible for the protracted delay. Though one of the strongest advocates of constitutional reform, he did not formally propose to Congress the holding of a convention for that purpose until the third year of his second term as president, and then he made it an integral part of the proposal that the reform should begin with the replacement of the presidency by a collegial executive. The issue of "collegialism" proved to be highly controversial and slowed down the whole process of reform. The framing and adoption of the new constitution by the convention was not completed until 1917, and it did not go into effect until 1919, after ratification by the people in a plebiscite.

The great innovation of the new constitution, collegialism, was adopted only in a modified version forced on Batlle by a coalition of the National (Blanco) Party and dissident members of the now divided Colorado Party. Collegialism was strongly opposed for many reasons: because it was new, because it was proposed by Batlle, because it was borrowed from abroad,* and because it was inappropriate in a developing country which needed a strong executive. Under the final compromise, the presidency did not appear but was cut in half. Instead of being wholly vested in a collegial body, the executive power was now divided between the president (foreign affairs, defense, internal order) and a new National Council of Administration (all other powers). Both were to be popularly elected, the president for four years and the national council for six. In the election of council members, voting was to be done under the same "incomplete list" system as the one recently adopted by Argentina in the Sáenz Peña Law, and in both countries its purpose was to assure minority representation, which would serve as a political safety valve. There was, however, a significant difference, for the representation was to be in a legislative body in Argentina, and in an executive body in Uruguay. "Coparticipation," which Batlle ended in 1904, was thus reintroduced at the highest executive level; but not for long. The whole collegial system was scrapped in 1934, and although revived in 1952, it was abandoned again in 1966.

The other striking innovation of the Constitution of 1919 was the

*From Switzerland, though there were also early American precedents in the provisions for plural executives in the 1814 constitutions of Mexico and Colombia. A plural executive was also considered, but quickly rejected, by the constitutional convention of 1787 in the United States.

separation of church and state. This was far less controversial than collegialism. It came as the culmination of a long process of secularization that as early as the 1870s and 1880s had divested the church of traditional functions of a cultural and social character. By the turn of the century compliance with the constitutional requirement that the government support the Roman Catholic Church had been confined to financial support and the amount of such support had been reduced to a mere token. Then, in anticlerical José Batlle's first term, the government had legalized divorce — a measure most strongly combated by Catholic leaders in Uruguay, as in all countries. Separation from the state, especially from a state as unfriendly as the Colorados had made it, was welcomed by most churchmen as a release and a protection against political meddling in ecclesiastical affairs.

No persecution accompanied or followed disestablishment, unless one includes under that heading what may have been only a rather tasteless joke. This was the secularization by a law of October 1919 of the names of certain holy days in the church's calendar, turning Holy Week into "Tourism Week" and the day of the Virgin (Immaculate Conception) into "Day of the Beaches." The church was permitted to keep its property and, in sharp contrast to the treatment the church in Mexico was receiving at that time, to continue its customary educational and religious activities. As compensation for the loss of even a claim to financial support by the state, a substantial fund was raised for the church by private subscription. While the separation had far less visible effect than the new collegial system, it also did less harm than that doctrinaire innovation and may even have helped the Roman Catholic Church in Uruguay to share in the revival of organized religion that took place in many Latin American countries, including Argentina, in the next generation.

A third new feature of the constitution was an article legalizing the autonomous agencies, for which there was no specific warrant in the Constitution of 1830, and strengthening their independence. The article identified these agencies as being those comprised in the state's "industrial dominion," in education (higher, secondary, and primary), in public aid, and in public health, and empowered Congress to create others. It provided for the administration of each agency by its own autonomous council, the members to be normally appointed by the national council, or, in special cases, elective. All the agency councils were to be subject only to supervision by the National Council, except for the ultimate authority of Congress, which in the nature of things could be exercised only rarely. As a result, in their normal operation the independent agencies were turned into an aggregation of separate satrapies. This was done in the name of each one's efficiency, but the overall, long-range results were deplorable.

The other noteworthy changes effected by the Constitution of 1919 can be stated briefly. More power was given to the municipal governments. Universal suffrage was established and the secret ballot adopted. Members of the military and police forces were prohibited from engaging in any political activity except voting. Amendment of the constitution was made easier by requiring only approval by two successive meetings of Congress. In short, the new constitution provided for a government that was more democratic, more secular, and much less centralized.

It was also a more flexible instrument, with two glaring exceptions. One was the assortment of bomb-proof bureaucratic shelters erected for the autonomous agencies. This made adaptation to new situations much more difficult and created what came to be described as administrative and budgetary chaos. The other exception was the bifurcation of executive functions between the diminished presidency and the new national council in such a way as to make disagreement and deadlock on controversial measures likely to occur and difficult to resolve. Its tendency was to maintain the status quo, which even its beneficiaries might sometimes wish to change. An additional brake on adaptation was the weakening of the dominant Colorado Party by schisms, which continued in the 1920s, and by what Carlos Real de Azúa calls a certain ambiguity in that party's majority group. By this he means the opposing thrusts of a proclivity for grass-roots democracy and the impulse of leaders to impose their leadership as a matter of conscience when they feel they are right. Batlle himself was the embodiment of this ambivalence. He was constantly torn between two aspirations: that no one should be in command, and that he should be the commander. He died in 1929 just at the beginning of the Great Depression with its imperative call for action, but the ambiguity lived on and so did the party's schisms.

Depression and Dictatorship

In 1921 Uruguay pioneered again by adopting women's suffrage; no other South American state had yet adopted it, and none, except

Brazil, was to adopt it for another quarter-century. By the mid-1920s, however, as Aldo Solari notes, Uruguay seems to have exhausted its capacity for innovation, which had been so notable during the first two decades of the century. Until the end of the 1920s, to be sure, there was no urgent pressure for new departures. Rather, many of its people felt that time should be taken to try out those already made. At first the system worked well; so well, in fact, that during this period Uruguay began to build up its reputation, untarnished until the 1950s, as a model of social justice and political democracy. The operation of the new system, which drew its main financial support from the pastoral sector, was made easier in the 1920s by the general prosperity in Uruguay, as in most of the Atlantic world; by the subsidence of ideological controversy at home and abroad, and by the prevalent spirit of détente expressed most clearly in the great powers' reduction of their navies under a Washington Conference pact of 1922 and the widespread adhesion of both great and small powers to the Kellogg-Briand Peace Pact of 1928. The international factor, already important to the economy, had now become an important one for Uruguayans politically as well, since their country's stability and growth had increased both the interest and the influence of their government in the affairs of the Atlantic world. They were consequently very responsive to changes in the international political and cultural climate as well as in the world market.

It is not at all surprising, then, that the drastic changes of the 1930s — the Great Depression, the fascist explosion, and other events culminating in the outbreak of World War II — had a heavy impact on the domestic situation in Uruguay as well as on its foreign relations. Its economy was paralyzed. Its government, though not overthrown by force, as happened in half the Latin American states, including Argentina, Chile, and Brazil, was converted into a dictatorship by its president. When he restored representative government under a new constitution, the collegial experiment was discarded. Also, the Colorado Party's hold on the government was broken for nearly a decade. There was, however, no change in the land system, or in the welfare system, or in the autonomous agency system, all of which were too deeply embedded in the national fabric for any of them to be greatly altered, much less destroyed, without a structural revolution; and for that the country was obviously not prepared.

When the Great Depression began, Uruguay had one of the two

most highly developed economies in South America (Argentina had the other) and in per capita income it ranked second only to Argentina. But its economy was highly vulnerable. Its per capita national debt, the highest in South America in 1900, was still in 1928-1930 one of the two highest (again the other was Argentina's). The service on its debt was a drag even in good times, and in the early 1930s the times were unprecedentedly hard for Uruguay; in South America, only Chile suffered as severely from the depression. From 1930 to 1932 Uruguay's exports of chilled and frozen beef fell 40 percent; of wool, 45 percent; and of frozen mutton, 75 percent. Since these were its principal exports, the total value dropped from $100 million to $58 million in these three years. For a country that had become dependent on its export economy, this was disastrous. To make matters worse, the collapse was due not only to economic but also to political factors. Chief among the latter were restrictions imposed on Uruguay's meat exports by its customers. Most painful were Britain's, adopted under the Ottawa Conference's imperial preference system. Australia was the chief gainer from it, and Uruguay the chief loser. Its share of British imports of chilled beef, for example, was cut almost in half (from 9.5 percent in 1930 to 5.7 percent in 1932).

The domestic repercussions in Uruguay were severe. The government's chief source of revenue, customs duties, dropped in 1932 to only 60 percent of the 1929 level. All other countries suffered similar losses, but Uruguay's were the more serious because its revenue service was so inefficient that the cost of collection was exceptionally high—twice as high as in Argentina, which had a similar revenue system. According to Hanson, writing about this situation later in the 1930s, a chief reason for this inefficiency was the tenure system, under which government employees were so well protected that it was often easier to hire a new man than to try to get rid of an inefficient one. The result was overstaffing, swollen payrolls, and inferior performance. Employment also declined sharply; the government could not take up all the slack, though it seemed to be trying to. Taking the 1931 figure as 100, employment fell to 80.5 percent in 1932 and slightly lower the following year. To protect the existing labor force, the immigration policy followed for generations was reversed. Formerly welcomed, encouraged, and even subsidized, immigration was closed in 1932 to all but skilled workers with jobs waiting for them. By the end of the ensuing year, the government had tried all the now familiar fiscal and other anti-depression devices, such as the imposition of exchange controls and the suspension of payments on the foreign debt; but hard times continued without remission.

One fruit of the depression may have been the creation in October 1931 of still another autonomous agency, ANCAP, for the administration of fuel, alcohol, and "Portland" (meaning cement). Proposals leading to its establishment, one of them by José Batlle himself, had been made as much as ten years earlier, but none had been adopted until now. There was a feeling of special urgency about fuels because of Uruguay's heavy dependence on foreign sources of supply; although it was one of the smallest of the ten South American states, it ranked third in volume of coal imported. It had no known coal deposits, and potential sources of hydroelectric power, already extensively exploited in contiguous southern Brazil, were too far from Montevideo for the existing technology and could not be tapped with the facilities and resources then available. There was, however, hope that petroleum deposits might be found in Uruguay, as they had been in Argentina some twenty years earlier. Accordingly, the law of 1931 vested in the state exclusive control of all such deposits and provided that all of them should be exploited by the state through ANCAP. Argentina had given private oil companies, all foreign, a substantial share in the exploitation of its petroleum resources; Uruguay gave them none at all. The obvious economic nationalism of this part of the law of 1931 ran through the whole of it and was reflected a year later in the description of ANCAP by Baltasar Brum, former president of the republic and formerly best known for his internationalism, as "one of the finest economic achievements of recent times in Latin America" and as "a step to the economic independence of Uruguay."

It was, however, a political controversy rather than the economic situation that provided the immediate occasion for the establishment of a dictatorship. After José Batlle's death, factionalism in the already divided Colorado Party was intensified. With the support of the majority factions in both the Colorados and the Blancos, Gabriel Terra, commander-in-chief of the army, was elected president, but the minority Colorado group, led by Batlle's sons, owners of the chief party newspaper, *El Día,* joined forces with the minority of Blancos and gained control of the other half of the executive power, the National Council of Administration. Thus divided against itself, the executive power could not work. Terra felt that the only remedy was to amend the constitution, for he was convinced that left-wing agitators, including Communists, posed a serious threat to national security. Montevideo had in fact become a center of Communist activity and of communications between southern South America and Moscow because it offered more freedom and facilities for the purpose than any other city in the area. Terra and his associates may have been particularly sensitive to the threat from Communism at this time because only six months earlier the new autonomous agency ANCAP's petroleum division had begun to import oil from Russia. This was a measure the mere planning of which by the Argentine Yrigoyen's administration is alleged to have contributed to his overthrow in 1930.

Under the Constitution of 1919, however, amendment of it required a two-thirds vote in two successive sessions of Congress, and Terra, who probably could not have got a two-thirds vote for his amendment even once, insisted that the need for action was too urgent to admit of delay. Accordingly, he proposed to ignore the constitution and submit the question to the sovereign will of the people in a plebiscite. The same argument, it will be recalled, was advanced by good Colorados early in the century when they wanted to amend the constitution then in force without following the procedure prescribed in it. Now, however, the Batlle faction of *El Día* turned a deaf ear to it and insisted on strict obedience to the letter of the constitution. On the ground that the national security was in imminent danger, President Terra, who had force on his side, then got what he wanted by decree—a device often used in Latin America, sometimes under the doctrine of inherent power, when there is no explicit authorization for it. His opponents, who controlled the lower house of Congress as well as the National Council, held a meeting of the former that same night and obtained the adoption of a resolution demanding the revocation of all decrees. All they got for their pains was another decree by Terra dissolving both bodies, establishing a junta of government headed by himself, and announcing a constitutional plebiscite.

Terra's assumption of dictatorial power took place early on March 31, 1933. It was followed the same day by a phenomenon that has become familiar in Latin America: the suicide of a statesman. Word of the coup reached Baltasar Brum, former president of the republic, until quite recently president of the national council, and still head of the Colorado Party. Taking his gun in hand to lead a counter-coup, he waited at home in the expectation that the party faithful and loyal elements of the army would rally around him. Time passed, but no one came except a few close friends and a cordon of police that was thrown around his house, not for his protection. Disillusioned, Brum shot himself before his friends could stop him. "A romantic gesture," one of his country's historians calls it. It was not the first gesture of its kind in this part of Latin America, nor the last. In the 1890s President Balmaceda of Chile and Leandro Alem, first head of Argentina's Radical Party, had committed suicide; a few years after Brum's death another Argentine leader, Lisandro de la Torre, was to do likewise, and in the 1950s so was President Vargas of Brazil. Another Chilean president, Salvador Allende, may join the list, but whether his death in 1973 was by suicide, as first reported but soon denied, is uncertain.

The plebiscite was held on schedule. As usual under dictatorships, the government won. This time it was aided by the abstention of the ousted parties. A convention was held and a new constitution adopted (1934). Besides suppressing the national council and making the president once more the sole executive head, the new constitution also eliminated minority representation in the Senate by dividing the seats in that body equally between the two major parties. A complementary electoral law then gave the majority group in any party sole ownership of the party name and the right to grant or deny its use to minority groups. It further provided that the votes cast in an election for all groups bearing the same party label should be counted for the one receiving the largest number of votes. The combined effect of the new law and constitution tended to strengthen the two major parties, but it did this by muffling dissent and innovation and thus further reducing the ability of the political system to meet the changing needs of society.

From another point of view these measures were an effort to save the system from the atomization that had already taken place in its economic and social sectors through the proliferation of autonomous agencies. A parallel effort to reduce the trend towards decentralization was begun by Terra after his coup of March 1933 and continued in another feature article of the Constitution of 1934 which deprived three of the most important autonomous agencies of their autonomy by placing them under the executive department's direct control. In the long run the effort failed, although it was continued by Terra to the end of his administration and for another three years by his hand-picked successor, General Alfredo Baldomir, who was a relative of his and had been chief of police at the time of the coup in 1933. As a result, while the extension of state control went on apace in many other countries during the depression decade, Uruguay, formerly in the vanguard of the movement, now lagged behind. But not for long: President Baldomir restored free elections in the last year of his term, the reanimated Colorado Party returned to power in 1942, and the extension of state control began again. In the next few years the Uruguayan version of the welfare state was rounded out.

Foreign Relations and Domestic Politics

The reversal just described was in part a result of the world crisis brought on by the rise of Nazi-fascism. The crisis helped to shape political developments in Uruguay as well as in Argentina, but in the opposite direction. In Argentina civilian was supplanted by military control and "50 percent democracy" by a dictatorship sympathetic to the Axis. In Uruguay, on the other hand, the movement was from the dictatorship of Terra in 1933-1934 to very limited self-government under two military presidents, Terra and Baldomir, and finally to the restoration of unfettered democracy under a civilian government strongly committed to the anti-Axis cause headed by the Grand Alliance of the United States, Great Britain, and the Soviet Union.

Since independent Uruguay had been created by an international agreement and lay between two large states in perpetual rivalry with each other, its people might have been expected to take a keen interest in the outside world from the start. Before 1914, however, it was too small and weak to participate actively in world affairs and its governments were too unstable and too preoccupied most of the time with domestic problems of growth and internal order to pay much attention to anything else. There were occasional exceptions, as when it was host to an important Spanish American juridical conference at Montevideo in 1888-1889. As a rule, however, in the field of foreign affairs it gave systematic and continuing attention only to its two big neighbors and its growing export trade.

A great change was brought about in this respect after 1904 by Uruguay's newly achieved political stability, combined with its economic and cultural development. Accordingly, during World War I its leaders' concern with international affairs was quickened, greatly broadened, and made constant. For the first time, Uruguay began to function regularly as a member of the family of nations.

What is more, circumstances combined with the domestic tradition of opposition to tyranny to identify Uruguay, in the minds of its own people, with the cause of freedom in that war. When the label "new Holy Alliance" was pinned on the Central powers—the German and Austro-Hungarian empires—reminding Uruguayans of their own struggle for independence against imperial Spain, their sympathies were naturally with the opposite side. Taking the side of France and Great Britain was all the easier because Uruguay's closest ties were with those two countries, and because during the war the British navy severed almost all communications with the Central Powers. The latter process was completed by the entrance of the United States into the war in the spring of 1917. A second feature was then added to the Uruguayan people's conception of their country's international role by its strong commitment to inter-American solidarity. The commitment was undertaken because it brought Uruguay closer to Brazil and the United States. The protection of these two might be needed against Argentina, which seemed to be moving in the opposite direction. Both features of the Uruguayan self-image thus imprinted during the war—identification with the free world and commitment to inter-American solidarity— were called up again and etched even more sharply when, two decades later, Hitler's Germany started another war and it had to be done all over again.

In this sense, World War I was epoch-making for Uruguay. Its leaders' experiences and observations at that time are therefore worth examining in some detail. How the international scene appeared to them at that time can be seen through the eyes of Carlos María de Pena, minister plenipotentiary to Washington from the time of his appointment by President Batlle in 1911 until his death there in 1918. Economist, lawyer, and professor of law as well as diplomat, Pena was one of Uruguay's late nineteenth-century "doctors" devoted to promoting "civilization over barbarism"—the terms of Domingo Sarmiento, with whom in his later years Pena had a close friendship and active correspondence. Before going to Washington, Pena had had some diplomatic experience in Brazil and Argentina, but had spent most of his life in Uruguay. There his political connections were of the best. In addition to President Batlle, he was well acquainted with three future presidents of the republic: Gabriel Terra and Juan José Amézaga, with both of whom he had served on delegations to international conferences, and Baltasar Brum, who had been a student of his at law school and who, before becoming president, was minister of foreign relations and in that capacity his former professor's immediate superior.

In July 1916, instructions from Foreign Minister Manuel B. Otero regarding "Pan American policy" (apparently in connection with President Wilson's projected Pan American pact) provided Pena, now a veteran of five years in his Washington post, with an occasion for sketching his own views regarding Uruguay's foreign relations and policy. After stating his complete agreement with the foreign minister's injunction to go along with the United States in policy matters, Pena gave the minister a short lecture on the great political, economic, and cultural importance of Europe to Uruguay, and then took up the principal countries of Europe and America one by one. France, he said, is the one with which Uruguay has the closest affinity and the "noblest ties." Next come Italy and Spain, which are actuated more by material interest and ethnic ties. England, with a long-standing special concern for the Plata area and obvious economic influence there, has since before the war had Germany as a rival; and these two nations are the most "expansive and absorbent" of all.

In America, he continued, relations with Argentina have been a mixture of conflict and cooperation, and its government may be tempted to revive its impossible claims to predominance. In addition, ancient rivalries are revived whenever it meddles in Uruguayan affairs. While the most serious dispute with Brazil has been settled by a boundary adjustment, some delicate questions—relating to the national debt, policing the frontier, and commerce and customs— are still outstanding. Chile, though it wants very much to cultivate the ABC entente, is today the only South American country whose international policy is determined unilaterally and in terms of national interest. If Chile would only settle its disputes with Bolivia and Peru, it would thereby consolidate its already great prestige and would always be Uruguay's good friend. If it should by any chance "try to upstage us, we could play Argentina and Brazil off against it."

Two of Pena's most interesting points were made in his discussion of the foreign policy of the United States. One was his reference to the Wilsonian projected pact (see chapter XVI), which provided for, among other things, Latin American participation in the maintenance of Western hemisphere security, and which the Uruguayan government had immediately endorsed. The greatest merit of the proposal, according to Pena, was that such a pact would set at rest Latin American fears arising from the unilateral character of the Monroe Doctrine. His second point, related to the first, concerned Foreign Minister Otero's own Pan American project, outlined in the instruction to which Pena was replying. This he described as a proposal to establish a Pan American assembly or court or senate which would "serve as the voice of America, regulate and resolve matters of interest to the continent, and forestall future conflicts."

The chief interest of Otero's project lies in the fact that it anticipated by four years the somewhat similar but much better known proposal of an American association of nations made in 1920 by Baltasar Brum, Otero's successor as minister of foreign relations and, by the time he launched it, president of the republic. Far from being a sudden inspiration or only one man's notion, Brum's Pan American proposal was the culmination of a durable policy development that began at least as early as 1916, with his government's quick endorsement of Wilson's similar proposal, and continued the same year with another of the same kind by Foreign Minister Otero. The policy in question was Uruguay's commitment to internationalism with a bias in favor of inter-American cooperation under leadership by the United States. Montevideo adhered to this policy through World War II and beyond.

It may seem surprising that such a policy should have been adopted by a government controlled by a Colorado Party still dominated by José Batlle. For his economic nationalism was designed to free his country from foreign domination, especially from domination by the great powers with extensive interests in South America — a description which by 1916 fitted the United States like a glove. Yet their concept of economic nationalism was moderate enough to permit new foreign investments regarded as beneficial on balance to Uruguay, such as those of Swift and Armour in the rapidly growing frigorífico business. In addition, Uruguay's leaders were favorably impressed by Wilson's new Latin American policy and still believed — as Pena wrote at this time — that Uruguay was remote enough from the Panama Canal to be out of range of the "hegemonic" Caribbean policy of the United States. Another reason is that during World War I Uruguay became wholly dependent on the United States for oil and the tankers to carry it, and for coal and the freighters to deliver it. The dependency would have extended to weapons of war, except that Uruguay's troops had been trained to use only German Mausers and other German weapons and the United States could not supply these, not even when it was reported that Uruguay was about to be invaded from contiguous southern Brazil, where many Germans lived.

Still another explanation, and one of special interest in a study of South America's Southern Cone, is that Uruguay's key decision, made public in a decree of June 18, 1918, in favor of "continental solidarity" under United States leadership, was "unquestionably inspired" by the example of Brazil. So says Uruguayan historian Oscar Abadie-Aicardi, who has recently defended his thesis of Brazilian inspiration strongly and convincingly. In addition to the documentary evidence he presented, it should be noted that an additional reason for joining the United States and Brazil was the unsatisfactory state of Uruguay's relations with Argentina for several years past, combined with the tone and tenor of Argentine foreign policy after President Yrigoyen took office in 1916. A constant irritant in the relations of the two countries was the question of jurisdiction in the Plata and Uruguay rivers and their islands. There was so much ill feeling over it at this time that a boundary treaty negotiated in 1916 failed of ratification and Argentine Ambassador Naón told Pena he thought it advisable to wait for the "present manifest antagonisms" to calm down before making any further effort to reach an agreement.

A particularly irksome detail in the complex of Plata problems was the dispute between the two countries over title to Martín García Island. The island is closer to Uruguay and, its spokesmen argued, is obviously a natural extension of its continental territory at this point. But after the island had changed hands several times in the first half of the nineteenth century (Garibaldi once occupied it, as also did a British force), it ended up in the possession of Argentina, which refused repeated demands by Montevideo to reopen the question. Another irritant was economic competition, in which Argentina had certain advantages, such as a soil better adapted to growing wheat and alfalfa, and, after both countries had improved their breeds of livestock, a breed of English sheep whose wool was preferred to that of Uruguay's merinos by buyers in the United States. In addition to specific disputes and rivalries, Uruguayans resented their bigger, richer, and stronger neighbor's assumption of superiority in all things. Even envoy Pena, who usually lived up to his motto, "keep cool," gave vent to the resentment on occasion. Although his personal relations with Ambassador Naón were close and friendly, he complained that Naón was typically Argentine in his mistaken ideas about Uruguay. In fact, wrote Pena, "I have never known but three Argentines who did not think about us as he does, and unfortunately all three are dead." If Pena had in mind at this point Palmerston's remark about the Schleswig-Holstein question, he did not say so.

The general lines of foreign policy established during the first world war remained substantially unchanged to and through the second. It was a policy of internationalism with an American accent. Uruguay took part in the Paris Peace Conference of 1919, became a charter member of the League of Nations, and joined the International Court of Justice (World Court), but the most conspicuous action it took just after the war was Pan American. This was President Brum's proposal in 1920 of an American association of nations. He made it only after it had become virtually certain that the United States was not going to join the League of Nations, but, as previously noted, it was in accord with a policy stand taken by Uruguay in 1916. Uruguay formally presented Brum's plan to the next Pan American conference, the one held in Santiago, Chile, in 1923, where it was pigeonholed when the United States showed that it had no more intention of joining a regional than the general international organization.

Beginning in 1929, Uruguay shared in the efforts made to prevent or stop the fighting between Paraguay and Bolivia, but during the full-fledged Chaco War between the two, from 1932 to 1935, Uruguay, after having been the first state to proclaim its neutrality, gave passive aid to Paraguay (as Chile did to Bolivia) by facilitating the transshipment of arms from overseas sources. In December 1933 it played host, though with considerable reluctance, to the seventh in the series of Pan American (restyled Inter-American) conferences. Its reluctance was due to various considerations, one of which was that the conference might be a fiasco because of the Chaco

War, then in progress, and the tension to which it had given rise in neighboring countries; another, that the Uruguayan government might at any time have to face a revolution against Terra's recently established dictatorship. Held in Montevideo, the conference was a pleasant surprise in coming peacefully to a successful conclusion, but its success did not extend to the efforts made during its course to end the Chaco War.

The task of ending the war finally devolved upon the Chaco Peace Conference of mediation held in Buenos Aires from 1935 to 1938. Again Uruguay was one of the participants, the others being Argentina, Brazil, Chile, Peru, and the United States. Just before it began, the Uruguayan minister in Washington took a strong stand against action by the League of Nations in the Chaco affair. The League's European members, he asserted, were trying to apply sanctions in this case so as to have a useful precedent for later disputes in which they themselves might be directly concerned; and in any case his government could not agree to the League's imposing sanctions on small Latin American countries when it had been unwilling or unable to impose them on powerful states such as Japan. Throughout the long conference that followed, Uruguay played a very minor role and its first delegate was described by his United States counterpart, Ambassador to Argentina Hugh Gibson, as tending to be "subservient to Saavedra Lamas." Since the latter was, of course, Argentine minister of foreign relations, the implication seems to be that Uruguay's foreign office was subservient to Argentina's. It is true that the two usually sided together, but this was more likely a matter of agreement than of subservience. Argentina's bias in favor of Paraguay during the conference was notorious, and Uruguay had aided Paraguay during the war by facilitating shipments of arms to it.

The area of agreement between Uruguay and Argentina, however, was limited and its duration brief. After the outbreak of World War II in 1939 the increasing intensity of ideological conflict tended to present problems of both domestic affairs and foreign relations in terms of a choice between democracy and totalitarianism, between the peace-and-freedom-loving nations and the Axis. It was a slow process, not completed until after Hitler's invasion of the Soviet Union and Japan's attack on Pearl Harbor. During its course Uruguay and Argentina moved further and further apart. The transition back to constitutional, representative government in Uruguay took place at the same time that President Castillo of Argentina was making the earlier years of the Conservative Restoration look almost democratic in comparison with his own administration. In foreign policy he was going back on concessions a previous administration had made to democracy and Pan Americanism at Inter-American meetings in 1938, 1939, and 1940. Uruguay, on the other hand, hewing to the line established during World War I, supported the same measures and thought not of turning back but of going forward. It did so at the next Inter-American meeting, one held in Rio de Janeiro in January 1942, in the wake of the Pearl Harbor attack. At that time the foreign policy rift with Argentina became a chasm. Of the many measures on which they disagreed, the one that underlined their disaccord most heavily was the creation of the Inter-American Emergency Advisory Committee for Political Defense, with Montevideo as its seat and, as its chairman, Foreign Minister Alberto Guani of Uruguay, who was an ardent supporter of Pan Americanism and the anti-Axis cause. In one of its first acts the new committee fulfilled expectations by investigating subversive activities in Argentina and then, over the protest of its Argentine member, publishing an exposé of them.

By no means all Uruguayans shared Alberto Guani's views. Nazi-fascism and the Hispanidad doctrines of Franco Spain had gained votaries in Uruguay as in Argentina, though on a smaller scale. In addition, there were conservative nationalists who needed no foreign prodding to look with distaste on the things treasured by Guani, and there was the *Ariel* tradition with its warning against embracing Caliban. All these currents were strengthened late in 1941 by the publication of the book *Hispanoamérica en guerra?* (Hispanic America at War?), whose author, Felipe Barreda Laos, was Peruvian ambassador to Uruguay as well as to Argentina. His emphatically negative answer to the policy question raised by his title and the Hispano-American doctrine with which he supported it, delighted conservative nationalists in both countries. One such was Luis Alberto de Herrera, now leader of the Blancos and well established in Fredrick Pike's words, as a "most eloquent spokesman of Catholic and Hispanic values." We encountered him earlier as an advocate in 1910 of close friendship with the United States and Brazil as insurance against the ever-present threat to Uruguay from Argentina. By the early 1940s, however, he had switched to cooperation with the politically influential conservative nationalists of

Argentina and was keeping up a drum-fire of denunciations of the Uruguayan government's cooperation with the United States in the defense of the South Atlantic. His long-delayed honeymoon with Argentina was soon over, for conservative nationalism had no more staying power in that country than in his own. Its apogee and quick decline in both countries were bound up with the early stages of the development of Peronism and will be discussed in that connection.

VII Chile from Centenary to World War II, 1910-1942

Members of Chile's ruling class liked to describe themselves as the Englishmen of South America and the period of congressional supremacy under their leadership as "parliamentary." James Bryce, describing Chile as he saw it in the centenary of its independence, amiably adopted their usage, but, with his characteristic perspicacity, he added that it was a parliamentary government of the kind England had had in the eighteenth century; an unreformed, rotten-borough, upper-class parliament. However, he did not go on to discuss the rising discontent with it and with the country's economic and social system as well — a discontent which, combined with disillusionment about Chile's past and misgivings about its future, was beginning to find expression in literary and other forms, among them mounting labor violence. In the course of the next three decades the forces of change gathered such intensity that, by the time the American republics became directly involved in World War II, Chile (at least upper- and middle-class Chile) had been catapulted into the modern age. Instead of the eighteenth-century parliament with which it began the period, it had now acquired a regime of the latest model, made in Moscow, a Popular Front government. Also by this time there had been equally sweeping and more lasting changes in other respects, notably in the adoption of a labor code and a social welfare system that were among the most advanced in the Western hemisphere. In economic policy, free enterprise was replaced by state interventionism and an ancillary "neo-orthodox" development policy. Still, the old regime was by no means done for, and World War II helped bring headlong change to a halt.

Centennial Stock-Taking

In the nineteenth century Chileans had come to regard theirs as the leading country in all Latin America. As 1910 and the centennial of its independence approached, however, and evidences of decline, stagnation, and social malaise multiplied, a piecemeal national stock-taking began, and thoughtful observers were troubled by what it revealed. As early as 1900, Radical leader Enrique Mac-Iver published a pamphlet in which he declared flatly that Chile had now been overtaken by its sister republics and that the root of the trouble was the Chilean people's loss of energy and enterprise. He called his pamphlet a discourse on "the moral crisis of the Republic," and other writers chimed in to make moral decline the central theme of the decade. One of them, Alejandro Venegas, who is described as a "humble school teacher," claimed to have discovered the origin of the decline. It began, he asserted, when "a responsible, energetic, progressive aristocracy transformed itself into a greedy, visionless plutocracy." The same indictment was brought against the Argentine upper class of that period, but, unlike Chile, the Argentina of 1910 felt itself still on the upward curve, and its bout of soul-searching still lay nearly a quarter of a century in the future.

There was no let-up in the Chilean inquest when the centenary ended. In a book published in 1912, Francisco A. Encina analyzed "our economic inferiority." He too stressed the moral factor, but not so much in terms of a decline of morality as of national character. Chile's national character, he said, was formed by a compound of solid Basques with less practical Castilians and Andalusians. It had served the country well under nineteenth-century conditions, but lacked the daring and imagination required in the twentieth century. However, Encina's main stress was on economic factors, among them inflation and foreign control of important sectors of the economy. He thereby gave the inquest a new dimension and at the same time provided a logical foundation for his belief that there was hope of salvation for Chile, for problems of national character are rather intractable, but one can hope to find solutions for economic problems. Furthermore, Encina proposed, as one means of coping with the latter, a drastic change in the educational system, and thereby gave the inquiry further depth.

The outlook did not seem gloomy to all Chileans. Writers in the Santiago newspaper *El Mercurio* in 1910 saw only good for their country in the approaching completion of the Panama Canal, as well as in the increasing interest shown by the United States and Europe in South America. Examples cited were articles by "our recent guest" William Jennings Bryan and former Secretary of State Elihu Root, and other articles in great newspapers such as the Paris *Figaro,* which welcomed the entry of South America—especially Argentina, Brazil, and Chile—into international politics, and the *Times* of London, which devoted an entire special issue, equivalent to a 224-page book, to South America. Also, Chile was one of the two countries in all Spanish America to which the great Spanish writer Miguel de Unamuno was beginning to give close attention.

For Chile in particular he expressed a "profound sympathy" as a country "which in spirit is so much like my own Basque people." It was because of his sympathy for Chile that, about this time, he excoriated two Chilean writers because they wrote so boastfully about their country as to make it look ridiculous. "Patrioteers," Unamuno called them, "what the French call chauvinists."

Finally, James Bryce's report on his visit to Chile in 1910 pictures a society that was sound on the whole and not apprehensive about the future, but rather living agreeably in the present. For those who could afford it, there was plenty of horsemanship and horse racing, and, at Viña del Mar, polo and golf. He even accorded Chile's "great historian and bibliographer," as he called José Toribio Medina, the almost unique distinction of mentioning his name; personal names rarely appear in Bryce's accounts of any of the South American countries he visited. He also paid a handsome tribute to Chile at large, saying that it "is of all the Latin-American states the one which best answers to European or North American notions of a free constitutional commonwealth." He noted that the government was "practically in the hands" of a small aristocracy (one hundred families, he had heard) and that there were "constant changes in the ministers," but, he went on, "the machine works . . . The level of capacity is . . . high, and so is the national spirit of the people."

Bryce clearly missed the malaise; *El Mercurio* failed to reflect it; and Unamuno, in Salamanca, was too far away to know about it. Yet there was reason for the apprehension that many Chileans felt about their country's situation and prospects and for the lack of élan in their centennial celebration of 1910 as compared with Argentina's. Evidence of decline and disarray was already at hand, and more was to come. Morals do not lend themselves to measurement, but for what the figures are worth, the percentage of illegitimate births in Chile rose from 21 to 1850 to 31 in 1900 and 38 in 1920. Generally said to be a by-product of Chile's booming wine industry, second to none in Latin America, alcoholism was already a serious problem by the 1890s. Campaigns against it were resisted by the producers of wine, who were well represented in the government; in the early 1920s, 14 were members of the national Senate.

On the economic front a big issue of paper money during the war scare of 1898 ushered in two decades of monetary inflation. The collapse of an industrial development boom in 1907 was followed by a depression that had hardly ended when World War I brought on another, though much shorter one, during which government revenue was reduced to barely more than one third its 1913 level. Wages were wretchedly low for rural workers, little better for most industrial workers, and the best paid of all, the nitrate workers, were exploited by company stores and wine shops. The rate of unemployment, though fluctuating, was often high, and by World War I, despite the slow growth of the country's total population, the urban rush had already given Santiago a mushrooming shantytown.

Relief and welfare measures were conspicuously lacking. As Pike says, all the writers talked about the horrors of the social problem, but no one did anything about it, and the upper classes and their middle-class allies were unwilling or unable to understand where the "worsening plight and rising expectations" of the lower classes were bound to lead. That their expectations were rising was due in part to labor leaders such as Recabarren of the Social Workers Party, who was also telling them how to find an issue out of their afflictions.

Declining Status in America

The decline of Chile's relative standing among its neighbors was already a source of disquiet to its leaders by the centennial year, and it became even more troubling to them in the next decade. They were particularly sensitive where Argentina was concerned. As regards population, they had every reason to be. In 1850 Chile's population was about 15 percent larger than Argentina's, but by 1900 the positions had been reversed and Argentina had a wide lead, with a population of 4.7 million to Chile's 2.9 million. In the next 30 years the gap widened greatly: in 1930 Argentina's population was nearly three times as large as Chile's (11.9 million and 4.4 million respectively). Much of the disparity, of course, was due to immigration, but that fact hardly made it less irksome to Chileans, who thought their country ought to have been more attractive to newcomers.

There was also a disturbing contrast between Chile's great success in foreign relations before 1890 and its frequent frustrations since then. First came the incident of the U.S.S. *Baltimore* of late 1891 at Valparaíso. Chileans on the winning side in the civil war just ended were resentful towards the United States because it had interpreted its neutrality policy in a way helpful to Balmaceda, just as, during the War of the Pacific, to the displeasure of all good Chileans, it had favored Peru.

In this atmosphere a tavern brawl between American sailors on shore leave and Chileans on the loose quickly blew up into a riot and troops had to be called out. By the time the fracas was over, two sailors had been killed. The affair gave rise to a dispute between the two governments that escalated to the threshold of war. The details need not detain us. What matters here is the way in which peace was preserved. The measures included the withdrawal of a Chilean note under heavy pressure from Washington, and the resignation of Chile's foreign minister as well as its minister to Washington. As a result, the Chilean people were left with the feeling that they had been humiliated by an arrogant American government. The resentment in Chile was so great and lasting that all classes sided with Spain against the United States in the war of 1898.

Chileans were again frustrated, though not humiliated, in a dispute with Argentina that in 1898 brought on another war scare. The issue involved the boundary line between the two countries. Their treaty of 1881 was thought to have settled this question, but, not for the first time, it turned out that honest men could disagree when it came to locating on the terrain a boundary line described in a treaty and drawn on a map. The dispute dragged on and on, and the Chileans became more and more impatient, as a considerable number of them would end up on foreign soil if Argentina's contention prevailed. By early 1898 the Argentine minister in Santiago was warning his government that "these people are fed up" with the delay. That was no exaggeration, if we may credit the account given by Chilean historian Mario Barros. According to him, the great bulk of the Chilean army, navy, and civilian population were saying: "Enough of conversations and documents! Prepare for action, cross the Andes, revive the historic expeditions of 1879, and don't stop until [we are in] Buenos Aires!" Their hope was to dictate peace to the Argentines in their own national capital, as happened to the Peruvians at the end of the War of the Pacific. As it turned out, war was avoided and a lasting peace agreed on in 1902 in the *Pactos de Mayo.*

Once again, though, a feeling of frustration lingered on among the Chileans. Their dreams of glory faded and became every day more fantastic as Argentina continued to increase its lead over Chile in population, wealth, and power. This was reflected in the changing balance of naval strength to Chile's great disadvantage. To make matters still worse, Chile was alone in South America, isolated by the smouldering resentment of Peru and Bolivia and the long-standing rivalry with Argentina. Since Paraguay was too weak to count, and Uruguay too small and far away, that left only Brazil, which was still more distant and, in that period, of doubtful utility as an ally even if it had been closer.

The realization that Chile was falling behind Argentina would have been less painful to its people if, despite obvious differences, the two countries had not been so much alike as to challenge comparison — alike both in basic factors and in their historical development since the 1870s. Community of Spanish race, language, and culture and Roman Catholic religion they shared in some degree with all the other Spanish American countries, but, except for Uruguay, only Chile and Argentina lay largely in the temperate zone and by 1900 had achieved both political stability and economic growth. Both had developed export economies, but these were non-competitive; in both, foreign capital and management, principally British, bulked large; and in both there were traditional ruling classes that were beginning to feel threatened from below. Moreover, there were striking parallels in their historical development in the quarter century just before 1900. In the 1870s and 1880s both countries adopted anticlerical legislation and severed relations with the Vatican. Between 1879 and 1882 both countries brought their centuries-long Indian wars to a successful conclusion, thereby opening large areas to settlement. In both, the 1880s were a Gilded Age and this was followed immediately in both by a civil war, though in Argentina the conflict was much briefer and less bloody. Finally, both countries began to professionalize their armies with the aid of German experts; Chile in the 1880s, Argentina in the late 1890s.

From Détente to Entente with Argentina

The thought of these similarities and resemblances heightened the Chileans' sense of national decline, but it also suggested to them, as to the Argentines, that the converging lines of their development should lead not to collision but to cooperation. After all, that would only be a return to their relationship during the struggle for independence. They did in fact move in that direction during the first two decades of the new century. After drawing back from the brink of war, they concluded the Pacts of May, which not only settled past differences but also looked to the future. In the next dozen years there was much talk about putting cooperation on a more formal basis. Brazil became involved in it, and in 1915, after the three governments had mediated in the dispute between Mexico and the United States, they established the ABC entente in a treaty negotiated in Santiago and signed in Buenos Aires, providing for the peaceful settlement of disputes. Although the treaty was never ratified, the three foreign ministers who had negotiated it maintained the entente on an informal basis and as a moral obligation. The entente lapsed, however, when Brazil entered World War I on the side of the United States, for Chile and Argentina remained neutral and followed parallel policies that provoked ill-founded charges of pro-Germanism against them. After the war, both became charter members of the League of Nations, which many people in both countries regarded as an escape hatch from a Pan American Union dominated by the United States.

While Yankeephobia was not rampant among the governing classes of either Chile or Argentina during these two decades, there was a certain coolness towards the United States that constituted a bond of sympathy between the two. Evidence of this feeling came out in connection with one of the many anticipations of the ABC entente, such as a speech given in Santiago in September 1910 by Argentine Foreign Minister Carlos Rodriguez Larreta during the centennial celebration of Chilean independence. In the course of his address he proposed that Chile, Argentina, and Brazil enter into an accord of "triple friendship" as a contribution to the maintenance of peace and order in South America. As he explained four years later, he followed this up at once with a fuller explanation at a secret meeting with a few colleagues, among whom were Chilean Foreign Minister Luis Izquierdo and American Minister Henry White. Undeterred by White's presence, he declared that the proposed triple accord would, "above all," create "a powerful force in the southern part of the continent, one capable of counterbalancing hereafter the influence of the United States." Commenting on this gloss some time later, Izquierdo, no longer foreign minister, matched the Argentine diplomat's cautionary tone in his references to the United States. He referred to the ABC mediation, then in progress, and warned that it would be a "pernicious error" for the three governments to confine themselves in such matters to the United States alone. While he was as warm a friend as any, he continued, of good relations with the United States, such relations could never be maintained except on a basis of mutual respect and equality, "at least that fictitious equality established by international law."

Chile's dislike for Wilson's Pan American Pact, xenophobe Yrigoyen's coming to power in Argentina, and the neutrality of both countries during the war, caused their relations with the United States to become cooler, and with each other closer, in the course of that decade. Both tendencies seemed likely to become definite trends when, in 1920, Arturo Alessandri was elected president of Chile, for he was in significant respects a Chilean counterpart of Yrigoyen. Batlle of Uruguay was a leader of the same type, but even an approximation to Southern Cone solidarity was doubtful because of the Uruguayans' resentment over being left out of the ABC entente, their traditional distrust of Argentina, and their government's cooperation with the United States in World War I. More likely was a flowering of the "hands across the Andes" spirit in the other two Cone countries, but that would depend in large measure on how Chile fared under Alessandri's government.

The Interwar Years: Accelerated Change

Chile changed greatly and at an accelerated pace in the interwar period, by which is meant here the period from the end of the first world war in November 1918 to the beginning of the American republics' direct involvement in the second, with the Pearl Harbor attack in December 1941. How greatly it had changed is apparent in political terms from a comparison of two coalitions that governed the country during this period, one at its start, the other at its close. The Liberal Alliance, which won the election of 1920 under colorful Arturo Alessandri's leadership, had been in existence since the late nineteenth century. It represented mainly the middle class, though in this election significant support came from the upper and lower social strata as well, and promised to renovate society from top to bottom. In the chaotic first four years of his administration, however, Alessandri accomplished little, and he owed the passage of the very important social reforms of his fifth and last year to help from a surprising source, the military. A new constitution, also adopted in his last year, institutionalized social reform, as Mexico and Uruguay had already done, but otherwise made no innovation of fundamental importance.

On the other hand, the Popular Front that elected President Aguirre Cerda in 1938 was an entirely new coalition and the only successful Popular Front in the western hemisphere. It conformed to Moscow's new strategy of drawing the liberal middle class into an alliance with the proletariat against the upper classes. The Chilean Communist Party was a principal component of the Front in that country and anti-imperialism was one of the three planks in its platform. Its major achievement was the establishment of a state Development Corporation (CORFO) to conduct national economic planning and development. The measure was adopted with some support from conservatives, but that fact only shows how far Chile had moved away from free enterprise capitalism since the beginning of the interwar period.

Two events of the years between the electoral victories of these two coalitions illustrate, if they do not explain, the main trends of the times in public affairs. These trends were towards class conflict, state socialism, and the adoption of a welfare system. The first event was the establishment of a virtual dictatorship under an army officer, Carlos Ibáñez del Campo, which came on the heels of Alessandri's disillusioning administration and lasted from 1927 to 1931. The other event was the disastrous economic depression of the early 1930s. The havoc it wrought combined with influences from Europe to produce a flock of new parties and movements of all hues, including Communist, Socialist, and Nazi-fascist. The result was a further complication of Chile's traditional multi-party system, which made coalitions necessary. Yet the coalitions and their opponents were almost always equally balanced. Thus, the Liberal Alliance won by the narrowest of margins in 1920, so did the Popular Front in 1938, and neither was able to maintain majority control after the initial victory. This unstable equilibrium was to continue to be a main feature of Chilean public life after World War II.

Democracy, Dictatorship, and Depression

In the campaign of 1920, says Eduardo Frei, "the romanticism of youth found popular expression for the first time." That was a year, he continues, when speeches full of beautiful promises made everything seem possible and solutions for all problems seem easy. Eloquent, fiery Arturo Alessandri was the caudillo called for by the occasion; he rose to it magnificently, and that was his great moment in history. In a somewhat different vein Alberto Edwards describes Alessandri as a man of Italian origin who, though brought up in the most aristocratic and reactionary circles of the oligarchy, nevertheless now came forth (at the age of 52) as the standard-bearer of the Chilean electorate's democratic rebellion against that same oligarchy and did not hesitate to preach an "unarmed revolution" against all the formulas of the past, with the pledge to remedy all grievances. His program, remarks Edwards rather drily, is difficult to define, for it was one of rebellion and protest rather than of reconstruction.

Nineteen hundred and twenty was full of hope for some Chileans, of foreboding for others. Commentators on it in later years likewise saw it in widely different ways. To Federico Gil it was the year when fundamental changes that had been under way for a long time — the growth of industry and an industrial proletariat, of the metropolis and an intellectual middle class — all reached a culmination. Eduardo Frei, on the other hand, wrote in the late 1940s that Chile had never had a true middle class, for what went by that name lacked consistency and was made up largely of transients, some on their way down from the upper class and the rest on their way up from the lower class; but even he admitted that Chile's so-called middle class provided leadership for the restless proletariat, which did not develop its own leaders from the labor unions until well after 1920. Still a third view was presented by Alberto Edwards, according to whom the main issue in the campaign of that year was the class conflict between the traditional ruling class and the petty bourgeoisie educated in the *liceos*. (The liceo is roughly equivalent to a combined high school and junior college.)

Since only 8 percent of the Chilean people voted in this election, one can understand why, although Alessandri made himself a popular hero in the campaign, the votes were so evenly divided that he won the national election only by winning enough contested district elections to overcome the initial majority gained by his conservative opponent, Luis Barros Borgoño. Described as elegant, rational, and a perfect expression of the past, Barros was the candidate of another coalition. This was the newly formed National Union, a powerful bloc comprising all the great forces of traditional Chile — landlords, bank, press, the Conservative Party, most of the National and Liberal parties, and part of the Balmacedistas.

The election gave the Liberal Alliance the presidency and a

majority in the Assembly but not in the Senate. Even in the Assembly Alessandri lost effective control when the Liberal Alliance fell apart before the year was out. From that point on, he suffered almost unrelieved frustration almost to the end of his five-year term. The even division of power between government and opposition was not, however, the only reason why Alessandri accomplished so little for so long. The middle-class Radicals, a major component of the Liberal Alliance, were readier to coalesce with left-wing forces before an election than to support left-wing measures after victory. In addition, according to Marcos Mamalakis, Robert J. Alexander, and others, Alessandri tied his own hands in 1920 by making a tacit agreement with the rural landlords to forget agrarian reform and prevent the unionization of agricultural workers in exchange for the landlords' concurrence in his policy of encouraging industrialization. That severely restricted the scope of reform, for it will be recalled that in the 1920s the population of Chile was more rural than urban by a wide margin. The agreement did not even bring Alessandri enough support to give him control of Congress.

The forces of government and opposition remained evenly balanced through his first four years, and the government itself was as unstable as in the worst days of the parliamentary period. The period, in fact, was still going on and so, says Frei, were its familiar ills of materialism, corruption, sterile politics, and a rapid succession of ministerial crises. In four years there were 18 different cabinets, and in all but two of these the change of personnel was total.

The conservative National Union made effective use of its control of the Senate to hamstring Alessandri's administration. It blocked his sweeping reform measures, which were aimed at strengthening the capitalist system, not abolishing it, and at improving the constitution. It even withheld appropriations, so that he had to resort to issuing paper money, thereby intensifying the inflation already stimulated by World War I. The postwar economic depression of the early 1920s followed, thus aggravating the already serious social discontent. This discontent had given rise in the preceding decade to 293 strikes, less than half of which were successful; they involved 155,000 workers, which was a very large fraction of Chile's still small organized labor force. In 1919 labor troubles provoked the imposition of a state of siege, and early in 1920 a coal strike paralyzed the nation's railroads. Although industrial workers in all countries suffered more than other groups from that postwar depression, in Chile their suffering was intensified by the decline of its nitrate industry, which, according to Alessandri, by 1922 had cost 47,000 nitrate workers their jobs. And now there was a new incitement to labor discord in the appearance of Communist agents from Bolshevik Russia.

In the election of 1924 Alessandri assumed active leadership of the Liberal Alliance's campaign, thereby shocking many who thought that the chief executive, as president of all the Chilean people, should remain aloof from partisan politics. His side won a majority of seats in both houses of Congress this time, but he still was unable to get his programs adopted. He then resorted to what critics denounced as a species of bribery by initiating a measure that provided salaries for all members of both houses, who had hitherto served without pay. This met with the expected cordial response from Congress, but provoked an invasion of its galleries by indignant and vociferous army officers, whose salaries, often in arrears, had lost much of their purchasing power during a decade of inflation. The government, unable to budge the demonstrators, threatened to punish them, but backed down in the face of the strong support given them by the officer corps of both army and navy.

In the meanwhile Alessandri had begun to court the military, even visiting them in their barracks, to enlist their backing for his reform program. They gave it in even greater measure than he expected or wanted. After pushing the reforms through a cowed Congress in a few days, along with salary increases for themselves, instead of going back to their barracks the military leaders set up a junta of senior officers to see to it that suitable follow-up measures were taken by the government. This intrusion was too much for Alessandri, who resigned on September 8, 1924, and left for Europe. In Chile, as in Argentina since the turn of the century, liberal and radical politicians were at least as active as conservatives in bringing about the armed forces' intervention in politics. And in both countries politicians of whatever stripe often got much more military intervention than they had bargained for.

The reform program so persuasively pushed through Congress on bayonets included laws for the protection of labor unions, the improvement of working conditions, and the provision of health insurance for workers. This accomplished, Congress was sent packing three days after the president's resignation, and the junta continued to rule the country with the apparent acquiescence of the civilian population. Among the military themselves, however, many officers of middle and junior rank were sharply critical of what they called the junta's conservatism. In late January 1925 they ousted it and set up a new junta nominally headed by a civilian but actually dominated by Major Carlos Ibáñez del Campo. In the next two months the new junta produced a mass of social legislation for the benefit of the workers. It also enacted Chile's first graduated income tax law.

This was the beginning of the political career of Carlos Ibáñez. He was 46 years old at the time, four years younger than was Colonel Juan Perón of Argentina when he emerged in mid-October 1945 as the undisputed leader of a somewhat similar reform movement based on a union of armed forces and workers.

The junta's reforms did not include the new constitution that Alessandri had long been trying to get adopted. Persuaded by the officers' promise that civilian government would be restored, he returned to Chile late in March 1925, but stayed only long enough to see to the adoption of his new constitution. Though not fundamentally different from its predecessor except in the firmer legal basis it provided for social reform, it made some interesting changes. The two most important were its restoration of a strong presidency, which brought the so-called parliamentary period to a close, and the separation of church and state. Neither change was in the least revolutionary. The new constitution did little more than restore the balance between executive and legislature established by its predecessor of 1833. This was accomplished mainly by depriving Congress of a power it had obtained in the 1870s, that of forcing cabinet changes by censuring cabinet ministers, for this power had been the chief prop of the "parliamentary" system. It is true that the new constitution somewhat reduced the congressional power of the purse, which had been another prop of that system. It was now provided that presidential budgets take effect unless altered by Congress within four months of receiving them. Nevertheless, Congress still had four months within which to make such alterations, and it frequently made use of this and its other powers to maintain a fairly even balance between these two departments of the government. In fact, competent critics have rated Chile's Congress since 1925 as one of the strongest legislative bodies in Latin America. As we shall see, its strength has been demonstrated time and again, notably at the expense of presidents Carlos Ibáñez in his second administration, in the 1950s, and Salvador Allende in the 1970s.

The other principal constitutional change, the separation of church and state, would have been revolutionary two or three generations earlier. By the 1920s, however, it had been under discussion so long, and the secularization of society had proceeded so far in both legislation and mental attitudes, that when it came at last, the separation seemed almost a matter of course. Not everyone took it so. In Chile, as in Uruguay a few years earlier, some church leaders even welcomed it as a liberation from bondage to a godless government, but the opposition among them was much stronger and more lasting in Chile. The hierarchy now ceased to participate directly in politics, but continued to speak on the conservative side for a substantially united church until the 1950s, when a strong social reform movement developed among Catholic clergy as well as laymen.

The strength Congress demonstrated in later years was not readily apparent for more than a decade after the adoption of the Constitution of 1925, but neither did a strong president put in an appearance quickly. As Eduardo Frei says, the process of political decomposition that had provoked military intervention in 1924 continued until 1927. Omitting details, it is enough to say that Alessandri, unable to control the situation, decamped again in a matter of months and that another civilian president, who had little talent and less liking for the job, was happily forced out in 1927. His successor was his own minister of war, Carlos Ibáñez.

In order to legitimize his power, Ibáñez submitted to the formality of an election. He won it by an overwhelming majority and to great public acclaim. Although he had none of the personal magnetism of his fellow countryman and contemporary Alessandri, or of his Argentine counterpart in the next generation, Juan Perón, he was vividly and, by many, most favorably remembered as the strong man of the military junta that had so recently given the common people a welcome package of long overdue social reforms. The masses loved him for that. The upper classes accepted him because of their faith in his ability to restore law and order. He did not disappoint them.

In the process, however, Ibáñez turned his presidency into a virtual dictatorship and showed the same contempt for constitutional restraints that Diego Portales had expressed so pungently in the 1830s. Ibáñez muzzled the press, tolerated no opposition even from Congress, and exiled outspoken critics. To keep the growing labor movement in line, he rewarded friendly unions with government support and castigated the recalcitrant. Among the latter were a Chilean affiliate of the Industrial Workers of the World, which had its headquarters in the United States, and Chile's oldest labor organization of national scope, the Chilean Labor Federation (FOCH). Founded in 1909, FOCH had come under Communist control in 1919 and soon thereafter became affiliated with the labor arm of the Communist International. By the time Ibáñez took office, it was claiming more than 100,000 members, but under his forceful ministrations it went into a decline from which it did not recover even with the onset of the Great Depression.

In exchange for the country's lost freedom, Ibáñez for three years conferred important material benefits upon it. Some of his measures were of the same kind that contemporary European dictators such as Mussolini of Italy and Primo de Rivera of Spain were already noted for: building highways and bridges, making the trains run on time, modernizing the cities, and creating an efficient national police force. In addition, he gave effect to the recent social reforms and greatly improved public administration by creating institutions, among them superintendencies of banks, insurance, and corporations, that became a permanent and valued part of the country's administrative system. Perhaps most surprising of all, Ibáñez spent far more on education than any previous president had done, opened schools all over the country, and granted the University of Chile autonomy.

Yet, despite his strong nationalist bias, he relied heavily, as his predecessors had done, on foreign capital in the shape of both loans and investments. Foreign investments shot up nearly 50 percent, from $723 million in 1925 to $1,017 in 1930. The United States led the procession with 60 percent of the total, and by the latter year, which was also the last full year of the Ibáñez regime, the Guggenheim interests had pushed to 70 percent their share in the nitrate industry, which once, if only briefly, had been dominated by Chileans, and then, for a longer period, by British interests.

It may be that the solid achievements and obvious vigor of the Ibáñez regime were what enabled it to survive the onset of the Great Depression twice as long as did the senile Yrigoyen's rudderless administration in Argentina. Counting from the Wall Street stock market crash of October 1929, the depression was just over 10 months old when Yrigoyen was toppled; another 11 months passed before Ibáñez fell. The order of the two rulers' disappearance might well have been reversed if the force of the depression's impact had been the only factor, for, according to a League of Nations report on the damage done by it in 27 selected countries, Chile was the hardest hit of all. Statistical measurements of the extent of the disaster there abound. From 1929 to 1932, Chile's total exports dropped 88 percent. Most of the loss was accounted for by a decline from $27 million to $3.5 million in export sales of copper and nitrates, which provided more than 70 percent of Chile's national income. The suffering was universal. A crop failure in 1931 set off a rise averaging over 100 percent in the cost of food stuffs in a two-year period during which real wages fell 40 percent.

An epidemic of strikes forced Ibáñez out at the end of July 1931. There was no shooting except by overzealous student strikers and overreacting police. Ibáñez resigned quietly and went into exile.

Reaction, Recovery, and Popular Front

Eighteen months after the Ibáñez dictatorship in Chile crumbled, President Terra set up a similar regime in Montevideo. This made previously democratic Uruguay the third and last of the Southern Cone countries to join the list of political casualties of the Great Depression. In all three countries the fall of the old regime was followed by several years of conservative reaction. Stricken Chile, however, differed from the other two in first passing through more than a year of near-chaos during which the reaction followed for a time a leftward course. The culmination of this phase came in June 1932 with the establishment of the Socialist Republic of Chile under the leadership of an air force colonel by the unlikely name of Marmaduke Grove. His Socialist Republic lasted only twelve days, but that was long enough to scare the wits out of the great majority of politically active Chileans. Its quick demise was followed in the next hundred days by a half-dozen assorted but equally short-lived regimes. This experience only strengthened the rightward trend of public opinion. As a result, the newly conservative—or perhaps better, the now more clearly conservative—Arturo Alessandri, who had been defeated in a presidential election held shortly after the fall of Ibáñez, won by a wide margin in the one held in late 1932.

There were five presidential candidates in this election. Three of them, including Alessandri, represented the center and right. The other two were Socialist Grove and a Communist. The three center and right candidates polled 80 percent of the total votes, and Alessandri received more than twice as many as the other two combined, and more than three times as many as Grove. The Communist Party's candidate lagged far behind, with only a trifle more than one percent of the vote. The results were to be strikingly different at the end of Alessandri's six-year term.

In his middle sixties by the beginning of this term, Alessandri made order, security, and defense of constitutional government (as defined by him) the political motto of his administration while he set about promoting economic recovery and growth. He had not lost his earlier zeal for social reform, but he believed that, as his Washington counterpart Franklin Roosevelt put it in his first inaugural address of March 4, 1933 (which almost coincided with Alessandri's second inaugural), that first things must come first and domestic economic recovery must come first of all. To Alessandri this meant recovery of the existing capitalist system, to be followed by its growth, as essential to the operation and extension of the welfare system built up in the 1920s but largely suspended by the shock of the depression. Accordingly, Alessandri and his talented finance minister Gustavo Ross concentrated on the promotion of industry, mainly through tariff protection and tax incentives. They were motivated partly by the nationalist spirit that the depression stimulated in Chile as in most other countries, but also by the economic doctrine of import substitution, which was to continue to enjoy a great vogue in Latin America for a generation to come.

Things worked out very much as planned, thanks to skillful administration, recovery among Chile's trading partners, and a growing demand for Chile's copper and other products as World War II approached. Both total exports and nitrate production increased about three-fold from 1932 to 1937. The principal nitrate corporation was brought under closer government supervision and made to share its profits with the treasury. Unemployment virtually disappeared and by the end of Alessandri's term the budget had been balanced and a surplus had begun to accumulate. Also, as planned, the social welfare system resumed its normal functioning and was extended in some respects, principally in public health and technical education.

That Alessandri's second administration was so much more successful than his first was due in large measure to the economic factors just mentioned, but part of the credit must be given to the fact that his political support was far more united, and his opposition even more divided, than in his first term. Whereas the Liberal Alliance that elected him in 1920 broke down in the first year and the break was never mended, his chief supporters in the 1930s, the Conservative Party and the right-of-center Liberal Party, soon came together in an alliance that worked well and held together until the end of his term. His most dedicated opponents, on the other hand, were the Socialist and Communist parties, which were almost as hostile to each other as to Alessandri and his cohorts. In addition, each of them suffered from multiple fractures, such as the Trotskyite schism in the Communist camp and the rift between Marmaduke Grove, a non-Marxian Socialist, and Carlos Dávila, a state Socialist. This rift helped to hasten the Chilean Socialist Republic of 1932 to an early grave.

Why, at the end of Alessandri's second term, did Chilean voters replace his successful conservative government with a left-wing Popular Front government? Part of the answer is that many Chileans regarded Alessandri's success as fortifying the privileged classes in a fundamentally unjust social system. In its baldest form this thesis was propagated by members of the relatively new Socialist and Communist parties. Their numbers were few, but their thesis gained credibility from the excessive rigor with which Alessandri combated them and all other dissidents. He formed a paramilitary Republican Militia of well-to-do youths, and dissolved a critical Congress, declaring a state of siege and muzzling the press during a railroad workers' strike in 1936 that brought business to a standstill. All this helped the Marxists to win converts in wider circles, particularly the Radical Party. Their task was all the easier because the need for a reordering of society had long since been recognized in Chile and organized efforts to bring it about dated at least as far back as the mid-nineteenth century, when the Society of Equality was established.

Another part of the answer to our question is that by the close of his second term the Chilean public was agitated by the same issues, originating largely in Europe, that we have already encountered in Argentina and Uruguay. As in those countries, quick dissemination of them in Chile was made possible by the new technologies of radio and airplane, and an attentive response was assured by the great and often excessive respect with which most educated Chileans viewed European works and ways. The foremost issue at this time was that of democracy versus fascism. By the end of 1936, with Germany and Italy openly aiding a military rebellion against the Spanish Republic and no one able to curb Nazi-fascist aggression there or elsewhere, it seemed the threat to democracy was a real one. It was taken seriously by many persons even in remote Chile because a veritable German colony was well established in the south and friendly to Hitler and because a party had been formed calling itself *nacista* and showing itself pro-Nazi. In these circumstances liberals felt that a continuation of Alessandri's authoritarian kind of government would be too high a price to pay for order and prosperity. There would be less risk, they thought, in accepting the alternative of cooperation with Marxists which was offered by Moscow's Popular Front strategy.

Formed during the railroad strike of 1936, the Chilean Popular Front quickly adopted a program that demanded the restoration of democratic liberties and the return of Chile to the Chileans, denounced imperialism (as indeed Alessandri was already doing), and promised economic and social justice to the exploited middle and lower classes. The Front's principal members were the Radical, Socialist, and Communist parties. The oldest and by far the largest of the three was the Radical Party, which dated from the 1860s and was essentially middle-class. Second in both respects was the Socialist Party; though not organized in its current form until 1933, it consisted of older elements, one of which was more than twenty years old. The Communist Party, founded in 1919, was much the smallest member of the Front.

The relative strength of these three parties at the time of the Front's formation is indicated by their respective percentages of the popular vote in the congressional election of 1937, which were Radicals 19, Socialists 11, and Communists 4. This represented a great gain in recent years for the two Marxist parties, but a reverse for the Radicals, for it was the worst showing they had made since 1912. That fact may have made the ever flexible, pragmatic Radicals all the more ready to team up with the Marxists. For the latter, ideology could have made joining the coalition less easy. For some Socialists it did, but both parties insisted that Marxism must be adapted to Chilean circumstances and these seemed, in and about 1936, to justify the experiment of a coalition that had not only the blessing of Moscow but also a fair prospect of victory at the polls.

As its presidential candidate in 1938, the Popular Front convention, after a bitter fight, chose right-wing Radical Pedro Aguirre Cerda over the much more dynamic Socialist leader Marmaduke Grove. Aguirre Cerda was rather colorless, but it was hoped that he would attract swing votes from the center, for he was a moderate reformer and reassuringly prosperous. It was thought that some might also be attracted by the Horatio Alger-like quality of his career. Rising from humble beginnings, he had made his way up through liceo and university to become a university professor and dean, member successively of both houses of Congress, cabinet minister, leading proponent of industrialization, and wealthy landowner. Ironically, he had opposed his party's joining the Popular Front.

The Front's platform stressed bread-and-butter issues in a bid for lower middle-class and labor support. Opposed to it was the Conservative-Liberal alliance, whose strong candidate was, appropriately, Alessandri's minister of finance, Gustavo Ross. The Popular Front won, but, as in 1920, the election could hardly have been closer. This time the winning margin was less than one percent of half a million votes. Aguirre Cerda fulfilled hopes to the extent of winning some prosperous as well as many working-class districts, but most of his slender margin of victory was provided, oddly enough, by Carlos Ibáñez and his nacista splinter group. They threw their support to the Front at the eleventh hour in retaliation for the Alessandri government's bloody suppression of an uprising by nacista students.

Continuing the parallel with 1920, the Popular Front, like the Liberal Alliance of that year, carried out few of its campaign promises and soon fell apart, though not quite so quickly. As Paul W. Drake has shown in his enlightening study of the Socialist Party in this period, the Front was wrecked by antagonism between its two Marxist parties. At that time the leadership of both was mainly middle-class, but the Socialist Party drew from a wider social spectrum, was more ideological, and less disciplined, whereas the smaller Communist Party had more support from organized labor, was more compact, and took orders from Moscow. After the secession of a minority group, the majority Socialists took the party out of the Front in 1940. They withdrew from it not in protest against the Radicals' failure to support thoroughgoing reform, but on the ground that continued alliance with the "anti-national and totalitarian" Communist Party was unacceptable.

The Front virtually disintegrated the following year. Electorally, it had been a distinct success for its members. In the 1941 congressional elections the Radicals rose to 21 percent of the total vote, the Socialists to 18 percent, and the Communists (proportionately the greatest gainers of all) to 12 percent. Its reform program, however, as already indicated, remained unrealized. Explanations are easy to find. First, there were the inherent weaknesses of all coalitions, especially this one. Then, the Front, which had been shaken by an exceptionally destructive earthquake just after taking office, suffered a still more severe shock from the news of Stalin's pact of August 1939 with Hitler, which made a mockery of the whole Popular Front idea. The pact also made the Chilean Communist Party's ties with the Kremlin once more a heavy handicap in Chilean politics, especially in dealing with its Socialist fellow members of the Popular Front. By the time Hitler broke the pact by attacking the Soviet Union in June 1941, the Front was too far gone to be salvaged.

In the meantime the Front had been dealt another heavy blow by the outbreak of World War II. It had been created to deal with domestic problems and its sharp focus on these was faithfully represented by its slogan in the 1938 campaign: "Bread, roof, and overcoat" (*Pan, techo, y abrigo*). The war, however, forced a shifting of the focus from domestic to foreign affairs and raised divisive issues about foreign policy. After Hitler's conquest of Europe from Norway to the Pyrenees in May and June of 1940, the diversion was massive, and at home, as Drake says, "industrialization took precedence over social reform." In early November of the following year ill health forced the resignation of President Aguirre Cerda. With his death two weeks later the last hope of resuscitating the Popular Front flickered out.

The most important of the Front's few achievements came early and was carried through with some support from the conservative opposition. This was the establishment of the Development Corporation, which was the first government institution of its kind in Latin America and proved a great success, especially in the 1940s. As indicated by its name in Spanish, Corporación de Fomento de la Producción (CORFO), its function was to promote production, and it did so on a broad front, in a variety of ways, and with considerable success. As will be shown in a later chapter, its main stress for several years was on industrializaton. In some of its enterprises ownership was vested solely in the government, while in others it was mixed governmental and private.

Flexible politics, good administration, and foreign aid contributed greatly to the Development Corporation's success. The war also helped in some ways, though it was a hindrance in others. By cutting off imports of manufactures from more advanced countries, for example, it forced postponement of work on a projected steel mill and other ambitious projects, while at the same time creating a boom market for such Chilean substitutes as could be produced and releasing more funds, public as well as private, for financing feasible development projects. Much of the increase in public funds came from Chile's largest industry, copper. Under pressure of wartime demand, its production of copper had already established new records by 1941, and as the volume and price increased, so did the government's taxes on it. In addition to an existing 33 percent tax on profits, which had been in effect for several years, the government in that same year imposed an excess profits tax of 58 percent on taxable income arising from any increase in the sales price of copper. Probably the worst of all the ill effects of the war for Chile, as for Argentina and Uruguay, was the fuel shortage, which was more painful to them than to the rest of Latin America because they were economically more advanced. Chile had the advantage over the other two of possessing a substantial domestic supply of coal, but it was worse off than either with regard to petroleum because of its greater remoteness from the main sources of supply and lack of a petroleum industry of its own,* such as Argentina had in YPF.

On the whole, however, the Chilean economy fared well in these early war years, thanks mainly to the increased demand for its principal products and to its new Development Corporation. One result was an easing of the tense political situation that had developed in the 1930s to the point of polarizing formerly polycentric forces. Tension still existed, but it was less severe, if only because the focus of controversy had shifted to foreign policy, which by definition lacked the immediacy of confrontations over domestic issues. While there was sharp disagreement over foreign policy and extremists were irreconcilable, most people in Chile, as in Argentina and Uruguay, were content through most of the war to have their government adhere to the neutrality agreed upon by all the American states just after hostilities broke out in 1939.

---

*Its present petroleum industry was established after the war. See chapter XIII.

There were many reasons for the Chileans' strong attachment to neutrality. Chief among these was their reluctance to break the rhythm of recovery from the disastrous Great Depression by involvement in a remote conflict which was none of Chile's making and whose outcome it could not affect, whereas it would be highly vulnerable to attack by sea. Also, they had too many grounds for satisfaction with the way things were going to have any desire to change course. Besides having made a notable economic recovery and set the pace for their neighbors by establishing a novel Development Corporation, they had gained recognition abroad in other fields as well. In 1941, for example, foreign writers bracketed Chile with Uruguay and Mexico as having the most advanced social welfare system and labor legislation in all Latin America, and with Uruguay again as outstanding in music and musicology. According to one of these writers, the year had been "almost revolutionary" in the cultural life of Chile, for in the course of it the tax-supported Institute of Musical Extension had brought about the establishment of national schools of drama and ballet and the formation of a national string quartet. By contrast with the devastated Chile of a decade earlier, the country was now becoming, for its ruling classes, a terrestrial paradise. It is not surprising that when the United States, on the heels of its entry into the war, pressed all the Latin American states to abandon neutrality, Chile held out for more than a year and was the last, except Argentina, to comply.

VIII Interwar
Comparisons

The interwar period as we have delimited it—from the armistice in November 1918 to Pearl Harbor in December 1941—is particularly rich in materials for a comparison of tendencies towards convergence or divergence among the Southern Cone countries in circumstances propitious to change. These tendencies had been present from the beginning of independence, as has been pointed out from time to time, and have continued down to the present time. Nevertheless, both kinds seem to have reached a peak of intensity in the interwar years. Why they did so is not hard to understand. By the beginning of the period all three countries had for several decades been incorporated in the world economy and, partly for that reason, had moved into an intermediate stage of political and cultural as well as economic development—the most advanced stage of all the Latin American countries. They were therefore open to change, including change in their traditional structures, and highly sensitive to influences from the North Atlantic world of the great industrial, financial, and military powers. Though peripheral to that world, they were bound to it firmly by many ties. Despite the depression, these ties were further strengthened during the interwar years, as all the leading Latin American countries were ardently courted by all the great-power rivals, including the United States with its Good Neighbor policy, and as multinational corporations became for the first time a major factor in Southern Cone affairs. Political sovereignty notwithstanding, the countries of the Cone had become economically and culturally so subordinate to the great powers that, intentionally or not, they were strongly influenced by them in the political field as well, and in domestic politics no less than in foreign relations.

As a result, all three were profoundly shaken in every aspect of national life by the depression, which began midway between two other seismic shocks, the first and second world wars. In the interwar years they were as sorely beset by public problems as the Europe that produced Mussolini, Primo de Rivera, and Hitler, and they shared in the same widespread loss of faith in representative government, the capitalist system, and Western civilization itself.

The severity of the challenges to our three countries during this period was matched by the intensity of their responses, and these moved them closer together in some ways and further apart in others. Two leading examples of historical development as it affected their convergence or divergence are new kinds of corporatism and development policy. They illustrate a fact which, however familiar, cannot be stressed too strongly: that periodization is as artificial as it is useful. Corporatism already had a long history behind it when this period began and is still very much alive today. As for the new kind of development policy, it was well established in Uruguay by 1918, but in Argentina its acceptance remained limited and piecemeal until the Perón regime embraced it, so that Chile is the only one of three in which the history of the policy's birth and maturation lies neatly enclosed within the limits of the interwar period. What is more, all three countries continued to follow the policy for more than a decade after the end of World War II.

New Corporatism

Exotic in the United States, corporatism is familiar in many other countries, including the Scandinavian. Mussolini and Hitler gave it an undeserved bad name, since they diverted it from its true purpose, which throughout its long history has been the harmonious integration of society by means of functional corporations representing its main sectors. Contemporary examples are industrial corporations, chambers of commerce, professional and managerial associations, and labor federations.

Some authorities find a special affinity for corporatism in the Iberian world on both sides of the Atlantic and trace its history in that world from Hispano-Roman antiquity to the contemporary Spain and Argentina of Franco and Perón. In the Iberian countries, as elsewhere, corporatism has passed through three phases in the modern age. It flourished until the eighteenth century in such institutions as *gremios* or guilds. In the nineteenth century it was overwhelmed by liberal pluralism based on individualism and free enterprise. In the twentieth century a recrudescence of corporatism took place as liberal pluralism came under fire for various reasons, among them the charge that it had increased the inequitable distribution of wealth, thus promoting social discord, and that it had shown itself unable to provide the strong, concerted planning and action required by the ever more complex problems of modern society.

In its revival since the turn of the century, corporatism has assumed various forms in different countries. In all of them, however, there is at least a touch of authoritarianism, and this brings us to the most important of several questions regarding corporatism about which there is disagreement among specialists. That question is, what is the nature of its relationship to the state? Some regard it as ancillary, others as coordinate, and still others as antithetical. Whatever the future may bring or the past has brought, it would seem clear that at the present time the first, or ancillary, relationship prevails. This fact excludes the coordinate relationship, which in any case is a highly artificial and unstable one in human affairs. As the old Spanish proverb has it, if two men ride a burro at the same time, one must ride in front. A stronger case has been made by those who argue for the antithetical relationship. It is also a more interesting one since its advocates contend that the growth of corporatism will eventually bring about the replacement of the state by syndicalism. In other words, the argument seems to run, under corporatism, just as under Socialism-Communism as seen by its devotees, the state will wither away. Perhaps so, although so far the state has not withered away anywhere under corporatism any more than it has under Communism.

However that may be, the possibility that corporatism and Socialism-Communism may meet in infinity over the dead body of the state should not be taken to mean that they can be expected to march together in harmony today. The fact is that, at least in Latin America, corporatism and Socialism-Communism have only one common bond, which is their hostility to democracy based on liberal pluralism. Otherwise, each is the other's worst enemy. As Fredrick Pike points out, corporatism owes its current revival in the Iberian world partly to the fact that it is perceived there to be "the best method for containing social revolution"; and social revolution is, of course, the goal of all true Communists in democratic countries. In short, Latin American corporatism most frequently serves as a prop to the upper class in a hierarchical society, though it should be added that its conservatism is not necessarily either rigid or reactionary.

In the Southern Cone countries, as well as elsewhere, corporatism is ancillary to the state today, as it was in the interwar period. The state sanctions or creates the corporations, gives each a monopoly of representation in its own category, and allows them a measure of autonomy, but acts as the moderating power among them and its decisions are final. Its success depends on its ability to moderate their demands, mediate among them, and achieve the harmony that is the system's chief goal. Viewed in this way, the function of the state is as much that of a policeman under corporatism as under free enterprise liberalism. There is, however, the important difference that under corporatism the state acts on and through corporations rather than individuals and territorial units. This fact, together with the bias of corporatism in favor of the upper class, explains why, in these countries, the phenomenon has taken the form, among others, of extensive social welfare and labor reforms enacted by conservative governments. For such reforms could be accurately described as safety valves for social discontent and sops to the dogs of class war. The clearest example of the type is provided by the second, or conservative, administration of Alessandri in Chile, which, as noted in an earlier chapter, was the Southern Cone country that had the most strongly entrenched and class-conscious upper class. At the other extreme, Argentina's Conservative Restoration did the least of the three conservative regimes of that decade to provide such sops and safety valves. One reason for this striking difference was probably that liberal pluralism was more deeply rooted in Argentina than in the other two countries, Another was that the Argentine ruling class felt no need to make such concessions, having just piloted the country through nearly half a century of phenomenal growth and so acquired a massive self-assurance that not even the Great Depression could destroy. There were still other reasons besides these, as will appear.

However, the most important expression that the new and strongly nationalistic corporatism found in these three countries during the interwar decades was in the adoption of a new development policy.

New Development Policy

A striking example of convergence is provided by William Glade's enlightening account of "neo-orthodoxy in development policy" in the Southern Cone countries in the first half of the present century. At different times and in different ways, all three adopted it. It had its start in Uruguay, its most complete expression in Chile, and its last and most "frenetic" application in Argentina. Moreover, as Glade says, there have been notable differences among the three with respect to emphasis, surrounding circumstances, and outcome.

Most features of the new development policy were applied in Uru-

guay in the first quarter of the present century. It was rounded out
and systematized by the Economic Commission for Latin America
(ECLA), a United Nations agency established in 1948 despite opposition by the United States. In contrast to the development policy
that prevailed in the nineteenth century, which aimed at bringing
underdeveloped countries into a world market economy based on
ideas of comparative advantage, free enterprise, and maximized
international trade, the neo-orthodox policy was nationalistic and
quasiautarkic. It called for national planning, nationalization of
natural resources, state intervention in the economy, industrialization, and promotion of the public sector, rather than, if not at the
expense of, the private sector, including foreign-controlled as well
as domestic interests.

The new policy had built-in guarantees of conflict in both foreign
and domestic affairs. Neo-orthodox developmentalism was obviously bound to collide head-on with neocolonialism, for the former
made rapid strides in this area in the 1920s and 1930s, just when—
and no doubt because—neocolonialism was nearing its peak there.
Likewise, on the domestic front the rise of the neo-orthodox doctrine, with its stress on state intervention in the economy, coincided
with a substantial increase in popular participation in politics which
posed a threat to the privileged classes' maintenance of their control
of the economy as well as of the government. That nevertheless no
major clash occurred during the interwar period on either the domestic or the foreign front was probably due to the fact that none of
these three countries pushed the new policy too far or too fast at that
time.

The pace and degree of the policy's application differed significantly in each country from the other two. In pioneering Uruguay, a
foretaste of things to come was provided by the tariff act of 1875,
which protected import-substitution manufactures. Neo-orthodoxy
did not definitely arrive, however, until nearly forty years later, in
José Batlle's second administration, when a systematic program of
nationalization was undertaken. Beginning with insurance, transportation, and public utilities, the process was carried out gradually
and acquisitions were made by purchase, not confiscation, thus
minimizing foreign friction. One aim of the policy was to industrialize, but the country's market and natural resources were too limited
for that. Moreover, it also aimed at social development, and to that
end it became the overriding purpose of Batlle's and subsequent

Colorado administrations to hold down the cost of living for workers and consumers at large. Out of this program came a great increase in the number of the autonomous entities—corporations—discussed in an earlier chapter and a generous and proliferating welfare system. Both became heavy burdens and contributed to the economic stagnation of later years. Until the end of the interwar period, however, the burden was borne rather easily with the help of generally favorable terms of trade, so that Uruguay's trail-blazing foray into neo-orthodox territory encouraged others to follow its lead.

Chile was the first to do so, beginning in 1924 and 1925 under the military intervention near the close of Alessandri's first term. The measures adopted at that time resembled Uruguay's in announcing the welfare theme, as they did by encouraging consumer cooperatives and establishing old-age pensions and insurance programs for illness and accidents. Also as in Uruguay, the government's role in labor relations was greatly strengthened. Measures of the latter type included not only the usual stipulations regarding collective bargaining, strikes, and the eight-hour day, but also a novel feature soon copied by other Latin American governments: the requirement that at least 75 percent of the employees of all firms operating in Chile consist of Chilean nationals. Under subsequent administrations, beginning in 1927 with that of Ibáñez, state intervention in the economy became massive. In that year the nationalist note was sounded again by reserving the insurance business for Chilean companies (a step taken by Uruguay several years earlier), though exempting already established foreign firms (as Argentina had done a few years earlier in setting up its state petroleum agency, YPF).

In Chile during the rest of the interwar period, still other measures were taken to extend government intervention in finance, industry, commerce, and agriculture. A favorite instrument was the special-purpose state bank, which engaged in entrepreneurial operations of many kinds as well as in normal banking activities, which used its control of credit to forward the government's projects for development, and which was widely copied in Latin America. The climax of state interventionism in the interwar years came with the establishment in 1939 of the Development Corporation, with whose broad scope and notable achievements the reader is already familiar. This corporation was still another Chilean initiative that was soon widely copied elsewhere in Latin America. Although Uruguay had been first in the field of state interventionism for development and social justice, by 1940 its interventionism had become so closely identified with social justice that Chile had supplanted it as leader in state intervention for economic development. In this respect Chile now led all Latin America, both in the comprehensiveness of its plans and operations and in the originality of its instruments and procedures for development.

Another major objective of interventionism, however, was to free the country from dependence on foreign capital, industry, enterprise, and markets, or, in the fighting words of left-wingers, to combat neocolonialism; and in this regard Chile had made little progress by the end of the period. It had indeed established a measure of government control over the nitrate monopoly COVENSA (organized in 1934), but that was a mixed enterprise in which foreign private capital held a majority interest, and, in any case, nitrates now played a very minor role in the Chilean economy. The copper industry, which played the leading role, though more and more heavily taxed, remained almost wholly owned and controlled by foreigners to the end of the period and beyond, as it had been from the beginning. The same was true of most other foreign interests in Chile. What is more, the Chilean economy had in a sense become more dependent than ever on foreigners, for the Development Corporation itself financed a substantial number of its enterprises with funds from the United States.

Argentina did not make a large-scale shift to neo-orthodox development policy until shortly after the end of the interwar period. It was, by a margin of more than a decade, the last of the Southern Cone countries to do so. In addition to opposition by the strongly entrenched export interests that dominated the Conservative party, the delay was probably due mainly to the lack of sustained effort by the only other major party, the Radicals, led by the politically-oriented Yrigoyen, to follow the path of neo-orthodox economic policy just blazed by Uruguay. The notion that the Radicals might have been expected to follow it because of their resemblance to Batlle's Colorado party has no merit. During their tenure of office too many of the Radicals belonged to occupational sectors, both business and professional, whose livelihood depended on that same export economy. Argentine investigators have recently pointed out that Radical policy might have been quite different if the middle class had been mobilized under the leadership of a vigorous "national bourgeoisie" of large industrialists, but such leadership was not available since at this time the great majority of Argentine industrialists were foreigners who took no part in politics.

Whatever the reason, little heed was paid to economist Alejandro Bunge's well-documented warning in the 1920s that the existing export economy had exhausted its potential for growth and must be diversified by state intervention. The sweeping change of economic policy recommended by him was not made until the 1940s. If Uriburu's dictatorship had lasted longer, he might have attempted it as a complement to the far-reaching constitutional change he proposed, which was likewise an expression of the new corporatism. As for a shift to the neo-orthodox development policy in particular, only a few piecemeal measures pointing in that direction were adopted before the end of the interwar period. What is more, most of them were, paradoxically, fashioned in that citadel of economic orthodoxy, the Conservative Party. Only two of any significance owed their adoption to the Radical government. These were the creation, in 1922, of the state petroleum agency YPF, and of a state fleet of tankers to carry its petroleum.

On the other hand, the restored Conservatives, chastened by the disaster of the depression, offset the orthodoxy of their surrender to Great Britain in the Roca-Runciman Pact and related actions by adopting, in the mid-1930s, several measures that not only presaged the shift to neo-orthodoxy under Perón in the next decade, but were in fact taken over and either continued or expanded by him. These included the establishment of a Central Bank and several national boards for the control of the principal products of the country's still basic agricultural-pastoral economy, among them grains, meat, dairy products, *yerba maté,* and cotton. One of the new creations, the National Grain Board, was later expanded by Perón into IAPI, which became the most important economic institution of his nine-year presidency.

Exchange and other trade controls imposed by the Conservatives in the 1930s stimulated the most rapid expansion of industry that had ever taken place in Argentina; in this respect, too, Perón was to continue and extend what had been well begun under the Conservative Restoration. But he extended it greatly and added other features, besides which he made a formal commitment to neo-orthodoxy, though not under that name. That was a major step that had not been anticipated by the Conservative Restoration or any of its predecessors.

We may conclude, then, that by the end of the interwar period

Argentina had begun to follow a line of development policy which, when continued, would converge with the lines already being followed by Uruguay and Chile in so far as economic development was the objective of intervention by the state, but that there was no convergence with them in the matter of social welfare development. Under the Conservative Restoration, the latter was conspicuously lacking.

Population Growth

Chile's rate of population increase was to accelerate rapidly after 1940, but throughout the interwar period it remained, as it had long been, one of the lowest in Latin America. Despite advances since 1920 in social welfare and health care, Chile's average annual growth rate in the 1930s was only 1.5 percent. Only in Uruguay (1.3) and El Salvador (1.2) were the rates lower, and the average for all Latin America was 1.9. Since the volume of immigration in Chile was still small, its population growth depended almost entirely on the excess of births over deaths. Sánchez Albornoz would add another factor, economic development as measured by GNP, which, as noted earlier, was substantially lower in Chile than in the other two Southern Cone countries. More obviously relevant, however, is the ratio of births to deaths, and the data for Chile show little change in the rates until the 1930s. From 1900 to 1924, for example, the birth and death rates declined only slightly: from 44.7 to 42.2 for births, and from 31.6 to 31.3 for deaths. The contrast with the other two countries in these years was striking. While their birth rates were of the same order of magnitude as Chile's, their death rates, already much lower, were still falling: in Argentina, from 20.0 in 1900 to 13.8 in 1924, and in Uruguay, from 13.7 to 12.6 in the same years.

By the 1930s, a substantial reduction of the infant mortality rate was under way in Chile. From 250 deaths per thousand live births in 1920-1924, it was reduced to 212 in 1930-1934 and to 170 in 1940-1944. As a result of this development and the shutting off of the immigrant flood by the depression, the other two countries ceased to outpace Chile's population growth, as they had been doing ever since the 1870s. From 1900 to 1930 Argentina's population had more than doubled and Uruguay's had almost doubled, but Chile's had increased by barely one half. From 1930 to 1940, however,

Chile's average annual growth rate of 1.5 was almost as high as Argentina's (1.7) and higher than Uruguay's (1.3). The population totals for each country in this period were as follows:

Population in thousands

	1900	1930	1940
Argentina	4,743	11,896	14,169
Chile	2,904	4,424	5,147
Uruguay	915	1,704	1,947

In both composition and distribution, substantial demographic changes took place in all three countries, though they were less noticeable in Chile than in the other two. The most striking change was in the volume of immigration, which fell from flood to trickle, partly spontaneously, as in all periods of economic depression, and partly under selective government restrictions. For a time, all immigrants were barred by Uruguay (1932-1933) and Argentina (1931-1935), but not by Chile, which had never had a superfluity of immigrants and even now only channeled them to the countryside — a measure copied by Argentina in 1940.

With immigration brought to a halt and hard times continuing in agriculture, internal migration accelerated greatly. Its volume was greatest in Argentina, where it rose in the late 1930s to new heights that were sustained in the next decade. Most of the migrants from the back country flocked to the metropolitan area of Buenos Aires. The number of them arriving there annually rose to 83,000 in 1936 and to more than 90,000 five years later, with a consequent reduction of the proportion of foreign-born in the city's population from a staggering one-half in 1914 to one-fourth in the mid-1940s. Smaller but still considerable migrations from the rural areas to the cities took place in the other two countries, and at mid-century the national capitals of the three still ranked among the largest cities in Latin America, as they had done in 1900, when urbanization had hardly begun in most of the other countries. In that year their rankings in the list of Latin American cities were Buenos Aires 1, Santiago 4, Montevideo 9: in 1950 they were still, respectively, 1, 5, and 13. In their own countries, two of the three had even increased their relative size: Buenos Aires from less than one fifth to nearly one fourth of the total population, and Montevideo from a little more than one fourth to one third. What is more, each of these was much larger than all the other large cities of their respective countries combined. Santiago, which had never overshadowed the rest of its country in the same way, still contained one tenth of the total population and remained the largest city in Chile by a wide margin.

Finally, Uruguay continued to be the only one of the three in which the whole country was settled and settlement was even approximately compact. In both Argentina and Chile there had been population movements into the far north and southward all the way to Tierra del Fuego, and both governments had staked out territorial claims in Antarctica and backed them up with expeditions to that frozen land. Yet in both countries large areas remained uninhabited or nearly so, and compact settlement was confined to the same regions as for generations past: in Chile, the Central Valley, and in Argentina, the Buenos Aires province and the River Plate-Paraná littoral.

Democracy and Participation

The lines of political development in Chile and Argentina might have continued to converge, as they had been doing for more than a decade past, if Arturo Alessandri and his Liberal Alliance, after winning the election of 1920, had consolidated their position as firmly as Yrigoyen and his Radical party had done since their first victory in a national election in 1916. The two leaders had much in common, and so did their respective cohorts. To be sure, the Alessandri of 1920 resembled Batlle of Uruguay rather than Yrigoyen in the open quality of his leadership and the social and economic content of his program, not to mention his social origin, which was a cut above Hipólito's. Nevertheless, at the time of that election Alessandri's public image was much like his Argentine counterpart's: both were tribunes of the people leading peaceful uprisings against the oligarchy.

These images did not quite coincide with the facts in either case, but the discrepancy was much the same in both. The "people" were actually the middle class in both, as also in Uruguay, and although the two leaders appealed to the masses, neither got much effective political support from them, nor, for that matter did they share power with them. In fact, power in these nominally participatory democracies continued to reside in interest groups that comprised a small minority of the population. None of the three countries was ruled by the traditional triad of power consisting of great land-owners, church, and army. The nearest approach to it in this period was the Argentine regime during the Conservative Restoration, and even in that the church had no direct voice, the army stayed in the background, and the great landowners shared power with their banking and business allies in the export economy. As for the other two countries, at the end of the period Uruguay was beginning to look like a city state run by the Montevideo bureaucracy and Chile was governed by a Popular Front composed of left-wing and left-of-center political parties. In fact, however, in all three countries power was divided among several different groups, which included the corporations discussed above, associations of landowners, industrialists, lawyers, political parties, chambers of commerce, and, oldest of all, the church, now disestablished in Uruguay and Chile, and the armed forces, wonderfully active in all three countries in the middle third of the period, but quiescent in all three at its close.

Labor organizations were still weak in Argentina and Chile at the close of the period. Even in the towns and cities the great majority of the workers did not belong to them, and rural workers were not only unorganized but, if they took any part in politics, were still likely to follow their landlords' lead, whether under pressure or from custom or choice. They were more likely to do so in Chile than in Argentina. Their lowly status in Chile is indicated by the fact that even the Popular Front government, in order to avoid a confrontation with the conservatives, prohibited efforts to unionize rural workers and that even the Front's two Marxist parties obeyed the prohibition.

In Uruguay the rural workers' situation was about the same as in Argentina, and if urban labor was better organized and fared better than in the other two countries, that was due less to the workers' or the unions' vigor than to Batlle's paternal protection. Yet, though his party controlled the national government from 1904 to 1932, even he was unable to push his program of labor legislation through Congress until the 1920s, and he succeeded then with the help of conservative landowners, who, like their Argentine and Chilean counterparts, were not averse to making things difficult for urban employers, especially since many if not most of the employers were foreigners.

Batlle was hardly more representative of the masses than Alessandri or Yrigoyen. In all three countries the masses were political ciphers so far as participation in the process was concerned. Their situation was worst in this respect in Chile, where the proportion of voters to total population never rose as high as 10 percent until the 1950s, and was only 8 and 9 percent, respectively, in the hotly contested elections of 1920 (Alessandri's first) and 1938 (Popular Front). One reason was the restriction of the suffrage to literate adult males, which reduced the eligibles to 20 percent of the total population. Then, for whatever reason, half of the eligibles never voted.

In Argentina, too, the suffrage was restricted to adult males, but for them voting was nominally compulsory under the Sáenz Peña law of 1912 and there was no literacy requirement. Yet the rate of participation in proportion to total population at the beginning of the period, 10 percent, was only slightly higher than in Chile and rose only to 12 percent by its close. The explanation is simple. The proportion of foreigners in Argentina—nearly 30 percent of the total population in 1918 and about 20 percent in 1941—was far higher than in Chile in this or any other period. Most of the foreigners were immigrants, most of the immigrants were adult males, and, for reasons given in an earlier chapter, only about 3 percent of the foreigners were naturalized at this time, although naturalization was easy and the only penalty for not being naturalized was loss of the right to vote in national elections. If the computation were adjusted to include in the population base only citizens, born or naturalized, the percentage of participation during the interwar period would be substantially higher than in Chile. That it was only slightly higher when based on the raw figures was a passing phenomenon. With the stoppage of the immigrant flood by the depression and a doubling of the naturalization rate, the rate of participation rose to 15 percent in 1946 (the first Perón election) and continued to rise thereafter.

As one might expect, the rate of voter participation during these years was highest in more democratic Uruguay. This was the result of a phenomenal increase in the number of voters during the Batlle period, from 46,000 in 1905 to 318,000 in 1930. The latter figure was more than 18 percent of the total population, a level not reached in either Argentina or Chile until the 1950s. It was not surpassed in Uruguay itself in the remainder of the interwar period. Of course, statistics of participation in elections do not tell the whole story. Since the Colorado party won all the elections, the main question is how much rank-and-file participation there was in that party's decisions and operations. The answer is that there was very little of it. Apparently the reason for it was not exclusion by the party bosses, but the failure of most members to take advantage of opportunities offered by the party's organization and procedures. Local party meetings, which might have been turned into something like a New England town meeting of yore, attracted only a handful of members, the great majority of whom seem to have preferred to leave most decisions to their *patrón* and caudillo, José Batlle. He ran the party, with the assistance of a small inner group, until his death in 1929, after which the group broke up and leaders of rival factions of the party took up where he left off. The most important point, however, is that during the interwar period most Uruguayans apparently had the feeling that, on the whole, theirs was a good government and that it was of and for, if not always by, the people. Even the Terra dictatorship was mild and brief and native enough not to destroy the sense of popular participation.

Even the women of Uruguay shared this feeling. They had reason to, for they were given the vote in 1922, more than twenty years ahead of the women in the other two countries, and Uruguay was also ahead of the other two in opening the professions to women, partly by law and partly by custom. The difference can be attributed in large part to the greater strength of the traditional order in the other two, but that is by no means the whole explanation. Part of it is the well-grounded fear of liberals and radicals at that time in both Argentina and Chile (as also in the Spanish Republic of the early 1930s) that votes for women would mean votes for conservatism. The apprehension did not apply with equal force to more secularized Uruguay, for the reasoning behind it was that because of women's greater attachment to the Catholic Church, which was a decidedly conservative institution at that time, on most public questions women would be sure to take the conservative side in greater proportion than men. This is not to say that the women's rights movement made no headway at all in Argentina and Chile. In fact, it had a promising development in the former from the late nineteenth into the early twentieth century. Then, however, it stopped growing until it was taken over by the Peronist movement in the 1940s. Its Argentine historian gives the perhaps oversimplified explanation that the wife of Juan B. Justo, founder and first head of the country's Socialist Party, became the most prominent leader of the feminists and thus identified their movement with that party, which was then very small and largely confined to the city of Buenos Aires.

In all three countries, though least effectively in Uruguay, lingering forces of the traditional order deterred many women from joining in such a campaign, which lumped all women together as equals. Class feeling was still strong among men and women alike, at all levels of society, and not only among those who considered themselves the aristocracy. White-collar workers (*empleados*), for example, who belonged to the middle class, regarded themselves as greatly superior to blue-collar workers (*obreros*), who were lower-class, and were supported in that assumption by the very social reform laws adopted by Uruguay and Chile during this period, which gave them preferential treatment. Likewise, members of the upper class took it for granted that they were beings above and apart from the nether world of the middle as well as the lower class. This was a poor return for the sincere flattery of imitation they received from members of the middle class, who adopted their social superiors' manners, styles, and standards to the extent that they were able to afford or bring it off. Aristocratic pretensions seemed to be most prevalent in Chile, which had had a titled nobility in colonial times. Commenting on them, one contemporary observer wrote that it was a common occurrence in social gatherings to boast about one's illustrious ancestry going all the way back to the conquest, although in fact the descendants of only three Chilean conquistadores—whom he named—had succeeded in maintaining the family's fortune and social standing from that time to the present.

Prejudices and pretensions of this kind, which were apparently stronger among women than among men, were a deterrent to the growth of a large-scale movement in favor of women's rights. For one thing, they kept it from attracting as much leadership talent as Socialism and Communism were drawing at this time from male constituencies of the middle class and even, occasionally, of the upper class. It was in the 1930s, for example, that young Salvador Allende, a physician, emerged as a leader of Chile's Socialist Party, as Juan B. Justo, also a physician, and Alfredo Palacios, a lawyer, had done in Argentina at the turn of the century. Ladies viewed such activities in a different light. Those of the upper class regarded it as unbecoming for their sex and class to engage in rough-and-tumble politics, which a crusade for women's rights would surely involve, and this was one of the upper-class value judgments that trickled down to the class below.

A companion belief held that there were much better ways than the vote for women to make their influence felt in public affairs. One of these was by taking the lead in charitable, literary, intellectual, or artistic activities, if only to conduct a salon in the centuries-old manner of the great ladies of France, which was still the cynosure of the social and literary elite in the Southern Cone countries. Even the men shared their esteem for such activities so fully that it was still no handicap, and could be an asset, for a political leader to be an intellectual, a philosopher, and even a poet. In leadership of this kind, women of all three countries achieved distinction during the interwar period, notably Victoria Ocampo of Argentina, who presided over the intellectual and literary circle of her generation, and Amanda Labarca of Chile, who was for many years an outstanding figure of international repute in the field of education.

Dictatorship and Conservative Reaction

Despite the many resemblances between the Alessandri and Yrigoyen regimes and the close similarity of the problems they faced — inflation and postwar depression, labor troubles, and control of the Senate by opposition parties — the two turned out quite differently in the short run. Yrigoyen not only survived all these trials and others besides, but strengthened his party's hold on the government, got his hand-picked successor elected in 1922, and won re-election for himself by a landslide in 1928. Alessandri, on the other hand, saw his Liberal Alliance fall apart within a year and suffered almost complete frustration until a military intervention which he had encouraged first aided him in enacting reforms and then virtually supplanted him. He soon bowed out, to be followed shortly by president-turned-dictator Carlos Ibáñez, an army officer.

Argentina seemed to be following the Chilean example of the Ibáñez dictatorship when, in 1930, it too produced a dictatorship under a military man, General Uriburu. In fact, however, that event only widened an already manifest divergence between developments in the two countries. The political intervention by Chile's armed forces had begun in 1924 because they felt aggrieved and threatened in their professional interests by the politicians, and yet the prolongation of it under Ibáñez was validated by a popular election, which he won handily. Uriburu, on the other hand, seized power by an armed revolt and was badly defeated in his only electoral test, and his motivation was less military than political. It represented a conservative reaction and, although his corporatist plans were rejected, it ushered in a restoration of conservative, upper-class rule. Here was another difference, for Ibáñez governed in what he conceived to be the interest of the whole nation, and not for the special benefit of any class. A no less striking difference between the two was in their attitudes towards education, as illustrated by the fact that Uriburu placed the formerly autonomous University of Buenos Aires under the control of a government "interventor," whereas Ibáñez made his country's national university autonomous for the first time. Finally, Ibáñez held on to power for four years, until his government's initial successes were wiped out by the Great Depression, while Uriburu, after less than eighteen months, gave up under pressure from his fellow officers.

Terra's dictatorship in Uruguay was as different from the other two as they were from each other. His conservatism did not have the fascist flavor of Uriburu's. Like Ibáñez he converted a constitutional presidency into a dictatorship, but he made the conversion formally, whereas Ibáñez made it without advertising the fact. The latter's regime was destroyed by the same depression that produced Terra's and facilitated the establishment of Uriburu's. Finally, Terra's was milder than the other two and, unlike them, it ended in a voluntary as well as orderly restoration of constitutional government—as might have been expected in view of Uruguay's better record of self-government in recent decades.

Convergence was closer in the conservative governments of the 1930s in all three countries than at any other time in the interwar years. The governments in question were those of Agustín Justo in Argentina, Alessandri in his second term in Chile, and dictator Terra in Uruguay. All three administrations were comprised in the period from 1932 to 1938, were authoritarian but not tyrannical, and were mainly concerned with economic recovery from the depression and political recovery from what their leaders now regarded as the twin afflictions of liberalism and disorder despite the fact that all three men had previously taken part in liberal governments. Although Justo and Terra were army officers, the former had served in a Radical cabinet and the latter had been elected president as a Colorado. Of the three, Alessandri best represents the conservatizing influence of the depression, for his seems the most obvious and most extreme case of reversal. A radical reformer in the early 1920s, he was charged a decade later with being the paladin of reaction. The charge has some basis in fact, although it is an over-simplification that involves some distortion. While Alessandri's career, ideas, and intentions are highly controversial, a case can be made for the proposition that his ends remained constant and only his means changed to match changing circumstances. In the early 1920s he did not seek to bring about a radical restructuring of the country's economic and social system any more than of its political system, but wished instead to strengthen them. As he saw it at that time, this called for extensive reforms in the interest of the middle class and the masses. By 1932, however, the whole system was so severely threatened as to require at the same time vigorous defense of law and order and of the whole system's citadel in the conservative classes. His defense was certainly vigorous. Justo and Terra sought the same ends with milder methods and, at least in the short term, equal success.

Social Welfare, Labor, and Neocolonialism

The convergence of the three countries in the 1930s did not extend for all of them to the related fields of social welfare and labor legislation. As noted above, in both fields Chile and Uruguay stood together at the end of the period with relatively advanced systems; Uruguay was the pioneer in both, beginning about 1915, and Chile followed a decade later. Their conservative governments of the next decade did not turn the clock back. Even if they had not been deterred by the self-serving new corporatism, the two systems were by that time too well established in both countries to be tampered with. In Argentina, little had been accomplished in either field at the end of the interwar period. This part of the Argentine Radicals' record from 1916 to 1930 was little better than that of the Conservative Restoration of the next dozen years. The Radicals were a middle-class party that showed no great concern for the masses, and maximum leader Yrigoyen thought about public problems in mainly political terms.

After the conservatives took over in 1930, they tolerated the newly established General Confederation of Labor (CGT) and other sparse creations of the Radical period in this field, but made no significant innovations of their own. Some of the reasons why they felt no need to do so even in defense of their class's interests have been suggested above. In addition to these and to the common unconcern of the upper classes for the masses except for dispensing charity, Argentina's conservatives had a strong strain of cultural nationalism which was nostalgic and easily passed over into xenophobia. They resented the inundation of their country by an endless flood of immigrants, though happy to employ them as peons. These immigrants made up a large part of the total labor force and an even larger part of the much smaller organized labor force and would therefore receive a correspondingly large share of any benefits from the adoption of social welfare and labor reforms. Though easy to understand, this coolness of the Conservative Restoration to such reforms left Argentina at the end of the interwar years lagging far behind its Southern Cone neighbors and even behind the Brazil of Getúlio Vargas in a course imperatively required by the rising demand for social justice.

Of the three conservative administrations, Justo's was weakest in economic nationalism. In fact, it was notoriously Anglophil and the epithet vendepatria, which is believed to have been coined to describe it, was certainly made a cliché by Justo's critics. Yet, at the end of the decade Argentina's national economy was not much more firmly controlled by Great Britain than was Chile's by the United States, for Alessandri's economic nationalism, like Yrigoyen's, was fervent but largely rhetorical. The suspicion naturally arises that it was proclaimed for political effect, for the depression's strong stimulus to nationalism was strongest in the economic field. It was good politics, therefore, to drape himself in the national flag when discussing economic affairs. By the beginning of his second term in 1932, however, foreign capital, with United States copper interests in the forefront, was so strongly entrenched in the Chilean economy and so closely intertwined with Chilean interests that to break the foreign hold would have required revolutionary action and created a revolutionary situation. That was hardly Alessandri's ticket, for his second administration was devoted to staving off revolution.

Some idea of the magnitude of the problem facing him is conveyed by the fact that, in 1940, direct investments of the United States in Chile, which amounted to $414 million, were larger than in any other South American country and made up one fourth of the total for all ten countries. In this list Chile was followed first by much larger Argentina, $388 million; then by oil-rich Venezuela, $262 million; and then by the largest of all, Brazil, $240 million. Near the bottom of the list stood Uruguay, $11 million. If the somewhat ambiguous Good Neighbor policy of the United States did not deter Alessandri from action against Yankee financial and business interests, the ties they had formed with influential Chileans did. It is worth repeating, however, that, above all, about the last thing he wanted to do was to take any action that might precipitate generally revolutionary action. Accordingly, he left the foreign owners undisturbed. So, for that matter, did the less united and less disciplined Popular Front administration that succeeded his, though its leaders may have told themselves that their reasons were different.

Justo and Terra, each for quite different reasons, did not face a comparable problem. In Argentina, nationalism flourished in several varieties and in several segments of the population, but none of them dissuaded Justo and his associates from actions that permitted a further strengthening of Britain's already firm hold on the Argentine economy. The segment that provided his administration with its main support was dominated by beef barons whose best market for their product was in Britain. As viewed by them and their influential allies in the frigoríficos, banks, export firms, social clubs, and professional circles, the concessions Justo made to the British to protect that market were the acts not of a vendepatria but, on the contrary, of a true patriot; what was good for the cattlemen was good for Argentina. As a result, by the end of the decade British interests controlled most of the key elements of the Argentine economy. Most of the rest were in other foreign hands, with the United States first, followed by Germany and France. Argentine critics were clamant but, for the time being, impotent.

In short, by the end of the interwar period the basis for the complaint against neocolonialism had been firmly laid in Argentina and Chile. In both cases, too, the chief ground for it, the engrossing multinational corporation, was by now well established. The most striking examples were provided by the United States. These were copper companies in Chile and frigoríficos in Argentina. They were not only owned in the United States but also operated by trained personnel from the United States and with sophisticated processes and machinery developed in its copper mines and meat packing plants. Although nationalism was probably as strong in Uruguay as in either of their countries, the process of nationalization begun by

Batlle early in the century had been carried so far in transportation, insurance, and other fields that the anti-imperialist animus did not reach nearly so high a degree of intensity in Uruguay as in Argentina and Chile. Terra was, therefore, under no such pressure as their leaders to defend foreign interests against his own countrymen or to match Alessandri's verbal assaults on the foreigners.

A serious and quite different problem was beginning to take shape during Terra's administration, though, fortunately for him, it did not become pressing until after the end of his term. This was the problem of moderating the claims of the numerous corporate institutions or entes autónomos that made Uruguay a prime example of the new corporatism, and of reconciling their respective claims with one another and with the claims of the not inconsiderable number of its people who were, so to speak, unincorporated. As a primarily domestic problem, this one engendered no hard feeling against foreign interests. It did among the latter, however, for as time went on some of them were taxed more and more heavily until they were taxed out of the country. Even this was done without xenophobe bitterness and with an almost kindly regret, as a necessary means of raising funds to help defray the heavy cost of maintaining the country's welfare system.

Foreign Relations

Partly because the Uruguayan people were better satisfied with their own country and comparatively friendly to "capitalist-imperialist" Britain and the United States, there was a divergence between Uruguay and the other two countries with respect to foreign ideologies and foreign policy. Since most of its people still had greater faith in the justice and equity of their government than Argentines and Chileans had in theirs and were sustained in it by admiring foreigners who used terms like Utopian to describe the Uruguayan system, fascism and Communism made far fewer converts in that country than in the other two. As a consequence, the reaction against both was correspondingly less violent. There was, for example, no movement there comparable to Chile's paramilitary Republican Militia of the 1930s and its Argentine counterpart. It is true that charges of fascism were leveled at Uruguay's best-known elder statesman, Luis Alberto de Herrera, but in fact he was a traditionalist Catholic conservative and was quite properly hailed in this period as one of their own by right-wing conservatives in Spain. Even so, the views he espoused gained wider acceptance in Chile and Argentina than in his own middle-of-the road country. During the Spanish civil war of 1936-1939 these two countries showed more sympathy than Uruguay for the rebels against the Republic, and the Chilean embassy in Madrid was one of the most active of all foreign embassies and legations in giving diplomatic asylum to the Republic's opponents.

There was also an important foreign policy difference between Uruguay and its two neighbors. Chile and Argentina, which had remained resolutely neutral throughout World War I, continued that policy for a considerable period in World War II even after the Pearl Harbor attack and after all the other American states had entered into the conflict, either as belligerents or by severing relations with the Axis powers and aiding the allies. Likewise, during the interwar period Santiago and Buenos Aires were generally cool if not flatly opposed to international cooperation involving security, especially to cooperative arrangements including the United States. This was reflected in their attitudes towards the evolving Good Neighbor policy. Both responded to it favorably on the whole so long as it was essentially a policy of good fellowship that committed the United States to nonintervention and, though rather vaguely, to economic cooperation. Both, however, drew back when, in the summer of 1940, the United States began to move away from neutrality on the road to war.

Although the two governments followed parallel courses during the interwar years, neither really trusted the other. In 1938, for instance, Major Juan Perón, Argentina's military attaché in Santiago, was expelled from Chile by its government for espionage which we may assume was authorized since, instead of punishing him, his government soon sent him on an important mission to warring Europe. Why despite mutual distrust, the two governments' foreign policies coincided so closely is best explained in terms of the particular circumstances and purposes of each of them.

In sharp contrast to the courses of Santiago and Buenos Aires, Montevideo showed itself ever ready for international cooperation, especially with the United States. Among the factors influencing its foreign policy were the country's small size, weakness, and great vulnerability owing to its long coast line and river front, and its uncomfortable buffer position between Argentina and Brazil. In this period Argentina was the greater threat because its armed forces were superior to Brazil's, because the viceregal tradition that Uruguay was rightfully a part of Argentina had not died out in that country, and because Argentina had chosen to tie itself to Chile and Brazil in the ABC Pact of 1915, from which Uruguay was not only omitted but excluded. In addition, part of the explanation probably lies in the relative economic independence that Uruguay had achieved through the success of its policy of nationalization — a policy carried out in the early years of the century, at the very time when United States capital was taking over Chile's two major industries, copper and nitrates, and when British capital, already dominant in Argentina, was gaining control of a new key position in that country's economy, the frigorífico industry. Whatever the explanation of its origin, Uruguay's choice of a foreign policy was to have important consequences during World War II and for several years thereafter.

Summary

On balance, the tendencies of the three countries of the Southern Cone to converge prevailed in public affairs during the interwar period. This is hardly surprising since they were so much alike in ethnic composition, culture, and social and political structure, lived in temperate climates and had for several decades had national economies based on exports to industrialized countries of the North Atlantic which dominated them to a large extent, mainly through capital investments and other interlocking interests with influential persons and institutions of each country. The strength of these forces is illustrated by an instance from the political field. Well before 1929, each country had adopted an important political device that differentiated its system from the other two. Proportional representation had been adopted in Chile for the benefit of minority parties and had helped foster a multi-party system; Argentina's Sáenz Peña electoral law, conversely, was aimed at promoting a two-party system; and Uruguay changed from a presidential to a collegial executive, mainly in order to curb executive power. Yet, under the impact of the Great Depression all three soon had governments that were fundamentally alike in being headed by a strong president and devoted to restoring law and order and the economy. Similarly, society in all three countries was becoming more and more complex, compartmentalized, and ready for the revival of corporatism that took place and, related to it, a new economic policy that required the state to play a major economic role for the general welfare.

Argentina, however, lagged far behind the other two in applying this policy, partly, one suspects, because of the smugness of the restored conservatives over successes described in an earlier chapter. Chief among these were the country's relatively quick economic recovery under their leadership and the international distinction it had won by serving as host to the Chaco Peace Conference of 1935-1938, which settled the first major Latin American war since 1883, and by the award of the Nobel Peace Prize to its foreign minister, Carlos Saavedra Lamas (the first Latin American ever to receive it), and his election as president of the League of Nations Assembly. Whether for these or other reasons, the country's political leaders were far from sharing the pessimism of its intellectual leaders, the *pensadores,* about its condition and prospects. (This is an instance of the compartmentalization just referred to. Political and intellectual leadership had overlapped and not infrequently coincided down through the Generation of 1880 so well described by Thomas McGann.) Instead, the regime's decision makers were so pleased with the way things were going that the only concessions they made to the new economic development policy were designed to shore up the status quo for their own benefit. They made none for the general welfare in the form of social reform or labor legislation. In effect, they dammed up for more than a decade a current that was running strong in this part of Latin America. How the dam burst, and with what enduring consequences, will be our next subject.

Part Three

From World War II to the Upheavals of 1973 and Their Aftermath

IX Postwar Disarray
in the Southern Cone

The relatively stable and prosperous early postwar years in the Southern Cone were followed by two decades of disarray that culminated in all three countries in the upheavals of 1973. In the present chapter we shall examine the reasons for this unhappy turn of events, with stress on the causes that were common to all three of them. Other factors of a local or individual kind will be noted in later chapters.

Signs of Disarray

Whether by contagion or for some other reason, similar signs of disarray also appeared in the United States and Europe in the course of this period, though some of the consequences were different. Among the signs were riots in cities of the United States, and in both the United States and Europe student revolts, rifts in Catholic and Protestant churches, and loss of faith in reform. Commenting on one aspect of this loss, disgust with politics, Milton Cummings and Francis Rourke pointed out in the *Johns Hopkins Magazine* for January 1975 that the "growing disbelief in the efficacy of political participation . . . is a phenomenon found in the whole Western world." Latin America, it should not be forgotten (though it often is), is a part of the Western world. As Gino Germani said, Latin America "is not exactly like other parts of the so-called Third World, such as Asia or Africa," for much of its culture is Western and "in many cases . . . the process of modernization started under the sign of the western model."* And, as we have noted before, the people of the Southern Cone are, in this sense, the most Western people in Latin America.

As if overeager to prove their Westernness, these three countries outdid the rest of Latin America in postwar disarray. So persistent and unceasing were their political, social, and economic troubles after the early 1950s that the attention of both foreign and domestic observers of Southern Cone affairs was distracted from developments of a more favorable kind in the cultural realm. Most foreigners' scant store of information about the area was largely confined to its coups and countercoups, its bankruptcies and other natural di-

*Gino Germani, "Main Stages of Modernization," *Social Change in Latin America*, Report of a seminar sponsored by the University of Texas in cooperation with the Southern Regional Education Board, ed. Richard P. Schaedel (n.p., n.d. [Austin, 1968]), 9.

sasters. They scarcely knew or cared, for example, that in the post-war period the Nobel Prize for Literature was twice won by Chilean poets, Gabriela Mistral in 1945 and Pablo Neruda in 1972, or that Nobel Prizes in science were twice awarded to Argentines, to Bernardo Houssay, for Medicine and Physiology, in 1947, and to Luis F. Leloir, for Chemistry, in 1970. Only to a handful of intellectuals and university students in Europe and America was Jorge Luis Borges of Argentina anything more than a name, though a long line of distinguished literary works had twice made him a leading candidate for the Nobel Prize for Literature.

Similarly, few of the many talented musicians from the Southern Cone were known or noticed beyond its borders except by specialists or through occasional performances with, for example, Leonard Bernstein's New York Philharmonic, Eugene Ormandy's Philadelphia Orchestra, or their European equivalents. Painters fared no better. It was frustrating. As a leading Argentine novelist and essayist, Manuel Gálvez, told the distinguished members of the international literary organization, the P.E.N. Club, at its congress in Buenos Aires in 1937, "Europeans can hardly imagine how tragic is our loneliness." That was said for Argentina; in the 1960s and 1970s it could still just as well have been said for the whole Southern Cone.

The outside world's attitude in these cultural matters is hardly surprising, though, when it is recalled that at times these countries' own cultural leaders likewise gave public affairs top priority. Pablo Neruda frequently spiced his poetry with politics and Yankeephobia; that he was a Communist is beside the point. Even Jorge Luis Borges, who had started his career in the 1920s as an apolitical, ivory-tower *littérateur,* in his later years took much time off from purely literary labors for public affairs. Perón's return to Argentina in 1973 made politics almost an obsession with him — not unnaturally since during his first administration President Perón had demoted the critical Borges from director of the National Library to poultry inspector. Now, with Perón returning, everyone else, according to Borges, was in a "great funk." The P.E.N. Club was "the only liberal element left," he lamented, adding, "I am the only one who speaks out."

What is not so easy to understand is the spreading loss of nerve and parallel rise of violence that became distinctive features of life in the Southern Cone in the 1960s. In Argentina these found cultural expression in the nihilism of Beatriz Guido's popular novels and the films of her husband, noted movie director Leopoldo Terre Nilsson; in the cynicism of Juan José Sebreli's best-selling exposé of daily life in Buenos Aires; and in the vogue of the nineteenth-century caudillos, archetype of the "barbarism" combated in the name of "civilization" by Sarmiento, against whom the vogue produced a reaction faintly reflected in the defilement of his statues.

Perhaps these phenomena are explained in part by the multiplying signs that Latin America was losing status in world affairs. In the political field, for instance, Latin America had slipped from a major to a minor component of the United Nations—from 40 percent of its total membership in 1945 to just over 15 percent by 1970 —with a consequent decline of its influence in UN affairs. It had also lost its formerly favored position in United States' foreign policy after 1945, and then briefly had the illusion of regaining it in the Alliance for Progress, only to lose it again at the end of the decade when Washington turned from the alliance to the "low profile." In the economic sphere, the evidence of slippage was only too clear, for, according to the UN Economic Commission for Latin America (ECLA), Latin America's share of world exports had been cut in half since the end of World War II, dropping from 11 percent of the world total in 1948 to 5 percent in 1968.

Yet puzzlement remains, for in the Southern Cone countries, as we shall see, economic and social conditions were in some important respects at least better than in the rest of Latin America and there was some improvement in the 1960s—chiefly in Argentina, to be sure, and least in Uruguay, with Chile in between. At any rate, if there is a solution to the puzzle, it must be sought in other factors besides Latin America's diminished international role. The hypothesis offered here is that it is most likely to be found in certain rather drastic changes in the Roman Catholic Church, the economy, and the middle class.

Opening to the Left in the Catholic Church

The principal change in the Roman Catholic Church in the Southern Cone during the postwar period was a pronounced swing to the left on the part of a substantial minority of the clergy. In Chile it even included the entire episcopacy, and the Archbishop of Santiago was conspicuously gracious to the head of that country's Socialist-Communist regime, Salvador Allende, and to his visitor from Cuba, Fidel Castro. In Uruguay, the council of bishops made a vigorous public protest against the government's stern suppression of the revolutionary organization known as Tupamaros. In Argentina, the hierarchy was more traditionally conservative, so that efforts of progressives to spread an ideology of social change met with little success there, although the efforts were pressed by a well-organized group of activists calling themselves rather inappropriately Third World Priests.

The church's opening to the left was, of course, not confined to the Southern Cone but worldwide, and it received a powerful stimulus from the Second Vatican Council and the reforms adopted there. Chief among earlier sources of the movement were the encyclicals of popes from Leo XIII to John XXIII. In Latin America the writings of Jacques Maritain were a major source until, in the 1960s, the continuing leftward swing reached the point where extremists took up the demand for violent revolution and dismissed the moderate Maritain as a milksop. In this area the opening to the left was facilitated by the creation in 1955 of the Latin American Episcopal Council (CELAM). Composed of diocesan bishops, CELAM held its first conference at Rio de Janeiro in that year. Thereafter it met annually; in the 1960s both of its meetings in the Southern Cone were held in Argentina (Buenos Aires in 1960 and Mar del Plata in 1966).

From the start, CELAM had a considerable variety of functions, but, as its clerical historian Cecilio de Loria notes, one of these—to serve as a means of communication among the national episcopal conferences—turned out to be particularly important because the environment was one in which social change and development were a major concern. Largely in connection with this function, CELAM's activities had, he says, an "almost explosive development." This entailed additions to the staff, particularly of persons trained in the social sciences. Most of those added were younger members of the clergy trained in seminaries from which they emerged with the conviction that the church had the right and duty to intervene in public affairs in defense of social justice and that social justice required extensive social reform, including a redistribution of national income for the benefit of the underprivileged classes. As a result, even when the bishops were personally inclined to maintain the traditionally right-wing stance of Latin American hierarchies, they were under constant leftward pressure from their staff and the position papers and other material prepared by them.

CELAM was by no means alone in its contribution, perhaps not initially intended, to the church's leftward swing. This received a strong impulse through other channels as well and from both regular and secular clergy. Among the former, the Jesuits were as outstanding in the Southern Cone, particularly Chile, as were the Dominicans in Brazil. There the latter helped to create a favorable atmosphere in some quarters for Dom Hélder Pessôa Câmara, Archbishop of Olinda and Recife, who preached that Che Guevara and Colombia's ex-priest guerrilla Camilo Torres deserved to be remembered with as much respect as Martin Luther King and that the "real promoters of violence" were those who "have hurt the cause of justice." Among the secular clergy of the Southern Cone, the relatively large proportion that, in this period as in the past, came from Belgium, France, and Spain, included some who, before the founding of CELAM, had already absorbed and were propagating advanced ideas about social justice and the church's mission.

The adoption and dissemination of such ideas had several consequences. One was to reverse the results of the long struggle it had taken to get the church out of politics on the side of the right wing and to bring it back into politics again, this time on the side of the left wing. Another was to help escalate the controversy over how far and how fast social change should go. Chile provided a better illustration than Uruguay, where the separation of church and state had taken place a few years earlier than in Chile and had been accepted by the clerical side with greater equanimity and finality than in Chile. The latter also provided a better illustration than Argentina. There, the church occupied a rather anomalous, half-in and half-out position, since it was supported by the state and yet was not an established state church in the same degree as the Church of England or the Roman Catholic Church in Spain, Colombia, or Peru. Government patronage in Argentina was terminated in 1966 and it was expected that other changes in church-state relations would follow, but the results are not yet clear.

In Chile, the separation of church and state in 1925 had been strongly opposed and at last only grudgingly acquiesced in by some clerical leaders. For nearly a generation thereafter the hierarchy maintained at least a nominal neutrality in politics. The proclivity for intervention in public affairs did not die out, however; what was changed when it was fanned into new life, which happened shortly, was its intended beneficiaries. These were no longer the conservative upper classes, but the common people. The form of its renaissance, which began to stir as early as the 1930s, was shaped by the newly ascendant ideas about social justice for the masses and the church's obligation to speed its coming. Though not without strong conservative opposition, which was never completely eliminated, the entire episcopacy in Chile was gradually brought by the 1960s to the point of asserting in pastoral letters what Ivan Vallier sympathetically describes as "the church's fundamental responsibility for serving the cause of radical social change." He acknowledges that this radicalization of the Chilean hierarchy, which was quite exceptional in Spanish America, was carried out partly as a means of meeting competition for the support of the masses from organized groups, both secular (Communists and Socialists) and religious (Pentecostal Protestants), both of which were likewise stronger in Chile than in the rest of Spanish America.

In this atmosphere, the non-confessional, moderately left-wing Christian Democratic Party of Chile flourished for a time, and it was apparently easy for the members of a religious order, the Jesuits, to become identified with the party as advisers and policy planners. No such connection between the church and a political party is known to have been formed in either Argentina or Uruguay. Soon, however, left-wing religious activists in all three countries concluded that mere reformers of the Christian Democratic type were an obstacle to the indispensable social revolution and were no better than collaborators with the fascist oligarchy. This conclusion contributed to the sharp decline of the party in Chile, where it had become the largest party for a time in the 1960s, and to the virtual disappearance of the Christian Democratic parties in Argentina and Uruguay, where they had never amounted to much.

Clerical advocates of radical social change in the Southern Cone generally counseled achieving it by peaceful means. Even Brazil's episcopal firebrand, Hélder Câmara, prayed for "the miracle of being violent as the prophets . . . revolutionary as the Gospel, but without offending against love." Yet when the imperative of revolutionary change has been made the fundamental rule of action, the next question becomes the means, and as the 1960s wore on, increasing numbers of people in the Southern Cone chose violent means on the ground that revolutionary change by peaceful means had become demonstrably impossible. The leftward swing in the church was not unrelated to the spread of this belief through secular circles and the mounting violence of guerrilla groups in all three countries in this decade and the next.

Some readers may doubt whether the situation in the church made any significant difference in this connection, since there is a rather widespread tendency to underrate the church's influence in Latin America, especially in the more developed countries of the Southern Cone. The principal ground for doing so seems to be that only a small part of the people of the area — the figure given is usually ten or fifteen percent — are practicing Catholics. In his study of social change in Latin America, however, Juan F. Marsal makes observations that point to a different conclusion, and he makes them with special reference to Argentina and Uruguay. Commenting on one of the potentially major consequences of the "modernizing tendencies" in the church, he observes that it has ceased to be the bulwark of "traditional society" and of that society's "congenital irrationalism." But, according to him, as the modernizing church proceeds from the irrationalism of Christian orthodoxy to scientific study of sociology, the Marxist leaders in these countries move in the opposite direction by rejecting sociology in conformity with Marxist orthodoxy. And so, he concludes, the traditional "irrationalism of the right" is now matched by the new "irrationalism of the left" and the combination of these with the "native emotionalism" of the people of the area forms an obstacle to the progress of scientific thought that at times seems insuperable.

Marsal's observations are germane to our question, since by "modernizing" he means substantially the same development that has been referred to here as the church's leftward swing or opening to the left. His conclusion should be pondered not only by academics but by officials of foreign governments who would like to know how to deal with those of the countries in question. It is also worth noting that implicit in his conclusion is his belief that, for all the modernizing they have undergone for more than a century past, traditionalism is still strong in these countries.

Economies in Trouble

"Stagnation" is the term most often used to describe the usual condition of the economies of all three Southern Cone countries since about 1950. Another term, which is not uncommon and which may give a more accurate picture of their performance, is "stop-go." The sense of the latter term is graphically conveyed by Albert Hirschman's description of the performance of the Argentine economy after its so-called "take-off" as less like a jet's than a helicopter's. However one describes them, the performances of all three economies have with good reason been deemed unsatisfactory by the people they serve. Once the economic leaders of Latin America, all three countries in the postwar period have lagged behind — sometimes far behind — Brazil, Mexico, and several other countries in rate of growth. Argentina, which long headed the Latin American list in gross national product, had already lost the lead to oil-rich Venezuela before OPEC was established on that country's initiative. As early as the beginning of 1962 the state of the Argentine economy was causing President Frondizi grave concern. If its growth rate since 1950 should be maintained, he warned, its per capita income would be reduced by 1975 from the current $460 to $420, whereas Brazil's on the same assumption would more than double by that time, rising from $230 to $511. There was a similar decline in Uruguay. Chile's per capita growth rate in the 1960s was better, but because the national income was accounted for so largely by copper and nitrates and was not distributed per capita, but increasingly concentrated in the top two or three percent of the population, the state of the Chilean economy remained a source of grave discontent.

For their economic troubles and the attendant ills, critics in all three countries held foreigners largely responsible through their "neocolonial" control of the respective national economies, and through the terms of trade, which according to the more imaginative critics were determined not by the market, but by a conspiracy. The control, it was generally charged, was exercised through investments and ties with influential but venal nationals, and the terms of trade, when not rigged, ran against developing nations by the very nature of the exchange of raw materials and foodstuffs for manufactures in a so-called free market. There is some merit in both charges, but the problem is more complicated than that. Uruguay, as we have seen, pioneered from about 1910 onwards with a successful policy of nationalizing its economy. At the very same time, the United States and Great Britain were tightening their hold on the economies of, respectively, Chile and Argentina. Yet Uruguay's experience with economic stagnation and related ills since mid-century has been strikingly similar to the experiences of the other two. Moreover, Aníbal Pinto, one of the ablest Chilean economists, wrote as far back as 1965 that in the development of Latin America, the "basic factors at present are domestic — and not foreign — investment and demand."

It is in order, then, to take a closer look at the serious problem of so-called stagnation in the economies of the three countries. The examination will focus on Argentina, which contains two-thirds of the population of the area and whose social scientists have produced unusually varied and interesting commentaries on the problem. It is so complex and they differ so widely about it that here we can offer only a brief sampling of a few diagnoses. One feature they share with one another and with Aníbal Pinto: all of them lay a considerable part of the responsibility for what has gone wrong on the people of Argentina.

According to sociologist and social historian Torcuato S. DiTella, writing in the late 1960s, Argentina has been stagnating not merely since 1950, but ever since the 1930s. Its stagnation, he says, has been due to a political stalemate among various contenders for power — large landowners, industrialists, army, church, middle classes, intellectuals, labor unions, the Peronist Party — and this stalemate has hamstrung economic policy. Economic historian Adolfo Dorfman, on the other hand, agrees with economist Alejandro Bunge that the stagnation began even earlier, just before World War I, and attributes it to Argentina's agrarian system, especially the latifundio or great estate, which prevented the proper growth of manufactures by reducing the purchasing power of the rural population. Aldo Ferrer, also an economic historian, likewise holds the land-tenure system responsible, but only in part. The factors he adds include lack of investment in strategic sectors and failure to integrate them, neglect of the country's interior provinces, deterioration of its traditional export trade, inflation, and the faulty economic policies followed by landowner and Peronist regimes alike.

Among recent foreign commentators, fresh analyses have come from Eldon Kenworthy and Peter H. Smith. Kenworthy rejects, as typical of American interpretations of Third World trends by economic determinism, the explanation of Argentina's troubles in terms of the economic and political damage done by Peronism. Yet there is a strain of economic determinism in his own explanation, which locates their source in the fact that Argentina made the wrong initial responses to the requirements of late industrialization: that national policy must be shaped by groups identified with industry, and that the rest of society must be brought to accept this distribution of power and the sacrifices it entails. Peter Smith bases his well-documented study of the period 1904-1955 on the political science concept of sequential crises (legitimacy, participation, distribution) and the weakening effect of each successive crisis on the then dominant political elite. Economics (with, again, a tilt towards economic determinism), and other social sciences are drawn on skillfully, but so single-mindedly and at such a high level of abstraction that, as an otherwise enthusiastic reviewer noted, Smith's book fails to capture the "flavor" of the era with which it deals.

An earlier and somewhat similar explanation is offered by José Luis de Imaz in his well-known essay *Those Who Command* (*Los que mandan*). He makes it highly persuasive, for it is sophisticated and comprehensive, yet simple, and it does convey the flavor of its era. According to the author, Argentina's stagnation, the cause or multiplier of many of its other troubles, has been due to the lack of an effective governing elite, which, in turn, is due to the lack of unity and coherence among those who since the 1920s have commanded the several sectors of Argentine society. The old oligarchical elite, he explains, was more successful because it was endowed with unity by its members' common background and values, whereas the sectoral leaders who have replaced them since the 1920s had widely different backgrounds owing to such factors as the flood of immigrants and the rise of the new middle class, and to the new leaders' highly compartmentalized training in their critical years between the ages of twenty and forty. The sons of businessmen, for example, were trained in Zurich or England, the young clergy in Rome, naval officers in southern Argentine posts, and so on; and self-made men and labor leaders, besides maturing in still other compartments, received no training at all in public affairs. Added to lack of unity and suitable training, the argument continues, was the Peronist regime's policy of excluding the opposition from any effective participation in public affairs — a policy which its opponents copied when their turn came. As a result, he concludes, the history of Argentina became a "succession of discontinuities," national policy lost touch with the requirements of a changing world, and despite Argentina's rich natural and human resources, economic stagnation became permanent.

It will be noted that all the foregoing explanations of that phenomenon lay heavy stress on the domestic Argentine sources of it, and not on the external factors so dear to the hearts of the country's politicians, such as foreign exploitation, imperialism, and decapitalization. But was there in fact any stagnation to be explained? In an ingenious 1966 study based on new data for the period 1949-1965, Clarence Zuvekas, Jr., answered "no" to the question. He maintained that the Argentine economy in those years should be described as "stop and go" rather than "stagnant," since although it halted and even lost ground at times, the new data showed an annual increase for the period of just over one percent in the GNP. The data apparently bear him out, but so small an average increase for so long a period seemed very much like stagnation in comparison with Argentina's high growth rates in earlier decades and with the recent and current growth rates of rival Brazil and several other Latin American countries. So the term will be used here, interchangeably with stop-go, in referring to the 1950s and early 1960s, after which Argentina sustained a moderate growth rate for several years.

Except that Uruguay made no such recovery after the mid-1960s, the story was much the same in the other two Southern Cone countries. Uruguay depended mainly on an agricultural-pastoral economy that resembled Argentina's and was similarly handicapped. Additional handicaps were Uruguay's smaller, over-protected, high-cost manufacturing sector, and its rigid, highly compartmentalized economic and social structure, which was dominated by over-staffed, inefficient autonomous government agencies (entes autónomos) and burdened with an excessively expensive social welfare system. Chile's economic performance was about the same as Argentina's. It too faced serious, long-standing economic problems, headed by an exceptionally high rate of inflation. With a population growth rate now the highest of the three countries and an agrarian sector sacrificed to the industrial-urban sector, Chile was transformed from an exporter into an importer of foodstuffs. In 1973 it remained, as always, the lowest of the three in per capita gross domestic product, which was $640, as compared with Argentina's $974 and Uruguay's $751.*

The upturn in Argentina after 1965 is reflected in the sharp increase of its gross domestic product growth rate from an average of one percent in 1950-1965 to 4 percent in 1965-1970. The corresponding figure for Chile in the latter period was 3.7 percent, which was at least an improvement over the disappointing 2.7 percent rate

---

*As estimated in *Statistical Abstract of Latin America, 1971,* Table 1, according to which the corresponding figure for the United States was $4,734.

during the first postwar decade. Uruguay had only a 1.4 percent growth rate for 1965-1970, despite a thumping but unrepresentative 4.5 percent in the last of those five years. The following year Uruguay fell back to a more normal 0.6 percent, while Chile leaped up to 8.5 percent. The Chilean increase was not only abnormal but artificial and short-lived; it was the result of unsound measures taken for political purposes by the new Allende government. Argentina's growth rate in 1971 declined slightly, to 3.8 percent. That was still substantial, but it was dwarfed by rival Brazil's rate of 11.3 percent for the same year, which climaxed an impressive growth rate of 7.5 percent for the period 1965-1970 and of 9.5 percent for its last year.*

Another and perhaps greater cause of dissatisfaction in the Southern Cone was the increasing concentration of wealth in a small-to-minute top income group in each country. In Argentina, this group, 5 percent of all families, received 27.3 percent of all personal income in 1953 (under Perón) and 29.4 percent in 1961 (under Frondizi), as compared with the lowest 20 percent groups's 7.5 percent in 1953 and 7.0 percent in 1961. In Uruguay the disparity was somewhat less, but in Chile it was much greater. In 1968 (under Frei) 2.4 percent of the population received 46 percent of the national income, as compared with the lowest 25 percent's 4.8 percent. Further details will be given in later chapters, but the few given here are enough to suggest why, in this postwar period, when a great increase in mass communications was giving the masses a heightened awareness of their condition compared with that of others, both at home and abroad, the countries of the Southern Cone were shaken by a swelling demand for a redistribution of wealth. In Chile the disparity was so great that people in the lowest one-third of the income groups, if they could read, could identify with the denizens of *Animal Farm* in the matter of material rewards as well as equality.

It could not be much solace to the lowest income groups in these countries to know that, according to an ECLA study of Latin American income distribution in the early 1960s, their opposite numbers in every other country were even worse off. They would hardly be happy to learn from the same study that their countries, which accounted for only about one-eighth of the total population of Latin

---

*The source of all figures in this paragraph is ECLA, *Economic Survey of Latin America, 1971*, 39, table 1.

America, nevertheless contained two-thirds of the top 20 percent income group of all Latin Americans. In that favored group, the Southern Cone accounted for 31.4 percent of the top 5 percent, and 34.5 percent of the next 15 percent.

The same ECLA study, made in 1971, contained some findings about the Argentine economy that should have been reassuring to most of its people. Some of the findings differentiated it, to its advantage, from the rest of Latin America, including Uruguay and Chile. One was that, by the tests applied, Argentina had the most equitable income distribution of all and that this provided it with a "greater basis for mass markets" than any of the other countries. Another finding was that, although Argentina had a greater-than-average concentration of income in a small group, an exceptionally high proportion of that group (four-fifths) were self-employed, not *rentiers*, and, unlike other Latin American top groups, did not spend all their income on consumption, with the result that Argentina had a "relatively high rate of savings" and capital formation. Although the study did not say so, this meant that Argentina was less dependent than most on foreign sources for development capital.

With regard to the possibility of reducing the inequality of income, the study in question offered two conclusions. One was that, while a redistribution of land ownership would help bring this about in most other Latin American countries, it would not do so in Argentina. The reason was simple: in Argentina (as in Venezuela and Mexico) the existing inequality of income was not much greater in the rural than in the urban sector, so that even an extreme degree of land distribution would reduce the top 5 percent's share of the national income by only 3 percentage points (that is, from about 30 to 27). The other conclusion was that, although the inequality of income could theoretically be reduced by a shift to an economy dominated by impersonal, corporate-type organizations, no such change was under way or in prospect in Argentina, where, despite the recent rapid growth of corporations, the economy was still based on "large numbers of relatively small producers" and the self-employed dominated the high-income group. The study did not refer in this connection to the encroachment of the public on the private sector, a process that had gone even further in Chile and Uruguay.

In these two countries the problem of income distribution at that time (1970) differed in other ways as well from the one in Argentina.

In Chile, the very small upper class in which there was such an exceedingly high concentration of income did not constitute an oligarchy, strictly speaking, but it was bound together by interlocking family and business ties that made it a powerful interest group, particularly as an impediment to change. In Uruguay, too, where the private sector was relatively small because of the mushrooming government-controlled autonomous agencies, there was a similar bar to income redistribution in that sector's two chief component parts: the large landowners and the industrialists, supported by their financial and commercial associates. The landlords by staving off agrarian reform, and the industrialists by obtaining fantastically high tariff protection at the expense of the consuming public, had demonstrated a degree of political effectiveness that was surprising in a country so long and deeply committed to social welfare and government intervention in the economy. The success of upper-class interests in resisting the demand for thoroughgoing structural reform — a demand that built up from the 1950s onward — increased the pressure for change and turned reformers into advocates of revolution by armed force.

Middle-Class Disarray

Until well into the 1960s most (though not all) specialists on Latin America gave the area's middle class a high rating as a force for political and social reform and economic development. Subsequent events, particularly in the Southern Cone, where that class was oldest and largest, brought about a downward revision of that appraisal. Large numbers of persons in all classes, it appeared, had become alienated, especially by the developments in the Catholic Church and the trend of the economy. The political consequences of this alienation were most important among the middle class — which, it turned out, was unstable and fragmented — and above all among the middle-class youth. Rather than reformers, this sector now provided leaders for extremist groups of both the right wing and the left, but principally the latter. This reminds one of the part played by the German youth in the rise of Hitlerism, but there was at least one great difference: many of the middle-class youth of the Southern Cone fought for, not against, Marxism, especially in its more radical and violent forms, including their version of Maoism. They provided the leadership for establishing left-wing control of university student federations and of the rural and urban terrorist groups that grew partly out of those federations, though the first impulse to violence of this kind seems to have come from Cuba, through Che Guevara, in the early 1960s. The activities of these terrorist groups sent a series of seismic shocks through all three countries from the middle of that decade to the close of our period in the next. The most dangerous of them were not suppressed until 1972 in Uruguay and the following year in Chile. Several of them remained active in Argentina until 1976, despite years of effort by the armed forces and the police to break them up.

While the Tupamaros of Uruguay, who will be discussed in a later chapter, were the most highly publicized of these guerrilla organizations, and while some in Argentina were the most durable, Chile produced the one that was politically the most effective. This was the MIR (Movement of the Revolutionary Left), organized in 1965, which became an influential factor on the extreme left of the Allende regime from 1970 to 1973. According to Robert Moss, the MIR was founded by young Socialist dissidents of Santiago and Concepción and in its first two years engaged mainly in stirring up university students, as in the hostile demonstrations that spoiled Robert F. Kennedy's visit to the University of Concepción in 1966. The following year a group of its extreme left-wing members—all young middle-class intellectuals—got control of that university's student federation. Outstanding among them was Luciano Cruz, who came of a landowning family in the Concepción area and had had a Catholic schooling. At the age of 21 he became a founder and the firebrand of MIR. Very few of the organization's leaders were of working-class origin.

Convinced that the necessary structural change in Chilean society could never be achieved through the peaceful political process, Luciano Cruz and his fellow activists set out to provoke a revolution by a campaign of violence conducted through MIR. The campaign was carried on with great success and almost complete freedom from government interference during Allende's administration. MIR was never officially part of it, but had ties with some who were, and Allende could never be persuaded to outlaw it or hamper its illegal activities in its chosen role as "accelerator of the revolution." Its activities included forcible seizures of land in south central Chile; building up in the Andes, along the Argentine frontier, a safe guerrilla base, a Chilean equivalent of Fidel Castro's Sierra Maestra; and constructing armed camps in and around Santiago and training paramilitary forces for the civil war that MIR's leaders were sure was coming and which they were trying to precipitate. They never gave up the conviction that the necessary social revolution could never be achieved peacefully through political channels, not even by Allende's government.

The middle classes were also well represented, though less dominant, in right-wing organizations of the Southern Cone, such as Chilean Patria y Libertad (Fatherland and Liberty), that combated those on the left. On both sides it was often armed combat, but combat by ambush and assassination — true guerrilla tactics. Assassination was much more common in Argentina than in Chile; at times it became so frequent that a war of attrition seemed in progress. In Uruguay there was no comparable right-wing reaction among middle-class elements. One reason may have been that the only major left-wing organization, the Tupamaros, not only drew most of its leaders from that class (though there were also some from the upper class), but also for several years won considerable popular sympathy among the middle as well as the upper and lower classes by professing an attractive policy and avoiding bloodshed. When it abandoned this course and began to follow a course like Chilean MIR's, it alienated its essential middle-class fellow-travellers and was soon liquidated by Army and police without the need of help from a right-wing guerrilla force.

As suggested above, Juan Marsal's perceptive comment, made in the mid-1960s, on the growth of an irrationalism of the left to match that of the right in Latin America, and particularly in Argentina and Uruguay, implies his belief that traditionalism was still a significant factor in those countries. Subsequent chapters will confirm that view as regards Chile as well. One symptom especially characteristic of the area's Hispanic culture was the accelerated revival of corporatism, but perhaps the most striking expression of traditionalism was the way in which even the new middle class drew back from reform when the old order was threatened with drastic change in the early 1970s. Here we shall note only one more sign, a rather quaint one, that the traditional society, which its critics often describe by the loaded term "archaic society," was still very much alive in the Southern Cone.

That symbol of traditionalism was duelling, still actively practiced there at the end of our period. It was still legal in Uruguay, provided a Court of Honor made proper arrangements. So arranged, two duels were fought in October and November of 1970. Both duels took place in the national military academy's court of honor in suburban Montevideo, and both were fought with sabers by the same national senator, whose opponent in the first was a member of the president's cabinet and in the second a member of the Batlle dynasty and (naturally) a candidate for the presidency. In the first duel, the senator was wounded badly enough to cause a three-week postponement of the second, but in this one no one was injured.

In Argentina duelling was nominally under the ban of a law that imposed a penalty of from one to four months in jail for wounding a man in a duel and stiffened the penalty to from one to four years for killing him. But the police never interfered unless one of the parties filed a formal complaint, and none ever did. So duelling continued to flourish in Argentina, too, and there, as in Uruguay, it flourished mainly among politicians. The duel master was a former member of Congress and the best-known duelist was a politician and newspaperman, Yolivan Alberto Biglieri. Biglieri's pen involved him in duels and his saber won him renown. He was scornful of swords because they "just cause a prick," a report in the *New York Times* of December 6, 1970, quoted him as saying. Duelling pistols he dismissed as "wildly inaccurate." For gentlemen (and duelling was only for gentlemen), that left only one choice, the saber, a fine weapon, with which, he explained, "you can really slash . . . and even kill." His most celebrated victory was won in 1968 over recently retired naval chief Benigno Varela, whose retirement Biglieri's newspaper had hailed with the headline, "Another Traitor Has Gone." Though Biglieri won, Varela survived to become ambassador to Belgium. Biglieri went on with his journalism, politics, and duelling, and duelling went on as usual. Efforts to stop it were made on both sides of the Plata, but on both sides it was successfully defended as the best way for gentlemen who felt aggrieved to square accounts. As the *Times* report said, duelling was "so much a part of the tradition of the region" that it was not likely to be supplanted by prosaic libel suits as a means of squaring them.

The survival of duelling is only one minuscule indication of the continuing strength of tradition in this area, among people of the middle as well as the upper class. Little noticed by students a generation ago except as a relic that was a hindrance to progress but happily on its way out, traditionalism is now widely recognized as a still vital force with a future as well as a past. This recognition has been expressed in terms that range from esoteric to earthy. Richard Morse, writing in the early 1960s about Hispanic patrimonialism, contended that in the seventeenth century Francisco Suárez "encapsulated certain assumptions about political man and certain political dilemmas that pervade Hispanic life today." Max Weber, he further maintained, by distinguishing patrimonialism as one form of "traditional domination," enabled us to trace the patrimonial state's persistence in modern Spanish America. Morse did not illustrate his thesis by concrete examples, nor did he differentiate one Spanish American country or sub-region from another.

Writing a few years later, José Nun did both things in an article on the "middle-class military coup" in Latin America, and more particularly in a group of countries headed by Argentina, Chile, and Uruguay. The only thing that can be postulated about the middle classes in these countries, Nun insisted, is their "basic lack of cohesion and unity," and these characteristics are mirrored in their armies, whose officer corps are drawn mainly from the middle classes and are their political instrument. The army in each country has its own special character, but—he continued in a passage especially relevant to our present theme—in all of them both army and middle class act in a frame of culture still controlled by the traditional upper class. This latter proposition, in both its parts, is one on which there is now widespread if not general agreement among students of society in the Southern Cone. To put it another way, in the "frame of culture" extending from fashions to values, the otherwise disunited middle class in all three countries now follows in the wake of the upper class, and the upper class is bound by tradition.

The traditionalism of the Latin American middle class is also stressed by Gino Germani, a leading authority on the growth and character of that class, especially in Argentina, where he lived and taught at the University of Buenos Aires for more than a quarter of a century. In the mid-1940s he and Sergio Bagú, another leading authority on the subject, published articles in which they stressed that class's lack of unity and homogeneity in Argentina. In 1967 Germani discussed its relationship to modernization in Latin America at large. He first noted Ben Hoselitz's hypothesis that the middle classes of that area consisted largely of office workers and salaried people, and not of entrepreneurs, and then the opinion of other social scientists that middle-class growth has contributed to social mobility and thus to the integration of one population sector. Germani then observes that "such integration has been accomplished within the so-called traditional or archaic social structure," one feature of which is highly concentrated land ownership. The middle class's increase in size, he continues, has not been accompanied by a modernization of attitudes; in fact, these attitudes are still "not very favorable to modernization" in such matters as rational thinking, scientific approach, and technological perspective.

In conclusion on this subject, Germani says the "traditional power structure" has succeeded in absorbing the force of reform. He leaves it an open question whether this came about through the power structure's own promotion of middle-class growth as a cushion and insulation against lower-class pretensions, or through the inherent tendency of the middle classes, once they are in power, to forget the aims they formerly sought to achieve by alliance with the lower class in populist movements with substantial, even drastic, programs of reform. At any rate, he notes, that is what happened to the Radicals in Argentina and Chile, and the Colorados in Uruguay: once in power, they forgot their quondam lower-class allies. He reserved judgment as to whether the new, Christian Democratic type of populist government (then in power in Chile) would turn out the same way. It is a question worth pondering whether the still more radical populist movement that overwhelmed the Christian Democrats of Chile in 1970 and produced the epidemic of left-wing terrorism of the years just before and just after that in all the Southern Cone, was in some measure a product of resentment over this desertion of the populist movement by the Radicals of Argentina and Chile, and the Colorados of Uruguay.

X The Perón Regime
and Its Legacy

Because of Argentina's strong economic, cultural, and military ties with Western Europe, the impact of World War II on that country was exceptionally heavy from the start, despite the intervening 6,000 miles of ocean. Besides soon beaten Poland, the original belligerents in 1939 were Argentina's principal trading partner and investor, Great Britain; the chief source of its governing classes' ideas about literature and the good life, France; and its army officers' mentor for the past forty years, Germany. In 1940 these three were joined by Italy, which was the principal source of the immigrant flood that since 1870 had changed Argentina's ethnic composition from largely mestizo-Indian-mulatto-Negro into almost all white and had turned the national capital into an Italianate city. The next largest source of that immigration and Argentina's mother country, Spain, though never a belligerent, was everywhere regarded as being in the Axis camp through most of the war.

Perhaps the most lasting result of the war for Argentina was that it contributed to the rise and consolidation of Juan Perón's regime. Among other things, the war took him to Italy, where he learned valuable lessons; it created problems for Argentina that opened the door to his rise; and it provided the country with the large foreign currency reserves with which Perón, as president for nine years, financed spectacular and politically useful measures that helped to consolidate his power. Possessing magnetism and considerable personal talents that enabled him to make the most of his opportunities, he built up a following and a reputation, mainly among organized workers, that survived his overthrow and flight in 1955 and brought him back to Argentina and to power eighteen years later. Throughout his long exile his followers remained the most numerous political aggregation in Argentina despite persecution and made Perón and Peronism always a major and often the dominant issue in Argentine public life through all those years. His General Confederation of Labor (CGT), which Perón himself near the end of his life described as the backbone of the Peronist movement from the start, is still the strongest labor organization in Latin America. Besides leaving a strong imprint on Argentine society and domestic and foreign policy, he first gave populistic nationalism and the Third Position—both the term and the policy—wide currency throughout Latin America. Consequently, it does not seem fanciful to call the whole period of Argentine history from his rise during

World War II to his death thirty years later the Perón Era. His many defects, errors, and backslidings are beside the point.

War Abroad and Drift at Home

In the early years of the war Argentine policy, both domestic and foreign, drifted first one way and then another in response to the opposing thrusts from abroad and from a now fragmented society. On the home front, there was, to begin with, a rift in the regime itself between the two parties composing the Concordancia. This was symbolized by the contrast between the president in 1940, Roberto Ortiz, an Antipersonalist Radical, and his Conservative vice-president, Roberto S. Castillo. Ortiz favored political reform, a neutrality policy benevolent towards the Allies, and loyal inter-American cooperation. Castillo, on the other hand, was committed to the existing political system of "patriotic fraud" (see chapter V) and, though pro-British in his sympathies (but not pro-American), favored a policy of strict neutrality except when Argentina needed arms from the Axis. Neither man supported industrialization except as a supplement to the agricultural-commercial export economy in which both were deeply involved.

President Ortiz, already crippled by ill health for more than a year, resigned in June 1942 and died the next month. Castillo succeeded him in normal course, but the strain between the Concordancia's component parties continued without relaxation. Still more serious was the growing antagonism between the pro-British political wing of the regime and the army officer corps. Though remaining discreetly in the background, the armed forces had been the ruling Concordancia's main prop, but many of the army officer's were pro-Axis and increasingly resentful of the government's failure to reciprocate their support of it by arming them adequately.

This was only one of many fissures in Argentine society. The chief opposition party, the Radicals, was likewise divided. As related earlier, its unity was breached in the late 1930s by the secession of its left-wing group, FORJA. Though small, FORJA expressed a widespread disillusionment with the Radical Party on the ground that it had been less the corrupt conservative regime's opponent than its collaborator. Organized labor too was divided. By early 1943 its main confederation, the CGT, had split into two wings of almost equal strength, one Communist-controlled, the other independent.

The employers' groups also, industrial as well as agricultural, were disunited. The Rural Society of Buenos Aires province was an economic and political powerhouse, but it spoke only for that province, and similar bodies in the interior operated independently and sometimes in opposition to it, as in their efforts to nationalize the foreign-owned frigorífico business, with which the Buenos Aires Society was intimately meshed.

Industry was no exception to the general rule of fragmentation. It continued its rapid growth of the late 1930s, the number of plants increasing from 54,000 in 1939 to 86,000 in 1946, and the number of their workers from 620,000 to 917,000 in the same period. With growth came disunity. Most of their production was intended to complement manufactured imports, not compete with them or substitute for them. Hence the employers' organization, the Industrial Union, which had been tamed by the irresistible agrarian-commercial combination, opposed the demand of the new group of industrialists for effective tariff protection of certain products, such as textiles, that were of the import substitution kind. This new breed of entrepreneurs (*empresarios*), though mostly of immigrant stock, as was the nonpolitical older generation also, had begun in the late 1930s to take an active part in politics. By the early 1940s they were developing a corporate sense which was soon, with a push from Perón, to lead to the creation of a rival industrial organization, thus formalizing the split in the industrial field.

There were other rifts as well, but the result of all these opposing thrusts was not so much immobilism as indecisive movement within a limited sphere. Until the military coup of June 4, 1943, that sphere was the Conservative Restoration in its final stage. During that stage the policy variations, both domestic and foreign, were confined within the bounds set in the 1930s in accordance with the interests and values of the restored oligarchy. In this respect Argentina's faltering response to the current world crisis contrasted sharply with Uruguay's and Chile's. In foreign policy, for example, Uruguay took a strong stand against the Axis at the Meeting of American Foreign Ministers in Rio de Janeiro following the Pearl Harbor attack, and the Uruguayan foreign minister and vice-president, Alberto Guani, provided energetic leadership as chairman of the wartime Inter-American Committee on Political Defense set up at Rio to combat Axis propaganda and sabotage. Argentina, on the other hand, first wavered, making a seeming commitment to hemispheric defense at the Havana conference in 1940, only to renege on it at the

Rio conference and then, with the world in flames, ended up with a negative policy of abstention worthy of its distinguished but sterile foreign minister through most of the 1930s, Carlos Saavedra Lamas.

The sharpest contrast with Chile was in domestic affairs. In this case too there was a variation in Argentine policy. In 1940 Federico Pinedo proposed a far-reaching plan to help the Argentine economy adapt to the changing world situation. He will be remembered as the chief architect of the Justo administration's economic policy and the author of the most important policy innovations of the 1930s. His measures, which were nationalizing and successful, were still in effect and he now proposed to move further along the same line of state intervention in the economy. His plan had much in common with the one that Chile had followed in establishing its Development Corporation the preceding year. As we have seen, however, Pinedo, a former Independent Socialist, was a maverick in the Concordancia, and the Conservatives and Antipersonalists who dominated it had had enough of chipping away at the free enterprise system on which their treasured export economy was based. Pinedo's plan never had a chance. It was left for Juan Perón to get Argentina's domestic and foreign policy off dead center and moving again.

Under Army Rule and Still Adrift

On June 4, 1943, Argentina's armed forces again took over the government in an almost bloodless coup. This one was started by General Arturo Rawson and a dozen officers of lower rank. It brought about the establishment of a military dictatorship that lasted three years to a day.

Rawson's group was immediately joined by the better organized Group of United Officers (GOU), of which Colonel Juan Perón was a leading member. Sealed by President Castillo's resignation the next day, the success of the coup was quick and complete, but in addition to the usual personal and interservice rivalries, the officers were deeply divided over domestic and foreign policy questions. They had not even agreed beforehand on the kind of government they would set up or who should head it. General Rawson assumed the acting presidency, but apparently he was believed by those with different ideas to be too sincere in his promises of a democratic and pro-Allied course. They were willing to pay only lip service to the same promises, in an effort, which soon succeeded, to obtain recognition from Argentina's Supreme Court, the United States and

Great Britain, and the other Latin American states. The officers most opposed to Rawson were those who favored an authoritarian government and a pro-Axis nonbelligerency. No one in Argentina favored going to war on either side.

On June 7 Rawson was forced out and succeeded by another general, Pedro Pablo Ramírez, who had been Castillo's minister of war and whose attempted dismissal by Castillo for disloyalty had precipitated the coup. Internal dissension and drift continued, however, until October 1945, when the struggle for power within the military regime ended with the definitive establishment of Perón's leadership.

This critical period falls into two parts. In the first phase, June 1943 to March 1944, Ramírez headed the administration. The most prominent of its several different elements were the conservative nationalists, who, as part of their effort to bolster up the traditional social order, restored compulsory religious instruction in the public schools. The period ended with the ousting of Ramírez because he had severed relations between Argentina and the Axis under heavy pressure from Washington and it was feared he might even take the country into the war. The GOU was dissolved at this time in order to free its members from the oath they had taken to support Ramírez. During the second phase, March 1944 to October 1945, General Edelmiro Farrell was president but his administration featured the rise of Perón and his populistic nationalism, accompanied by a crescendo of attacks on him as pro-Nazi and a demagogue. The period ended with Perón's unexpected and dramatic victory over his enemies within and outside the regime on October 17, 1945. It still remained for him to be elected constitutional president of the republic in February 1946, but, though no one knew it, that was a foregone conclusion. The period of drift was over and so also, though not for long, was the constant bickering within the armed services.

One of the questions most often asked about the critical period from 1943 to 1945 is why the military corporately seized and held political power. Formerly an answer often given was that they acted under the influence of Germany on the Argentine army, mainly as it had been exercised through military channels for decades past. Recent studies by Robert Potash and others, however, have largely discredited this facile explanation. They have shown that, while German influence through training the Argentine army officers since the turn of the century was indeed great in military matters ranging from uniforms to organization and weapons, it was never decisive and seldom even substantial in the political sphere. As the discussion now stands, it seems reasonable to conclude that German influence helps to explain why the armed forces' intervention was corporate, but not why it took place. If an answer is to be sought outside Argentina, the inquiry should also take into account the examples set in the 1920s and 1930s by the military in Chile under Carlos Ibáñez; in Brazil under first the *tenentes* (lieutenants) and then Getúlio Vargas (whose labor policy Perón certainly imitated); and in Spain under, successively, Miguel Primo de Rivera and Francisco Franco.

In a persuasive article published in 1972, George Atkins and Larry Thompson concluded that the military intervention was due mainly to domestic conditions in Argentina, including the "weakness of countervailing political forces." This last factor was probably decisive, especially if we add to it the Argentine military's sense of mission to "save the country from the politicians" (as did the military in many countries at that time), together with technical training and a near-monopoly of weapons.

More immediately, the officers took over the government because the civilians were not making adequate provision for the armed forces or national security, and because the Concordancia was Anglophil, whereas by 1943 most of the officers expected, and many of them wanted, the Axis powers to win. They had already come close to turning Castillo out of office in 1941, and now, two years later, their grievances became fiercer as they could only watch while Argentina lost its generation-old military primacy in South America to Brazil, its hereditary rival. Brazil's armed forces were forging ahead because its president, Getúlio Vargas, was giving them more generous funds and far more enthusiastic support than Argentina's military were receiving, and a steel mill—the first, and at that time the only, such plant in South America—and because the United States was pouring into Brazil more than half of all its Lend Lease aid to Latin America, whereas it gave none at all to Argentina, which was not cooperating in the war effort.

Evidence of the great importance that the military attached to the situation in Brazil was soon forthcoming. In July 1943 President Ramírez justified a request to Germany for weapons on the ground that they were needed to defend Argentina against "much better armed Brazil." The next month his government pocketed its pride and, in a locally sensational note from Foreign Minister Storni to

Secretary of State Hull, asked for a share of Lend Lease aid and said
it was needed in order to restore the balance of power in South
America, which the United States had upset by giving such aid to
Brazil but not to Argentina. The request was rejected. (See chapter
XVII.)

The breaking point between the military and Castillo came when
he picked as his successor a man of his own stripe who, if the election
were held in September 1943 as scheduled, would be sure to win it
with customary aid of "patriotic fraud" that the government would
provide. Thus a regime would be perpetuated that many in the
armed forces had come to regard as insufferable. Originally planned
for a later date, the coup was precipitated by the news that President Castillo was about to dismiss Minister of War Ramírez, thus
endangering its success. So on June 4 they struck.

By some extraordinary trick of legerdemain, Juan Perón, already
47 years old at the time of the coup, proceeded to rise from comparative obscurity to unrivaled — though not uncontested — national
leadership within the short space of two years and a few months. It
was a phenomenal achievement, considering his rather ordinary
background and career up to this time. Born on October 8, 1895, in
Buenos Aires province, he came of a middle-class family and, like
thousands of other Argentines, was of Spanish-Italian parentage
(both parents born in Argentina) and grew up on adventure stories
about gauchos, including the mythical Martín Fierro. He followed
in the footsteps of an uncle and a cousin in becoming a professional
soldier. In March 1911 he entered the Colegio Militar as a cadet; he
was a captain by the time of Uriburu's coup, and just before it took
place he defected from that general's army faction to Justo's. In the
1930s he taught for several years in the Army War College; wrote
military books and was charged with plagiarism; served as military
attaché in Chile and was expelled for espionage; and in 1939 was
sent to Italy with several other officers to "perfect his studies." He
remained in war-torn Europe until 1941, visiting other countries as
well, among them Germany, France, and Spain, the last-named still
devastated from its civil war. After his return to Argentina he was
promoted to colonel and became a member of the GOU, most of
whose members were of the same rank. The formation of such
lodges or conspiratorial groups was routine in Argentina and this
one played a secondary role at the beginning of the 1943 coup. Altogether it was not a remarkable career so far.

There must have been much more to Perón than is even hinted at by his service record to this point. The missing element is suggested by a description of him which was written in July 1945 and has stood the test of time extraordinarily well. That the writer, *New York Times* correspondent Arnaldo Cortesi, himself of Italian background, was critical of Perón's politics only validates his tribute to the leader's "great personal charm." If "charisma" had been in vogue among journalists at that time, Cortesi would no doubt have used it in this description of the man.

"Colonel Perón," he wrote, "is a strong, vigorous man of medium height, dark-haired, clean-shaven, with an aquiline nose and ruddy complexion. He is close to 50, but considerably younger in appearance, and looks very smart and handsome in his uniform. He is endowed with great personal charm and speaks well and convincingly, both in private conversation and in public. His energy is unbounded and one can see at a glance that he is one of those men who know what they want and are ready to fight to obtain it. All these things fit him admirably for the task he has set himself of having himself elected the next President of Argentina."

While Perón was a man of action and pleasure, he also read widely — in Italy he studied social sciences and fascism as well as military matters — thought about what he had read, and tried to learn from experience. For future use he noted in Italy Mussolini's mistakes as well as his achievements, in Spain the horrors of a civil war brought on by a conflict between the armed forces and organized labor, and at home, a decade earlier, Uriburu's two greatest blunders. These were his efforts first to make a revolution without strong support, either military or popular, and second to impose on the nation a corporatist political system at odds with Argentine traditions, institutions, and the myth that Argentina was a democratic country.

How did Perón go about "the task he had set himself," as Cortesi put it? Friendship with a rising star gave him his first opportunity. General Edelmiro Farrell, the new minister of war, in June 1943 made him head of the ministry's secretariat (a key post). A few months later Farrell helped him get appointed secretary of labor, and after becoming in rapid succession acting president and president, appointed Perón minister of war (February 26) and vice-president (July 7). The only one of these posts that Perón surrendered during his ascent was the secretariat of the war ministry when he became minister of war. So, by early July 1944 he was wearing three hats and was clearly the strong man of the regime, second only to President Farrell in rank and not even to him in the day-to-day exercise of power. But as it turned out, in a regime dominated by a rank-conscious officer corps, Perón, though promoted to brigadier general early in 1944, still needed the support of Farrell, a senior general; and Farrell stood by him when the crisis came in October 1945.

One important source of Perón's popular appeal was his skillful blend of Argentina's various types of nationalism. During his rise to power, however, he had to rely mainly on his three government offices and the considerable measure of control these gave him over three sectors of society: workers, employers, and the armed forces. Through the secretariat of labor he reached both workers and employers and the respective organizations of each; and through the war ministry, the armed forces, which not only were the regime's indispensable support but also provided the sanctions for his measures in the other fields. Because he was a vice-president with broad ideas and easy access to the president, his activities extended beyond his own bailiwick into such fields as industry, education, and communications.

Here only a sampling of his measures in his own domain can be given. For the armed forces, the 1943 budget was doubled in 1944 and the officer corps increased by 30 percent, mainly in the higher ranks, so that there were many promotions. Modern arms from abroad were still not available, but in order to promote armaments manufactures and industries related to defense, such as steel and chemicals, the General Directorate of Military Factories, founded in 1941 and now headed by General Manuel Savio, was given increased funds and other support, including the authority to form mixed public-private companies for these purposes. Perón also, in 1944, made the air force a separate service and built it up rapidly.

For the workers, Perón from the start, in August 1943, promoted the formation of more unions (centered in the CGT), wage increases, fringe benefits, and dignity. By June 1944 his life-long identification with the labor movement had begun, and by the following June he was able to talk—with only the expected exaggeration—about his "army" of four million workers. Actually, the CGT had only half a million members at that time, but a better guide to the size of his army is the number of workers eligible for the social security program inaugurated in 1943, and that increased from its half million in 1943 to three times as many in 1946. Perón's strength lay largely in the newer unions, of which many were formed in the interior as well as in Buenos Aires with the aid of experienced labor leaders such as Cipriano Reyes and Luis Gay. The older unions were inclined to be reserved or even hostile towards Perón. The reasons ranged from a justifiable fear of losing their independence to the fact that about half of the CGT unions were controlled by Communists, most of whom opposed Perón from the start, while he denounced them as agents of a foreign power and purveyors of alien, anti-Argentine ideas. He also pressured the members into electing cooperative officers, but once that was done and the officers (and members) really cooperated, he allowed them and the other unions a large measure of autonomy. In his regimentation of labor he made more use of the carrot than the club, and the wartime and postwar boom in Argentina enabled him to provide labor with a steady diet of succulent carrots until the end of the decade.

Perón's relations with the two principal employers' organizations had turned sour by late 1944. With the Rural Society of Buenos Aires, pillar of the old order, they were never good and Perón's Statute of the Peón, issued in mid-1944 for the benefit of rural workers, made them even worse. At first, his relations with the Industrial Union were very pleasant. The Union's president, Luis Colombo, was one of Perón's first callers when he became secretary of labor and brought him assurances of its cooperation. Perón reciprocated in kind and apparently all went well between them at least until August 1944, for then, according to Dardo Cúneo, Perón assured Colombo that he too was a capitalist and that his "syndicalism" was designed to organize the workers "totally" under state direction in order to neutralize revolutionary currents that might imperil "our capitalist society." By January 1945, however, the Industrial Union had broken with Perón, partly over his social security measures but mainly over what its spokesmen denounced as his increasingly incendiary harangues inciting the workers to class warfare.

This was also one reason why many of Perón's fellow officers now turned against him. Another was his violation of the officers' code of conduct by living openly with his mistress, the stage and screen actress Eva Duarte, and even bringing her to the sacred precincts of the main army base, the Campo de Mayo, just outside Buenos Aires. Still another was the example of the vigorous anti-Peronist move-

ment launched in early 1945 by most of the leaders of the civilian
upper classes, with which many of the officers liked to be identified.
The movement gained momentum rapidly with the defeat of Germany, the end of the war in Europe, the moral support of U.S.
Ambassador Spruille Braden, and the lifting of the two-year-old
state of siege and its restrictions on freedom of speech and assembly
in preparation for early elections and a return to civilian rule.

In the commotion that followed, Perón's undeclared but obvious
bid for the presidency and use of the government apparatus to
harass his enemies precipitated another military coup, this time
against him. It came early in October and again, as in 1943, when
he had been one of Rawson's spearhead group, Eduardo Avalos was
a principal actor. Now a general and commander of the Campo de
Mayo army base — and also, before the crisis was over, minister of
war and acting minister of interior — Avalos was the most powerful
man in Argentina, and, while he tried to moderate the storm, he
was against Perón.

The crisis lasted eight days. On October 9, as a slightly tardy
birthday greeting to Perón, who had turned fifty the day before, he
was forced by his fellow officers to resign all three of his offices. The
next day he was permitted to deliver a farewell radio address to the
workers. Again it was incendiary, whereupon the exasperated leaders of the drive against Perón made the reluctant President Farrell
arrest him and one group tried to assassinate him. At this point Perón
seems to have lost his nerve, and the miracle of his comeback was
the work of his friends. Farrell sent him to Martín García Island for
his own protection on October 13. Now would have been the time
for his enemies to make the rout complete by filling the power
vacuum, but the civilian and military groups among them were too
distrustful of each other and divided among themselves to agree on
any course of action. While they procrastinated, the Peronists re-
grouped for a counteroffensive and time ran out.

On the morning of October 17 Farrell had the ailing Perón
brought back to the capital, nominally for hospitalization, but actually, as it turned out, just in time for "the most revolutionary mass
action" in the history of Argentina. This is Argentine historian
DiTella's characterization of the general strike and menacing mass
demonstration in Perón's behalf that same day. The demonstration
was arranged partly by Cipriano Reyes and other labor leaders, with
some assistance from Eva Duarte, but it was also a spontaneous out-

pouring of workers, among whom members of the metallurgical, slaughterhouse, and other newer unions predominated. All day long they kept pouring into the great Plaza de Mayo in front of the executive office building, the Casa Rosada. Many of them were roughly dressed (hence *descamisados,* "shirtless ones") and all of them demanded Perón's instant return.

Fearful of a riot or worse and unwilling to use military force (the police, friendly to Perón, were no help), his enemies came to terms with him. They agreed to let him go free and run for the presidency, and in return he resigned all his posts, and his commission as well. That night, with President Farrell standing by him as usual, Perón appeared on a balcony of the Casa Rosada overlooking the crowd of scores of thousands of devotees who jammed the plaza. After receiving a tremendous ovation, he made a short speech in which he claimed to be reviving "the almost forgotten civilian tradition of Argentina," reaffirmed his devotion to the "sweating, suffering mass of laborers who are building the greatness of this nation," and closed by asking the crowd to go quietly home and return to work after taking one day off for rest and the celebration of their triumph, as he himself was going to do. Shortly thereafter Perón and Eva Duarte, by now best known to all as Evita, were married, first in a civil ceremony and six weeks later in a church wedding.

October 17 has remained the greatest of Peronism's red-letter days, but there is no film, photograph, or any live recording of its climactic scene in the Plaza de Mayo — a fact which argues for its high degree of spontaneity. In his excellent book about the Argentine army and politics, Robert Potash's account of the October crisis reaches the afternoon of the seventeenth, but stops short of Perón's ovation and speech that evening. He does, however, make an interesting venture into psychohistory in explaining the failure of General Avalos, the most powerful man in Argentina at that time and an anti-Peronist, to use the military force at his disposal to "keep Perón from gaining complete control that day." His explanation is that Avalos was "psychologically disarmed" by guilt feelings arising from the fact that he was one of the two men responsible for a clash that had caused the only heavy loss of life during the coup of June 4, 1943.

That may be the reason why Avalos refrained from sending his troops into action against the Peronists. Yet the question arises whether his fellow officers would have acted differently. The Peronists on that day were a bellicose host, though unarmed and militarily unorganized, and the use of military force against them would have led to such a blood-letting as the Westernized, cultivated upper- and middle-class Argentines of the 1940s could not have borne to contemplate. The officer corps was drawn from those classes and the professional training of its members had not changed their values and standards in this respect. A century earlier the order to fire on the mob might have been given by the Sarmiento who fathered the dictum that the blood of gauchos was fit only to fertilize the soil. By the turn of the century, however, customs had changed—gone soft, old timers complained—and even defeated rebels were no longer put to death. As Carlos Pellegrini pointed out in 1906 in his last speech, nowadays one Argentine revolt after another was regularly followed by one amnesty after another. The great respect for human life implicit in these facts continued to prevail until past mid-century.

Yet violence is even more a part of the national tradition in Argentina than it is in the United States, and in the Argentina of the early Perón era it was strongest among those of his followers who were recent migrants from the interior, and had rarely been exposed to the debilitating influence of modern Western culture. In encounters like the one in Buenos Aires in October 1945, those who are willing to kill and be killed win out. That time it was Perón's followers who won; almost ten years later the tables were turned and, like Charles II after Worcester, he went traveling for his health.

The Perón Regime

After that October crisis Perón's victory in the presidential election the following February was almost an anticlimax. This was not because it was expected that he would win, for in fact his opponents were so sure he would lose that they feared another military coup to forestall the election. Rather, it was because the campaign was drab and uninteresting. His opponents included nearly all the leaders of the press and intellectual, social, and economic life as well as the established political parties. Again, however, they muffed their chance, partly because they were divided and partly because of over-confidence. They put together a paper coalition of the parties, but after much haggling they came up with a colorless candidate, (José Tamborini), and a negative program. As for Perón, he had no party of his own, for he claimed, as Yrigoyen had done, that he was the leader of a nationwide, patriotic movement, whereas political parties were by nature factional and selfish. His organized support in this election came from the new Laborista Party, which emulated the British Labor Party, and from a splinter group of dissident Radicals. He gained some support from the Catholic Church by opposing the legalization of divorce, which some of his opponents advocated, and by his adroit blending of the "cross and sword" brand of nationalism with other and vastly different brands.

The highlight of the campaign was provided near its close by the publication of the U.S. State Department's sensational "Blue Book on Argentina," nominally prepared only for the information of the other American governments. This contained what it claimed was "incontrovertible" evidence, drawn from captured German documents, that Perón and other high Argentine officials were "seriously compromised with the [Nazi-Fascist] enemy" during the war just ended. In view of the timing and the fact that Spruille Braden, well-known anti-Peronist ambassador to Argentina in mid-1945 and now assistant secretary of state, was responsible for it, the publication of the Blue Book was generally believed to have been intended to divert votes from Perón in this election. If so, it backfired, for, as a glaring example of foreign interference, it gave added plausibility to Perón's self-appointed role as defender of Argentine national independence against Yankee imperialism. Now, he said, the issue in this election was clearly "Braden or Perón." The effect of all this on the outcome is impossible to measure, but the probability is that it was more a help than a hindrance to Perón in the election. Yet it was not decisive since he would in all likelihood have won without it on domestic issues.

At any rate, he won by a comfortable margin in an election that his opponents described as free and honest until the votes were counted and they learned to their great surprise that they had lost it. Their first appraisal was probably right, for the election was supervised by the army, most of whose officers still were not enthusiastic about Perón. It was certainly the most representative in the nation's history in the sense of voter participation. He received 56 percent of the votes cast. They numbered 2,734,386, which was a far larger proportion of the total population (some 15 million in 1946) than in any previous election. Carrying all but four of the fourteen provinces, he received 304 votes in the Electoral College to Tamborini's

72, and his followers won two thirds of the seats in the Chamber of Deputies and three fourths of the Senate seats. If this was not a clear mandate, it was at least a very clean sweep.

Inaugurated on June 4, 1946, the third anniversary of the coup that had started his public career and rise to power, Perón ended the long period of drift by suppressing opposition to the nationalistic policies — some populistic, others bourgeois — that he had already begun to develop. He was re-elected for another six years in 1951 but ousted in September 1955, so that he headed the government for just over nine years. The first three were gladdened by a prosperity due mainly to the large reserve of gold and foreign currency built up during the war and to the boom market for Argentine food stuffs just after the war. During those years he consolidated his power at home in an almost unbroken series of successes and fared only a little less well abroad. Then, almost imperceptibly at first, clouds began to gather and his last five years were a time of troubles. The difficulties were various, including a military revolt in 1951, the beginning of a rift with the Roman Catholic Church, and the death in 1952 of Evita, who had become a great asset to him in his dealings with the masses. Worst of all, though, was the economic depression that reached bottom in 1952; because it hurt everyone, caused dissension within the regime, and lessened its prestige. Perón's abandonment of populistic nationalism in an effort to save the situation contributed to his overthrow by offending the populace and incensing nationalists.

During the sunshine years from 1946 to 1949, he consolidated his regime and his own position by measures, both positive and negative, that introduced sweeping changes into many aspects of Argentine life. He talked tirelessly about producing a "New Argentina" and came up with a new doctrine called Justicialism and a new policy called the Third Position. The latter signified, in domestic policy, a position between capitalism and Communism, and in foreign policy, a free hand to side with the United States or the Soviet Union or neither, as the national interest of Argentina might require. As the cardinal principles of Justicialism he replaced the old triad Liberty, Equality, Fraternity, with a new one: Economic Independence, Social Justice, Political Sovereignty.

Yet, viewed in historical perspective, change is no more striking a feature of Perón's nine years in power than continuity; which is another way of saying that his regime was essentially Argentine. He borrowed from several foreign systems, but copied wholesale from none. His borrowing from fascism was extensive enough to warrant calling his regime neofascist, provided the stress is on "neo." But it could just as well be called authoritarian, and most of the features that justify this characterization were of legitimate Argentine descent; if ultimately of foreign origin, at least naturalized. IAPI is one of several cases in point.

IAPI is the acronym for the name in Spanish of the Argentine Trade Promotion Institute. The creation of that institute by decree in 1946 was one of the first positive measures of Perón's administration. For the next five years it had a monopoly of the foreign marketing of agricultural and livestock products, and from the proceeds it purchased goods for its own use and for other government agencies. Its origin was in the economic control boards set up in Argentina under Justo in the 1930s. Another example is the CGT. This labor confederation had been in existence since 1930. What Perón did was to expand its membership many times over and have his own men put in charge after purging the old-line leaders who had been hostile to him in the crisis of October 1945 and even later.

Still another illustration comes from the political field. Unlike Mussolini, Hitler, and Franco, he retained his country's long-established political institutions and nomenclature. Though he changed his mind about political parties and had one, named for himself, definitely organized in 1949, with a women's branch headed by Evita, he never established a one-party system, but instead permitted opposition parties to function (not very freely, to be sure). And when he wanted to change the old Constitution of 1853 to permit his re-election, he had it duly amended by a properly elected convention. Some of the amendments were highly innovative, particularly those that guaranteed the rights of labor and asserted the social character of property and the state's ownership of the country's natural resources and its right to "intervene in the economy and monopolize any given activity." Yet the amended constitution still provided a place for "free private enterprise" and the profit system and made no change in relations between the state and the Roman Catholic Church and no substantial change in the framework of government. Continuity was apparent in many other ways as well, among them Perón's linking his regime to Argentina's past by encouraging the revival of old folk dances and music and the treatment of gaucho themes in books, plays and movies, and by a year-long celebration of 1950 as "The year of the Liberator San Martín."

In addition to nationalism, a tendency to autarky, and certain trappings, the principal mark of fascism in Perón's regime was a strong strain of corporatism, which was apparent in his use of interest groups. Chief among these were the Chamber of Commerce and the Rural Society, which quickly came to heel after the famous October 17, and the Industrial Union, which held out too long and was placed under a government interventor in July 1946, on the grounds that it had helped finance the anti-Peronist coalition in the February election and had failed to carry out government orders to make itself more representative of industry in all parts of Argentina. In December 1952 the same three groups, in response to government pressure, joined together in forming the General Economic Confederation (CGE), which was denounced (privately, until after Perón's fall) as totalitarian.

Despite the democratic structure and populist doctrine of his regime, Perón made ruthless use of his great power to extend and fortify it. When possible, he operated within the letter of the law, as just noted in the case of amending the constitution. This was possible most of the time, thanks to a subservient Congress and the ever-present threat of violence by Peronist gangs given their head by the Peronist police and the generally obedient if not always sympathetic armed forces. Other notable examples are his destruction of the too-independent Laborista Party, which had played a leading part in getting him elected, and his imprisonment for several years of his formerly indispensable ally, Cipriano Reyes; his purging of a refractory Supreme Court through the perfectly legal process of impeachment by his lackeys in Congress; his purge of the universities by a likewise legal combination of interventors and congressional action; his domination of radio stations through the licensing power and of the press by assorted means, such as rationing newsprint, harassment of troublesome journals by the government's sanitation inspectors, and, in the most celebrated case, that of the newspaper *La Prensa,* seizure through court action in a law suit brought by a Peronist labor union.

Perón reached the pinnacle of his prestige at home and abroad in the late 1940s with the aid of the beautiful Evita, now in all her glory as a national image of pin-up girl, fairy godmother to the poor, and an orator no true descamisado could resist. Her trip to Europe turned out badly, with snubs everywhere except in Franco's

Spain, but they did her no harm at home and him no harm anywhere. Perón himself was not always successful. Uruguay remained
his severest critic and a haven for his Argentine enemies (as it had
been a hundred years earlier for the enemies of Rosas) despite all he
could do. That did not include the use of force, but it did include
economic reprisals, such as making Uruguay and its delightful
beaches off bounds to Argentine vacationers — a short-lived measure
that seemed to hurt his own people as much as it did the Uruguayans. Even favorable circumstances did not result in gains. In backward Paraguay a general friendly to Perón shot his way to power,
and in Chile another friendly general made his way back to power
via the ballot box in 1952. This was Carlos Ibáñez; and as another
friend, Getúlio Vargas, had already done likewise in Brazil, Perón
in 1953 proposed to them seriously the formation of what was sometimes referred to as "a new ABC," but which he intended to develop
into an economic and military "union" of Argentina, Brazil, and
Chile. Both the other presidents responded favorably, but the plan
was opposed by the Brazilian foreign minister for being in conflict
with the Inter-American System, and any chance of success it might
still have had after that disappeared with the suicide of Vargas in
1954. All Perón got for his trouble, which included a trip to Santiago to develop the project with Ibáñez, was a bilateral trade agreement with Chile looking towards a customs union, and the agreement met with so much opposition there that it was never ratified.

Perón's experiment with sending labor attachés to spread the
Peronist gospel throughout Latin America turned out much better.
His greatest success, however, was won in his dealings with the
United States. In 1945 and 1946, while trying to unhorse him,
Washington refused to sit down at an Inter-American security conference table with Perón's government; but in 1947 it did just that in
negotiating the Rio Treaty of hemispheric defence. In the next few
years, instead of talking back when he denounced Yankee imperialism to his descamisados, the authorities in Washington stuck to their
task of making Argentina a better field for American enterprise. By
1953 they had reached the point of publicly praising him and sending President Eisenhower's brother Milton to call on him. Perón
responded in kind to the laudation, but not to the mission. It looked
as if Washington were doing the courting.

It would have been better for Perón if he had kept the feud with
the "Yankee imperialists" alive, but because of the depression into

which Argentina had fallen, he needed the help of the United States. Though deepened by a succession of droughts and an unfavorable change in the terms of trade, the depression was due in part to the government's misguided economic policy, which sacrificed the basic agricultural-pastoral economy to a program of rapid industrialization. Measured in billions of pesos at 1950 prices, the gross national product fell from a high of 62.3 in 1948 to 53.6 in 1950 and 49.3 in 1952. To make matters still worse, industrial development was concentrated on consumer goods, and this led to an increase in Argentina's dependence on imports and to the neglect of basic production industries. The neglect extended not only to the nationalists' sacred cow, the YPF, whose petroleum production fell further and further behind domestic consumption, but even to the armed forces' favorite project, the building at San Nicolás of a big steel mill such as Brazil and Chile already had. Although its construction by a mixed public-private company called SOMISA had been authorized in 1949, it was still in the drawing-board stage five years later.

The depression brought about a reversal of policy in favor of agriculture, which was embodied in the Second Five-Year Plan and which William Glade describes as marking a return from neo-orthodox towards orthodox economic policy on the government's part. Two other consequences of the depression were disastrous to the regime. The first was an aggravation of the Jacobin and antireligious strains in Peronism. The former was fostered by Eva Perón to the end. She devoted her brief farewell speech, on May Day 1952, to inciting her "dear descamisados, the real Argentina," against the "traitorous and corrupt oligarchy and their foreign masters" and the effect remained strong after her death from cancer in July 1952. These strains found expression in, for example, the sacking of the upper-class Jockey Club in April 1953 and in efforts to legalize divorce and prostitution, to separate church and state, and to arm the workers as a counterpoise to the military. Symptoms of this kind combined with a reactivated totalitarian trend to alienate many Roman Catholics and a large part of the officer corps from the regime.

The second disastrous consequence of the depression was Perón's reversal of policy in two adjoining fields. This he accomplished by cultivating friendly relations with the United States, formerly his favorite whipping boy, and by welcoming foreign enterprise and capital investments into Argentina. In short, he was now seeking support from the capitalist system, whose "remaining redoubts" in Argentina, he had assured Congress as recently as May 1952, "will be the objects of our implacable destruction." Both reversals could be defended on the ground that they were aimed at obtaining aid to speed Argentina's economic recovery and development, but they were so abrupt and fundamental that, together with the simultaneous stoppage of labor coddling, they shook the regime's hold on its own faithful. Probably the most offensive of all his measures was the signing of a contract early in 1955 that gave a subsidiary of Standard Oil of California exclusive rights in a large area of Argentina. This was widely regarded as a sell-out to Yankee imperialists at the expense of Argentina's own petroleum agency, YPF, and Perón was unable to induce his own party to support it.

In June 1955 the sharpening conflict with the Catholic Church precipitated an uprising that failed, but three months later another, called the Liberating Revolution, which was better planned on a larger scale, succeeded in three days. Starting at Córdoba on September 15 under the leadership of General Eduardo Lonardi, a conservative Catholic, armed forces in the interior isolated loyal troops in the Buenos Aires area. At the same time, the battle fleet, commanded by Admiral Isaac Rojas, a ferocious anti-Peronist, steamed around from its base at Bahía Blanca to Buenos Aires. Anchored in the river within point blank range of the Casa Rosada and other principal government and business buildings in the heart of the capital, it threatened to blow the city to bits. Thereupon, on September 18, Perón surrendered and went into exile, first in Paraguay, later in Panama (where he met the dancer who was to become his third wife), Venezuela, the Dominican Republic, and finally Spain, the first and the last three then ruled by presumably sympathetic dictators.

It was by no means a bloodless revolution. Remarkably enough, however, hardly a blow was struck in Perón's defense in Greater Buenos Aires, although that was his citadel. It contained the country's largest concentration of troops, labor unions, and Peronist Party members, all of whom were nominally loyal to him. Apparently, what happened was that he again lost his nerve, the leaders of the military in the area were relieved that he did, and the descamisados, who in August had threatened to stage "another October 17," had no stomach for it when their challenge was met in September. To be sure, they had again asked to be armed and again been

denied arms; but lack of arms had not deterred them ten years earlier. The most probable explanation of the difference is that on this
second occasion their enthusiasm for Perón had been dampened by
the conservative turn of his policy since 1953; but its revival was not
long delayed.

The Regime in Perspective

Reconsidered two decades after its abrupt termination, Perón's
regime looks neither so good nor so bad as it seemed at the time to
most observers both at home and abroad. The oft-repeated charge
that he wrecked the Argentine economy has been defused by closer
study of the data and by the failure of subsequent governments to
cope with the country's economic problems much more successfully
than he did. Also, there is at least palliation in the fact that the
economies of Chile and Uruguay, under governments that differed
widely from Perón's, functioned little if any better than Argentina's
during this period. Again, for better or for worse, Perón did not
carry out his heralded revolution to create a "New Argentina."
Indeed, in a recent analysis, Kalman Silvert, one of the most sophisticated students of the phenomenon, describes Peronism as an "essentially rightist . . . reaction to certain critical social issues" in a
sorely beset Argentina. Certainly, Perón in 1955 left the Argentine
economy substantially the same in structure as he had found it; that
is, a capitalist economy strongly linked to foreign countries by their
investments and trade and considerably modified by state intervention, which he increased but did not initiate.

Similarly, Perón stimulated industrialization, but that process,
too, was well begun before he came to power and in fact it had been
more rapid in the decade before 1946 than it was during Perón's
nine years. The agricultural-pastoral sector continued to be dominated by great estates. It also remained the basis of the national
economy, as he recognized in his return to an orthodox development
policy in his Second Five-Year Plan. His few expropriations of great
estates were made for political reasons and not as part of an agrarian reform, which he never undertook. So the economic and social
basis of the already politically weak oligarchy remained firm.

The middle class continued to grow along with urbanization and
to lack unity and coherence, as it had done before Perón's advent.
The upper middle class, called *burguesía* in recognition of its differ-

ence from the middle and lower middle class, was acquiring these qualities. Its industrialist members of foreign extraction were taking a more active part in public affairs than formerly. The workers were doing likewise, and it was Perón's principal achievement that he gave them a higher standard of living and a sense of dignity and made them — especially the labor unions — a major plitical force, as they have been ever since. As Gino Germani has pointed out, however, it was a misfortune for Argentina that the induction of the masses into political life took place in the fundamentally antidemocratic atmosphere of Perón's regime.

Perón did not convert Argentina into a citadel of fascism, as was charged at the time. His political performance was very mixed, for as he himself put it, "I have a right hand and a left hand, and I use them both," but his principal legacy was a left-wing, populistic, and primarily Yankeephobe nationalism that stirred up strife both within the country and in its foreign relations and that, ironically, rose to haunt him when he regained the presidency in 1973. Although when he first voiced it, this brand of nationalism aroused a favorable response in some circles in Chile and Uruguay that was to bear fruit later, its chief effect was to alienate the ruling groups in both countries. The other chief items in his political legacy were two shibboleths: regarding domestic affairs, Justicialism, and in foreign policy, the Third Position. The latter, which gained common currency in Latin America, is not to be confused with Third World, of which no Southern Cone country, least of all Argentina, is or was then a part, their left wingers' assertions to the contrary notwithstanding.

Liberalism and Stagnation

The revival of Peronism, which was to be the central fact of Argentine public life for the next twenty years, was stimulated by the character of the government set up after the victory of the Liberating Revolution. Despite its name, what that revolution gave the Argentine people was another military dictatorship and again, as after the coup of 1943, the dictatorship lasted three years. At first it was headed by General Lonardi. If his brief administration's policy of national reconciliation had been adhered to, Peronism might never have recovered. "Neither victors nor vanquished" was the motto now, as after the fall of Rosas, and Lonardi not only preached but practiced it. This did not, however, prevent him from denouncing the Perón regime time and again. In his pronunciamento at the beginning of the revolt he had charged that it "endangers the future of the Republic through the surrender of its sources of wealth." A week later, after victory, he made the allusion to Perón's contract with the Standard Oil of California subsidiary explicit, let the uncompleted contract lapse, and turned the job envisaged in it over to Argentina's own YPF, with the assurance that his government would "attach special importance to the exploitation of petroleum." In a sensational radio broadcast on October 26 he charged that the Perón regime's "ten years of irresponsibility and corruption" had created the "gravest problem before us, namely, the economic situation," which he described as "disastrous." If anyone, he continued, had set out deliberately to wreck "our economy" and annihilate its "dynamic forces," he could not have accomplished his purpose more completely than Perón had done.

These charges were based on a report prepared by a group of Argentine economists headed by a special adviser, Raúl Prebisch, former manager of Argentina's Central Bank. An anti-Peronist, Prebisch had gone into exile and, since 1948, had been chairman of the United Nations Economic Commission for Latin America (ECLA). Through ECLA he had given wide currency to economic doctrines anathema to the United States: opposing free enterprise, counselling large-scale state intervention in the economy, and favoring the "buy from those who buy from us" rule that had hurt the United States and helped Great Britain in trade with the Plata area in the 1930s. Prebisch was therefore cordially disliked in Washington. According to a report by Simon Hanson dated October 8, 1955, the State Department cited his appointment as Lonardi's special economic adviser as proof that the United States had been right to stand by Perón to the end. The apprehensions about Prebisch proved to be hardly justified on this occasion. Whether in view of the special circumstances in Argentina or under the influence of other members of the group, he closed the report with recommendations favorable to foreign private enterprise and capital investment in Argentina.

Despite Lonardi's verbal anti-Peronism, many of his fellow military officers and some civilian leaders thought him too soft on Peronists, especially in the CGT, besides being much under the influence of conservative Catholics and Nazi-fascist sympathizers. Their view prevailed. On November 13 he was forced out and replaced by a five-man military junta headed by General Pedro Aramburu as acting president. Aramburu remained at the helm until May 1, 1958, when constitutional government was restored.

Aramburu had a civilian advisory board made up of representatives of all the principal political parties except the Peronists and the Communists. The decisions, however, were made by him in consultation with the other members of the junta, who were Admiral Rojas, as acting vice-president, and the three heads of the armed services. It was as if the United States were ruled from the Pentagon by the chairman of the joint chiefs of staff. Civilians had even less voice in the government now than they had had in the administration of General Ramírez just after the coup of 1943. Aramburu's administration remained wholly military to the end. Its military character was important for the future of Argentina, for this was the beginning of a long period in which most of the officers seemed to be trying to do penance for having produced and supported Perón by destroying Peronism. Aramburu went about that task by purging the armed forces and labor organizations, intervening in the CGT, disqualifying Peronist labor leaders for both union office and public office, abolishing the men's and women's Peronist parties, and prohibiting the formation of any replacement for them.

There was no general roll-back of the workers' gains and in fact Aramburu promised to protect them, but they were whittled down in one way or another, as, for instance, by the initiation of an austerity program early in 1956 and by the cancellation in April of all the Peronist amendments to the constitution, including the article that stipulated the rights of the worker. As Samuel Baily has shown, although real wages fluctuated with the rest of the economy at this time, there was a decline in the workers' share of the GNP from 55.5 in 1955 to 52.1 in 1957, and the slight rise to 53.1 in 1958 (Aramburu's last year) was followed by a sharp drop to 45.8 in 1959.*

---

*The general impression of these statistics is confirmed by a subsequent ECLA analysis of the distribution of family income in Argentina in 1953, 1959, and 1961. However, there was a recovery, though slight, from 1959 to 1961 in the shares of Lowest, Middle, and Upper Middle groups, comprising 90 percent of the total, and the greatest disparity was in the top 5 percent group, which in 1961 received an income more than five times the average of the Upper Middle 20 percent (71 to 90), nearly six times the national average, and seventeen times the average of the poorest group (Lowest 20). ECLA also points out that even this poorest Argentine group had a relatively high average income in comparison with the rest of Latin America.

Peronists, who made up 70 percent of the organized labor force, soon came to describe Aramburu's administration as *la revancha,* the oligarchy's revenge for a decade of Peronist domination. Out of this situation came a revolt in June 1956, led by two former generals, both purged as Peronists, who made a bid for labor support. Although they got some, the revolt was quickly and ruthlessly suppressed by Vice-President Rojas, who took charge during President Aramburu's absence on a visit to the interior. Rojas shocked anti-Peronists as well as Peronists by having nearly thirty of the rebels, including one army general, summarily executed, contrary to the country's long-unbroken custom of sparing the lives of prisoners. This blood-letting was the alleged reason for the assassination, years later, of General Aramburu, who apparently was not responsible for it. It certainly marked another stage in the growing resort to violence in Argentina, which roughly coincided with sinister developments of the same kind in Chile and Uruguay.

Having lost their power (or their illusion of power) with Perón's fall, and now seeing their social conquests imperiled, the workers naturally sensed a causal relationship and felt they must look to the return of Perón, or perhaps only to the return of Peronism, for their salvation. By the end of Aramburu's administration, this way of looking at things was as firmly established among the workers as was the anti-Peronist focus among the great bulk of the officer corps. Even after Lonardi's ouster and the ensuing purge of Peronists, however, the officers constantly disagreed among themselves, sometimes to the point of armed conflict, over how to deal with the Peronist problem, principally over whether to follow a hard line or a soft one.

The divisions among the Peronists were equally deep and much more numerous. Some were between those who were for Peronism with Perón and those who wanted it without him; between union and nonunion members; between right-wing gradualists and left-wing revolutionaries; between the young Peronists and their elders; and, in addition, fragmentation along provincial, local, and personal lines. Yet there was a basic dichotomy between Peronists and armed forces that kept Argentina in a ferment for nearly twenty years after Perón's overthrow. It did not disappear completely even when, in 1973, the armed forces finally gave in and permitted him to return to Argentina and become president again. This dichotomy had no counterpart in either of the other two Southern Cone countries until, just as the schism was being healed in Argentina, one like it began to open up in Chile. Until then, the nearest approach to a match for it anywhere in the Western hemisphere had been the long feud between Apristas and armed forces in Peru.

XI The Perón Era:
Fragmentation and Finale

The economic policy followed by General Aramburu provides the principal link between his administration and that of his civilian successor in the presidency, Arturo Frondizi. It may help explain why, after pursuing a policy of rigorous "de-Peronization" for nearly three years, Aramburu overrode a strong movement among his fellow officers in favor of preventing the inauguration of Frondizi, who had won the election of 1958 through a deal with Perón. It may even help explain why they gave in without a fight. At any rate, the economic policy that Frondizi adopted soon after taking office was different from the one he had given the public reason to expect and had much in common with the one that Aramburu had followed from January 1956 to the end of his administration more than two years later. Under it government controls on industry and agriculture were removed, the Central Bank denationalized, foreign investors welcomed, and the austerity program adopted. In addition, Argentina joined the World Bank and the International Monetary Fund.

In some respects Aramburu's policy resembled not only the one Frondizi was to adopt a little later, but also the one that Perón had followed after 1952 in his return from neo-orthodoxy and corporatism towards orthodoxy and free enterprise. It is rather remarkable that men who were as different as Perón, Aramburu, and Frondizi, and who represented such different constituencies and aspirations, ended up with economic policies which, though never identical, were much alike in important respects. It is an attractive hypothesis that they were spurred by the contrast between the painful circumstances prevailing in Argentina in the 1950s, and the remarkable economic recovery that was taking place simultaneously in war-torn Europe with aid provided by the United States under a policy of free enterprise and international cooperation.

Stabilization and Violence under Frondizi

In preparation for the restoration of constitutional government, a national election was held in February 1958. Since the men's and women's Peronist parties had been outlawed, the two principal parties in this election were the products of a split during the preceding year in the ever-schismatic Radical Party: the left-wing Intransigent Radicals (UCRI), led by Frondizi, and the People's Radicals (UCRP), led by Ricardo Balbín.* Frondizi and his Intransigents had been bidding for the Peronists' support ever since 1955, so that it was no surprise when he won their votes through an unacknowledged but well-known deal with Perón, still in exile but still their leader. Since neither Radical party could muster more than about 25 percent of the total vote, the Peronists, who turned out to attract about 30 percent of it, held the balance of power. With their support and that of the Communists, who polled some 70,000 votes in this election, Frondizi received nearly two thirds of the popular vote and an even larger proportion of the electoral vote. His party gained control of both houses of Congress by similar margins.

Frondizi had won a smashing victory, but it was his last. In the next election, 1960 (for members of Congress), his party was routed, and in 1962 he was ousted by the military to as general applause as had greeted the overthrow of Yrigoyen in 1930 and of Castillo in 1943. Among the sources of his troubles the chief one seems to have been the failure of his effort to carry water on both shoulders. The failure was most obvious in the field of economic policy, and the nature of the choices before him here is illustrated by the emergence in June 1958, a little more than a month after his inauguration, of two rival industrial organizations, both of which were strong and which represented sharply conflicting economic and political ideas. One was the General Economic Confederation (CGE), founded by Perón in 1952, dissolved by Aramburu in December 1955, and now revived by Frondizi. It was Peronist, nationalist, and allegedly totalitarian; it represented the medium-sized and small industrial firms and the interior of the country and aimed at modernization, particularly through economic development, and national economic independence. Its rival, ACIEL, was a coalition, initiated in 1956 and given definitive form in June 1958, of three associations representing the free enterprise system: the Rural Society, the Industrial Union, and the Stock Exchange, which were made up of the big landowners, industrial firms, and financial-commercial firms, mainly of Buenos Aires province. According to the unsympathetic Dardo Cúneo, ACIEL embodied what was coming to be called "gorilla-ism," that is, intolerance and persecution of the popular elements represented, after its fashion, by Peronism. With little exaggeration he further

---

*UCRI stands for Unión Cívica Radical Intransigente, and UCRP for Unión Cívica Radical del Pueblo. In 1951 Balbín and Frondizi had been the candidates of a united Radical Party for president and vice-president, respectively.

describes it as a pillar of anachronistic forces that tied Argentina to its traditional export-import economy, kept it dependent on countries that were economically more advanced, and stunted its own economic development.

Six months before Frondizi came forth with his solution of this policy problem, he had assured it of a hot reception by adopting a provocative measure in a politically sensitive field: in July he had initiated a series of contracts for the opening up of Argentine oil fields by American and other foreign firms. Despite his plausible defence of these contracts, they created a highly unfavorable atmosphere for his solution of the policy problem by his Stabilization Agreement of December 1958 with the International Monetary Fund. The agreement was designed to please both sides in the controversy; the partisans of ACIEL by the Stabilization Plan itself, and those on the CGE side by a companion program of economic development and modernization.

The Stabilization Plan aimed first of all at controlling inflation. To this end it set limits on credits to the private sector, raised the rediscount rate, eliminated price controls, and restricted wage increases to productivity. It was in effect an austerity plan, especially for small industrialists and industrial workers. The development program, which was very ambitious, was not embodied in a single document. Rather, it was a strategy devised by Frondizi and his special adviser, self-made millionaire entrepreneur Rogelio Frigerio, and expressed in numerous measures designed to increase production of petroleum, natural gas, coal, iron ore, and steel. The plan also sought to create a national network of highways and airports, to develop sources of electric energy, and to stimulate the production by private industry of motor vehicles, machinery, and several other goods.

The results were quite disappointing. Despite a resolute enforcement of austerity at the outset — which may have been responsible for the 20 percent reduction of real wages in industry during 1959 — inflation continued at a high rate and the cost of living increased three-fold from 1958 to 1961. On a scale of 1966 = 100, it climbed from 36.8 in 1958 to 113.7 in 1961. In 1960 and 1961 there was an increase in industrial production, especially of petroleum, but by the end of the latter year a decline had set in and by early 1962, before Frondizi's overthrow late in March, the economy was well into a recession and a balance-of-payments crisis. Argentina was once more back in its familiar stop-and-go pattern.

This failure has been widely attributed to defects in the Stabilization Plan, but there is reason to doubt whether they provide a sufficient explanation of it. For one thing, in July 1959, only seven months after the adoption of Argentina's Stabilization Agreement, Spain too entered into an agreement of the same kind with the International Monetary Fund. Both agreements were made with encouragement (not to say prodding) from the United States government and the assurance of financial support from U.S. commercial banks and other foreign sources. Yet, in Spain, the sequel was a decade of extraordinarily rapid economic expansion and rising living standards for most Spaniards, combined with relative stability in prices, currency, and foreign exchange. After making generous allowance for the different circumstances in the two countries, one must conclude that the defects of the Stabilization Plan alone can hardly account for the widely different sequel to its conclusion in Argentina.

Perhaps the difference was due in part to the great disparity between their political systems. In both countries austerity and other features aroused widespread opposition, but in Spain this was suppressed quite handily by the Franco dictatorship, whereas in democratic Argentina it contributed not only to the failure of the program by crippling Frondizi's congressional support and weakening his own prestige and authority, but also to his ultimate overthrow. On economic grounds the stabilization plan is exonerated in a careful study by Clarence Zuvekas, Jr. He concludes that the failure of Frondizi's economic policy was due rather to the shortcomings of the accompanying economic development plan, particularly to its underestimate of the program's foreign exchange cost, its "severe redistribution of income in favor of non-wage earners," and faulty implementation of agricultural policies.

Politically, Frondizi's economic policy had disastrous consequences. It amounted to a reversal of the nationalistic platform on which he had campaigned and won in 1958 by gaining the Peronists' support. After the adoption of the stabilization plan, he never had their support again; they made up the bulk of the industrial labor force, which was the principal sufferer from the plan's austerity. From nearly two thirds of the total vote in 1958, Frondizi's party's share plummeted to 25 percent two years later, and he remained a minority president by about the same wide margin to the end, increasingly harassed by the devotees of Fidel Castro and the anti-Castro military alike.

Despite all this, Frondizi's administration had its bright side. He was partially successful in his efforts to stimulate provincial growth (as Perón had done) and in other parts of his development program. His most striking success was in increasing petroleum production, thanks to his much criticized contracts with foreign oil companies. He let Argentina become an early "showcase" for the Alliance for Progress while warmly supporting the economic integration of Latin America. Under his leadership Argentina in 1960 joined with six other Latin American states, among them Chile and Uruguay, in founding the Latin American Free Trade Association (LAFTA) at a conference in Montevideo. The new organization was set up partly as a protection against possible injury from the recently formed European Common Market and its concessions to France's former colonies in Africa. In the promotion of this and other Argentine interests he traveled tirelessly—to the United States, Europe, India —and was easily the most peripatetic president in the history of his country.

Some of his best-intentioned actions, however, added to the number of his enemies. One example is his strong support of an act of Congress that gave degrees granted by the Catholic University of Buenos Aires equal validity with those granted by the public universities. This was done in the name of freedom of instruction (*enseñanza libre*), but it shocked many liberals, including members of his own party, who had been brought up in the tradition of secular education. Troubles multiplied for his administration as the capital city suffered a campaign of violence reminiscent of the anarchist terrorism of the early years of the century, only more sustained and more difficult to deal with. Perón is said to have promoted it after withdrawing his brief and unavowed support of Frondizi. Unlike later such campaigns in Argentina, this one was not characterized by assassination—when deaths resulted from bombing, they seemed incidental—nor by kidnapping or theft. Rather, it gave the impression of being aimed at spreading sabotage and confusion to discredit the government. If so, it succeeded, thereby increasing Frondizi's dependence on the armed forces, which were themselves the source of much of the violence through several attempted coups.

Unable to cope with the campaign of violence through the ordinary channels of police and civil courts, Frondizi called on the armed forces for help and joined with Congress in empowering them, through military courts, to deal summarily with crimes endangering national security — a conveniently flexible term. This further weakened his support among civilians without bolstering it up among the military. Many of the officers had never forgiven him for his deal with the Peronists in 1958, and in 1961 he compounded the offence by turning all the CGT unions back over to the workers (most of whom, it will be recalled, were Peronists) for the first time since Aramburu intervened and purged them in 1956. Henceforth the Peronists controlled the CGT organization and about two thirds of the component unions, which numbered nearly one hundred.*

The military and Frondizi nearly reached the breaking point in January 1962 over his opposition to the expulsion of Fidel Castro's government from the Organization of American States at the Punta del Este conference. He averted the break momentarily by severing Argentina's diplomatic relations with Cuba, but it came only six weeks later over a domestic issue, which, as might have been expected, was Peronism. In an election held in March he permitted the Peronist† parties to participate as parties for the first time since 1955. In doing so, he overrode the objections of the military and many civilians, partly because he wanted to reintegrate the Peronists into the body politic and partly because some minor victories of his own Intransigent Radical Party in recent local elections had given him the strange notion that it could win this national election. Instead, the Peronists won a smashing victory. They polled only 35 percent of the total vote, but the other 65 percent was so divided among Intransigent Radicals, People's Radicals, and several minor parties that they came in far ahead of the second-place Intransigents, who led the other Radical party by a nose. If the two Radical parties had stayed together, their combined vote would have been more than 50 percent of the total, and that would have given them a landslide victory over the Peronists. As it was, the latter gained control of ten provinces, including Buenos Aires province, by far the largest of all, and a substantial representation in both houses of Congress.

This was more than the military could bear. They forced Frondizi first to intervene against the Peronists in the ten provinces they had

---

*The rest, called "independents," were the older unions (railroad, garment, commercial, bank workers, printers, government). Politically, about half of them were Communist, the rest Socialist and Radical.

†Not under that name, since the use of Perón's name in any form by a political party was still prohibited by law. Many called themselves Justicialist.

won, and shortly thereafter to resign (March 30). No force rallied to his defense. Imprisoned on Martín García Island, as Yrigoyen and Perón had been, after some months he was moved further away from his political supporters in Buenos Aires to the Andean lake country resort of San Carlos de Bariloche. There he was kept until his release shortly after the next election, which took place in July 1963.

The leaders of the armed forces need not have let the possibility of Frondizi's making a political recovery worry them. Though he tried hard, he never came anywhere near bringing it off, as Perón was to do and as Carlos Ibáñez of Chile and Getúlio Vargas of Brazil had already done. Frondizi had acquired a reputation for duplicity and made too many enemies. His populist nationalism was too much like Perón's, while his personal magnetism was far less; and his tardy shift to bourgeois nationalism was no more convincing than it was successful. Yet in making that shift he did offer his countrymen a plan for recovery that might have succeeded, as did Franco Spain's similar plan, if he had been equipped with the Spanish dictator's power. And he was surely wise in insisting that Argentina's basic social and political problems could not be solved without restoring the massive Peronist minority to first-class citizenship.

A New Argentina

Unfortunately for that country, the members of the officer corps remained captives of an unreasoning anti-Peronist obsession. This was mainly responsible for the subjection of its people to military rule in all but three of the eleven years between Arturo Frondizi's fall from power and Juan Perón's return to it. Yet during those years the officers disagreed so violently among themselves about how to deal with Peronism and other problems that street fighting broke out among them more than once and several military coups against military regimes were attempted, two of them successful. Civilians, including the organized workers, were similarly divided. Political apathy became widespread although social tensions remained high, extremists on the right and the left made acts of violence routine, and the economy continued its frustrating stop-and-go course. All of this contributed to the "brain drain" which by the 1960s was seen as a serious national problem. All told, the experiences of the period generated a feeling of being caught in a blind alley and at last increased from a one-third plurality in 1962 to a two-thirds majority in 1973 the number of Argentine voters who wanted to give Peronism another try.

For all the impression of history going around in circles during Perón's long exile, there was in fact so much change that the Argentina to which the old man returned in 1973 was new to him, though it was far from being the "New Argentina" he had promised his people a quarter-century earlier.

The eleven-year interval between Frondizi's fall and Perón's return began with eighteen months of thinly disguised military dictatorship during which there was fighting between the two main officer groups, but with few casualties, mostly civilian. The moderate group won out and held a national election in July 1963. The new government, which took office on October 12, was headed by President Arturo Illia, a kindly small-town physician who had long been a wheel-horse of the People's Radical Party. The auguries were not good. Illia had won only 26 percent of the popular vote in the election and gained a majority in the Electoral College only through the temporary support of other parties. His own party was also in the minority in the Chamber of Deputies, whose approximately 200 members were divided among 24 parties through the working of the proportional representation system adopted for this election. His administration never recovered from its bad start. He struck out boldly enough by cancelling Frondizi's contracts with foreign oil companies, but that appeal to nationalism was better politics than economics. Then he made two political errors that offended the military. One was in letting the Peronists campaign again in 1965, this time under the label "Popular Union." They received only 31 percent of the total vote, but the total was divided among a score of parties and again the Peronists' share was the largest by a wide margin. Illia's other serious blunder was in making military appointments that were contrary to custom and otherwise unacceptable to the officers. One of the most important men in the hierarchy, Army Commander General Juan Carlos Onganía, resigned in protest.

On broader grounds than these, a junta of the three service chiefs led a coup that evicted Illia in June 1966 and established another military dictatorship. Before striking, however, they proved their modernity by taking a poll among their fellow officers on the proposition that "What we need is a strong man to lead us" and getting an overwhelmingly affirmative response. In a pronunciamento called

"Act of the Argentine Revolution," they made a detailed statement of their grounds for the coup. These were, in essence, that the country was going to pieces economically, socially, and politically under Illia, and that the fault lay not only in him but in the existing political and economic system, which was divisive, rigid, and anachronistic. Hence, the Act concluded, the object of the revolution was to transform and modernize that system. In effect, this was a repetition of Perón's 20-year-old promise to create a "New Argentina," but the authors of this document envisaged a very different kind of Argentina and one purged of Peronism.

A beginning of the transformation was made by suspending the constitution, dissolving Congress and the political parties, and vesting supreme authority in the junta, which governed by decree. Once that had been done, however, the military leaders were unable to agree on what to do next, the main division being between those who were relatively liberal and the hard-line nationalists. Consequently, during the seven years that this dictatorship lasted, each of the three generals who successively headed it gave it a different focus.

The first of the three was General Onganía (1966-1970). He tried to devise a policy combining economic liberalism and political nationalism, but tilted toward the latter. One typical measure was his much needed attack on featherbedding in the state-owned institutions, which had multiplied under Perón, especially in the nationalized railroads; in three years Onganía cut the number of railroad employees from 240,000 to 153,000. Typical also were his forcible interventions in the universities and his tentative proposal, reminiscent of Uriburu's in 1930 and soon abandoned, of a corporatist replacement for the political parties. In what José Luis de Imaz describes as a neo-Bismarckian policy, Onganía gave high priority to economic growth and a paternalistic social policy, and founded a National Development Council (CONADE), which soon became a model of its kind.

The economy performed better than for years past, but labor troubles multiplied and contributed to a new wave of violence that Onganía was unable to control. It reached a climax in two shocking events of mid-1969: the bloody *"Cordobazo,"* a riot in the now heavily industrialized city of Córdoba in which some fifteen people were killed, and the kidnapping and subsequent murder of General Pedro Aramburu. This was too much for Onganía's fellow service chiefs, who were already resentful of what they regarded as his high-handed methods. One of them, Army Commander Alejandro Lanusse, also objected strongly to Onganía's refusal even to discuss the holding of elections.

Accordingly, with Lanusse in the lead, the service chiefs eased Onganía out in June 1970 on the heels of Aramburu's kidnapping. As his successor they chose General Marcelo Levingston, probably in the expectation that he would do as he was told because he was an intelligence officer who had no troops under his command and no personal following among the officers who did. For a few months all went well, but in October of the same year Levingston appointed a cabinet that was wholly nationalist, both economically and politically. His new minister of the economy, Aldo Ferrer, a well-known structural economist, proposed a plan which was biased in favor of the interior provinces (as the nationalist-populist line in Argentina had generally been) and which called for an increase in the state's already deep penetration of the Argentine economy at the expense of private enterprise, domestic as well as foreign. Opposition to the Ferrer-Levingston economic policy took shape at once and was bolstered by such incidents as a beef shortage and a doubling of its price in two months, the adoption of an easy-money policy that intensified what was already being called "stagflation," and the bias in favor of labor that the government was showing in a period of multiplying strikes and mounting labor violence. The opposition to Levingston on political grounds was even stronger, for he coolly announced that there would be no elections for at least another four or five years, and his associates feared that he was trying to establish himself as a popular dictator, a democratic Caesar. This brought on a ten-hour confrontation with Lanusse on March 23, 1971, which ended with Levingston's resignation.

The Joint Chiefs of Staff then designated General Lanusse head of the nation, with the mission of completing "the Argentine Revolution," begun in 1966. To that end he sought a "Great National Accord," legalized political parties again, announced elections to be held in March 1973, and even moved in various ways towards a reconciliation with the Peronists. Surely none of these ways was more singular than his returning the hitherto secretly guarded remains of Eva Perón to Juan Perón, long since remarried.

Terrorism and Perón's Return

The armed forces' bid for a national accord on these terms was a great concession on their part. Probably the chief reason why they made it was that no one up to this point had been able to check the mounting wave of organized terrorism, which had been brought home to them by the kidnapping and murder of General Aramburu, one of the most prestigious officers in the nation's armed services. That was the work of the Montoneros, a left-wing Peronist group, as their Robespierre, Mario Firmenich, admitted, or rather boasted, in an article published in September 1974. It was a cold-blooded murder, committed after a long "trial" of Aramburu by his captors, who sat as a "court" and condemned him to death because he was too intelligent and hence dangerous to their cause. They were uncompromising populist-nationalists, whereas he advocated (in 1969) the policy of "national accord" later adopted by the junta. They feared he might be successful—so he had to die.

There were two other principal terrorist groups, and it was some consolation to ordinary citizens that each of the three was as hostile to the other two as it was different from them. The Argentine Anti-Communist Alliance (AAA) was a right-wing Peronist organization. The victims of the political assassinations with which it was credited included Montoneros, other left-wing Peronists, and members of the third of these terrorist organizations, the ERP (People's Revolutionary Army). ERP, a Communist group, was originally part of an "army of liberation" established in Bolivia by Argentine-born Che Guevara. From the point of view of the present study, ERP is particularly interesting not only because Perón is said to have used it before his return to Argentina, after which it turned against him, but also because it had ties with similar groups in the other Southern Cone countries: with the Tupamaros in Uruguay and the MIR (Movement of the Revolutionary Left) in Chile, as well as with the original Bolivian group. All four organizations were coordinated and advised by a committee in the Paris headquarters of the Revolutionary Workers Party.

Like the other two Argentine organizations, ERP engaged not only in assassination but also in fund-raising activities such as bank robberies and kidnapping for ransom, and in assorted bombings and assaults on police stations and army installations. The general idea was to create chaos and bring about a revolution, for the sequel to which each group had its own scenario. By 1970 it seemed only too likely that they would get the first part of their wish. The size of their membership was mainly a matter of guesswork (one guess gave the largest of them, ERP, 200,000 members in 1973), but its quality was high. The leaders and many members of these organizations were trained technicians, professional men and women, and other members of the middle class. If the old myth of the middle class as a stabilizing, democratizing influence on Latin America still needed exploding, Argentina now provided explosives in abundance, and so did Chile and Uruguay. Ground between the elite and the state enterprises above and the hard-bargaining labor organizations below, the Argentine middle class had become the principal source of leadership in the development of a pervasive revolutionary spirit that might have been irresistible if it had not sought to move in so many contrary directions at once.

In the economic field Lanusse was at least as generous in the matter of wage increases as Levingston had been, and relaxed the latter's restrictions on foreign investments, though his policy was still nationalistic enough to draw protests from the private enterprise association, ACIEL. Opposition also came from a variety of other quarters, ranging from corporatist army officers to the terrorists. In between were quite a few labor leaders, who thought they could get better terms from an authoritarian than from a democratic government. But the great bulk of the armed forces supported Lanusse, while most civilians did likewise or else waited to see what would come of his quest for a national accord.

In the course of 1973 the political plan for the accord was carried successfully through all the stages of party organization, Peronist participation, campaigns, elections, and inauguration, but in the last stage, the achievement of a true national accord, it failed dismally. Although Perón himself came back as the great pacificator and won a landslide victory at the polls, terrorism and inflation continued unabated, by the end of the year Perón's party had split wide open, and he had become the leader of the conservative wing which had the CGT as its core, against the Marxist wing, which was largely a youth movement.

A brief review of the political events of the year will indicate some of the chief factors involved and suggest why the outcome was deeply disappointing. On March 11 the presidential election was won by a coalition headed by the justicialist candidate, Hector J. Cámpora, who had been Perón's personal agent in Argentina for several years past. His vote fell a fraction of one percent short of the 50 percent required by law, but Lanusse nevertheless declared him "virtually elected." He then went to Spain to talk with Perón again before taking office, but was recalled for a conference on May 3 with the "deeply concerned" military junta. The issue was escalating terrorism and the report by a Peronist youth leader, also just back from a visit to Perón, that a militia of Justicialist Youth Groups (like the Red Guard of the People's Republic of China) was about to be formed. Perón quickly denied the report and fired the youth leader who had made it. At this point the navy chief of staff was assassinated in reprisal for the execution some time earlier of sixteen young revolutionaries who had broken out of a naval prison. ERP claimed credit for this murder.

On May 25 Cámpora was inaugurated as president and on June 20 Perón returned to Argentina for the first time since 1955, except for a visit in November and December of 1972 that had failed to spark popular enthusiasm. This time too, despite his campaign managers' best efforts, things started out badly, though in a different way: the triumphal welcome they had planned for him at the Ezeiza (Buenos Aires) airport was ruined by a pitched battle between rival Peronist youth factions. The official death count was fifteen; all other reports said that was only a fraction of the number killed. Perón's special plane was diverted to a military field, the reception canceled, and his planned speech postponed until the following day. After a few days in semi-seclusion, he returned to Madrid with no fanfare.

The violence continued. Unable to check it, President Cámpora and the vice-president resigned on July 13 after 49 days in office. As acting president, Congress chose Raúl Alberto Lastiri, president of the Chamber of Deputies and son-in-law of Perón's former secretary in Spain, José López Rega, at this time minister of social welfare. In accordance with the constitution, Congress called for a new presidential election. On August 4 the Justicialist Party convention nominated Perón for president and his wife, Isabel María Estela Martínez de Perón, for vice-president. They arrived in Buenos Aires quietly on August 31 and began their campaign promptly.

On September 3 a long and important televised interview with Perón was broadcast over Channel 13 by 45 stations to an estimated audience of more than one million persons. An independent rating service reported its rating as an average 33, with a peak of 39, compared with 25 for the most popular regular program, "Rolando Rivas, Taxi Driver." The complete text of the interview was published two days later in the Peronist newspaper *La Opinión,* along with a summary of other journals' reports of it the day before.

During the interview Perón spoke as disdainfully as ever of politicians and described himself as no politician but a professional soldier with 45 years of service. The interviewers asked a wide range of questions about both domestic and foreign affairs, and Perón replied so fully and clearly (though not frankly) that the report of the interview was in effect his platform for the campaign. It was conciliatory in the sense that it called for a union of the whole nation to meet the current national emergency. According to a friendly commentator, Heriberto Kahn, however, Perón's replies were addressed primarily to the middle class and non-Peronists, in line with his instructions to the managers of his campaign to "orient it towards the bourgeois sectors."

In his summons to national reconciliation, Perón described himself as an advocate of nonviolence and of reform, not revolution. He insisted that Argentina's key problem was not economic but political, and pointed to Salvador Allende's Chile, then on the brink of disaster, as an example of the consequences of too rapid change. Although during his exile he had promoted organized terrorism in Argentina, he now urged his fellow countrymen and women to stop regarding a political opponent as an enemy and had kind words about those, both lay and clerical, who differed with him, including Argentina's "Third World" priests, who had been and still were preaching violent revolution. Yet he himself gave some replies that were divisive and that seem to indicate that he was out of touch with the situation in Argentina. They certainly help us to understand the dismal failure of his effort to promote peace and order and national unity during his brief presidency.

Perón and his wife won the election with 62 percent of the 12 million votes cast (total population, 24 million). Among the other candidates Ricardo Balbín, Radical, received 24.4 percent and Francisco Manrique, Conservative, 12.3 percent. The election took place in relative calm, but the very next day José Rucci, the head of CGT and a strong supporter of Perón, was machine-gunned in front of his residence. Credit for this assassination too was claimed by ERP, which had turned against Perón when his campaign calls for national reconciliation and for reform, not revolution, cast him in ERP eyes in the role of defender of the status quo and collaborator with the oligarchy, the imperialists, and all other wickedness.

On October 12 Perón and his wife were inaugurated during a truce between left- and right-wing Justicialists, who had been fighting each other ever since Rucci's murder. One of Perón's first acts was to remove the rector of the University of Buenos Aires, left-wing Peronist Rodolfo Puiggrós, who had been appointed only a few months earlier by President Cámpora. In November Perón intensified his verbal attack on leftist "traitors" in the Peronist movement and on December 21 he established a new Security Council with increased powers to deal with terrorism. He admitted that it was a dangerous problem but denied that it was a national threat and rejected a proposal that a counterpart of the Brazilian "Death Squadron" be set up to deal with it. Such drastic measures would not be adopted by his government, he declared, for the country had already suffered more than enough oppression under the military.

As the year 1973 ended, that was as good a face as Perón could put on the problem of terrorism, which, in the judgment of others, was indeed threatening to tear the country apart. In his view the military, who ought to be the chief guarantors of internal security, still could not be trusted and presented at least as serious a threat to his government as the terrorists. Accordingly he balanced the creation of the new Security Council by removing the heads of the army and navy and forcing a dozen colonels into retirement. The army commander, General Jorge Raúl Carcagno, who was regarded by some as too friendly with left-wing Peronists, had been appointed to that post the preceding May by President Cámpora. This is one more indication that Perón and Cámpora, once very close, had by the end of 1973 at the latest drifted far apart. (To Cámpora's relief, they did so literally: with alacrity he accepted diplomatic exile as ambassador to Mexico.) By that time a generational gap, encouraged at first by Perón, had opened up in his movement between the organized Peronist Youth and their elders. There was also a rift in the movement between its organized labor component, with which Perón identified himself when he had to choose, and its non-labor, primarily political component, to which Dr. Cámpora belonged.

All these problems were still as far from solution as ever when Juan Perón died on July 1, 1974. He had been completely unable to cope with any of them in the nine months since his extraordinary success in winning power again after a humiliating overthrow and eighteen years of exile. There were many reasons for his failure, beginning with his age, 78, and the short time allowed him. Besides the fact that others had failed, too, another reason must surely have been that the Argentina to which he returned was so new and strange to him that he did not know how to deal with it.

What Was New

Among the most obvious changes during Peron's absence was the proliferation of parties. This was of limited benefit to the Peronist Party. Although it meant a fragmentation of the opposition, Jeanne Kirkpatrick's field study showed that in the mid-1960s the Peronists' own hard core had been reduced to about one fifth of the voting population, so that the votes it obtained above that level came from a floating and fluctuating population of pro-Peronists. Moreover, the issues that mattered most to the hard-core Peronists were no longer economic and political, but only economic, nor were they revolutionaries, but reformers who wanted only minor structural changes. They were only the upper crust of the masses and one third of them did not belong to the masses at all but to the middle class, and only one twentieth of them gave foreign affairs high priority. In a study also made in the mid-1960s Peter Ranis found that in all the political parties ideological considerations were not a primary factor and that the parties had come to be regarded as existing for the promotion of certain programs and interests, rather than as "integral parts of a democratic political system." This attitude, he believed, encouraged military interventions and the judging of each of them on its individual merits.

The public attitude most commonly reported by both domestic and foreign observers in the decade before Perón's return was one of widespread apathy about public affairs. This was hardly to be expected in a period when violence in various forms was on the increase and when masses of people were anything but apathetic about the seemingly endless succession of horse races and soccer games. Smaller but still considerable numbers of them took time off even for the rich man's game, polo, in which at this time Argentina had more top-ranking players than any other country in the world. Perhaps a clue to the puzzle is provided by the report of an experienced observer, Francisco Ayala, that on his return to Argentina in 1962 after several years' absence he found its people profoundly discouraged by Frondizi's failure and the spectacle of corruption revealed after his fall, for he had started his administration in 1958 with everything in his favor. He did the country even more harm than Perón, concluded Ayala, because, although these experiences had had the salutary effect of reducing the Argentines' national pride to reasonable proportions, fatal consequences might ensue from the shame and skepticism with which they now regarded themselves.

The political and economic frustrations of the next ten years did nothing to restore public morale, and there was much to keep it low, particularly among the intellectual and literary leaders, who in Latin America often exert an influence well beyond the borders of their esoteric circle. Alienation was the central theme of brilliant young Juan José Sebreli's portrait of porteño society in the mid-1960s, which became a bestseller. Veteran Jorge Luis Borges saw the country still continuing its decades-long decline and now exhibiting two especially painful traits: a deficiency of imagination, illustrated in the country's provincial cities, which were merely modest fragments of Buenos Aires scattered across the pampa, and a lack of moral sense, shown by an Argentine's asking about a proposed action, "Will it pay?," where a North American, in his Protestant way, would ask, "Is it right?" (Borges is cited here for his knowledge of Argentina, not of the United States.) It is hard for Argentines, he added, to conceive of impersonal relations and consequently they have so few scruples in dealing with the impersonal state that smuggling and bribery are respectable and even envied.

Borges himself was now a target for shafts from younger writers. One of the most prominent of them, Jorge Abelardo Ramos, a Marxist, described Borges contemptuously as a child of the upper-class Barrio del Norte, "whose titles of nobility still smell of alfalfa" and, while admitting that the aging Borges was considered Argentina's leading writer, declared that "in our opinion [he is] one of the most flagrant examples of the irresponsibility of our literature of importation." This last phrase was an expression of literary nationalism and echoed the complaint by Ricardo Rojas in the first decade of the century that Argentina's intellectuals lived from day to day for the next shipload of books and magazines from Europe. The phrase also hints at the animus Ramos's severe strictures on Ezequiel Martínez Estrada, whose influence, especially on the younger intellectuals, had exceeded even that of Borges for a decade after World War II. Ramos then attacked both of them and other "mandarins and mystifiers" in a book which by the 1960s had, the author flattered himself, cut them all down to size. The chief ground of his criticism of Martinez Estrada was the latter's misinterpretation of the protagonist of *Martín Fierro* as a victim of fate, for he thereby evaded the famous poem's central problem, which was the implacable destruction of Argentina's natural economy by the imposition of a capitalist type of agriculture and stockraising tied to Europe. In short, he charged, though born a provincial, Martínez Estrada became a creature of the porteño oligarchy and the foreign imperialism it served.

By the 1960s Marxist influence among Argentine intellectuals was so great that Borges, Martínez Estrada, and all the other non-Marxist leaders of the preceding generation had been deposed. They had not been replaced, however, for the Marxists quarreled endlessly among themselves, and intellectual-literary circles were in a state of as great confusion as that prevailing among the politicians. To make matters worse, the growing "irrationalism of the left" described by Juan F. Marsal (see chapter IX), not only barred the development of scientific sociology because its findings did not always square with Marxist beliefs; it also increased the likelihood that orderly self-government would be impossible. A potential source of similar conflict and confusion in Argentine foreign affairs was brought out in another study of Marsal's. This was an analysis in Weberian terms of the current "boom" in Argentine right-wing thought and its background in that country and Spain and France. One of the chief features of that thought, he found, was a right-wing nationalism whose "anticapitalist and anti-Yankee" position, opposed to both "exploitative capitalism and atheistic communism," linked it to Perón's Third Position. The conservatives opened vistas of a "right-wing populism," but, he warned, once such regimes are established, the popular element is soon eliminated under all kinds of fascist governments. Although Marsal did not say so, this right-wing nationalism, if put into practice, could also make serious trouble between Argentina and the economically advanced countries that had always taken first place in that country's foreign relations.

One of the most important changes in Argentina during Perón's long absence remains to be noted. His first government had been sustained by two power groups that had no rival in the country— organized labor and the armed forces—and he had had no rival for control of them until he weakened his hold by a sudden change of course shortly before his fall. Now, eighteen years later, Argentina was fast becoming what David Jordan describes as a society of bureaucratic oligarchies, atop of which stood not two but three organized groups, labor and the military having been joined by the state enterprises; and the three of them, autonomous but interlocking, knew no master such as Perón had formerly been. Instead, they could and did obtain from the government a larger share of the national income from the country's stop-and-go economy.

To be sure, the economy had already suffered a long "stop" under Perón in the early 1950s, but, with help from the United States, he was getting it moving again when he was overthrown. Now, in the mid-1970s, any such invocation of foreign aid was almost certainly ruled out by the economic nationalism rampant in all three bureaucratic oligarchies. The officer corps, divided about it in the 1940s, had been won over to it by the subsequent growth of an Argentine "military-industrial complex." This phenomenon was noted in 1967 by Mariano Grondona, who, writing in *Primera Plana,* Argentina's leading weekly newsmagazine, described as something "entirely new" the emergence in that country, as well as in Brazil and Mexico, of "a political-military-entrepreneurial oligarchy determined to industrialize." Two years later the same phenomenon drew from social and political historian Darío Canton the comment that "in contrast to 1945, a much more extensive connection of the military with the economic-financial apparatus has grown up of late."

The connection Canton referred to was obvious in the large and growing number of military officers among the directors of the huge state enterprises that now dominated the Argentine economy and were the principal promoters of economic nationalism. These state enterprises included the Bank of the Argentine Nation, which accounted for more than half of all the deposits and commercial banking in the country, and the state monopolies of oil exploration (YPF), meat (CAP), steel (SOMISA), petrochemicals, and electric power. In addition, the movies, theatres, transport, communications, and the General Economic Confederation (CGE), were under state control. The officers were also appearing with increasing frequency on the boards of private companies, but these were clearly losing ground to state enterprise. An outstanding and very recent example was the largest of them all, the Italian entrepreneur Torcuato DiTella's S.A.M. complex, in which the state bought a controlling interest in 1971. As a consequence of this process, the armed forces were less ready than formerly to defend private property and enterprise, domestic or foreign, and more than ever disposed to join hands with an economic-financial apparatus "determined to industrialize."

This is one of the subjects on which Perón's replies in his highly publicized interview on September 3, 1973, help us to understand his failure to achieve his proclaimed goal of peace, order, and national unity. The power interests set on industrializing cannot have been happy with his emphatic declaration that it was now time for Argentina to concentrate on a massive effort to increase agricultural and livestock production. (He even announced specific goals: 200 million tons of wheat and 250 million head of cattle.) No matter how true it may have been, there was little comfort for those interests in his assertion that a soil exceptionally rich in phosphates and iodine equipped Argentina admirably for this task and gave it a precious advantage in the "world war of proteins" which had broken out, with nations all over a hungry world planting soy beans and trying to breed cattle.

Other responses given by Perón on that occasion could hardly have failed to offend both the younger generation and their elders. Asked what role the youth of 18 to 20 ought to play, he replied that they were wonderful people and the hope of the country and that it was the corresponding generation that had been the making of the great October 17 (in 1945, of course), but that the youth of today were beside themselves, needed to cool off, and must wait three years to play a "protagonist" role. Impartially he then stepped on the toes of their fathers' generation by calling it a "destroyed or at least frustrated generation" and advised the young people to avoid "contamination" by it by forming a separate youth organization of their own. That left only their grandfathers' generation, Perón's own, without a black mark against it. Then, as if to make Peronist Party members of all ages unhappy, he stressed the fact that that party was only one sector of the Peronist Movement and that the movement's "vertebral" sector was and always had been the CGT.

These replies give the impression that, after his long exile, Perón was somewhat out of touch with reality in Argentina. By encouraging the formation of a separate youth organization to save the young people from contamination, he showed that he still did not realize the extent to which youth was the source of the campaign of violence. Another example is his reply to a question about this campaign. He was in Paris, he said, when organized terrorism started there on May 30-31, 1968 (a reference to the anti-De Gaulle riots).

From there, he continued, it grew into a worldwide terrorist movement directed from Paris, supported by Marxists and other left-wing
malcontents, and aimed at destroying the industrial society and
consumerism, and it "is still managed from Paris." That he gave no
hint of his own responsibility for the growth of violence in Argentina
was only to be expected, but it is surprising that he showed no awareness of its native background and no appreciation of the significance
of the parallel developments then going on in Chile and Uruguay.

The spread of organized violence was not the only convergence in
the history of Argentina and its two Southern Cone neighbors in the
1960s and 1970s. Though the processes were different, by 1973 Argentina had moved about as far along the road to state socialism
through proliferation of state enterprises as Chile had done under
Frei's Christian Democrats and Allende's Socialist-Communist coalition, or as even Uruguay had done, despite its much earlier start
under Batlle y Ordóñez. The Argentine state enterprises developed
a political influence and a de facto autonomy that made them first
cousins to the autonomous entities of Uruguay. In Argentina, as in
Uruguay, that caused a fragmentation of society in its political as
well as its economic aspect — as if Argentina were not already fragmented enough. Another convergence of the three countries was in
respect to political intervention by the military. In this instance Argentina led the way. Such intervention was increasingly frequent
there from 1930 on, and, although in Chile and Uruguay from
about 1940 to 1970 it was rare and never total, at the end of 1973
the military were in full control in both countries, as we have noted
more than once. Just at that point the convergence seemed to end
when the Argentine military withdrew in favor of a civilian government headed by Perón, but he was well aware that they were looking
over his shoulder the whole time and might take over again at any
time if they felt the need.

Areas of Development and Balance of Power

Although in some aspects the three countries shared common
trends, this is not to say that Argentina was losing its individuality.*
In some important ways that was becoming more sharply marked

---

*It was still outstanding for its comparatively even distribution of national income below
the top 5 percent of the population, as described in chapter X.

than ever. Examples are military arms, the economy, and sources of energy. In all three respects the country was more nearly self-sufficient by the early 1970s than its two Southern Cone neighbors and more than it had been for many years past, if ever.

In 1950, as Geoffrey Kemp has shown, Argentina and Brazil were the only Latin American countries that had even a limited competence in aircraft assembly and ship building capability. In 1972 the two were far ahead of all the rest in the proportion of military supplies received from domestic sources, and specifically in manufacturing and assembling capabilities in small arms and ordnance, heavy trucks, tanks and armored vehicles, and warships. Chile at this time was capable in only one field, warships; it had manufactured small arms in 1950, but only as a consequence of allied requirements in World War II, and by 1960 the installations built to meet these requirements had been shut down.* The account does not mention Uruguay, which apparently had no capability at all and imported all the arms needed by its armed forces.

Since it is often assumed in the United States that some Latin American countries, especially "militaristic" Argentina, have disproportionately large military budgets, it should be noted that, in a list of 31 selected Third World countries ranked according to defense expenditure as a percentage of GNP, Argentina stood almost at the foot of the list in 1966; to be precise, it was 28th, with 1.5 percent. Even in 1969, after three years of military dictatorship, Argentina still had one of the smallest military budgets, ranking 20th in the list of 31, with a budget of 2.6 percent. Chile dropped from 26th, with 1.9 percent, in 1966 to 30th (next to last), with 1.7 percent, in 1969. Again little Uruguay was omitted.

At the close of our period the Argentine economy was still dependent on foreign nations in technology, but in foreign trade and investments its dependence on them had decreased greatly in the last half century. In its foreign trade an ECLA study showed that imports as a percentage of the Argentine GNP declined from a twentieth-century peak of 28.7 in 1905-1914 to 14.8 in 1930-1939 and 7.3 in 1950-1954. After that imports continued to fluctuate around the latter low figure, which is almost as low as the corresponding figure for the United States since the 1930s, and far lower

---

*Chilean factories had supplied the army and navy with arms during the War of the Pacific, 1879-1884, but later succumbed to foreign competition.

than that for Chile and Uruguay. The ECLA study shows an even
sharper drop in the ratio of foreign to aggregate fixed capital in Argentina. In 1913, the peak year, the ratio was 47.7, from which it
declined to 32.0 in 1929, to 15.4 in 1945 (the year before Perón took
over) and then dropped to 5.1 in 1955, around which low figure it
remained for the rest of our period. All this while, foreign capital
likewise diminished steadily in volume, though less rapidly; in 1950
prices, the volume fell from $8.23 billion in 1913 to $1.86 billion in
1955. In the same years the volume of domestic capital increased
from $9.0 billion to $34.9 billion. In this matter of foreign investments there was no great difference between Argentina's experience
and Uruguay's, except that in the latter country Batlle started their
sharp decline earlier. There was a substantial difference in the case
of Chile, where the ratio of foreign capital remained comparatively
high until the Allende government forced it down.

As these figures suggest, by the 1960s Argentina no longer lived
under that export-import economy, dominated by foreign capital
and dependent on foreign markets, that for so many years had provided nationalists and Marxists with the text for so many furious
philippics. The statistics of agricultural and livestock production
point to the same conclusion. Between 1900 and 1954, production
increased 300 percent, but exports in the last five-year period were
only 25 percent higher than in the first five-year period, and the
ratio of exports to production had declined from 52 to 21 percent.
The ratio continued to decline after 1954, with the result that when
in 1973 the world woke up to the fact that it faced a food shortage, it
found that Argentina was no longer its breadbasket, as it had been
in the first half of the century. As we noted, Perón (of all people)
now proposed to restore it to its breadbasket role, but the indications were that, if the thing could be done at all, it would require a
heroic effort, for the country appeared to be well started on a cycle
of internal development.

This development necessarily took place to a large extent in the
provinces of the interior, so long overshadowed, exploited, and even
stunted by megalopolis Buenos Aires. One example is the rapid
industrialization after 1940 of Córdoba. Another, seldom noticed
outside Argentina, is the emergence of that country since the turn of
the century as a large-scale producer of wine and by 1970 one of the
world's five largest producers, the other four being France, Spain,
Italy, and the Soviet Union. Chile's wine industry is older, produces

excellent wines, and has a well-established foreign market for them, but it is much smaller and has a much more limited capacity for growth than Argentina's. Uruguay's wine industry is not remotely comparable to the other two.

The growth of Argentina's wine industry is a fine example of the exploitation of great natural resources made possible by the use of modern technology. Virtually the whole industry is concentrated in what is commonly called the Mendoza district, although its extends across all three provinces of the Cuyo region: San Luis and San Juan as well as Mendoza. All three provinces lie in western Argentina, with the snow-covered Andes in the background. There is so little rainfall that, without water piped from the Andes to irrigate the fields, vineyards could not grow even in the extraordinarily fertile soil of the Mendoza district, which produces 35 tons of grapes per acre, as compared with 15 tons in the best California vineyards. If the Andes were not there, rainfall might be abundant, but things are better as they are, for irrigation never fails. The supply of fertile land, too, seems endless. Sunshine is abundant and in summer so hot that the vines have to be protected from it by vast awnings.

Although grapes were introduced here by the Spaniards in the sixteenth century, all the natural advantages of the Mendoza district were of little use commercially until the mid-1880s, when the construction of a railroad to Buenos Aires 700 miles away made it possible to build up a national market for the wines of the district. This was done with the aid of vintners and new varieties of grapes brought over from Europe, a national control system, and a National Wine Institute, located in Mendoza, which by the 1970s was using banks of computers to process information poured in by 66,000 growers, 4,000 vintners, and 700 field inspectors. One of the vintners owned a 1.1 million gallon blending tank, the largest in the world. Only five percent of the wine produced was shipped abroad and until the 1970s little effort was made to develop a foreign market. The other 95 percent of this huge production was consumed in Argentina at the rate (in 1970) of 24.5 gallons a year for every man, woman, and child in the country. Long noted as great meat eaters, the Argentines deserve to be no less famous as wine bibbers.

In energy resources Argentina was by the 1970s unique in the Southern Cone and outstanding in Latin America. Its situation in this respect had improved vastly since World War I, when it produced no fuel except wood and most of its inhabitants lived on or near the almost treeless pampa. There had been a great improvement even since the first post-World War II decade, during which imports of fuels and lubricants doubled as a share of total imports and YPF was never able to meet half the country's petroleum requirements. By 1973 it was able to meet most of them. Coal of passable quality and in substantial volume was being produced by Argentine mines that had barely begun operations in the earlier period, while large hydroelectric plants were in operation and others in various stages of planning. Among the latter was an international project at Iguassú Falls (larger than Niagara, we are constantly reminded), on the borders of Argentina, Brazil, and Uruguay. Chile, though better supplied than Argentina with coal and hydroelectric power, was far behind Argentina in petroleum production and, as far as was known, reserves; and Uruguay had none of these sources except the hydroelectric.

The greatest difference of all in this field, however, was in the production of atomic energy, in which Argentina led all Latin America in resources and facilities as well as production, while Chile and Uruguay had nothing. Argentina's atomic energy program had its beginning in Perón's establishment of the National Atomic Energy Commission (CNEA) on May 31, 1950. Its first director, Ronald Richter, an Austrian, had carried on nuclear fusion research in Germany during World War II. Perón provided him with expensive facilities and on his advice broadcast extravagant claims for the program. When these soon made Argentina look ridiculous, he fired Richter (November 1952). As J. R. Redick tells the story, Argentine interest in the program continued and was stimulated by the conclusion of an "Atoms for Peace" agreement between Argentina and the United States in 1955. Two years later the Argentine government decided not to buy any more foreign research reactors, but to construct them in Argentina as an aid to the development of its own nuclear capability.

In the same spirit CNEA decided to make use of Argentina's own plentiful sources of uranium (estimated at 10,000 tons, ten times as large as those of Brazil, the only other South American country with any uranium to speak of). Its first nuclear power station, Atocha, was started in 1968 and completed in 1972, to serve Greater Buenos Aires. Despite its high cost, the use of uranium gave Argentina a completely free hand in the development of its nuclear energy program. The alternative method had strong advocates on the ground of economy, but it would have made Argentina dependent on the enrichment services of the United States, which, under the Nonproliferation Treaty, would have required guarantees to be given that the product would be used for peaceful purposes only. Argentina was not a party to that treaty, nor, along with Chile and Brazil, to the Latin American Treaty of Tlaltelalco for the prohibition of nuclear weapons in Latin America.

So far as is known, however, Argentina has confined its nuclear program exclusively to peaceful purposes. Despite delays caused by the troubled state of public affairs, by 1972 five research reactors and six major centers for related studies in physics, biology, mineralogy, and chemistry had been established; researchers were receiving advanced training in the United States and Europe; and plans for the construction of additional nuclear power stations to serve Bahía Blanca and Córdoba had been announced. Three extracting and refining plants were producing an estimated 88 tons of nuclear fuel by this time. Experts in the United Nations and at Stockholm were estimating that Argentina's annual plutonium production would be 145 kilos by 1976 and 400 kilos by 1977, as compared with Brazilian production of only 100 and 190 kilos respectively. Also, Argentina was the only Latin American nation that had a plant capable of extracting plutonium from irradiated nuclear fuel. The program had obvious economic value, especially in view of the opening of a new era of high petroleum prices by OPEC in late 1973. The rise meant serious trouble for Brazil, and even Argentina could not remain indifferent to it, though it was less vulnerable because better supplied with its own petroleum.

Despite pacific appearances and assurances, this program had martial overtones, and there was comfort for security-conscious Argentines in its progress. In the 1940s Argentina had lost to Brazil its generation-old military primacy in South America, and had fallen further and further behind ever since. In these thirty years Brazil's population had grown so much more rapidly that it now dwarfed Argentina's by a margin which—almost overnight, it seemed—had jumped from 3 to 1 to more than 4 to 1. In addition, since the military takeover at Rio in 1964, Brazil's economic growth had proceeded unbrokenly at a fantastic annual rate which was more than twice as fast as Argentina's, although this was the best rate Argentina had been able to sustain for any period of the same length since 1950. As computed by ECLA in 1973, the growth rates of gross domestic product of the two countries from 1965 to 1971 were as follows:

	1965-1970	1970	1971
Argentina	4.0	4.1	3.8
Brazil	7.5	9.5	11.3

What Argentina should do in the face of the dismal prospect opened up by these developments was a question for which no one had had a ready answer. For a time about 1970 its government gave top priority to the more immediate threat that left-wing extremists might come to power in Uruguay, and accordingly made common cause with Brazil against it. As the danger from that quarter diminished, however, relations between the two military governments cooled rapidly. The Buenos Aires government, now under General Lanusse, was moving towards an accommodation with the Peronists, which would be unacceptable to the generals in Rio. The Argentine authorities, on their part, were irritated by Brazil's dam construction on the upper Paraná River and bids for influence through a new foreign aid program in countries bordering on Argentina: Paraguay, Bolivia, and even Uruguay. And there was, as always, the traditional power rivalry between the two. This surfaced in March 1972, when at a banquet in his honor in Brasilia, General Lanusse shocked his Brazilian hosts by declaring that Argentina would never "under any circumstances accept a second-rate destiny" —which could only mean second to Brazil. Argentina now reverted to its traditional policy of seeking support among the Spanish American countries bordering Brazil on the north, west, and south. To this end Lanusse visited all of them and even had two meetings with President Allende of Chile, although it would have been hard to find a regime more unpalatable to Lanusse's fellow officers than the one headed by Allende.

For a variety of reasons, beginning with the explosive situation in Chile, the weakness of Paraguay and Bolivia, and the remoteness of the other countries, this was not a very promising line for the Argentine authorities to follow. So it must have seemed to them a providential coincidence that skyrocketing petroleum prices checked Brazil's headlong economic growth just as Argentina established itself as a substantial producer of atomic energy, far superior in this respect to Brazil, not to mention the other South American countries. It is perhaps significant that Argentina refused to deny itself the possibility of making whatever use it chose of its nuclear power and rejected a nuclear process which, while relatively cheap, would have made Argentina's production of atomic energy dependent on Brazil's virtual ally, the United States.

XII Uruguay: From Democracy
to Dictatorship, 1942-1973

As the account of Uruguay's time of troubles since the early 1940s unfolds, it may seem a twice-told tale after the chapters on Argentina and Chile in the same period. There is indeed much again about the exploitation of countryside by city, of rural workers by their landlords, and of the whole country by foreign imperialists headed by the United States. We also find rising social and political tensions, frustrated aspirations for development and a better life, and a strong left-wing movement for revolutionary change which was capped by the growth of a terrorist movement successful for a time, but then beaten back by forces of the center and right.

The three cases are not identical, however. The most obvious difference appeared in the last stage, when the military established a dictatorship in Uruguay as in Chile, whereas the Argentine armed forces terminated their six-year rule and helped restore constitutional government. Another striking difference is that, perhaps because it was much smaller and weaker, had fewer natural resources, and had fallen from a greater height, Uruguay suffered more from its afflictions than the other two from theirs, as is indicated by the fact that the unhappy inhabitants of that quondam Utopia emigrated on a much larger scale. There were still other differences between it and the other two Southern Cone countries, and, as the period ended, the trend in their interrelations was away from unity, for the new quasi-military dictatorship in Montevideo formed increasingly close ties with the older and wholly military dictatorship in Brazil, traditional rival of Argentina.

Political and Economic Downturn

After Uruguay recovered from the first shock of World War II, it came through the rest of the conflict in apparently good shape. At the close, the vitally important export trade was booming: from 1944 to 1945 it increased about 40 percent. Most of the exports went to the United States and the United Kingdom, in that order. Another encouraging indication was the growth of Uruguay's holdings of gold and foreign exchange from $104 million at the end of 1941 to $240 million in November 1945. Politically, the country was back on even keel after the stormy weather of the depression decade. It once more had a stable, democratic government under control by the Colorado Party. During the war there had been apprehension that it might by upset by the allegedly pro-Axis Herrera faction of the Blanco Party, with aid from the military dictatorship across the Plata, but nothing came of this except a naval demonstration by the United States as a warning to the porteño government to keep hands off.

In foreign affairs Uruguay gave the United States close wartime cooperation and gained exceptional international prominence through Alberto Guani's activity as chairman of the Inter-American political warfare committee. His committee proposed and the American states adopted a new doctrine of recognition, commonly referred to as the Guani Doctrine, which attracted wide public attention. The war was hardly over when Montevideo produced another well-publicized international doctrine. This was the proposal made by Foreign Minister Eduardo Rodríguez Larreta in November 1945 that the American states adopt a policy of collective intervention when one of their number failed to give its citizens their essential rights. This "doctrine" was aimed at the threatening dictatorial regime in Buenos Aires, but most of the other Latin American governments, including some that shared Montevideo's aversion for the regime of its neighbor, rejected the proposal out of hand for fear that it might somehow open the door to intervention by the United States in their own countries.

The cold reception and quick demise of Rodríguez Larreta's proposal will serve as a symbol of the downturn that took place soon after the war in Uruguay's whole condition. As the country's own writers looked back later on, they dated the beginning of its time of troubles from these years. One of them, Carlos Real de Azúa, pinpoints the first realization of its presence in 1945. He cites some earlier indications of a "retreat from pride and confidence" among Uruguayans, but, noting that 1945 is usually taken as marking the emergence of a new generation in that country, he asserts that, with the aid of developmental economists, its stagnation and other problems were clearly perceived in that year for the first time.

The statistics show that the people of Uruguay had reason to worry. For one thing, this once food-exporting country was increasingly having trouble feeding itself. According to its own Bank of the Republic's report for 1945, there had been an almost uninterrupted decline of the area under cultivation for wheat from 556,000 hectares in 1937-1938 to 346,000 hectares in 1944-1945, and an even sharper drop in the size of the wheat harvest, from 451,000 tons to

177,000 tons in the same period. Population figures, too, were disturbing. A rapid increase in population had for many years been a source of pride to the people of Uruguay, as well as an important factor in the growth of their economy, but after World War II the rate of increase was even slower than in the worst years of the depression (1930-1934), and the volume of immigration was only one-third as large as in those years and one-seventh as large as in the 1920s. The total population grew, in round numbers, from 1.9 million in 1940 to only 2.2 million in 1950 and 2.5 million in 1960. To make matters worse, there was a slowing down after the war in the growth of light, import-substitution industry, until it came almost to a halt in the mid-1950s. In the 1930s its growth had helped offset the decline of the pastoral sector, once the welfare state's chief support. As a result, while the economy of its big neighbor Brazil was enjoying a rapid if irregular growth, Uruguay's own economic growth rate from 1945 to 1960 was, as Jacques Lambert notes, a slightly negative −0.2 percent.

There was no improvement in the next decade. In fact, the diagnosticians who examined the patient in the 1960s found so many things wrong with Uruguay—the society and the polity, as well as the economy—that it seemed a wonder that the whole structure had not already broken down. To begin with, Real de Azúa found that since 1940 Uruguay had become a "group society" of distinct social nuclei uncommitted to any political party and bargaining with the parties from the outside. Consequently, power in this fragmented society had been displaced from the state to a "para-state" and the parties only tagged along after it, though at times they made a great noise about their autonomy. Uruguay, he continued, had become a nation of checks and balances, quasi-bourgeois in tone, whose social conformity made it hostile to any structural reform, above all to any reform that would entail a redistribution of income.

Aldo Solari probed more deeply, but he too found the spirit of conformity prevalent in that period. It permeated even the body of university students, which contained the highest proportion of nonconformists. Polls, he said, showed that the students almost unanimously expressed approval of the education they had received, and planned to educate their children the same way. Thus, he commented, the family seems to have satisfied the expectations of its members. He went on, however, to point out that the educational sphere had grown substantially without any increase in its connection with other spheres, thereby illustrating the general tendency in Uruguay towards the growth of "independent—or, if one prefers, autonomous—institutions." (His reference here is to the entes autónomos discussed previously.) He found further that the political parties reflected this increasing fragmentation (the stronger "atomization" was his word for it), for, instead of trying to build up a single normative system for all people in their dealings with the different institutions, the parties employed the value systems and images of each institutional group. The result was the emergence of a series of absolutely autonomous state organizations and the end of any parallel process of integration.

This last observation brings us back to Real de Azúa's point about the appearance in Uruguay of a "para-state," although Solari did not use that term in this connection. He went on, however, to make the highly important point that a system such as Uruguay's was almost impenetrable to major change, since it could only absorb a change that was limited to a single institutional sphere and did not sensibly affect the rest. "Changes of greater magnitude," he concluded, "can be absorbed only by a rupture of the system." For a country urgently in need of "changes of great magnitude," this was a grim conclusion. It was probably sound, but Solari was less successful when he moved on from diagnosis to prognosis. Here he tripped over a facile paradox. Paradoxically, he asserted, the very weakness of Uruguay's social system reinforces its power of survival, for none of its beneficiary groups is strong enough, or if strong enough, would dare, to break it up. That was said in 1967. The events of the next six years belied it.

In a more down-to-earth analysis of Uruguay's situation, Abraham Guillén Arapey stressed as sources of its troubles inflation, declining economic productivity, and overloaded government payrolls. Its public employees, for example, included one in every 13 inhabitants, as compared with one to 59 in The Netherlands and one to 125 in Belgium. That did not include pensioners, and social security pensions absorbed another 15 percent of Uruguay's GNP. Data from other sources reinforce his argument. Retirement at the age of 50 was easy and common. So also at that age was a new career and a second job, for pensions were low, expectations high, and time hung heavy. Job tenure was secure under one of the most liberal labor codes in the world. Perhaps as a result labor was inefficient, especially in the overmanned state offices. These problems were already appearing before the war, but they had become progressively more acute until, after the war, Uruguay found itself saddled with a social welfare system beyond the ability of the existing economy to maintain. The system broke down with increasing frequency as the economy deteriorated, rising prices outpaced pensions, and pensions were in arrears. The International Monetary Fund's statistics show that, with 1958 = 100, the cost of living in Uruguay nearly doubled from 1951 (43) to 1957 (83), nearly doubled again in only two years (1959 = 148), and continued to shoot up in 1960 (202) and 1961 (223).

Moreover, the benefits of the system were very largely confined to Montevideo and paid for at first by the pastoral economy. When that declined after 1930, financing also came from the new industries. Unfortunately, the latter, established under the protection afforded by the depression and World War II, could hardly compete with imported goods after the war, even with tariff protection. By the 1950s, industrial production in Uruguay was notoriously high cost. With limited natural resources and a very limited national market (a population of 2.8 million in 1960), the prospect of improvement was not good. In Uruguay pressure to change the system itself built up.

By the late 1950s foreign observers who had once been fascinated by Uruguay's novel and seemingly successful experiment were aware that something had gone wrong in utopia. The reversal of opinion among them was neither sudden nor complete. Rather, as Real de Azua said, the change was a gradual one from dithyrambic to neutral to apprehensive, and, he might have added, to censorious in the next stage. Why they did not reach this last stage more quickly is easy to understand. Most writers whose observations were published* were either academics or journalists, and Uruguay had statistically attractive distinctions that appealed to each group—to academics, its 85 to 90 percent literacy rate, the highest in Latin America; to journalists, its voracious newspaper-reading public, whose per capita rate was again the highest in Latin America. Well into the 1960s some leading Latin Americanists continued to rank Uruguay, along with Chile, at the top of the Latin American group for stable political democracy, often, to be sure, with the admission that the competition was not keen.

*Some of the best were confidential observations by diplomats, and often these were not published until years later.

It was, as it should have been, the specialists on Uruguay who hoisted the first storm signals, and even they did so tentatively and almost apologetically; the utopian myth died hard. In England, George Pendle in 1957 omitted the first edition's subtitle, "South America's First Welfare State," from the second edition of his excellent little book on Uruguay. In the United States two years later Russell H. Fitzgibbon raised serious questions about the favorable judgments in his own earlier, longer, and likewise firstrate study of that country. In 1960 Philip B. Taylor, a newcomer to the field, echoed the past in calling Uruguay "a wholesome and progressive society," but then went on to negate that judgment with such comments as that "conservative or even antiquated standards" and business practices "preclude expansion"; that the political system was marked by personalism, confusion, and "inefficiency throughout the government"; that "the country has fallen on economically difficult times" and has gone on increasing its social commitments at a time when it "has been decreasingly able to pay the high cost of its version of the good life"; and, finally, that "the future is dim."

A few years after that was written, the question of economic "expansion" was given a new twist in a statistical study by a group of scholars headed by Aldo Solari. One of their tables showed the distribution by sectors of the economically active population in selected countries of the world. According to this table, the tertiary (service) sector in Uruguay in 1963 was 50.3 percent. The analysts described it as "enormously high" in relation to the country's economic development—higher than in better developed Argentina in 1947 and almost as high as in the United States in 1950 (51.8 percent), although the per capita income in Uruguay in 1963 was less than half that in the United States in 1950. A high service figure usually results from high economic development, but in Uruguay, the analysts suggested, the figure might be abnormally high precisely because of *lack* of economic development. This, they continued, had led the government to stimulate the tertiary sector's growth artificially— which was to say that more and more people were put on the government payroll.

The analysts then went on to point out that the primary (agricultural-pastoral) sector in Uruguay had been greatly reduced in size without any corresponding increase in productivity and that this might be one of several reasons for "the weakness of our economy." As for the secondary (industrial) sector, they found that, although it had grown, not until 1963 did it reach the level Argentina had attained in 1947, and that Uruguay's industrial sector in 1963 contained a high proportion of small, inefficient plants. (This, we may interject, was partly because of the persistence of family ownership and traditional methods and practices—Taylor's "antiquated standards"—and of the same type of resistance that the rural proprietors put up in rejecting fertilizers and insecticides.) Finally, a table of the distribution by sex of workers in selected occupations showed that women made up 27 percent of the largest group, office employees. In the next largest group, professional and technical workers, they outnumbered the men by 35,000 to 25,000. This was only partly because the group included schoolteachers; already in the 1940s, for example, many of the dentists in Montevideo were women. In the management-directors group, however, women fell to 8 percent, and in the diplomatic-consular group they disappeared altogether. As the country's sociologists and left-wing politicians noted without pleasure, the hold of the traditional culture was still strong in the economic and social aspects of Uruguayan life in the 1960s.

Responses by the System

To attentive Uruguayans who noted the storm warnings of this period, the heart of their country's problems was economic. Like Argentina, though less acutely, Uruguay suffered from a slackening of the European demand for its foodstuffs in the late 1940s. The Korean War brought it only temporary relief. Long-term improvement might have been achieved by shifting the stress—as the Perón regime tried to do in the early 1950s—from pastoral to agricultural production, but in Uruguay that did not seem politically feasible. Instead, its government moved in the opposite direction and concentrated on the implementation of a livestock and pasture improvement project recommended in 1951 by a joint mission of the World Bank and the Food and Agriculture Organization (FAO). Some fifteen years later Albert O. Hirschman made a study of the project in which he concluded that in the rest of the 1950s the results were nil except for some valuable experiments by a few wealthy landowners. Some of the blame for this he laid on the project's use of the "pseudo-comprehensive-program" technique that makes it seem as if the experts who drew it up had solved all the problems. But he also blamed the Uruguyan farmers, who kept up the stubborn resistance they had long offered to improvements of the kind recommended in the project.

It may have been as a result of the country's economic difficulties that it returned in 1952 to the collegiate, plural executive form of government under a new constitution. Although the constitution was backed by both major parties, it was ratified by a rather narrow margin of 232,076 votes to 197,684. The change was unfortunate politically, for it impeded decision making, and it was no help to the economy, which went from bad to worse and at one point in the late 1950s was not far from collapse because of a sharp drop in the price of wool. There were strikes and even meat shortages, inflation got out of hand, and the International Monetary Fund refused to help. In their desperation the Uruguayans adopted an income tax — a mild one, but their first. Matching Chile's treatment of the big foreign-owned copper companies, they also raised the already high taxes on the foreign-owned meat packers, Swift and Armour. The unexpected result was that both closed down their plants and moved out, thereby leaving the cupboard even barer than before.

It was a sign of the hard times that the National or Blanco Party was returned to power in 1958 for the first time in nearly a century — since 1865, to be exact. The sign should not be misread. The Blanco victory did express public dissatisfaction with the state of the nation, for which the Colorados, as the party in power, were of course held responsible. Yet the dissatisfaction was neither very deep nor very lasting. The Blancos won by a narrow margin and the Colorados were soon back in control. On the other hand, while the failure of the former to win a national election for so many years is unequaled by any other major party in the world history of party politics, it does not mean that their party was in the minority by a wide margin, much less that its following was confined to the rural areas or that it dominated all the latter. In a recent study Ronald McDonald pointed out that the Blancos polled 35 percent of the Montevideo vote in 1954, 55 percent in 1958, 43 percent in 1962, and 40 percent in 1966. Conversely, the Colorados' strength was so far from being confined to Montevideo that they were usually sure of carrying 9 rural departments to the Blancos' 7.

The two parties were, in fact, so evenly balanced that the outcome of elections often depended on personal popularity and the alliance of party factions called *sub-lemas*. Such factional alliances facilitated the displacment of the parties by the para-state system and the interests they represented. Yet, since the parties were enshrined in the successive constitutions, the political process had to be carried on through them. Failure to observe that rule would be a serious matter in the eyes of most Uruguayans, for among traditionalists, who in this respect were the majority, respect for the letter of the law was profound — as deep as in Argentina, often called a nation of lawyers in that generation. And so the checks and balances of party, sub-party, and para-state institutions and interests as these had developed by mid-century combined to reinforce the constitutional rigidity of the system. Effective national action of any kind had become difficult and significant innovations within the law next to impossible.

It would hardly be fair, then, to say that the Blancos muffed the long-delayed opportunity afforded by their victory in 1958. Given their inner divisions (which, like those of the Colorados, were numerous) and the state of the nation and the world, they never had a chance. They did badly, but no worse than the other party had done for many years. They at least had the excuse that they were beset by new troubles, both economic and political. The terms of trade were now running against Uruguay, with no new war to relieve it with a rise in the prices of wool and meat. The infection of Castroism had begun to spread through the country soon after the Blancos took office and not a few of its people were happy to be infected. There was even a sour note in what had become the traditionally friendly relations of Uruguay with the United States, for President Eisenhower's visit to Montevideo in 1960 was marred by a hostile demonstration. That was only a foretaste of the Yankeephobia that was to well up in Uruguay in the rest of the decade. In 1965 it found expression even in a book by a sober professor at the University of Montevideo, Carlos M. Rama, whose interpretation of his country's history is discussed in Chapter III. Although he had done some very creditable historical writing on other occasions, on this one Rama took it into his head to blame the economic woes of Uruguay largely on Yankee imperialism despite the fact that the United States' economic position in Uruguay had never been strong. When Rama wrote, its position there was still represented, as it had been for many years past, by a total investment that stood at $55 million in 1950, rose to $74 million in 1955, and fell back to $47 million in 1960. At its peak this was only a tiny fraction of total investments in that country. Commercial statistics tell the same story. The foreign trade of Uruguay in this postwar period was spread fairly evenly among several countries, and if the United States held first place in imports or exports from time to time, its share was always exceeded by a wide margin by Europe's. The military position of the United States in relation to Uruguay was likewise too limited to sustain a charge of imperialism, and in any case it had nothing to do with that country's economic difficulties. The most plausible explanation of the author's spleen is that it expressed the angry mood of his fellow countrymen, who had good reason to be irritable and gloomy.

Yet, not all of them shared that mood. In 1966 an Uruguayan sociologist, Isaac Ganón, published a book whose title, *The Social Structure of Uruguay*, implied scientific objectivity, but whose contents suggested nothing so much as whistling in the dark. Even if the country had been booming, the book's optimism would have been remarkable. It did contain some solid material, but its keynote, struck in the prologue, was Uruguay's "national social unity." When the author said unity, he meant it and explicitly refused to settle for "coexistential pluralism" of diverse ethnic groups living together more or less peacefully. Instead, he insisted that Uruguay had achieved the "integration" of its various groups into a single "global society," and was even free from the conflicts between groups and classes that might have been expected to arise in the absence of ethnic conflicts. Instead of conflict, there had only been competition. Even that was not severe, and there was free movement between groups or classes and "social mobility in the highest degree." Ganón made it sound too good to be true, as indeed it was. Yet many of his compatriots may have believed it, whether because they wanted to or because they were apathetic or indifferent about public affairs. Such apathy and indifference had become widespread. That was probably one source of Uruguay's mounting troubles.

Those of its people who felt less serene made another effort to find a political remedy for their country's ills. This took the form of yet another new constitution, which was adopted in 1966. Drawn up by representatives of factions of both parties, it was known before its ratification as the Inter-party Plan. It changed the framework of government once more by reverting from the collegiate to the presidential form, from a plural to a single executive. It also strengthened the executive, thus reversing the process of weakening it that had been going on ever since the adoption of Uruguay's first constitution in 1830. The change was effected mainly by making the president the coordinator of the national economy, with new powers of intervention in it and a new office of planning and budget, and by giving him closer control over the autonomous agencies. Other changes were aimed at streamlining the administration in the interest of efficiency, economy, and political morality and at facilitating the adoption of security measures. The last-named alteration soon turned out to have been most timely.

The leading commentators on this Constitution of 1966, J. M. Sanguinetti and A. Pacheco, say that its main purpose was to promote the planning and carrying out of economic development. They describe it as a bold step taken to fortify democracy in Uruguay at a critical moment. The crisis, according to them, was not only economic and social, but also one of public confidence in the political leaders and in republican institutions themselves.

Bold steps provoke opposition and this one was no exception. From various quarters it was denounced as fascist. Marxists joined in this denunciation, but their attack was motivated by a desire to keep the government weak until they could take over. Right-wing nationalists drafted a plan of their own. This together with the Inter-party Plan and still a third plan were all submitted to the voters at the same time. The Inter-party Plan was adopted by a majority of more than 60 percent (674,522 votes in a total of 1,085,287) and took effect in February 1967.

The adoption of the new constitution was soon followed by a worsening of the political situation and the economy continued to deteriorate. The reform had left untouched a unique electoral system which, according to McDonald, produced some pernicious consequences. Under this system, every national election was also a party primary. Each officially recognized faction (*sub-lema*) of a national party (*lema*) could present its own candidates, but all the votes were counted for the parent party. Then, to determine who had been elected, there was one procedure for the presidency and another for the Congress. In the former case, the sub-lema candidate with the largest vote in the national party with the largest vote was declared elected president. In the case of Congress, the seats were distributed among the sub-lemas in proportion to the votes each had contributed to the total. In the late 1960s the Colorados had 7 sub-lemas, the Blancos 4, and the two small parties none. Of the members of the Senate and Chamber of Deputies, respectively, the Colorados had 16 and 50, the Blancos 13 and 41, FIDEL (a left-wing coalition) 1 and 5, and the Christian Democrats 0 and 3.

The electoral system was written into the constitution, and both the national parties and their sub-lemas were subsidized by the government. Among the results so far as Congress was concerned were the perpetuation of the two historic parties in power and their inability to maintain party discipline. Real power resided in the sub-lemas, each of which was tied to the neighborhood political clubs and these functioned with the efficiency of the old-time ward machines in the United States. Unique though the electoral system was, the congresses elected under it developed some familiar Latin American traits and that body became factionalized, personalistic, and bound to a static social order increasingly infected by the economic blight.

The blight grew progressively worse. Instead of fulfilling the "main purpose" of the constitutional reform by rising, Uruguay's gross national product declined 12 percent and per capita income 15 percent between 1965 and 1970. Inflation moved the other way: up to 135 percent in 1967 and 147 percent in 1968. The Colorados, traditionally the party of development, recovered control of the government in the 1966 elections, but their problems were complicated at the outset by the death of the new president shortly after taking office. His successor, Jorge Pacheco Areco, stretched the new presidential powers to the utmost in breaking strikes and combating the Tupamaros. The majority in Congress tried to curb him, but when the military supported him with a threat to intervene, the legislators backed down and so did the strikers. Not so the Tupamaros, who helped to complete the politicization of the military by intensifying their campaign of violence.

The Tupamaro Response

The Tupamaros were an urban guerrilla organization in Uruguay. Collectively they called themselves the Movement for National Liberation (MLN), but they were usually referred to by the other name. Their early history is sometimes related with more assurance than the evidence warrants. In *La Nación* of Buenos Aires for June 16, 1972, its Montevideo correspondent took it for granted that everybody knew the founder of the movement was a bricklayer named Eduardo Pinela, who became the first casualty on either side in its violent history when he was killed by falling from the fourth storey of the scaffolding on which he was working at a Montevideo hospital. Most accounts, however, say the organization was founded in or about 1962 by Raúl Sendic, a University of Montevideo law student (or former student), who had already had some experience as an activist in the country's Socialist Party. It is also said that this movement was patterned after the one in Brazil described by its leader, Carlos Marighela, in a book subsequently published in the United States under the title *For the Liberation of Brazil.*

The name Tupamaro, a contraction of Tupac Amaro (the organization's spelling), was adopted, at least according to one account, because it was the name the gauchos of Uruguay gave themselves during the war of independence against Spain in memory of the Inca of that name who had led a rebellion in Spanish Peru in the late eighteenth century. Our urban guerrillas may have forgotten that the real Tupac Amaru (the correct spelling) was defeated and put to death most barbarously. At any rate, that was not their only link with the past. They also projected a Robin Hood image of themselves: while their overriding purpose was to undermine the government by discrediting it, until 1967 their depredations seemed confined mainly to taking from the rich to give to the poor. However, the anti-imperialist strain connoted by the "national liberation" in their title drowned out its Sherwood Forest note before long, and the United States and its supposed henchmen in the oligarchy of Uruguay joined its government as principal targets of the MLN.

"Gentlemen amateurs," the Tupamaros have been called because many of them came from the middle and upper classes and were not — at least in the first few years — professional hoods or rebels. After executing a robbery, kidnapping, or other service to the cause, they would return to their regular tasks or avocations as if nothing out of the ordinary had happened. There were women as well as men in the organization and members of both sexes were drawn from the lower as well as the upper classes. Upper-class members were officers, the rest soldiers; but in the hope of preventing betrayal and leaks under torture or by accident, a cellular form of organization was adopted instead of one of the conventional military type.

For several years the Tupamaros were remarkably successful in evading detection and capture while carrying out daring operations, sometimes under the nose of the police. While their objective was political and social revolution, they proposed to drive the government out not by a military coup but by destroying its credibility. For a time it looked as if they might do just that. Their success was due in large part to their own careful planning, technical skills, and courage, and to advice and aid from abroad; but it could not have been so great if they had not received substantial support and sympathy among the people at large. The way had been prepared for them among more literate Uruguayans by younger writers, of the "Generation of 1945," who were disillusioned with the welfare state. Some felt that its founding father, José Batlle, had given it the wrong direction from the start; others, that it had been corrupted by his successors and that he would be the first to rebel against it if he were still alive. Shades of Garibaldi and Artigas too were invoked against a welfare state that had fared so ill.

One representative of this generation (the term is flexible) was Alberto Methol Ferré. Born in 1929 of a Blanco family, he was given a conventional Catholic education. He developed a keen interest in nationalism, Peronism, and anti-imperialism at an early stage. Later he turned to Marxism, and formed close ties with a prominent Argentine writer and Trotskyite, Jorge Abelardo Ramos. Like so many other left-wing intellectuals of that period, Methol Ferré had an urge to justify his nationalism historically, and for that purpose to "restore truth" to the record of his country's past.* This he undertook to do, but he was also deeply concerned with the problems of his own day and devoted himself with "almost religious zeal," as one writer put it, to the task of rescuing Uruguay and a united Latin America from neocolonialism and the stagnation and despair spawned by it. Though not a prolific writer, he reached a large public with his message through a variety of channels. These included, besides his books, articles in one of the best-known left-wing periodicals in Latin America. This was *Marcha* of Montevideo, which an economist, Carlos Quijano, founded in 1939, and which anticipated even Perón in advocating that Latin America take an independent "third position" between the two superpowers.

Vivián Trías, born in 1922, was a more prolific and more combative member of that generation, and contributed more directly to propagating what we may call the Tupamaro spirit. He joined the Socialist Party in 1946 and, as a militant from the start and later its secretary-general, helped to transform the party. Since its foundation in 1910 by Emilio Frugoni, it had followed the model of European socialism that was parliamentary, pacific, educational, and internationalist. Now, with Trías urging it on, it espoused Uru-

*For a similar effort by his contemporary Luis Vignolo, see chapter V.

guayan nationalism and condemned its former error of holding that only electoral and parliamentary methods should be used in promoting reform. The clear implication was that violent methods could be legitimate. The themes of his books are anti-imperialism, agrarian reform (one of his ancestors had been an officer under Saravia about the turn of the century), and the quest for truth in the history of Uruguay. In one book, *Imperialism in the Río de la Plata* (1960), he bracketed Uruguay's "national bourgeoisie" with the imperialists and held both responsible for that country's stagnation and attendant ills. In *El plan Kennedy* (1961) he warned against the Alliance for Progress as a Trojan horse of Yankee imperialism. His own prescription, contained in the latter work, was what he called "the new nationalism," although in fact it had been anticipated by Juan Perón and others several years before. As he described it, it was a "revolutionary nationalism of the colonial periphery" (meaning the Third World) which was characterized by the imperative demand of the periphery's peoples for social justice and national liberation from imperialism. Without such liberation, he asserted, they could not overcome their underdevelopment, and that must be done before it would be possible to relieve the people's poverty and achieve social justice.

Add a blast against the oligarchy, which Trías was happy to sound on many occasions, and we have a definition of the new nationalism that was familiar fare by the 1960s in left-wing circles of the other two Southern Cone countries as well as Uruguay. Also, the other two produced organizations like the Tupamaros, notably ERP in Argentina and MIR in Chile. Why, then, did Uruguay's organization emerge earlier and achieve so much greater prominence than they or any other organization of this kind in the area? Without attempting an exhaustive reply, we may suggest, first, that the incitement of the new Castroite influence was felt with double or triple force in Uruguay because Cuba and Castro were uppermost in the minds of those who took any interest in two Inter-American conferences held at Punta del Este, only sixty miles from Montevideo, in August 1961 and February 1962. The first one adopted the charter of the Alliance for Progress as an insurance against the spread of Castroism; the second excluded Cuba under the Castro regime from the OAS and the Inter-American system; and in both conferences — and Montevideo as well, we may be sure — Castro's apologists and champions made a deep impression. His prestige had reached its peak by this time and many Uruguayans were susceptible to his appeal. They had suffered much for a long time and had lost faith in their political system. It had become too rigid for the growing stresses and its safety-valve was too small to relieve the pent-up discontents of a nation nearly half of whose inhabitants were piled up on each other in the metropolitan area of a single city.

It was an exceptionally open city. Press, speech, and travel and communications in and out of the country were free and remained so decade after decade, except in time of war. This, together with the fact that the Communist Party of Uruguay had never been outlawed since its founding in 1920, is probably why Moscow had all along used Montevideo as its South American headquarters. To be sure, in the 1960s the Communist Party line in Uruguay as in all other countries condemned revolutionary violence such as that of the Tupamaros, but Montevideo and Uruguay were as open to all comers, including the Tupamaros at first, as to the Communists.

By 1967 the Tupamaros, still an urban organization, were strong enough to become beneficiaries of the reaction in favor of urban as against rural guerrilla warfare that followed the defeat and death of Che Guevara in Bolivia that year. Said to number about 2,000 at this time, they responded in kind to the growing harshness of the government's futile campaign against them under Pacheco Areco. Except in one case, however, they did not kill hostages they had kidnapped, even when the demanded ransom was not forthcoming. The single exception was the case of Daniel Mitrione, whom they murdered in August 1970 after his kidnapping led to an extraordinarily thorough search by the police and the capture of more than fifty Tupamaros. Their release was demanded as the price of Mitrione's life, the government refused to comply, and he was executed.

Mitrione was one of a number of police advisers furnished the government of Uruguay by the United States under its AID program, which at this time provided more money and personnel for police training there than in far larger Argentina and Brazil. The purpose was, of course, to increase the efficiency of the campaign against the Tupamaros, and Mitrione played an important part in it as instructor in surveillance and investigation. It was charged that he also introduced the Uruguayan police to the systematic use of the latest and most refined (if that is the right word) methods of torture. The rumor lacks plausibility. Beginning in Hitler's Germany, torture has had a sensational revival in the civilized West and it has been easy for the police of any interested country to keep abreast of technological advances. If the Montevideo police in the 1960s needed instruction, they must have been living in an ivory tower. Just across the Plata River, the Peronist police of Buenos Aires had been adept in torture in the 1940s and it is doubtful the art had been lost there.

The kidnapping and murder of Mitrione inspired a left-wing movie, *State of Siege*, released in 1973, which was clearly, though not explicitly, about the Uruguayan situation, and presented a very distorted and very Yankeephobe view of it. The picture created a sensation in Europe and some American countries, including Argentina, but was barred in Allende's Chile as well as in Uruguay. In Uruguay the murder cost the Tupamaros heavily in public support. This loss, together with improved police methods, may help to explain why many of them were captured in the course of the year following the murder.

In September 1971, however, they effected a spectacular jail delivery of 106 of their number in a single operation that won them admiration for the skill it required, as well as for the scale of the operation. In celebration of it they released unharmed the most distinguished of their hostages, the British ambassador to Uruguay, Sir Geoffrey Jackson, whom they had kidnapped eight months previously. The almost simultaneous escape of a contingent of Tupamaro women from the women's prison sent the organization's stock soaring and made the government look ridiculous — and that with a national election only two months away. Shortly before it took place, Robert Moss, correspondent of *The Economist* of London and an authority on guerrillas in Latin America, wrote that the Tupamaros had proved that "urban guerrillas can be a very real threat to the state." The political future of Uruguay, he continued, would depend on whether the traditional parties could turn back a new competitor, the Broad Front, which the Tupamaros had endorsed.

Political Response: The Broad Front

The Broad Front (*Frente Amplio*) was a coalition formed by the opposition parties of the left as the election of November 28, 1971, approached. Their 1966 coalition, FIDEL, had polled hardly one-tenth of the total vote, but this time they were heartened by the success of Allende's left-wing coalition in Chile in the preceding year, and their prospects were much better, if only because the public was weary of the unending violence, hard times continued, and both of the major parties were now discredited by their dismal failure to cope with the nation's problems.

As its candidate for the presidency the Broad Front chose a 54-year-old retired Army officer, General Liber Seregni. His strongest claim on the nomination was that two years previously he had retired rather than carry out repressive measures against students, workers, and suspected Tupamaros. The coalition's strongest member was the Communist Party. Originally, its other members were the Christian Democrats, the Socialists, and one dissident left-wing fragment from each of the two major parties. Liking its platform, the Tupamaros decided to go back, for this election, from bullets to ballots. Accordingly their organization declared a moratorium on violence through election day and, being a secret organization, set up a front organ of its own to represent it in the Broad Front.

During the campaign, Chilean politicians from Popular Unity came to Uruguay to tell the Broad Front how to conduct it. They should have felt at home. Its platform was much like the Chilean coalition's in 1970, and identical with it at several points, including its promise of agrarian reform, nationalization of all private banks and foreign trade, and milk every day for the children. As *New York Times* correspondent Joseph Novitski pointed out, however, there were fundamental differences between the two coalitions. Unlike Dr. Allende, General Seregni was not a Marxist and never promised to transform Uruguay into a socialist society, and the Christian Democrats were a part of the Broad Front in Uruguay, but the chief anti-Allende party in Chile.

In August a Gallup poll showed that the Broad Front was making a close race of it, well ahead of the National Party and not far behind the Colorados. That conclusion proved wrong, but the poll also contained information about class attitudes that is more dependable since it dealt with present opinions and not with future behavior. The most interesting indications in it were those that related to the Broad Front, because, as a new group, it did not depend for its votes on inherited attitudes, as the Colorados and Nationals (Blancos) did to a considerable extent. The indications were that in Montevideo the Broad Front's least strength lay in the middle class, which revealed that class to be the opposite of the progressive, left-tilted stereotype. The Front's greatest strength, according to the poll, was in the upper class in Montevideo and in the upper and middle classes equally in the interior, where the population was largely rural. The Front was weakest by a wide margin among the rural lower class (which was to be expected), and its appeal to the young (the 18-25 age group) was twice as strong as to the voters at large.

The Colorados won the election by a narrow margin over the National Party (681,624 votes to 668, 822) and each received more than twice as many votes as the Broad Front (304, 275). Yet the latter did rather well in Montevideo, where it polled 31 percent of the vote (nearly twice as large a share as FIDEL's in 1966), and came in ahead of the Nationals (29 percent). Outside the capital, however, the Front received less than one-tenth of the popular vote. Its poor showing there had been predicted, and interestingly enough it was due to the presence not of the violent Tupamaros but of the relatively tame Communists among the Front's components.

In the northern range country around Tacuarembó, for example, *Times* correspondent Novitski found, two weeks before the election, that disillusionment with the major parties and the state of the nation could bring the Broad Front some protest votes, but probably not many. The few it got would come from the middle- and upper-class townsmen, not the country folk. The Front, a cattle dealer told him, had a good program, but it also had the Communist Party, "so now what do we do?" In the election of 1966 the party had polled less than one thousand of the district's 41,000 votes, and that did not augur well for the Front, of which it was the principal member. Another man, a ranch owner, said he was afraid of the Communist Party, but had no use for either the Blancos or the Colorados, for they had never given the country a good government and this time all their candidates were "tainted if not rotten with speculation or buying votes with state jobs." "So," he concluded, "I'm going to vote a blank ballot." If this rancher's opinion was any guide, the Tupamaros had gone a long way towards winning their campaign to discredit the existing political system, for one of their major charges against it was that the two parties that always dominated it were hopelessly corrupt.

The 1971 election was so close that it gave rise to the longest dispute in the history of Uruguay over which party had won. At last, on February 15, 1972, it was decided in favor of the Colorados and

Juan María Bordaberry was proclaimed president-elect for a five-year term beginning March 1. In the meantime an incident occurred that showed how high feeling ran over the political conflict and what a strong hold traditional ways still retained in Uruguay. This was a duel between the Broad Front's defeated presidential candidate, General Seregni, and another retired general, Juan Ribas, 70 years of age, who had called him a deserter, a traitor, and a disgrace to the army for consorting with Socialists and Communists. Seregni challenged his detractor to a duel, which was perfectly legal in Uruguay, so long as a Court of Honor made proper arrangements. That was done and the duel fought with pistols, at 25 paces, two shots each. No one was injured.

President Bordaberry, a wealthy 44-year-old rancher, had been a member of Pacheco Areco's cabinet and proposed to continue the latter's campaign against the Tupamaros. Soon, however, he ran into opposition in Congress that brought on a struggle for power in which the armed forces became involved. The introduction of that element led ultimately to the dissolution of Congress and the establishment of a dictatorship. Two main factors in the struggle were opposition in Congress to the rigor of the campaign against the Tupamaros, and the latter's escalation of the conflict. The escalation came on April 15, 1972, six weeks after the inauguration of the new president. On that day Tupamaro guerrillas ambushed and assassinated four persons connected with the government. One was a police intelligence officer and another a captain in the navy who was shot down outside Montevideo by a guerrilla disguised as a garbage collector. The president immediately called on Congress to declare a "state of internal war" (much like martial law) for an indefinite period. Congress gave him the declaration the same day, but limited it to 30 days. He came back at the close of that period with a request for a 45-day extension. This time, to his disgust and that of the security forces that had to do the fighting, Congress debated the question heatedly for four days before authorizing the extension by the uncomfortably close margin of 68 to 56. As the struggle became more intense in the next few weeks, the mood in Congress changed and in June, with only the Broad Front members opposing, it enacted a law for the security of the state which made it unnecessary for Bordaberry to keep coming back to that body for extensions of the decree.

In late April the situation had been exacerbated by the involvement of the Communists. Following the Moscow line, they disapproved of the Tupamaros' terrorism, but, because of the never-ending inflation, the Communist-controlled unions — transport, municipal workers, schoolteachers — struck for higher wages just after the declaration of internal war on April 15. While the strike was in progress, the police came to Communist headquarters looking for Tupamaro fugitives reported to be hiding in the building. Someone fired a shot (each side blamed the other for it) that started a general fight, and when it was over, seven Communists were dead. The affair did not bring the party into the "internal war" on the side of the Tupamaros, but it is significant as a sign of the growing tension and violence in the capital city. With the added trial of economic stagnation, things were now so bad that the owner of a textile mill that had been fire-bombed after some of the workers were laid off, said, "A year ago I used to worry that they would burn the place down. Now I worry that they won't. I would like to collect the insurance and get out."

Enter the Armed Forces

The declaration of internal war on April 15 meant, among other things, that the armed forces were now in charge of the anti-Tupamaro campaign. The police continued to take part in it, but as a junior partner. In 1972 Carlos Rama, the Uruguayan historian quoted above, voiced another complaint common among critics of the United States in Latin America. This was that his country had been militarized by the northern colossus, which, since World War II, had supplanted France in providing the largest of Uruguay's three armed services, the army, with advanced training. Whether a country has been militarized is easier to sense than to prove. In the present instance the charge seems exaggerated. One indication is that military service in Uruguay remained voluntary throughout the postwar period with which we are concerned. Another is that in mid-1973, more than a year after the declaration of internal war, the total number of men in its armed services, 21,000, was about the same, in proportion to population, as in Chile and only slightly larger than in Argentina, neither of whose people could be properly called militarized, even though in that year one of them came under military rule and the other ended a long domination by it.

What happened in Uruguay in the 1960s and early 1970s was not that its people were militarized by the United States, but that its military were politicized by the Tupamaros. And one of the most interesting things about this is that not all the officers were politicized in the same direction. All of them, it appears, condemned the guerrilla movement for its lawless violence, but some were convinced of the rightness of the Tupamaros' demand for radical reform by the capture of proofs they had assembled of extensive injustice and corruption in the existing regime.

The offensive begun against the guerrillas in April 1972 was the biggest of its kind in the ten-year history of their organization. The armed forces, which now headed it, were slightly inferior in numbers to the police (22,000), but, besides having an army reserve of 100,000, they were much better armed and trained, and probably better disciplined. The army had its expected complement of armored regiments, infantry regiments, and artillery and engineer battalions, and, in addition, one remarkable feature: 9 cavalry squadrons. These might prove quite useful, for by early 1972 it was noted that the Tupamaros were extending their operations on a considerable scale to thinly settled departments. Certain to be useful was the antisubversive training given by the United States under its military assistance pact of 1952 with Uruguay; this was the kind of training stressed in its aid under all pacts of this kind with Latin American countries since the Castro revolution in Cuba. Uruguay's other armed services were a navy of 3,000 men, a few destroyer escorts and patrol vessels for its extensive ocean and river coastline, and about two dozen helicopters; and an air force of 2,000 men, with a grand total of 12 combat aircraft and a number of trainers and helicopters.

The tide turned against the Tupamaros almost from the beginning of the April offensive against them. Before the end of that month the myth of their infallibility was shattered by the discovery of their principal "people's jails" and the release of several prisoners. Among these were two prominent men who had been kidnapped more than a year earlier. One was the head of the state electric power and telephone company, and the other a former minister of agriculture; both were wealthy ranchers. This coup was followed in ensuing weeks by the discovery of many Tupamaro hideouts, including a medical clinic, a financial office, and two information centers, and by the capture of scores of guerrillas and several arms caches of machine guns, bazookas, and other weapons and ammunition.

Under the hammer blows rained on them in Montevideo, these

urban guerrillas accelerated their dispersion into the interior, but there too the armed forces harried them and many Tupamaros were rounded up as early as June, the second month after the offensive began. The captures that month as reported in the Buenos Aires press (*La Nacíon, La Razón, Clarín, Crónica*) show how widely dispersed they were and illustrate the great diversity of their membership in age, sex, and occupation, which were specified in enough cases to provide a fair sample. Some of the captures were made at the opposite end of the country from Montevideo, in departments ranged along the whole length of the Brazilian border from Treinta y Tres in the east to Artigas in the west. Others were on a line stretching from the town of San José some 30 miles west of Montevideo northward through Fray Bentos and Paysandú to, again, Artigas, the country's northwesternmost department. Still other captures were made in its central department of Durazno. Sex was indicated by the reports in most cases. The great majority of the prisoners taken were men, but in one group of 43, six were women, and there were a few more in other groups. One of the women was described as a leader and a member of the old guard.

In age, the captives ranged from three "minors" and several "students" (admittedly a flexible category in temporal terms) to a man aged 68, who was described simply as retired, no occupation stated. Most of the rest whose ages were indicated were in their thirties or forties. In respect to occupation, twelve were described as schoolteachers, five as doctors, unstated numbers as builders, municipal functionaries, office workers, and (in only one instance) as rural laborers, two as priests, and one each as professor, landowner, nurse, tradesman, "radio-telegrapher," and traveling salesman. One of the priests was said to be an Italian (except for one Chilean, he was the only foreigner among the captives), aged 30, whose parish in the department of Treinta y Tres bore the appropriate name of San José Obrero (workman). Plain workmen, though, were a conspicuously minuscule fraction of these captured Tupamaros. They were, overwhelmingly, a middle-class lot. Yet, at the polls the middle class gave only weak support to the Broad Front, which the Tupamaros joined; that is one more evidence of the lack of unity, the fragmentation, of the middle class.

For a campaign in which, as *The Economist* said, the state itself was threatened, the number of casualties was surprisingly small. In the first two months, from April 15 to June 15, which seems to have been the most critical period, there were only 31 killed, according to one count, and 30 according to another. But charges multiplied that the Tupamaros taken prisoner were being tortured. Most of the Roman Catholic hierarchy in Uruguay had by this time espoused the cause of radical reform in the interest of social justice. Appalled by the unending violence, they met in an Episcopal Conference and on June 15, 1972, issued a 16-point declaration calling on "all men of good will" to work together for the restoration of peace. The declaration was of course focused on the confrontation between the guerrillas and the armed forces, that is, the government. It was couched in the language of the reformers. Ostensibly, it did equal justice to both sides. The Tupamaros, it said, had "suffered a mutation of values" that led to a contradiction between, on the one hand, their asserted struggle for justice and, on the other hand, their commission of "tremendous injustices" such as kidnapping and acts that led to loss of life—an elegant periphrasis unmatched in the bishops' references to the Tupamaros' opponents. After a brief acknowledgment of the government's right to defend itself, the declaration said that "the bishops severely condemn the illegal pressures and tortures attributed to the organs of security." The declaration went on to suggest repeatedly that the Tupamaros were not only not to blame for what they had done, but were even justified in doing it. Their actions were a product of the nation's "stagnation, dependence, and despair," said the bishops, which was brought on by the crisis in the economy, in education, housing, social welfare, and production, and which was translated into protest on the part of those who were unjustly treated and had neither help nor hope. The source of the trouble, they said, lay in structural defects in society, for which no individual was to blame, except those who did not try to correct them. "We think, then," they said, "that illegitimate resistance to change, skepticism about the future, and the gravity of the injustices appear as some of the motivations of those who began subversive action in this country."

This was, in effect, an admonition to the government to lay down its arms. President Bordaberry published a vigorous reply to the bishops the same evening. The use of torture, he declared, had never been ordered or tolerated by the government; but he defended its right to use other pressures on prisoners on the ground that it produced information essential for dealing with a secret subversive movement. To the argument that this movement was a protest of victims of poverty and was justified by illegitimate resistance to change, he replied that most of the Tupamaros belonged to the middle and upper classes and that his own administration had from the start made change in the interest of "distributive justice" one of its chief aims, only to be attacked by the guerrillas in its first few months in office. Finally, he countercharged that the intransigence of the Tupamaros made the pacification called for by the bishops a practical impossibility.

The campaign against the Tupamaros continued as if the bishops had never spoken. By late August, 1,600 of them and their accomplices were reported to have been imprisoned. In February 1973 the correspondent of *The Economist* reported from Montevideo that since President Bordaberry gave the army sweeping powers "last April" it had dealt with them so effectively that now "most of the guerrilla leaders are in jail, and the urban groups have distintegrated." The following August *The Times of the Americas* (Washington, D. C.) published a report from Buenos Aires, which the Argentine government would not permit to be published there, of a defiant statement issued jointly by the leaders of "the once-powerful Uruguayan Tupamaros" and their Argentine counterpart, ERP, announcing that they would fight on against "imperialism and capitalism" and that the Chilean MIR was affiliated with them in this "second war of independence, reviving the unity of our peoples, who were triumphant in the first battle of independence fought against the Spanish." These were brave words, but the Tupamaro leaders who uttered them were refugees and the other leaders were in jail. One of their number recently sent back to Montevideo by the allied ERP had just been caught and killed by the police.

The success of the anti-guerrilla campaign was due in part to the cooperation of the military dictatorship in Brazil, which gave the authorities in Montevideo the benefit of its experience in its own recent and highly successful handling of a similar problem. It is ironical that the Tupamaro movement, which drew early inspiration and guidance from Brazil, was put down with aid from the same country.

Coup on the Installment Plan

Under the caption "Uruguay: The colonels get ideas," *The Economist* of August 26, 1972, reported that the progress of the campaign against the Tupamaros was being offset by a decline of the gross national product and a shortage of beef for export that had led to the imposition of a four-month ban on the slaughter of beef for domestic consumption, and that the army officers had developed political ideas of their own. There was a three-fold political division among the armed forces, the report continued. First, there were the constitutionalists, who wanted to maintain the status quo. The army commander-in-chief was one of this group. Second, there were the *peruanistas* (Peruvianists), who were impressed by the left-wing military dictatorship in Peru and had even negotiated with the Tupamaros with the promise of sweeping reforms, "like land redistribution and the nationalization of the banks," on condition that they lay down their arms. In this group was a sub-group of naval officers who had recently gone so far as to issue a declaration that subversion includes corruption and the looting of national resources as well as assassination.

The third group, on the other hand, was impressed by the Brazilian style of government. This group, said *The Economist,* "may well emerge as the victor in any internal power struggle," given the Brazilians' influence over President Bordaberry and "their increasing financial hold on Uruguay" through, for example, a new credit of $15 million and land purchases in northern Uruguay. As it turned out, the first of these groups was the weakest, and although the second group, the Peruvianists, prevailed at the beginning of the take-over of the government by the military in early 1973, it was supplanted later that year by the third group, the Brazilianists, as *The Economist* had guardedly predicted a year earlier.

The military takeover in 1973, still not quite complete at the end of the year, was conducted by stages; a coup on the installment plan, Uruguayans called it. It began on February 12, when President Bordaberry yielded to "a brief show of force" by "14 vintage tanks" lumbering through a park uncomfortably close to his residence. He placated the officers by agreeing to share power with them and get on with badly needed reforms. As a first step he was to set up a National Security Council for development as well as security, with strong military representation and a reform program but, at the outset, without clearly defined powers. The 18-point reform program, which was issued by the military commanders, called for "the punishing of 'socio-economic' crimes, land redistribution and workers' participation in industry" — "fiery stuff, coming from the generals," commented *The Economist*, and continued, "It is starting to look as if the 'Peruvians' in the Uruguayan officer corps may be getting their way." The "program of national reconstruction," as the military called it, was welcomed by the Broad Front parties, including even the Communist Party, despite the fact that one of its points called for blocking the infiltration of Marxism-Leninism. At the other political extreme, the conservative National Party denounced the National Security Council as an extra-constitutional organ that would break the country's civilian tradition by placing control of the government in military hands.

The second installment of the coup, which carried it from halfway to the three-quarters mark, came on June 27. Among the military there was still dissatisfaction with the president, mainly over the slow pace of reconstruction, reform, and anti-left wing action. The prime target of the officers' discontents, however, was Congress, in which the majority, opposed to the president, had the temerity to resist the military too, whereas the only trouble Bordaberry gave them was to drag his feet occasionally. What precipitated the June 27 coup was the refusal of Congress to lift the parliamentary immunity of one of its members, Senator Enrique Erro, which had been demanded by the military so that he might be tried on charges of aiding and abetting the Tupamaros. In a similar case in 1972, Congress had finally yielded, and the military leaders, now in an even stronger position than the year before, were not going to settle for anything less this time.

Accordingly, they put pressure on the president to rid them of the obstructionist Congress. (They later denied having done so, but the denial was not convincing.) He may not have found it too difficult to comply with a demand for the elimination of a body, controlled by his opponents, that was a constant vexation to him too. At any rate, his compliance was thorough. He abolished Congress, dissolved the 19 municipal councils, and joined with the National Security Council in setting up a hand-picked Council of State to replace those bodies. When the Communist-dominated National Confederation of Workers (CNT) called for a general strike in protest against these actions, he dissolved it too. Uruguay was now ruled by a dictatorship, but it was civilian, for Bordaberry, a constitutionally elected president, still held that office. He was reported to have strong military support led by the commanding officer of the Montevideo garrison and a colonel who, as minister of interior, was in command of the police.

One reason why Bordaberry was able to retain his hold on the presidency seems to have been that most of the officer corps, warned by the political failures of the Argentine military, had salutary doubts about their own ability to run a government. One may wonder why, instead, they were not encouraged to try their hand at it by the political success of the military leaders in Brazil, with whom they had close ties and under whose rule since 1964 that country had achieved a quite remarkable economic development. Perhaps a clue to the answer is suggested by the question itself. Like many other Uruguayans, the military were preoccupied with the central problem of economic development; they wanted Brazil's succesful development policy followed in Uruguay, but did not want to risk botching the job by trying to do it themselves, and did not need to risk it, for in Bordaberry they had an experienced civilian leader who was much better qualified for it and whom they could trust to follow the Brazilian model. They had reason for thinking so. As *The Economist* noted just after the coup of June 27, Bordaberry had already declared that he admired Brazil's conservative government and believed that a liberal attitude towards foreign investment was the key to economic development. That belief was shared by Brazil's military rulers and their economic policy had been shaped in accordance with it.

Consolidating the Dictatorship

The coup of June 27 provoked a wave of opposition which, to judge from newspaper reports, was formidable. The National Workers Confederation defied Bordaberry's decree of dissolution and continued the general strike. The workers were joined by crowds of students in demonstrations that were, of course, angry. Shopkeepers, fearing broken windows and looting, suspended business and lowered their metal shutters. Traffic in city and port came to a standstill and food shortages became acute. All the opposition parties denounced the coup and five civilian members of the president's own cabinet resigned. Efforts were made by the police, mounted and on foot, and by soldiers with tanks to break up the demonstrations, but the demonstrators only dispersed to reform in another place. After two weeks of this, one would have concluded from reports in the *New York Times* that the government had little chance of survival. On July 10 the paper reported that a Resistance Front had been formed by the leaders of the main political parties and the labor unions and student associations and that the president was having difficulty filling the vacancies in his cabinet. It also reported rumors of "dissent within the armed forces" that "persist despite a denial recently by the joint command." On the same day, in connection with the general strike, it described the rather weak National Workers Confederation as "powerful," even reporting as a fact the confederation's inflated claim of 500,000 members, which would have been one-sixth of all the men, women, and children in Uruguay. The next day, July 11, the *Times* reported that this same confederation, whose general strike was already "the longest . . . in this country's history," had "announced today that its unions would stand firm 'until Mr. Bordaberry falls.' " The very next day the confederation called off the strike and the resistance to the dictatorship collapsed.

What had happened? *Pravda*, trying to put the best possible face on the bad news, claimed on July 13 that "the CNT [the Communist-controlled Workers Confederation] called off its two-week old strike because it had forced the government to enter into discussions with the Broad Front and the Nationlist Party." That was absurd. Perhaps *The Times of the Americas* erred as far in the other direction by reporting that apparently the only concession the labor leaders got out of secret talks with the government before calling off the strike was its promise "to release some labor prisoners"—the same labor prisoners, no doubt, who had been taken on Bordaberry's orders in order to break the strike. However that may be, the fact is that the strike had already collapsed before it was called off. Its collapse was probably due to the strong measures Bordaberry took to break it and suppress the opposition and to the effective support he received from the armed forces and the police.

One of the most interesting things about this strike is its quick failure after a promising start. According to the same report in *The Times of the Americas,* the strike was "extremely effective for about a week, but after that stores reopened, transportation was once more "about average," and by the end of the second week, "the capital city had returned to almost normal." This indicates that middle-class people did not even support their own leaders, for all the parties had joined in the Resistance Front set up to overthrow Bordaberry and the dictatorship. The measures taken by the government to put down the opposition included wholesale arrests of demonstrators, political leaders (among them General Seregni of Broad

Front), and labor leaders. So effective was the sweep that during the second week the CNT leaders who escaped arrest had to direct the strike from hideouts.

The collapse of the strike and the opposition left the civil-military dictatorship in a strong position, which it consolidated during the rest of the year. In August it proceeded to "democratize" the CNT unions by such measures as the requirement that in all union elections and other decisions made by the membership, voting must in future be done by secret ballot instead of by voice or show of hands, as had been the practice under Marxist domination. Another new requirement was that all unions must file with the government membership lists signed by all their members. This was expected to bring about a drastic reduction of the CNT's membership figures, which it could not fail to do if properly enforced.

In September the government felt sure enough of itself to permit student elections at the nation's only university, the one in Montevideo. It was described at the time, probably without exaggeration, as one of the "most leftist" universities in Latin America, in its faculty as well as its student body. As in the universities of Argentina, Chile, and other Latin American countries, the students were highly politicized and the political groups corresponded to the national parties. The September elections resulted in a sweeping victory for the Broad Front candidates, which was a blow to the government. It bided its time, but not for long.

Late in October a student was killed by a bomb blast in the engineering school, whereupon the government violated the traditional immunity of the university buildings and grounds by occupying them with troops and making scores of arrests of students, faculty, and officers of administration, including the rector and all the deans except one who was in Buenos Aires at the time. At the same time a decree was issued closing the university indefinitely and placing its administration in the hands of the minister of education and culture, Edmundo Narancio, a distinguished historian and university professor of the older generation.

The government justified these drastic actions on the grounds that the dead student was a subversive who had been killed by the accidental explosion of a bomb he was making; that the failure of the university authorities to maintain order in this and other respects made it necessary for the government to intervene; that the intervention had revealed abundant evidence of the involvement of university personnel in the "indoctrination of youths in the Marxist ideology," and in making the university a "refuge for conspiracy against the fatherland [*patria*], its institutions, and the security of its inhabitants." In one precious passage this dictatorial decree condemned Marxism because it was "opposed to the nation's democratic representative system of government."

With the university closed, the Tupamaros crushed, and the unions castrated, the government had disposed of all the most likely centers of subversion. As additional precautions, however, it was still holding the Broad Front's leader, General Seregni, under house arrest in the country at the end of the year, and it celebrated the beginning of the new year by outlawing the Communist Party, along with all other Marxist groups. This was a novel experience for the party, now more than half a century old. Even when, in 1932, the Terra dictatorship closed its headquarters and newspaper and jailed several of its members, the party was not outlawed. As suggested above, its long undisturbed life in Uruguay helps to explain why Montevideo became a kind of central postoffice for Soviet communications and propaganda in South America. Fear of losing it may also help explain why the Soviet press took a very hard line against Uruguay's military dictatorship from its beginning in the semi-coup of February 1973, whereas it remained discreetly silent about the dictatorship in Brazil, with which it appeared to have a tacit truce.

By the end of the year the Bordaberry regime had achieved its aim of restoring law and order in Uruguay. It had not had much success in coping with the country's basic economic problems. There was still inflation at a high rate—about 80 percent for the year—and there were still food shortages, of which the ban on beef and the use of wheat substitutes in bread were evidences. Production of the nation's chief export commodities, beef, lamb, and wool, still lagged. At the close of the year its troubles were aggravated by the skyrocketing price of petroleum, which was exceptionally painful to Uruguay. Its massive social welfare burden was as heavy as ever and there were fewer productive workers to sustain it, for emigration still soared. Hard figures were not available, but a careful estimate earlier in the year indicated that there had already been a loss through emigration of almost 300,000 persons, or one-tenth of the total population. Among the emigrants were many skilled workers and technicians, and the drain showed no sign of ending.

Nevertheless, at least in Montevideo conditions were reported to be somewhat better than in recent years, now that there was peace and security for most people. Some of them were even hopeful about the economic future. No reason why they should be hopeful about the near future was readily apparent. Looking further ahead, the prospect improved somewhat, particularly with regard to sources of power, in which the country had always been deficient. In December 1972 the Inter-American Development Bank made a loan of $80 million in support of the first stage of a joint project of Uruguay and Argentina for the construction of a very large (1,620,000 kilowatt) hydroelectric power plant at Salto Grande ("Great Falls") on the Uruguay River. When completed, the plant would provide electric power for an area of about 116,000 square miles, which was not far from twice the size of Uruguay. It would cover most of that country, including its principal zones of population and economic production, and a large part of the Argentine Littoral. To Uruguay it would render the inestimable service of greatly reducing that country's dependence on imported coal and petroleum. Politically, if this big joint venture developed successfully, it might check the growing rapprochement with Brazil and even replace it by one with Argentina. The completion of the project lay several years in the future. For the mid-1970s, most hopeful were the people who shared President Bordaberry's view that a liberal attitude towards foreign investment was the key to economic development and who trusted him to carry out a policy based on that view. Some Montevideo mind-readers predicted at the end of 1973 that the military leaders, so firmly entrenched that they did not need to keep up the least pretense of constitutionalism, would in a matter of months complete their takeover by discarding the president. That did not happen until 1976.

Seers in the Southern Cone, from the depression decade to the end of our period, seemed to have a special knack for misreading the minds of the military. That was particularly unfortunate in this turbulent period of great expectations and great disappointments, of decay of the old order and the only partial emergence of its disorderly successor. It was a period of flux during which the professionalized armed forces' almost unique stability pushed them to the fore in public affairs, and a period of violence that turned their near-monopoly of organized force into a standing temptation to take a hand in cleaning up the mess the civilians were making of things. So it would have been better if civilians had had a better understanding of this power group, for then, in Uruguay as in the other two countries, the power of the military might have been put to better use for all concerned.

XIII Poverty, Progress, and Politics in Chile, 1942-1970

In 1942 Chile's Popular Front government — the only one in the Western hemisphere — completed its disintegration with its term of office. In 1973 that country's Socialist government — one of only two in the hemisphere, and the only one voted into power — was overthrown by a military coup. During most of the intervening 30-odd years Chile shared with Argentina and Uruguay the pains of a stop-go economy and suffered even more than they from perennial inflation. It faced a still worse problem, though, in the extreme maldistribution of the national income. The gravity of the problem is not apparent from the cold statistics of income distribution in all Latin America, for these show that, again as in Argentina and Uruguay, the poorest people in Chile were better off than the poorest in all the other Latin American countries. But what this really shows is how misleading bare statistics can be, for the evidence supports Fredrick Pike's assertion that in this period most Chileans lived in a "culture of poverty" (a phrase borrowed, with due acknowledgment, from Oscar Lewis). Incredible though it seems, an estimate believed to be reliable indicated that in 1942, when things were not yet at their worst, 77 percent of the working force did not earn enough to enable a single man (not to mention one with wife and children) to live decently. At the other extreme, the top 2.4 percent of the population in 1968 received nearly half (45.9 percent) of the national income.

Poverty Amidst Plenty

Matters were made worse by the acceleration after the 1930s of Chile's previously slow rate of population growth. The acceleration continued until the end of our period and made Chile one of the faster growing Latin American nations, while Argentina and Uruguay became two of the slowest. From 8.5 million in 1964, Chile's population grew to 10.23 million in 1973.* For Argentina the figures in the same years were 21.17 million and 24.29 million, respectively, and for Uruguay, which had almost ceased to grow at all, 2.71 million and 2.99 million. Its accelerated population growth, together with industrialization, urbanization, and other factors converted Chile, traditionally an exporter of foodstuffs, into an importer on

---

*Population estimates are from United Nations *Monthly Bulletin of Statistics*, December 1974, pp. 1-4, table I, which for Chile are adjusted for underenumeration in the censuses of 1960 and 1970.

an ever-increasing scale throughout the three decades under consideration. Social problems increased somewhat in number and greatly in intensity in the countryside as well as the cities but reached their peak (or seemed to because of its high visibility) in the teeming shantytown of Santiago. By 1970 that city had developed as acute a case of elephantiasis as the capitals of Argentina and Uruguay, for one-third of the nation's total population was now crowded into its metropolitan area.

Politically, this state of affairs was reflected in a swing to the left, but, in terms of popular support, that movement travelled neither as far nor as fast as might have been expected. At the beginning of the period, in 1942, the Popular Front Government which was just leaving office was a coalition of Socialists, Communists, and the essentially middle-class and not-so-radical Radicals. Not until 28 years later was control of the government won by an exclusively left-wing coalition — the one called Popular Unity, which consisted of Socialists, Communists, and left-wing splinter groups and was headed by Salvador Allende. Even then the coalition won only the powerful presidency and polled less than 37 percent of the popular vote. What is more, during the three years it remained in power, it never gained control of either house of Congress and never polled a majority of the popular vote, although it was favored by two changes in the electoral law after the election of 1970: the abolition of the literacy requirement and the lowering of the voting age from 21 to 18.

Even allowing for the rise in the 1960s of the left-of-center Christian Democratic Party, the limited extent of the shift to the left calls for an explanation. None is readily apparent in the political history of the period. First there were ten years of Radical rule (1942-1952), which was, on balance, moderate and was featured by the treatment accorded the Communists, who were taken into the government for a time and then, in response to the Cold War, outlawed in 1947 and thereafter rigorously repressed for nearly a decade. The Radicals were followed by another six years under Carlos Ibáñez, who, now in his seventies, promised much and delivered little. His ties with Perón of Argentina, already mentioned in another connection, caused excitement for a time, but the outstanding measure of his administration was the "New Deal" (*Nuevo Trato*) copper law designed to stimulate production in the largely U.S.-owned copper mines, which had become the chief symbol of Yankee imperialism to many conservative as well as to all radical Chileans. After Ibáñez came the only conservative government of the period, that of Jorge Alessandri. His sound-money policy checked growth more than it did inflation, which had begun to gallop under his predecessors. The result was to prepare the way for the smashing victory in the elections of 1964 and 1965 of the Christian Democrats under the leadership of Eduardo Frei Montalva, but they won it with aid given by the conservatives as the only way of defeating the much more radical Socialist leader, Salvador Allende. Frei tried hard to keep his promise of a "revolution in liberty," but his party lost ground steadily and ended up a bad third in the election of 1970. The chief contenders in that election were the right-wing National Party and the left-wing coalition, Popular Unity. Three-fourths of the popular vote was divided almost evenly between the two.

Here we have a clue to the reason why the swing to the left in Chile's postwar generation was so limited, for the great bulk of the National Party's 37 percent of the vote must have come from the middle class. This was an indication of the conservative trend that had been going on for some time in that amorphous class. It provided Popular Unity with some of its most extreme left-wing leaders but must also have been the source of most of the surprisingly large number of votes cast for the right-wing ticket in the elections of 1970 and the rest of the Allende period. Here then is the most plausible explanation of his left-wing coalition's failure to live up to its "popular" name by winning a majority in any election.

This is by no means to deny that the conservatives, topped by the oligarchy, constituted a formidable political phalanx through its economic power in the sectors of finance, commerce, industry, agriculture, and communications. Yet, faced by a phalanx at least as formidable and backed by an even weaker labor movement than Allende's in 1970, Juan Perón in 1946 had won a clear-cut victory at the polls and had gone on from there to increase his popularity in the next few years. Perhaps a charismatic leader on either side might have done as well in Chile, but the country produced none after the first Alessandri. The second Alessandri, Jorge, was no "Lion of Tarapacá"; rather, he was the lion of Santiago's upper-class Club de la Unión, the Chilean counterpart of the Buenos Aires Jockey Club. Eduardo Frei had many admirers but was too cerebral for mass appeal. Allende was a skillful politician who had a social conscience and other attractive attributes, but lacked personal magnetism. If he had possessed it, his coalition might not have failed to win a popular majority or control of either house of Congress.

Inflation and Development

In the first half of World War II Chile was severely shaken, both politically and economically, by that conflict. As the prospect of an Axis victory receded, however, and along with it the fear of raids on the long, exposed Chilean coast by Japanese or German submarines or warships—a danger that helped to keep Chile neutral until January 1943—life seemed to go on much as before except for economic adjustments to wartime changes. Even these were relatively minor. Typical of them were a rise of copper production to a new peak and a modest revival of the manufacture of arms and ammunition. In politics, Aguirre Cerda was succeeded by another Radical, Juan Antonio Ríos. When he died just after the end of the war, his place, too, was filled by a Radical, Gabriel González Videla. He belonged to his party's left wing, whereas Ríos had belonged to its right wing, but that was normal in the Radical Party, which was as loose-jointed and heterogeneous as the middle class which it mainly represented.

More changes, however, were taking place during the war years than met the eye, even the eye of so keen an observer as George Wythe, Latin American specialist in the U.S. Department of Commerce and leading authority on the growth of industry in that part of the world. As he viewed the scene in Chile near the end of the war, the first thing that impressed him was that the Great Depression of the 1930s had made its people excessively pessimistic about the minerals export trade and excessively optimistic about industrialization, whereas in fact during the war copper exports had set a new record and nitrate exports had held up well in volume, although competition (from synthetic nitrates) had reduced the price. Before the war, he noted, agricultural exports too were moving upward, and yet the Chileans were still counting on manufacturing to raise income and living standards, since minerals are exhaustible and Chile's arable land area is limited; and they were holding up Switzerland and Finland, both small countries and successful in industry, as models for their own country to follow.

This report rightly stressed Chilean interest in industrialization, which was soon to become an obsession there as in most other Latin American countries. Yet the report missed another long-range economic factor of prime importance, which, though present in some degree throughout Latin America, attained its greatest intensity in Chile, and lasted longer there than in any other country in America, possibly in the world. That factor was inflation. That it was over-looked, or at any rate not mentioned, is not at all surprising, for in most countries it was checked or concealed until the close of the war. In Chile, however, its headlong rise had already begun by that time. Taking 1940 as 100, the cost of living index had risen to 205 by 1945. Much more and much worse was to come. In the next ten years the index skyrocketed to 2,887. In the next eight years after that, the consumer price index (on a basis of 1958 = 100) shot up from 42 in 1955 to 205 in 1963, despite the earnest efforts of the conservative administration of Jorge Alessandri, which began in 1958, to curb inflation.

Inflation and industrialization were closely interrelated in both theory and practice. "Development" was the watchword of the post-war generation. In the early years it was conceived of almost exclu-sively in terms of economic development, the heart of which was industrialization, and the crowning glory of industrialization could only be a steel mill. Such development entailed heavy expense, but both investment capital and patience were in short supply in Chile, and since its people were not conditioned to achieve development through forced savings on the Soviet Union's model, the solution became development by inflation, which already had a long history in Chile. It was not as simple as that, of course, but that was the heart of it. Development, whether economic or of any other kind, was financed in very large part by increasing the supply of money and credit or by borrowing from a foreign national or international agency, such as the U.S. Export-Import Bank, the World Bank, or, after its founding in 1960, the Inter-American Development Bank. Tax revenues from the big foreign copper companies, the Gran Minería, were also used to some extent in support of development but to a much greater extent for current expenses in order to keep the Chilean people's taxes down. As a result, the process of develop-ment remained highly inflationary. By the early 1950s it had be-come accepted doctrine in Chile's Central Bank as in all structural-ist circles that inflation was a good thing, not only necessary but proper since the only alternative was economic stagnation. Also, the fact that continued inflation does more harm to the poor than to the rich was ignored and only its immediate stimulus to wages and jobs considered. Thus it was another article of the new faith that anyone who opposed inflation was a reactionary defender of the status quo and a minion of the oligarchy.

Government intervention in the Chilean economy was already well advanced by the 1940s. The chief development agency was, not surprisingly, CORFO, which was established in 1939 by the Popular Front Government. CORFO provided an outstanding example of the neo-orthodox policy of internally oriented development and its limitations. CORFO had some notable achievements to its credit, but in the period of its most intense activity, 1945-1955, Chile's gross product increased at an annual rate of only 2.7 percent, as compared with a general Latin American average of 6.3 percent, and Chile's rate of capital formation, too, was one of the lowest.

CORFO was responsible for two particularly important new departures in the postwar period. One was the establishment in 1946 of the Huachipato steel plant of the Pacific Steel Company, near Concepción, which began production in 1950. The United States played an important part in getting it started. The plant was built with the aid of a loan of $110 million obtained from the Export-Import Bank by CORFO, personnel from the United States trained Chileans to operate the plant, and it obtained its iron ore from the Bethlehem Steel Company's mines at La Serena (north of Valparaíso). Coal for the plant came from Chile's best coal mines, which were only about 15 miles away, and Concepción is, of course, one of Chile's principal cities and had one of its best ports. With all these advantages, it is not surprising that the Huachipato steel mill soon became an important addition to the Chilean economy.

CORFO's second innovation, and one of its major undertakings for several years, was the establishment of Chile's petroleum industry. This was conducted by a government-owned monopoly, ENAP, and began production in 1949. All the wells were on either side of the Strait of Magellan in the vicinity of Punta Arenas, the world's southernmost city, some of them on Tierra del Fuego and the rest just across on the mainland. They produced petroleum and natural gas. By 1970 two refineries were in operation, the older one at Concón, near Valparaíso and the other near Concepción and hence much closer to the wells. By the time the second refinery was completed, in 1966, however, production had begun to decline. For the first fifteen years, crude oil production had grown at an encouraging rate, but after 1964 the old wells began to give out and the search for new sources was so unrewarding that the number of oil wells drilled fell from 99 in 1964 to 47 in 1965 and 37 in 1966. The decline was still going on in 1973. The refineries, on the other hand, were able by the late 1960s to meet nearly all the country's requirements of gasoline and diesel oil, and three-fourths of its fuel oil requirements. The catch, however, was that they were increasingly dependent on crude oil imports, which between 1960 and 1967 rose from one-third to more than a half of the refineries' total consumption; and the rise continued after 1967. This was the opposite of the trend during these same years in Argentina's petroleum industry, which was towards national independence.

The largest allocation ever made by CORFO was for the development of electric power, both thermal and hydroelectric, through the Empresa Nacional de Electricidad (ENDESA), which it set up just before the end of World War II. With extensive aid from the World Bank, ENDESA in the next quarter-century established a national transmission system and became the country's principal producer of electric power. Another major producer, a subsidiary of American and Foreign Power, was nationalized by purchase during Frei's administration. Yet even so, when Allende took office in 1970, plants generating two-fifths of the country's electric power were the property of the largely foreign-owned mining companies. The total output at that time was about equally divided between thermal and hydroelectric, and Chile's potential for both kinds is substantial because of its extensive coal deposits and the snow-capped Andes at its back door. Nevertheless, the government followed the fashion of the times by setting up a Nuclear Power Commission in 1964. The commission was made directly responsible to the president, obtained the cooperation of the United States, and in 1967 made a rather optimistic announcement of its plans for the development of nuclear energy for industrial uses. Disillusionment was not long delayed. In 1969 the commission's former chairman, Igor Saavedra, told a sad story of repeated frustrations. The climax came when his request for an indispensable nuclear accelerator was turned down by a cabinet minister who, after figuring how many buses could be bought for what the accelerator would cost, and how many people the buses would serve, decided that it would be more democratic to buy the buses. At that point Saavedra resigned and his best student, though reluctant to leave the country, added to the brain drain by accepting an appointment at the Massachusetts Institute of Technology.

Despite its determined effort to industrialize, mining retained the key role it had long played in Chile's national economy and public policy, and in public opinion. Among the minerals, copper led by a wide margin in all these respects, as it had done ever since the 1920s, but in the face of competition from Africa, Chile's share of the world production of copper declined from 20 percent in 1946 to 13 percent ten years later. This decline was partly responsible for a sharp increase in government intervention in the copper industry. The main target of its intervention was the Gran Minería, or three largest mines, and the intervention deepened by stages until they were expropriated in 1971. All three companies in this category, it will be recalled, were subsidiaries of companies owned in the United States, two of Anaconda and one of Kennecott; and two of the mines were still the largest in the world of their respective kinds: open-face Chuquicamata (Anaconda) and underground El Teniente (Kennecott).

Important to the national economy as producer of the chief export item and employer of between 15,000 and 20,000 Chileans, the copper industry was also one of the government's main sources of revenue. In 1952-1954 it provided 15.7 percent of total tax revenues, and the government let itself become increasingly dependent on the proceeds for current expenses instead of setting them aside for economic development. The tax rate had gone up steadily since it was first imposed in 1925. In that year it was a rounded 5 percent of the total value of the copper produced; by 1955 it had risen to 40 percent. In addition, a price-fixing agreement concluded with the Gran Minería by the United States government in June 1950 for the duration of the Korean War provoked a reaction in Chile that led two years later to the adoption of a law establishing a virtual monopoly of copper exports by the government and permitting the Central Bank to buy copper at the low New York price and sell at the best obtainable price. As intended, the measure resulted in substantial profits for the Chilean treasury. Nevertheless, there continued to be a strong demand that the copper industry be made to render better service to Chile's long-range interests so that this precious natural resource would not be frittered away, as had happened with the country's great wealth in natural nitrates.

It was in these circumstances that, in May 1955, Congress adopted the New Deal (Nuevo Trato) law already referred to. Reynolds describes the law as revolutionary and a pioneering effort both to use the copper industry for the promotion of the nation's economic development and also to integrate the "foreign enclave" of the Gran Minería into Chile's national economy. A major purpose was to stimulate production and recover Chile's leading role in world production. To this end, the provisions of the act included, besides a 50 percent tax on profits, a sliding surtax that would diminish for each firm as it exceeded its assigned quota. Production did in fact increase substantially in the next ten years. With 1960 = 100 as the base, the index of the Gran Minería's output rose from 82.5 in 1955 to 110 in 1964, and copper tax revenues from an average of 97.6 in 1956-1958 to 119 in 1964. During this period from 10 to 19 percent of Chile's total annual taxes came from the copper tax.

This too failed to satisfy. In the presidential campaign of 1964, the future of "big copper" was a leading issue and the only two serious contenders, Socialist Allende and Christian Democrat Frei, offered the voters just two choices: gradual, compensated "Chileanization" (Frei) or outright nationalization (Allende). With conservative support, Frei won and Chileanization proceeded through the government's purchase of a controlling interest first in Kennecott and then in Anaconda, with stipulations for expansion that would double the capacity of Gran Minería by 1972. Even that was not enough and in 1971 Allende's new government nationalized the mines by expropriation, with the support of right, center, and left in Congress. That upset plans made in the meanwhile by many-faceted International Telephone and Telegraph Company (ITT), which in 1968 had further diversified its already extensive interests in Chile by contracting with the Frei administration to undertake a 10-year copper exploration-and-development program.

Nitrates were still one of the country's principal exports, but by the 1960s they had been pushed into third place by iron ore; in 1970 the two accounted respectively for 7 percent and 9 percent of total exports. Chile's iron ore was of better quality than Argentina's and was produced on a far larger scale—nearly one million metric tons annually in 1967-1971, compared with Argentina's 20-25,000 tons. The chief Chilean producer still was Bethlehem Chile Iron Mines Company, which besides supplying the Huachipato steel plant, exported much of its ore to the United States. By the late 1960s, however, it had a serious competitor in the Pacific Steel Company, which not only operated the Huachipato plant but also—and in some years more profitably—engaged in iron mining. In 1968 the

Frei administration carried government intervention in the economy a long step ahead by purchasing enough stock from private owners to give it control of this leading steel and iron mining company.

Economic Ills and Diagnoses

Noting that in the election of 1964 both the leading candidates, Frei and Allende, were reformers, Federico Gil and Charles Parrish identified the sluggishness of the economy as a major problem: it had failed to respond to the rising expectations of a rapidly growing population. In 1963, they noted, the unadjusted GNP increased only 2.5 percent, which meant no per capita growth at all, for population increased at exactly the same rate, as it had been doing for the past decade. After commenting briefly on the problems of copper and inflation, they took up what they called one of the most difficult problems, namely, the low level of agricultural productivity: during the 1950s agricultural production increased only 6 percent, whereas the population increase was 26 percent. (They might have added that Chile was spending constantly growing sums on imported foodstuffs, which rose from only 8 percent of total imports in 1947 to 25 percent a decade later.) The causes of this complex problem, they said, could be summed up under the heading of the *fundo* or large estate system. Under that system 8.5 percent of all farms contained more than two-thirds of the arable land, and the landlords were generally well off when they were not rich, but most of the rural people were poor when they were not poverty-stricken.

For these and other reasons, the experts all agree, the fundo system was very defective, but there was more to the agrarian problem than that. Markos Mamalakis, in his study of Chilean development from 1940 to 1948, describes agriculture as a "neglected" sector of the Chilean economy, in contrast to the "dominant" industrial consumer goods sector. Jay Kinsbruner makes the charge stronger than one of neglect, pointing out that until 1964 not only did CORFO, bent on industrialization, give very little help to agriculture, but the government actually "frustrated agricultural incentive" by such measures as imposing price controls on many Chilean farm products while subsidizing imported foodstuffs. In 1967, at last, Frei's administration adopted an agrarian reform measure—the first since the abolition of entailed estates in 1857, except for a rather timid venture in the same direction under the preceding administration of Jorge Alessandri. Under the Frei measure, a Land Reform Corporation was set up which expropriated abandoned or poorly managed farms to a total of 3.56 million hectares, mainly in Chile's fertile, irrigated Central Valley, and set up associations among the 28,700 families affected, with a view to the ultimate division of the land into small individual farms. In the rest of the decade, 1965-1970, the overall annual growth rate of agricultural production, according to ECLA, was 2.5 percent, and in the last year, 1970, 5 percent. That was hardly a stupendous performance and, as we shall see, some of Frei's followers seceded from the party on the ground that the agrarian reform did not go nearly far enough. Yet Chile's growth rate was at least better than the corresponding growth rates in the other Southern Cone countries, which were, in Argentina, an average of 0.4 percent for the five years and 0.8 percent for 1970 alone, and, in Uruguay, 1.5 percent and 3.0 percent, respectively.

Taking a larger view of agriculture as an integral part of the national economy, Marxist André Frank in 1969 pictured Chile as a satellite in the world capitalist market and as containing within itself a domestic metropolis and its own satellite. The inner metropolis is the group of the country's most powerful interests, linked with foreign imperialism, and whose exploited satellite is Chile's provincial hinterland. As a result, he says, "Chile is becoming ever more underdeveloped." He is scornful of the notion that a "landed, feudal oligarchy" rules Chile, or ever ruled it, and that a "progressive national bourgeoisie" will wrest the state from its feudal grasp. Chile has never been feudal, the argument runs, but capitalist from the start, and the so-called "new" middle classes have a vested interest in maintaining the capitalist system imposed on Chile by its own world metropolis, the imperialists (meaning first and foremost, of course, the United States). Nothing except a social revolution, he concludes, will save Chile from its increasing underdevelopment; not only in agriculture but in all sectors. Whatever one may think of this way of looking at Chile's problems, it helps to explain the course of the Marxist experiment of the Allende triennium that began in the year following the publication of Frank's book.

Its author acknowledges his indebtedness to Chilean economist Aníbal Pinto for the term "frustrated," which both writers apply to that country's development. But they explain the frustration in very different ways. To begin with, Pinto's explanation is not doctrinaire.

His chief clue is inflation. Responsibility for the inflation, he says, is discussed in Chile in a way that reminds one of detective stories in which all the characters are under suspicion. Each sector of society has its favorite guilty party. Businessmen blame it on government expenditures or wage increases; labor organizations blame it on upper-class greed and speculation; others, on monetary expansion and the abuse of credit. In fact, he continues, in any long period of inflation, all these factors contribute to it as in a relay race: when one drops out, another takes its place. As regards monetary policy, it is idle to try to fix particular responsibility for what is a collective fault, for, as the IMF has pointed out, the powerful instruments of Chile's Central Bank were never used to check inflation, except for brief periods and in an inadequate way. Pinto also notes that many Chileans have the mistaken notion that their country has made a mighty effort to develop, whereas in fact it has ploughed back far less of its income into development than Norway, Holland, Great Britain, and Denmark, and less even than several Latin American countries, among them Mexico, Brazil, and Colombia. Moreover, he asserts, it has done very little for "basic industries" such as agriculture, and important sectors of private industry have been decapitalized as a result of the "mirage of inflation," which has sustained good dividends while depleting capital investment.

The urban middle class too has been charged by others besides André Frank with retarding Chile's economic development. At least as early as 1941, Pike tells us, this charge was stressed by a Chilean writer, Francisco Pinto Salvatierra. Several writers in the United States have done likewise in recent years. Some of their publications preceded Frank's, and none has taken his all-out Marxist approach to the question. As conveniently summarized in a study of it by Mario Rothschild (1973), the two who discussed the question in terms most relevant to the present account were David Felix (1961) and Tom Davis (1969). The former held that the conservatism of the urban middle class adversely affected Chilean development, first in copper and agriculture and then in the industrial sector. Davis included other retarding factors as well, such as Chile's political structure and land tenure system, but stressed the responsibility of the urban middle classes, which supported liberal emissions of paper money for expanding white-collar employment, but refused either to increase taxes or to pay more for social services or food.

Chile's sluggish and uneven development was reflected in the statistics of income distribution, though the image was not always what one might have expected. Perhaps the most surprising fact revealed by the statistics was that, despite all that has been said about the extreme poverty of Chile's poorest class, ECLA's study of the composition of the major Latin American income groups in the early 1960s showed that Chile (with Argentina and Uruguay) was completely unrepresented in the lowest 20 percent of the population of Latin America. For purposes of comparison, Mexico contributed nearly one-tenth of that group, and Brazil nearly half of it. The same study showed that more than four-fifths of the Chilean people were in the income groups above the Latin American median.

It could, of course, have been little or no consolation to undernourished Chileans to know that many Latin Americans were even worse off than they. The most significant comparison for anyone, rich or poor, is with one's neighbors and other fellow countrymen. From this point of view the statistics tell a very different story. Those for 1968 showed that the top 2.4 percent of the population received 46 percent of the national income, and that the lowest 25 percent received only 4.8 percent of it. A similar table for 1964 showed that the lowest 29 percent of the population received only 4.1 percent of the national income, and that most of those in this bottom group were identified as rural workers.* Another striking feature of the available income data is the wide — one is tempted to say enormous — chasm separating the highest income group from the upper middle class. In the 1968 table, the figures were, respectively, 2.4 percent and 1.8 percent of the population and 46 percent and a mere 3.6 percent of the income; financially speaking, the two groups lived in different worlds. If we add to this the fact that the gradations below the next-highest group were comparatively small and quite regular, it might seem a foregone conclusion that the middle sectors would line up against the super-rich oligarchy. But that did not happen, and we are brought back again to a strain of what might be called flunkeyism in the Chilean middle class. The strain was so strong that, as Pike has shown, there is a special Chilean word for it: *siútico,* which denotes a middle-class individual who imitates the upper class and hankers to be identified with it.

---

*This 1964 table was an Allende campaign document, but was probably fairly accurate, and at least it illustrates the kind of information that was being broadcast among the voters.

Politics from Right to Left: Ibáñez, Alessandri, Frei

Though with important exceptions here and there and from time to time, the salient feature of Latin American political development in the postwar generation was the swing from right to left. In recognition of it such phrases as "the revolution of rising expectations" and "the coming explosion in Latin America" had become clichés by the early 1960s and the Alliance for Progress was launched in 1961 in the hope of making the inevitable revolution a peaceful one. Among illustrations of the leftward trend, the most spectacular was the Cuban revolution led by Fidel Castro. Others include the contrast between the first and second administrations of Getúlio Vargas in Brazil, the establishment of a left-wing military dictatorship in Peru in the late 1960s, the spread of populistic nationalism in a large part of Latin America, and the whole course of development in Chile from World War II to the 1970s. Perhaps the most striking exceptions to the trend were the right-wing military governments set up in Brazil in 1964 and Argentina two years later, and the emergence about the same time of something like a military-industrial complex in each of those two countries and Mexico, as noted in an earlier chapter. Yet even in the three countries just mentioned, which contain two-thirds of the population of Latin America, it was obvious that the leftward trend, though checked, was still strong; and in two of them, Argentina and Mexico, it seemed at the end of our period on its way to breaking through the restraints imposed on it.

Chile's political system was the most orderly and democratic in Latin America from World War II to 1970. Perhaps for that reason Chile provides the clearest illustration of this swing from right to left. The first and last signposts along the way leave no room for doubt about the reality of the movement. Near its start, in 1947, we have seen President González Videla, a left-wing Radical, opening the Cold War in Chile and outlawing the Chilean Communist Party under oppressive laws that were not repealed until ten years later. At the end of our period, on the other hand, that party was a senior partner, and the most moderate partner, in a government headed by a Socialist who was committed to transforming Chile into a socialist republic.

Each of the three intervening administrations marked a new stage in the trend. The first, headed by Carlos Ibáñez, is the least obvious illustration of it. He was not the candidate of a regular party, the one improvised for him was not readily identifiable as either left or right, and his platform was notable chiefly for his promise that, as a new broom (*escoba*), he would sweep clean. Hence his followers were known as *escobistas*. Nevertheless, and despite his hostility to the oligarchy, he belongs with the right wing. Like his friend Juan Perón he was, as Donald Bray has shown, an authoritarian and a nationalist. Moreover, one of his most influential cabinet members, Minister of Finance Jorge Prat, was an extreme right winger who used the full power of the government to cripple the labor confederation when it defied him by opposing anti-inflationary measures recommended by the Klein-Saks mission from the United States. Yet Ibáñez himself was by no means an extreme right winger. So far as communism was concerned, he moved to the left of Radical González Videla, for it was under Ibáñez that the act outlawing the Communist Party was repealed. It was also under him that the government took a long step toward intervention in the copper industry by enacting the "New Deal" law of 1955.

In the next administration, that of Jorge Alessandri Rodríguez, the movement away from the right continued; though slight, it was clear. Politically independent, Alessandri had a cabinet that was definitely conservative, for it was made up of Conservatives, Liberals, and right-wing Radicals, but his own conservatism was moderate and his administration even produced an agrarian reform act — a very mild one, but the first of its kind. His main objective was to curb inflation. He tried to do this by measures that put the burden of curbing on the workers, as Ibáñez had done, but the resulting confrontation with organized labor was not carried to as great extremes. Even so, it was serious enough. It arose out of a strike by the workers of the National Health Service, which, as a result of the adoption of a compulsory health program, now cared for 90 percent of the nation's hospitals and three-fourths of its population. After several weeks the strike ended in a draw: loans for the workers and no reprisals, but no immediate wage increase and only a promise that provision for one in the coming year's budget would be considered in due course.

In January 1964, as Alessandri's administration drew to its close, the government brought about the adoption of the so-called "Gag Law," which imposed heavy penalties for the publication in print or the spreading by radio, television, or other means of false news, slanderous statements, classified government documents, and pornographic material. It naturally provoked indignant protests, mainly from the opposition press, which charged that one of its main purposes was to cripple the opposition parties in the national election to be held later that year. The adoption of such a measure might seem to mark Alessandri as an ultra-conservative, but the urge to muzzle dissenters seems to have little to do with right, left, or center. Although Alessandri's successor, left-of-center Christian Democrat Frei, did indeed lessen the worst constraints of the Gag Law, he turned right around and had the chief officers of the opposition National Party (just formed by merging the Conservative and Liberal parties) arrested for sedition and prosecuted under the Internal Security Law because they criticized his administration. The Supreme Court dismissed the charges as groundless.

In the election of 1964 for the first time none of the old-line parties was a chief contender. As the campaign developed, the contest narrowed down to a duel between the Christian Democratic Party and FRAP (Popular Action Front), both of which had made their initial appearance on the national stage in the election of 1958. Both newcomers had done remarkably well in it. The Christian Democrats, who had taken that name only the preceding year, after going under the name of Falange Nacional ever since they first organized in 1938, jumped from a mere three percent of the vote in 1953 to nearly 25 percent in 1958. In the latter election Eduardo Frei was their presidential candidate for the first time. FRAP polled an even larger share of the vote. In fact, its candidate, Salvador Allende, lost to Alessandri by only about 30,000 votes, or one percent of the total.

It was clear in 1964 that FRAP, again led by Allende, was about as strong as in 1958 and that in the interval the Christian Democrats, again led by Frei, had grown stronger and the right-wing parties weaker. Obviously, then, the Socialist-Communist FRAP was virtually certain to win if the other two groups split the rest of the vote between them. Faced by this horrid prospect, the great bulk of the right-wing party members came around tardily and reluctantly to supporting left-of-center Frei as the only alternative to left-wing Allende.

Despite their political differences, Allende and Frei had much in common. Both were successful professional men: Allende a physician (no longer practicing), Frei a lawyer. Both were in their fifties (Allende 56, Frei 53) and both came of mixed Chilean-foreign families, Allende Dutch on his mother's side, Frei German on his father's. Both had begun their political careers in the 1930s; Allende as a Socialist deputy from Valparaíso, Frei as a founder of his party's parent organization, Falange Nacional, and both had served in the Chilean Senate. Both were highly critical of the capitalist system and of the United States, which they had visited together in the 1940s. Allende was the first to achieve political prominence, for he became a leader of his relatively large party and a vice-president of the Senate in the 1940s, while Frei's Falange was still an obscure splinter group and he himself was hardly known to the public except as the author of books on politics and political history. By 1964, however, Frei was at no disadvantage in this respect. The Christian Democrats' meteoric rise since 1957 had turned the political spotlight on him. He was a better public speaker than Allende, and, as Paul Sigmund has pointed out, his party's combination of criticism of the capitalist system with resolute defense of democracy had made a particularly strong appeal in the last few years. Except for COPEI in Venezuela, his was by 1964 much the strongest Christian Democratic party in any Latin American country, including Argentina and Uruguay.

Both leaders likewise drew inspiration from Europe and aid and comfort from the Roman Catholic Church. Allende's prophet, however, was Karl Marx and his balm from the Catholic Church came at this time largely in the form of its traditional anti-capitalism. (Later, after Allende's victory in 1970, the Chilean hierarchy made the benediction more specific.) On the other hand, while Frei's party was not confessional (that is, it was independent of the church authorities and membership in it was open to non-Catholics), its ideas and platform were drawn in large part from papal pronouncements, the writings of the famous Roman Catholic philosopher Jacques Maritain, and other Catholic sources, both clerical and lay, and Jesuits had a hand in ordering these materials for the party's use. What is more, most of the Chilean party's political inspiration and some financial contributions came from the older Christian Democratic parties in Europe, and Conrad Adenauer was Frei's hero. There was a difference, however, for the Chilean branch laid much stronger emphasis than the European trunk on anti-capitalism. In this respect Frei stood somewhere between the European Christian

Democrats and Allende, from whom he differed in his firmer commitment to gradualism, to the avoidance of a confrontation with the United States, and to the economic and political integration of Latin America, regardless of the position of the other Latin American states on the question of capitalism.

With the conservatives' grudging help, the Christian Democrats won a smashing victory, first in the presidential election in September 1964 and then in the congressional election the following March. Frei received a majority of the popular vote; no previous president in this century had received more than a plurality.* In the congressional elections the Christian Democrats won 82 seats in the 150-member Chamber of Deputies and all twelve of the seats they contested in the Senate. In the latter, however, only half the seats are at stake in any election, and as the Christian Democrats had held only one seat before the election, they ended up with only one-third of the membership.

Because Frei and Allende together polled 95 percent of the popular vote in this election, it has been asserted that "95 percent of Chileans voted for revolution, either Christian Democratic or Marxist." Whether one agrees depends partly on one's definition of revolution —but only partly. The conservatives, whose votes enabled Frei to win, did not vote for any kind of revolution, not even the "revolution in liberty" that he promised. Their votes were cast against Allende and any kind of revolution; and the combined vote of the conservative parties (merged as the National Party in 1966) in the next presidential election was slightly more than one-third of the total vote. Unless one keeps in mind the strength of the anti-revolutionary spirit in Chile during this period, and the diversity of meaning given to the term "revolution," it is impossible to understand the course of events in that country in the nine years following Frei's election.

The Interest Groups and Frei's Administration

At least as important in these years as the political parties were the country's four chief interest groups. As described in Burnett's helpful study of Chile during the Frei administration, the four were

*Frei's popular vote (rounded) was 1.409 million (56.1 percent), and Allende's .978 million (38.9 percent). The remaining 5 percent went to Julio Durán, a right-wing Radical who started out as the candidate of a conservative coalition, Democratic Front, but had been deserted by most of its original membership for Frei.

the oligarchy, the Catholic Church, organized labor, and the armed forces. A fifth group, the intellectuals, consisting mainly of university faculty and students, had formerly played an important part in public affairs. Individual members or fragments of it continued to do so. The University of Chile's Department of Education, for example, was said to shape educational policy for Allende's party. In the 1960s, however, the intellectuals were too deeply divided to have anything remotely approaching group unity, and the divisions deepened in the next decade. To take the University of Chile again as an example, the Social Sciences division, too, was pro-Marxist, whereas the Law School was a citadel of the opposition to the Allendists.

What is commonly called the oligarchy did possess some degree of group unity. This was based on the nexus of landowning, financial, industrial, and commercial interests, whose leaders were interrelated by personal as well as economic ties. It was a management as well as an ownership group. That such a thing as an oligarchy existed in Chile in the postwar period has been affirmed by some writers and denied by others with equal assurance. Strictly speaking, the latter seem to have the better of the argument, for the unity of the group appeared to be undependable except when all its component elements were under attack. Also, the group had not ruled since 1938 except, at most, during the administration of Jorge Alessandri. If, however, the term is used loosely, as signifying a coalition rather than a class and as not necessarily connoting political rule, then there seems to be no good reason why we should not use so useful a shorthand term. For while the group had the weakness of a coalition, its members did draw together when attacked; and even when not attacked they had enough in common to act together on a good many occasions. Their coordinator or guiding force on such occasions was most likely to be *la banca,* a handy Spanish term meaning the banking community.

Detailed information about the holdings and operations of the Chilean oligarchy comes mainly from its critics, such as Ricardo Lagos, author of a book published in 1961 on the concentration of economic power in that country, and also a Communist periodical of Santiago, *Vistazo,* of the same period. Their findings seem plausible and the situation as they described it in the early 1960s presumably prevailed until 1970 and was largely revived after 1973. Its main features were the concentration of control of 70 percent of total invested private capital in eleven groups, which consisted of eight banks and three business groups, and the control of these in turn, through interlocking directorates and other devices, by a few families — the oligarchy. Foremost among these was the Edwards family, whose members owned one of the three largest banks, various important enterprises, and a publishing empire that culminated in the country's leading newspaper, *El Mercurio* of Santiago. Prior to changes introduced by Frei, the oligarchy had another lever for controlling the national economy. This was through representation by its members, as directors or otherwise, in the numerous government agencies, created mainly since 1930, which, as we have seen, had by the 1960s extended state control over a very large part of the economy, from economic development, investment, mining, and electric power to public health, social security, and education.

As an interest group, the Chilean Catholic Church was increasingly identified in this decade with reform in the interest of social justice, rather than with the maintenance of the status quo for the benefit of the upper classes, as it had been until mid-century. One indication of the shift was the rapid rise of the Christian Democratic Party. Although, as already noted, that party was not confessional, it was largely Catholic in inspiration and leadership. Thanks partly to its still important role in education, the church exercised a strong, pervasive influence throughout the country. This was impossible to measure and difficult to estimate, but it was probably a good deal stronger than might be inferred from the fact that in this nominally 95-percent Catholic nation, only about 10 to 20 percent of the people were practicing members of the church. As the decade wore on, the radicals among the clergy, though always in the minority, gained strength in this as in most other countries. By its close those in Chile were moving on from reform to revolution in much the same way as the Third World Priests in Argentina, Brazilian archbishop Dom Hélder Câmara, and Camilo Torres of Colombia. Even the Cardinal Primate of Chile said openly that he found "more of the Gospel's values in socialism than in capitalism"; that was after Allende's election in 1970.

Organized labor was not one of the strong interest groups in Chile at this time. In the early 1940s, with encouragement from the Popular Front government, it showed more promise than its Argentine counterpart. Reports from the respective central organizations in

1944 gave the Workers Confederation of Chile 400,000 members, as compared with 250,000 in much more populous Argentina's CGT.* In 1943, a projected customs union of the two countries was opposed by many Chilean workers on the ground that it might undermine their social gains, which were much greater than those so far won by the Argentine workers. In the next few years, however, the CGT was greatly strengthened and enlarged by Juan Perón, while the Chilean confederation, largely controlled by Communists and Socialists, was crippled after 1947 by the hostile administration of Gabriel González Videla. There were other unions not connected with the confederation, but the whole movement passed its peak in the late 1940s. After that it remained on a plateau until the late 1950s, when it declined. The story is told in the unionized percentage of the total Chilean labor force. From 3.0 in 1932 this rose rapidly through 9.0 in 1940 to an average of 11.4 in the first half of the 1940s, and then leveled off at 12.3 in the rest of that decade and 12.4 through the early 1950s, after which it declined to 10.8 from 1956 to 1959.

In 1953 the Chilean Confederation was supplanted by a new organization, the Single Central of Chilean Workers (CUT), which remained the country's largest labor organization until the end of the Allende regime. In the late 1960s, however, it had only about 300,000 members (though it claimed twice as many) and a large part of organized labor had no connection with it. The others included the new Christian Democratic unions and some that belonged to neither group. Also, there were sharper distinctions than in most countries between unions of white-collar workers (*empleados*) and blue-collar workers (*obreros*). Rivalry and controversy among these fragments of organized labor was one main source of its weakness in Chile. Another was its subordination to the political parties. Yet, even if the workers could not provide leadership, they still retained enough independence to defy the political leaders on occasion, as both Frei and Allende learned to their grief.

The armed forces were the most compact and best organized interest group in Chile. They were obviously by far the strongest if it should come to the use of force, as seemed increasingly likely because of the spreading violence in most of Latin America, including

---

*These figures, produced at the Latin American Confederation of Labor Conference in Cali, Colombia, in 1944, are no doubt inflated, but since both were inflated they will serve for comparative purposes.

Chile's nearest neighbors. That violence never became as serious a problem in Chile as in, for example, Argentina and Uruguay in the 1960s may have been largely due to the quality of the Chilean armed forces. It could hardly have been due to their numbers, which were not large. At that time the strictly military forces consisted of an army of about 22,000, a navy of 17,500, and an air force of 7,500, which were distributed throughout the country. There was no such massive concentration as that of the Argentine army at the Campo de Mayo on the outskirts of Buenos Aires. All three Chilean services were made up of well-trained professionals, apolitical and generally respected. For the maintenance of public order, the armed forces had a vanguard, so to speak, in the paramilitary national police force consisting of 22,000 *carabineros,* who were likewise well trained and generally well thought of.

Throughout the 1960s and until the military coup of 1973, all commentators agreed that the Chilean armed forces were exceptionally apolitical by Latin American standards. It was also agreed that they had been so since the end of the Ibáñez dictatorship in 1931. Two decades later some junior officers, looking enviously at the Argentine regime of Ibáñez's good friend Perón, plotted a military coup to put the former at the head of one like it in Chile. Nothing came of that, however, and for another score of years all of Chile's military leaders appear to have sedulously avoided involvement in party politics. Nevertheless, these military leaders had a strong esprit de corps and jealously guarded the corps' integrity while vigorously promoting its interests. The commentators seem to be in agreement on this point too, and the Chilean political leaders certainly concurred, for every one of the presidents — left-wing Allende and left-of-center Frei as well as right-wing Alessandri — courted the military during the election campaigns with promises to maintain them in proper style, which included respecting their power position. Alessandri and Frei kept the promise after their inauguration. This point should be kept firmly in mind, for it was to be one of the rocks on which Allende's government would founder.

Political action by another of the interest groups frustrated Frei's administration from just after its beginning to its bitter end. This was the owner-manager group headed by the oligarchy, whose political conservatism found expression in the Conservative and Liberal parties and the right wing of the Radical Party. Even with their support in the congressional election of early 1965, Frei's party had fallen far short of gaining control of the Senate. Shortly thereafter the conservatives of all parties turned against him as he began to press for the enactment of the agrarian and other structural reforms to which he was committed. As a consequence of their defection, Frei had to fight a two-front war through virtually the whole of his administration, which was constantly harried by left-wing attacks as well. These came not only from FRAP but also, increasingly, from extremists among his fellow Christian Democrats. Internal dissension weakened the party's hold on the general public and its situation deteriorated steadily. In the municipal elections of 1967 it polled only 49 percent of the popular vote, which was 7 percent less than it received in 1965. Its share dropped in 1969 to 31 percent and in the presidential election of 1970 to little more than one-fourth of the total vote.

The lack of a large constituency firmly based in one of the four chief interest groups was fatal to Frei's administration. The defection of the owners and managers and the neutrality of the armed forces, which he respected, left only the Catholic Church and labor, neither of which provided the support he needed. His base among Catholics was comparatively strong until the mid-1960s and his slogan "Revolution in Liberty" never lost its appeal to those among them who were liberal. Among the numerous remainder, however, he met with rapidly growing opposition from, on the one hand, conservative laymen and, on the other, priests as well as laymen who were impatient with the slow pace of his administration's promised structural revolution. As for the fourth and last group, organized labor, its usefulness to his party would have been limited even if it had been much stronger than it was, for he and his associates never succeeded in breaking the hold of Communists and Socialists on most of the labor unions.

XIV Socialism in Chile:
An Unfinished Experiment

Chile's socialist experiment began tentatively under Eduardo Frei and was greatly accelerated under Salvador Allende. Frei's administration, launched with éclat in 1964, ended in gloom after a crushing defeat at the polls six years later. In a larger sense his administration may be viewed as sharing the fate of the Alliance for Progress, which was still stimulating the revolution of rising expectations when Frei took office. During his term Chile received enough aid from the United States under the alliance label to identify him and his Christian Democratic Party with the alliance, and so involve them in the discredit into which that new noble experiment had fallen by 1970. Even if the alliance had been a thundering success, however, Frei would still almost certainly have been undone by the polarization of Chilean society to which his middle-of-the-road measures contributed. For they seemed to the exasperated left wing of his own party so weak that it went over to the Socialist-Communist camp, and to his recent conservative allies so drastic that they moved back further to the right.

The conservatives were undone by hubris. Perhaps misled by the trend to the right then dominant in Argentina and Brazil, the Chilean conservatives in 1970 shut their eyes to the lessons of the last dozen years, risked a confrontation with the left wing, and lost, by a slender margin but definitively. That loss exposed their whole class and its supporting economic system to destruction by bringing to power a Communist-Socialist government headed by Salvador Allende and bent on transforming Chile into a socialist society. As Frei's administration had done in 1964, Allende's began with high hopes and ended in grief. The United States, which tried as hard to hinder Allende as it had tried to help Frei, has been held responsible for the failure of this socialist experiment, but its power as a puppeteer has been vastly overrated. Allende was undone by an economic disaster and consequent chaos for which he and his associates were mainly responsible and which provoked a military coup that destroyed his socialist regime and resulted in his own death. In the reaction that followed, the pendulum swung far back, not towards a restoration of the pre-Allende liberal type of government and society, but to a revival of corporatism that harked back through the age of Mussolini to the guild system of the Middle Ages.

From Frei to Allende

Frei's troubles began at once and multiplied as he went along, from the desertion by the conservatives at the outset to the schism in his own party near the end. His achievements in six years were limited, but he deserves credit for accomplishing anything at all, especially since he respected the limitations of the constitution on his power as chief executive.*

In his fifth and semi-final annual message to Congress on May 21, 1969, Frei offered his own rather optimistic appraisal of his administration's accomplishments. Those he stressed were the Chileanization of the copper mines and agrarian reform, which we have already noted. In education he pointed to the building of two new schools per day and an enrollment increase of 30 percent in the schools, public and private, and 73 percent in the universities; in agriculture and stockraising to a doubling of the growth rate; in housing to the solution of the housing problems of 1.8 million persons while the population increased by 830,000; and to "Popular Promotion," a program of community organization "aimed at incorporating the popular sectors into the active life of the country" (which many regarded as a signal failure). Reducing inflation, he claimed, was "perhaps the only basic point in my program that has not been fulfilled." Even here he excused himself by adding that in his efforts to combat inflation he had received "practically no help from the political parties or from the professional and trade-union organizations."

To this list of achievements, some additions should be made. One of the most important was his government's leading part in the formation in 1969 of the Andean Group and its ancillary Andean Corporation. This was a sub-regional group of five South American states, Chile, Bolivia, Peru, Ecuador, and Colombia, set up within the Latin American Free Trade Association (LAFTA) to promote trade among its members. It was highly successful at first, for by 1973 trade in the group had doubled. But there should also be more entries on the other side of the ledger. In housing, for example, it turned out at the end of Frei's administration that in fact it had not

---

*An apparent exception is the case, mentioned above, of his arrest of the National Party officers, but even in that case it has been argued that there was enough doubt about the interpretation of the law to justify his forcing the issue, and he accepted the Supreme Court's adverse decision without demur.

made a dent in the huge housing deficit. Again, in education the advance was more quantitative than qualitative, and much of whatever credit was due here belonged to the foreign governments, international organizations, and private foundations that had contributed heavily to financing the improvement of education in Chile. In proportion to population, Chile in the Frei period received more foreign aid for study abroad than any other Latin American country.

Much more serious, according to Frei's critics, among them members of his own party as well as FRAP, was his failure to Chileanize the foreign-owned telephone and electric companies, and to move far enough and fast enough in agrarian reform. The latter program turned out to be the most explosive issue of all. As Robert Kaufman has brought out most clearly, it weakened Frei's party in two ways: first, by stirring up urban opposition to his agrarian reform because, among other reasons, it cost too much, and second, by creating dissension that let to a schism in the party over its pace and limits. By 1967 a workable reform law had been adopted, peasant labor organizations formed, and expropriation and redistribution of the land begun for the first time in Chilean history. But the law provided for compensation to the expropriated owners and when the bills started coming in, leaders of the urban sector, which would have to foot most of them, balked. On the other hand, a minority of the party, headed by the program's leader, Jacques Chonchol, were acutely unhappy about it.

As a member of a United Nations team, Chonchol had worked on agrarian reform in Cuba in 1962-1963. In Frei's administration he was one of a group of young intellectuals who were strongest in the department concerned with agriculture and land policy. They wanted to get on with the structural transformation of Chilean society more rapidly than the older and more professionally political leaders of the party were prepared to move. The party had originally promised to create 20,000 new proprietors a year, but at the peak of the reform in 1968 and 1969 the number actually created was only (in rounded numbers) 5,600 and 6,400, respectively, and the total for Frei's six-year term was just over 28,000. There was also dissatisfaction with the reform's orientation towards private ownership, whereas the structuralists demanded permanent and exclusive collectivization; to them, peasant landowners were a prop to conservatism, capitalism, and the old order. In 1968 Chonchol resigned his government post and in 1969 he and a number of other left-wing dissidents seceded from the party. The next year they joined Allende's Popular Unity coalition, and after his victory Chonchol was rewarded with a cabinet post in his special field: agriculture and agrarian reform.

Allende gained an even greater advantage from the hardening of the conservatives' resolve never again to vote for Frei or his party. One of the developments that brought them to this determination was that Frei upset the cozy relationship under which management had previously played a leading role in the formation and execution of official policy. With little exaggeration, Frei's minister of economy said in 1966 that formerly the directors of banks and corporations always had influential friends and relatives in government, so that if "they had a problem they would just call them on the phone. Now it was different and they sit and fret." That this was substantially true was demonstrated at the 1968 convention of the national confederation of industrial, agricultural, mining, and commercial organizations (the Chilean counterpart of Argentine ACIEL). With Frei himself present, their representatives pitched into his government for its mistreatment of them, and high on the speakers' bill of particulars was the complaint that the government had deprived them of the representation they had long had on official agencies. From this they went on to charge it with discriminatory and confiscatory policies.

How much ground the Christian Democrats had lost was indicated by the congressional elections of March 1969. Analyzing the results, the conservative *El Mercurio* offered an interpretation that showed good judgment and foresight. It began by noting that, though the Christian Democrats remained the strongest party, they had lost ground;* that the National Party had "increased its vote significantly" and come in second; that the Communist and Socialist parties, respectively third and fourth, had made "solid" and "appreciable" gains; and that the Radicals "remained stationary and the smaller parties disappeared." The editorial then commented that the "general tendency" of the voters was to "search for defined and logical positions" — which we may translate as a tendency to polarize

---

*They had indeed. Polling only 31 percent of the vote, they lost 26 seats in the 147-member Chamber of Deputies, so that they no longer had a majority. In 1965 they won 82 seats and a comfortable majority.

—and illustrated this by pointing out that in both the Christian Democratic and Radical parties the factions that prevailed in the election were those that took clear-cut positions. Voters once counted among the active Radicals, it continued, "now give their support to the National Party or to the Marxist left, thus showing their preference for a clear definition in one direction or the other." Without pretending to prophesy, the editor went on to observe that "the opinion of the Chilean left is [now] concentrated in the Communist and Socialist parties" and that the Christian Democrats, thinking to render their control of power permanent, had made the mistake of cultivating the peasants and the "marginal poor," to the neglect of Chile's middle class, "which is decisive in a country with such a high income redistribution as ours." This concluding remark about "high income redistribution" indicates the bias to be expected of *El Mercurio* in such matters, but that does not invalidate its suggestion of a strain of conservatism in the middle class, much less its comments on the tendency to polarize. The conclusion was obvious: that tendency was hastening the disappearance of Chile's traditional multi-party system and a regrouping around the opposite poles of the National Party and the Marxist parties, with the Christian Democrats occupying the exposed field of fire between them.

The constitution barred Frei from succeeding himself and the person chosen to head his party's ticket in the unpromising situation it faced in 1970 was Radomiro Tomič, one of its founders and until recently ambassador to the United States. Tomič was one of the surprisingly large number of Chileans of Croatian origin who, brought up in either hot Antofagasta or cold Punta Arenas, had by the 1960s achieved cultural or political prominence in temperate Santiago. He achieved it in both respects, for besides being a leader of his party, he was professor of economics at the Catholic University in Santiago, editor of a periodical, and author of several books. *Christian Foundations for a New Social-Economic Order in Chile* (1945) was his first book and *Latin America at the Eleventh Hour* (1958) one of the most recent. He spoke well and wittily in English as well as Spanish, to the delight of audiences in both languages when his hearers were not put off by his politics, which were considerably more radical and Yankeephobe than Frei's. In fact, although Tomič came back early from Washington to help unite the Christian Democrats for the campaign of 1970, the stand he took during its course was very much like Allende's. Conservatives even charged afterward that the two had made a secret mutual aid agreement for the eventuality that none of the presidential candidates won a majority of the popular vote and that they two received the largest shares of it.

The other two candidates needed, and need, no introduction. They were Jorge Alessandri for the National Party and Salvador Allende for the Popular Unity coalition (UP, for Unidad Popular). Replacing FRAP, Popular Unity comprised the Socialist and Communist parties and some splinter groups. One of the latter was made up of left-wing members of the Radical Party; another was the schismatic Christian Democratic left-wing group led by Chonchol.

When the votes were counted, they showed Allende in the lead with 36.3 percent of the total, which was smaller than the share (38.9 percent) with which he had lost in the 1964 election. Alessandri came in second, one percent behind Allende. Tomič trailed with a mere 28.4 percent. Some commentators think Frei would have been re-elected if he had not been ineligible under the constitution. That seems quite unlikely. He would not again have had the conservative support that had enabled him to win in 1964, for the right-wing parties, now united in the National Party, reanimated by the powerful interests they represented, and over-confident, were in no mood to tag along behind any Christian Democrat, including Frei. The left-wing parties, too, though less cohesive, were united under a new name but the same leader, whose vote-getting power had been demonstrated in previous elections; he had almost certainly lost in the most recent one because his conservative and Christian Democratic opponents united against him, and now they were divided. As for Frei's own party, it is difficult to believe that he would have been more successful as candidate for re-election than he had been as president in soothing dissension among its members, bringing the rebels back into the fold, and raising the party's share of the total vote above the low level to which it had sunk under his leadership between 1965 and 1970.

The failure of any candidate to win a majority of the popular vote threw the presidential election into Congress. The constitution required that body to choose between the two candidates who ranked first and second in the popular vote, but unbroken custom required it to choose the one with the highest vote. Allende's followers reinforced custom with threats of violence if he were denied the presidency. The Christian Democrats, under pressure from the party's left wing, gave in. First, however, they exacted from Allende his promise to honor a Statute of Guarantees, adopted by Congress for this occasion, which purported to strengthen the protection of civil rights. Their insistence on this commitment is quite understandable. Allende had close ties with Fidel Castro, whom he had visited nine times since 1959, and his daughter Beatriz was married to a Moscow-trained Communist whom she met while on one of these visits with her father. Allende had also taken part in the Tri-Continental Congress in Havana in January 1966 that had set up a special organization for promoting armed revolution in the Western hemisphere.

Allende's election was greeted with dancing in the streets and general jubilation by his followers but caused a near panic among conservatives. Capital took flight and so did many people, though the exodus was less massive than those from Cuba in the early 1960s and from Uruguay concurrently with Chile's. Whether or not they emigrated, so many wealthy Chileans shipped what valuables they could to Argentina that art dealers in Buenos Aires were soon reporting the local market glutted with paintings and objets d'art from Chile. To make matters worse for the conservatives, the Christian Democratic Party continued to try to collaborate with Allende during his first year. As a result, although the anti-Allende forces had a majority in Congress, they could not even count on offering effective opposition in that body, for what little its action was worth in a political system loaded in favor of the presidency.

The Allende Regime

On October 22, two weeks before inauguration day, the army's commanding officer, General René Schneider, was assassinated while driving to his office. It became known at once that the assassination was the work of right-wingers (later, a right-wing officer who had been dismissed from the army for political activity was convicted of plotting it) and this fact created a wave of public sentiment in favor of Allende.* His ready agreement to the Statute of Guarantees added to the good will.

Inaugurated for a six-year term on November 4, 1970, Allende and his lieutenants went to work with exemplary vigor. In his first five months he completed the five major steps to which he was committed for the "collectivization of Chile." So reported in May 1971

---

*It came out later that the Central Intelligence Agency was involved but had intended kidnapping, not assassination.

an official of the International Telephone and Telegraph Company (ITT), who was hardly a friendly observer. These major steps he identified as the nationalization of the copper industry, private banking and credit, and "basic monopolies" (steel, textiles); the establishment of state control of imports and exports, and the radicalization of agrarian reform.

Nationalization of the copper industry required a constitutional amendment. This was adopted quickly and with the overwhelming support of both houses of Congress—a unique occurrence in this administration. Government appraisers then announced they had made the happy discovery that the U.S. owners had improperly taken out of Chile so much more in excess profits than they had ever put into the mines that, instead of being entitled to compensation, they owed the Chilean government huge sums, which turned out to be more than the mines were worth. This action gave the government in Washington an excuse for manifesting the dislike with which it had viewed Socialist Allende's government from the start. Allende, however, was not deterred by the frowns of a government whose paramilitary and economic sanctions over a period of ten years had failed to topple his friend Fidel Castro's Cuban regime. So far was Allende from retreating that, under pressure from the far-left members of UP, he turned the heralded transition of Chile to socialism into a headlong rush. During the campaign he had declared that he would nationalize only 90 basic firms. Within a year his government had nationalized three times that many firms, which were industrial, financial, and commerical, and both Chilean- and foreign-owned. The agrarian reform effort, too, was greatly intensified and aimed at establishing collective farming everywhere, to the complete exclusion of the independent farmer.

For several months Allende's team met with a success that seems to have astonished everyone but themselves. Inflation was checked and real wages shot up. In a wave of "socialist consumerism" factories hummed while shop shelves were quickly emptied and as quickly filled again, and the masses were happy that they had at last come into their own.

It was too good to last. Soon Allende was grappling with the thorny problems that were to plague him the rest of the time until his overthrow and death. They arose partly from the control of both houses of Congress by the opposition, which he never broke. Another source was dissension among his own heterogeneous coalition

of parties and splinters. The focus of the disputes was the *vía pacífica,* the peaceful way of gradual transition to socialism. This was
Allende's chosen way, and it had been prescribed by Moscow and
dutifully adopted by the Communist Party of Chile, whereas paradoxically Allende's fellow Socialists were more extreme and impatient to impose their ideas and institutions on the country forthwith.
The explanation may be that Allende, once considered a left-wing
activist in his party, had learned moderation as he accumulated
years and experience; he was 62 in 1970 and a veteran of some forty
years of service in the party. His coalition also included other varieties of left-wingers — Maoists, Castroites, Radicals, Christian Democratic rebels — and observers came to the conclusion that he spent
too much time trying to hold the coalition together, to the neglect of
other matters of at least equal importance, and that he made too
many concessions to the extremists, thereby stiffening the opposition
and preparing the way for the final disaster.

Still a third major problem was the intractability of the workers,
both urban and rural, whom he could not induce to defer present
benefits for greater future gains. Among the results were a decline
in production, foreign exchange holdings, and all imports except
foodstuffs, which had to be increased to make good the food shortages caused by the decline of farm as well as factory and mine production. Soon, in fact, there seemed to be shortages of everything
except violence and extremism. To cap the climax, inflation, after
its brief check in the first few months, began to mount rapidly until,
by mid-1973, the annual rate had reached 300 percent. The United
States had a hand in this and in aggravating Allende's other troubles
too, through the Central Intelligence Agency and otherwise, but
how much effect its efforts had is uncertain. The view taken here is
that they were a work of supererogation. Allende never had a majority of the Chilean people on his side; among his opponents were
powerful domestic forces that needed no prodding from the outside;
and the Allende team's own fumbles and factions helped to bring on
the destruction of his regime.

That Popular Unity was already in trouble at the end of its first
year in power was admitted by Allende himself in a speech he gave
that marked rather than celebrated the occasion. Inflation, he con-
fessed, was already on the march again, and, at 30 percent for the
year, had reached a higher point than in the first year of Frei's
administration. The food shortage was beginning to pinch and

violence was spreading so fast that he felt called on to warn his followers against undisciplined seizures of farms and housing and against all seizures of small and medium industries by the workers, which he condemned. To the workers in the copper mines he addressed an urgent plea to remember that they were now part owners of the mines and to reconsider their demands for high wages, which would feed inflation. Showing the frustration he was suffering at the hands of a hostile Congress, he proposed in this speech, as he had done before and was to do on many subsequent occasions, that it be reduced to a single chamber. At the same time, in the face of increasing inflation, he proposed an increase in health and housing benefits, presumably in the hope that this popular measure would enable his coalition to gain control of the new unicameral assembly. We may note here that he never got his unicameral assembly. It was constitutionally possible for him to override congressional opposition to the change by a plebiscite, but he never called for one, probably because he was always unsure of winning a majority of the popular vote.

The reference in Allende's speech to undisciplined seizures points to one of the chief causes of the growing political and social tension. Public opposition to enforced collectivism was growing, but so was the impatience of extreme left-wing groups with what they regarded as the leisurely course of Allende's *vía pacífica*. The principal group of this kind was MIR (Leftist Revolutionary Movement). Originally a Castroite guerrilla organization like the terrorist groups in Argentina and Uruguay (see chapter IX), MIR at this time was operating in the open as a participant in the political process. Despite its nominal moratorium on terrorism, it was carrying on a low-key campaign of violence which it threatened to intensify unless Allende got on with his social revolution. Whether he tried hard to discipline MIR is not clear, but at any rate he never succeeded in doing so, and its activities played an important part in hardening the determination of the anti-Allende forces to put an end to his government by showing what they could expect sooner or later if it remained in power.

Although the euphoria of Popular Unity's first months in office was gone by the end of its first year, the outlook for it was by no means bleak. As a *Wall Street Journal* correspondent reported from Santiago in late August 1971, the Christian Democrats, who were the principal opposition party, "seem too busy squabbling among themselves to organize effective opposition" and Allende, "a consummate politician," had "two more years to turn his growing control of the economy into a strong power base" before facing his first test at the polls in the congressional elections of 1973.

Three events of the following November were good for the regime's morale. The Nobel Prize for Literature was awarded to Pablo Neruda, Chilean ambassador to France, a personal friend of Allende's, and a lifelong Communist. Neruda's statement to the press on the award several times stressed that the honor was for the Chilean people and all Latin America, "a little of whose soul I have tried to interpret." In this same month no less a personage than Fidel Castro arrived for a visit that he stretched out to three weeks, possibly in order to repay all at once Allende's nine visits to Cuba in the last ten years. Castro was given a hero's welcome by an enormous crowd. Even the archbishop of Santiago, Raúl Cardinal Silva Enríquez, was on hand to greet him. Before his long visit ended, the crowds seemed to tire of him and he became critical of Allende's failure to mobilize them and of their failure to respond with more enthusiastic support, harder work, and readiness to accept austerity for the good of the cause. "A Marxist revolution," Castro said, "is production; Chile's revolution is consumption." Yet throughout his stay he gave Allende his support and Chile's Marxists the advice Allende felt they most needed: above all, to maintain revolutionary unity.

The third heartening event of that November was the arrival of the already famous Régis Debray, recently released from his Bolivian captivity following the liquidation of Che Guevara and his little band of guerrillas. Debray stayed much longer than Castro and did even better by Allende. He became an enthusiastic admirer of Allende personally and gave stronger approval than Fidel had given to Allende's vía pacífica as the best strategy for Chile. What is more, in a new book, *The Chilean Revolution,* he endorsed two of its features, the use of compromise and participation in elections, in a revision of his own revolutionary strategy as set forth in the 1967 essay that made him famous, "Revolution in the Revolution?" Debray, too, urged revolutionary unity on the Chilean Marxists and his exhortation was directed particularly to Allende's critics on the far left.

The lift provided by Neruda, Castro, and Debray was shortlived. In mid-March 1972 two reports appeared that were severely critical of Allende's administration. They came neither from the opposition nor from the far left of his UP coalition, but from the central committees of the coalition's two main parties. In one of them the Communist Party's economic expert Orlando Millas warned its central committee that the nationalized enterprises — copper mines, cement plants, textile mills, and others — were costing more and producing less and that their large losses were being covered by inflationary currency issues which, if continued, would soon have the government "sitting on top of a volcano about to explode." The central problem, he said, was to improve the operation of these enterprises so that they would produce "the same immense profits that they used to give the capitalists." As usual, the Socialists were the more aggressive of the two parties. Their central committee's report also painted a gloomy picture of the situation, but its solution was to launch an all-out attack on the economic base of the anti-Marxists. That base, it asserted, lay in private enterprise, "which must be destroyed." Accordingly, the report continued, "the masses, the unions, the parties can and should go beyond the legal limitations on the government, employing all forms of struggle," among which the report specified the seizure of "factories whose expropriation has been blocked by Congress."

Polarization and Military Coup

These two reports marked a decisive stage in the progressive polarization of forces in Chile. One important move in that direction was made a few weeks earlier, when the Christian Democratic leaders, indignant over a personal attack on Frei by Allende's supporters, definitely joined the opposition to his government. Now the two government parties' reports mentioned above gave the solidifying opposition a strong stimulus. There was encouragement for it in the Communist report's frank confession of the government's wretched performance so far in the financial and economic fields, while the report of the president's own Socialist Party was highly provocative in its call for the destruction of private enterprise by force and its incitement to violation of legal limitations and democratic procedures. There was little or no reassurance in the fact that the president himself did not take this extreme position, for he had already let himself be pushed further to the left than he had said he would go.

As might have been expected, countermeasures were taken by leaders in the field of private enterprise. This still included a substantial part of the Chilean economy and, directly or indirectly, probably involved close to half the Chilean people. These leaders belonged to the oligarchy-management group described above, which played the most continuously active part in the struggle that culminated a year and a half later in the overthrow of Allende's regime. Two other groups joined in at times. One was made up of Chilean women, probably most if not all of the middle and upper classes, who, in a sense, started the struggle, helped more than once to keep it going, and were in at the finish. The other was the armed forces, which did the actual ousting but until two weeks before that either remained neutral or supported the government.

Group action by Chilean women in public affairs was relatively new. Even individual participation by them was rare until 1949, when they were at last given the vote—one year and twenty years, respectively, after the women of Argentina and Uruguay. Before long they were quite active, but still acted individually in the elections of 1964 and 1965, when they turned out in great numbers and were responsible for the Christian Democrats' wide margin of victory over Socialist-Communist FRAP. Sixty percent of them voted for Frei, to only 40 percent for Allende. When the latter won six years later, the women took to group action and were the first to stage a demonstration against his government, in December 1971. This was their highly publicized housewives' "march of the empty pots," in protest against the already severe food shortage. Some observers pointed to that as the beginning of the anti-Marxists' recovery from the loss of nerve they had suffered at the time of Allende's election a year earlier. Women also took a prominent part in subsequent activities of the same kind, notably the general strike of October 1972, which forced Allende to call on the armed forces for help, and the truckers' strike, started in mid-1973, that led straight to his overthrow in September. Finally, it was under pressure from a protest march by the wives of his fellow officers that Allende's last strong military supporter, General Carlos Prats González, resigned from his cabinet. The president's overthrow followed less than three weeks later.

The influential management group, as noted earlier, had been deprived by Frei's administration of its many official channels of influence on an already largely state-controlled economy, but had not been seriously molested otherwise. Allende's government, on the other hand, made an attack on it that started piecemeal with the seizure of one factory, farm, or other property after another, but gained scope and intensity until it began to look like a war of extermination of the whole private sector, as demanded by the Socialist Party's central committee in March 1972. The reaction was spearheaded by the gremial associations and its leader, according to a *New York Times* report on October 28, 1973, was Jorge Fontaine, president of Chile's principal management association, the National Confederation of Production and Commerce, which comprised the Chamber of Commerce and the organizations of mineowners, landowners, manufacturers, and builders. The Confederation had already started a mass movement in the 1960s to put pressure on Frei's government to restore management's channels of influence in government agencies. It now mounted a counterattack on Allende's.

According to the report just mentioned, the new phase opened with a general strike in October 1972, which began as a truckers' strike but quickly mushroomed. The effort behind it was aimed at uniting small and middle-class private associations, small businesses, merchants, farmers, and the truckers, with the elite groups in a mass movement against the regime. A theory of government and society as well as a nexus of economic interests was represented by this effort. "Gremial" came from *gremio,* meaning guild (as in merchant guild), which was a word used in Spain and its dominions from the Middle Ages through the eighteenth century to designate occupational groups that were vital elements in government and society. Revived in the twentieth century, the concept of the gremio was central to plans, including fascist plans, for a corporate reorganization of contemporary society in all its aspects, including the political system. The truckers' 40,000-member union was regarded by theorists of this school as being a gremio. It certainly had the requisite autonomy, for it did not belong to the pro-government labor confederation CUT, which was controlled by the Socialist and Communist parties. Instead, the truckers' union had close ties with a group of organizations of professionals and white-collar workers.

That group was headed by young Jaime Guzmán, who until recently had been a Catholic student leader and was now a professor at the Catholic University, editor, publicist, gremialist leader, and, it was thought, a coming leader of the National Party. From an article published in 1972 and written by Arturo Fontaine, professor of law and an editor of *El Mercurio,* we learn that the gremialist movement had by that time spread to the universities, cooperative societies, and other sectors, including trade unions, in which it worked against affiliation with political parties. In all cases, according to this article, the gremialists "defend the autonomy of the group they belong to"—a statement that again suggests the strain of corporatism in the movement. More to the present purpose, however, was its use, according to the *Times* report cited above, of confrontation tactics designed to bring on economic and political chaos and thus provoke military intervention.

The strategy worked, but only after the nation's armed forces had made a prolonged effort to maintain their tradition of noninvolvement in politics and had abandoned it at last to support the government at Allende's request. They not only supported it by helping to maintain public order but also on two occasions some officers became part of the government as members of the president's cabinet. The first occasion began with the general strike of October 1972 and lasted into early 1973. The second began on August 9, 1973, when in the midst of another crisis brought on by the truckers' strike, Allende again drew the military into his cabinet. This time there were four of them: the commanding officers of the army, navy, and air force, and of the paramilitary carabineros. The first three of these had trained at military installations in the United States, but at least one of them—top-ranking General Carlos Prats—took an attitude towards Allende's government that was the opposite of the one that the United States government had taken from the start.

The military contingent in Allende's cabinet on this second occasion was headed by General Prats. He had quite recently demonstrated his support of the regime by taking the lead in suppressing an attempted military coup in June. Allende now made him minister of defense, a post which, in this situation, was the most powerful in the government except for that of the president himself. For the moment at least, the situation seemed well in hand, for the well-trained armed forces were strategically located in the six military districts into which the country was divided. In mid-1973, according to the generally well-informed *The Military Balance,* the army numbered 32,000, the navy 18,000, and the air force 10,000, to which should be added the 160,000 army reservists and the 30,000 carabineros. The army consisted of five divisions, which included two armored regiments, one helicopter-borne regiment, and

10 motorized infantry regiments, and its arms included just under 150 light and medium tanks. The air force had 50 combat planes and 30 helicopters; the navy, 3 submarines, 3 cruisers, and six each of destroyers, landing craft, and patrol vessels. The same source indicates that, at least in recent years, Chile's armed forces had been financially well provided for. In 1973 its per capita defense budget was considerably larger than those of the seven other Latin American countries listed and almost four times as large as Brazil's; this may be an indication of Allende's eagerness to retain the good will and support of the military. In this list Chile was followed by Argentina, Venezuela, Uruguay, Peru, and Brazil, in that order. As a percentage of GNP, however, Chile's 1973 military budget (2.7) took second place, slightly behind Peru (2.9).

Allende's efforts to keep the military on his side were frustrated by the spreading political and economic chaos. They had been in his cabinet hardly a week when one of them, the air force commander, resigned his post as minister of public works on the ground that he had not been given sufficient authority to cope with the strike. Allende promptly removed him as commanding officer of the air force on the basis of evidence that he was in league with the opposition. From that point the conflict escalated rapidly to the military coup. Convinced that one was imminent, the Central Labor Federation (CUT) on August 23 ordered its members to fortify the factories for defense. If a coup was not already a certainty, this made it so, for the armed forces in Chile, as in most other Latin American countries, have been very jealous of their arms monopolies, especially since the liquidation of the Cuban army by Fidel Castro when he came to power.

A few hours after CUT issued the order to fortify the factories, General Prats resigned both his posts, as defense minister and as commander in chief of the army. He did so under pressure from his fellow generals and their wives. The ladies joined a demonstration in front of his suburban home in protest against his presence in the cabinet, and the generals invited him to resign as their commanding officer. In a letter to his friend the president, Prats explained that he gave up both posts "so as not to serve as a pretext for those persons determined to overthrow the government."*

---

*General Prats and his wife soon left for Argentina and were assassinated there in 1974.

General Prats's double resignation may have been a noble gesture, but it was utterly futile, for at this point one pretext more or less made no difference. Each side was now accusing the other of planning to attack it, and both were probably right. After the coup took place it was widely reported to have been in gestation for several months (eleven, according to óne report) and Prats, in his letter to Allende explaining his resignation, as good as said a coup was being prepared, though he did not indicate how long the preparation had been going on. On the other side, there was plenty of evidence that the Marxists were arming; in self-defense, they insisted, but one's own arms are always defensive. Before the Central Labor Federation issued its order of August 23, workers were already arming their factories to form cordons around Santiago and other cities. Arms were being shipped in from Cuba under diplomatic immunity via the Cuban embassy and left-wing vigilante groups were arming for combat (as were similar right-wing groups). Since 1971 the men of MIR had dominated what amounted to a military enclave in a large forested area in southern Chile. The army had been instructed to dislodge them, but General Prats had excused it on the ground that since MIR had no heavy weapons, this was a job for the carabineros; and the carabineros had always found themselves otherwise occupied. By mid-1973 problems of this kind and left-wing efforts to infiltrate and subvert the armed forces had apparently convinced most of the military leaders that the already serious threat from the left to their corps and, as they now saw it, to the country would go on growing so long as Allende's Popular Unity coalition retained control of the powerful presidency.

His coalition had been assured of retaining that control at least until 1976 by the failure of the opposition parties to win a large enough majority in the congressional elections of March 4, 1973, to remove Allende by impeachment. Popular Unity polled less than 44 percent of the popular vote. It thus remained definitely a minority coalition, although in this election for the first time there was no literacy requirement and the age requirement was lowered from 21 to 18 years, both of which changes were presumably to Allende's advantage. Yet, while the opposition parties, Christian Democratic and National, had won by a comfortable margin and remained in control of Congress, they had not won by the decisive majority they needed to oust Allende. In short, the election settled nothing. The opposition faced another three years of Allende, and he faced another three years of congressional obstruction. It was a situation that both sides were beginning to find intolerable, and observers predicted serious trouble soon. As the *Wall Street Journal*'s Latin American specialist, Everett Martin, reported from Santiago on March 1, three days before the voting took place:

> If the elections turn out to be as inconclusive as it seems they will be, Chileans are freely predicting more national strikes with armed extremists on both the right and the left resorting to more and more violence. At that point, the reluctant armed forces, who thus far remain the major question mark, may decide they have to step in forcefully. That could well mark the end of the Chilean experiment but not the end of Chile's problems.

What finally decided the armed forces to "step in forcefully" appears to have been the alleged discovery of a left-wing plot, known as Plan Z, to assassinate the military leaders on September 26. Whether or not there was such a plan, the military leaders seem to have believed it was a reality. When the coup came on September 11, the armed forces lived up to the reputation for efficiency that they had enjoyed for years past. The incident that was reported to have precipitated it was a left-wing seizure of a naval installation in Valparaíso. Naval forces promptly retook it and went on to seize all government offices and communications centers in the city. Within a few hours the army contingents in the Santiago area followed suit and were joined by the carabineros. A junta consisting of the heads of the armed forces demanded President Allende's resignation. He refused, shut himself up in the Moneda, the executive office building, and prepared to put up a resistance he must have known was hopeless. Dating from colonial times, the low, squat Moneda is solidly built but impossible to defend against the tanks immediately brought into action against it by the army.

It was all over in a few hours and Salvador Allende was dead. How he died is still uncertain. The first reports were that he committed suicide, as a predecessor, President Balmaceda, had done after his defeat in the civil war of 1891. Allende's widow, who talked with him by telephone while the siege was going on, at first confirmed this version and added that he had killed himself with a submachine gun presented to him by Fidel Castro. A few days later she changed her account from suicide to murder, but she was, of course, not an eyewitness, and on the evidence now available no one can be sure just how Allende died.

After Allende

The military junta, presided over by Army General Augusto Pinochet Ugarte, took over the government at once. At the end of the year, which is as far as the present chapter goes, it was still in power and had set no limit on its tenure. So far, its political performance had been well below the standard set by its military performance in executing the coup. This was to be expected. The senior officers in Chile were even less well prepared than those in Argentina to govern a country, for the latter's advanced schools provided a more thorough study of all major national problems, political, economic, and social, as well as military, than it was possible for Chile's only institution of that kind to offer. Two years before the coup a Chilean legislator, whose name was withheld for his protection, informed officials of ITT that the Chilean military's realization of their deficiency in this respect was one thing that was deterring them from intervening against Allende. Another deterrent, he went on, was their realization that any government that followed Allende's was going to "have a most difficult time." When at last they intervened, they brought civilians into high posts in the new government but did not always heed their advice.

The junta's first task was to complete its conquest of power. Although this required some mopping up at various points throughout the country, on the whole it was surprisingly easy. As in Argentina when Perón was ousted in 1955, there was no uprising by the organized workers and unorganized masses in defense of a regime that had cultivated them assiduously and designated them as its chief beneficiaries. In the Chilean case it may be explanation enough that Allende's death on the first day of the intervention left his side without a leader of sufficient stature to rally the resistance. Or it may be that the supposed beneficiaries had benefited too little from his regime to bind them firmly to it. On Fidel Castro's visit to Chile, it will be recalled, he complained that Allende had failed to mobilize the masses. That was at the end of Allende's first and best year; from then on, it was downhill for almost everyone in Chile, economically and in most other respects. Yet again, it may be that the left-wing Chileans were not nearly so well armed and otherwise prepared for combat as their political and military opponents would have us believe. This is a hypothesis that requires careful investigation of a kind not likely to be feasible for some time to come.

The government set up by the junta was a military dictatorship along the lines of the one in Argentina headed by General Aramburu after Perón's fall. It dissolved Congress, the Marxist political parties, and the Central Federation of Labor, prohibited political meetings, governed by decree, and set no time limit on its duration. It promised to respect the Supreme Court but did not let that prevent it from carrying out a harsh repression through measures ranging from censorship and arbitrary arrests to torture and executions. The repression was still going on at the end of the year and was conservatively estimated to have cost 2,000 lives by that time. The junta promised not to deprive the workers of their social conquests, but it established a regime of austerity which, as usual, bore hardest on the poor. Their lot was worsened by the continuing inflation and the worldwide petroleum crisis. The junta had barely been established when this crisis began and it caught C' 'le at a time when its own already inadequate petroleum production was declining. Some help came from foreign sources, including the United States, but on a scale that was hardly enough to mitigate the widespread suffering, which was not confined to the lower income groups. The character of the junta and a wave of propaganda against it did not encourage an outpouring of aid by other countries.

The private sector's vigorous promotion of the campaign against Allende had its reward. The junta left the gremios and professional associations intact. In December it announced the return to their former owners of 115 companies, including 12 controlled by foreign capital, that had been nationalized by the Allende government without compensation. Those it had purchased from the owners were not returned to them, even when the latter had been harassed into selling at a bargain price. The nationalized fundos and farms were returned to their owners on the same basis. The big copper mines were not among the properties thus returned, for they had been nationalized under a constitutional amendment and—even more to the point— to return them would have been, politically, the height of folly, for the nationalization of these U.S.-owned mines had been enthusiastically supported by the great majority of Chileans, including many people on the right as well as virtually everybody on the left. The junta did, however, agree to reopen the question of compensation for the former owners.

Looking to the future, the junta, whose members disliked the political party system almost as much as they did socialism, appointed a commission to draw up a new constitution for Chile. The commission's chairman, Minister of Justice Gonzalo Prieto Gándara, let it be known that the gremios would have a decisive voice in Congress under the new charter. This was in accordance with the thinking of Jaime Guzmán, who, as already noted, was a leader of the gremial movement and who, although only 27 years old at the time of his appointment to the commission was regarded as one of its most influential members. Since the gremial movement connoted corporatism and corporatism was redolent of fascism, some observers naturally compared young Guzmán to Portugal's fascist dictator for several decades after 1929, António de Oliveira Salazar. There was some ground for the comparison. Guzmán, like Salazar, was not only a corporatist but also an ardent conservative Catholic and a university professor, and had achieved considerable intellectual and political prominence at an early age. Moreover, if Guzmán insisted that his corporatism was democratic, so, too, had Salazar done when he was very young. Yet it appeared that Guzmán's profession of democratic faith was, if not more genuine, at least likely to be more lasting, for he proposed to institutionalize it by incorporating democratic features in the forthcoming constitution. Among other things, political parties would still be a part of the system and would share power with the gremios. Also, he had said in an article published in 1971 that Chile needed to be profoundly transformed selectively while building on the past. There was democracy in Chile's past, but hardly in Portugal's. Perhaps, then, it would be more appropriate to compare Guzmán to Chile's own Diego Portales, a hero to Chilean conservatives and particularly to the country's military leaders at this time. As the reader may recall, in the early 1830s, after Chile had gone through a decade of turmoil climaxed by two years of what was for those days a revolutionary left-wing regime and a civil war, Portales gave it a conservative constitution, built on its past, under which Chile became one of the leading countries of South America for the rest of the century.

What would come of these and all the other elements that would go into the making of the new constitution and the new order in Chile was not at all likely to be clear any time soon. Many Chileans, of whom young Jaime Guzmán was one, insisted that the armed forces should remain in control of the country for at least three years to come. At the end of 1973 there was no indication that the military junta, which made all the decisions, had any shorter period in mind.

XV Aftermath of the Upheavals
of 1973

The upheavals that brought about sweeping political change in all three Southern Cone countries in the latter half of 1973 had several sources in common; economic and social as well as political. Their sequels, too, were similar in important respects. Of the two most obvious exceptions, one was the displacement of civilian by military rule, partially in Uruguay and wholly in Chile, whereas the process was reversed in Argentina; the other, the crushing of organized guerrilla bands in the first two countries, while they continued to grow in Argentina. The differences were more apparent than real. The new civilian regime in Argentina, headed first by the restored Perón and, after his death, by his widow, took a turn to the right which was almost as pronounced as that of the military rulers of Chile and Uruguay. As for the guerrillas, although their organizations had been smashed in both countries, their recovery still seemed possible at the close of 1975. In all three countries the new governments were in serious trouble, and in none of them had there been a noticeable abatement of the other common sources of the upheavals of 1973.

The prospect of further trouble loomed closer as the world oil crisis that began in late 1973 bore with special weight on the developing world and not least heavily on the already staggering economies of the Southern Cone. Yet common problems and common trends did not unite them in a common front in dealing with either their domestic or their foreign affairs. Still, their leaders kept trying and if all previous Latin American cooperative ventures had not so uniformly failed, it would have been possible to believe that one of the potentially most significant events of 1974 and 1975 was the emergence of fresh efforts at cooperation in arrangements excluding, or simply not including, the United States.

After noting a striking though imperfect parallel with Western Europe in this period, the present chapter sketches the trials of the Southern cone countries in the two-year aftermath of their political earthquakes of 1973.

Crisis of Democracy: Southern Cone and Western Europe

In previous chapters it has been pointed out that the Southern Cone has shared with other parts of the world, especially Western Europe, many experiences of various kinds, including a sharp decline of faith in democracy. Fresh evidence of this decline in the

Northern hemisphere was provided in 1975 by the Trilateral Commission's publication of *The Crisis of Democracy,* by Michel Crozier and others. Described in its subtitle as a report to the commission "on the Governability of Democracies," the book contains one chapter on each of the three geographical divisions of the Trilateral area: Western Europe, Japan, and the United States. Although Latin America lies outside the commission's chosen bailiwick and hence is not discussed in the report, the events of 1973-1975 showed that there was a crisis of democracy in the Southern Cone too, and that the chapter on Western Europe was particularly relevant to Argentina, Chile, and Uruguay, which should not surprise anyone who knows both regions.

The report opens with two introductory chapters on the current pessimism about democracy and the challenges that confront democratic governments in the Trilateral area. These are followed by the chapter on Western Europe, whose author, Michel Crozier, was founder and director of the Centre de Sociologie des Organisations, in Paris. His analysis identifies six "Social, Economic and Cultural Causes" of the current crisis of democracy in Western Europe: "1. Increase of Social Interactions" (society grows more complex, citizens make incompatible claims and require more social control, but resist any kind that "is associated with the hierarchical values they have learned to discard and reject"). "2. The Impact of Economic Growth" (material progress, far from appeasing tensions, as hoped, has exacerbated them by raising expectations that cannot be met, and in other ways). "3. The Collapse of Traditional Institutions" (less a political or economic than a moral collapse, affecting churches, universities, schools, and other cultural institutions, with the Catholic Church "hit the hardest"). "4. The Upsetting of the Intellectual World" (the contemporary cultural revolution explains "the ungovernability of the masses," which is a "cultural failure"). "5. The Mass Media" (because of the "cultural void," anomic rebellion and alienation have "dangerously progressed" in education as elsewhere, and because the media, particularly television, which have become an "autonomous power," are a "very important source of disintegration of social control"). "6. Inflation" (inflation is an "easy answer to the tensions of growth," but when it goes into double digits its costs become unbearable and with its twin evil, economic depression, it makes the problem of governability "immediate and practical").

Every one of these six causes has also contributed notably to the current crisis of democracy in the Southern Cone. The parallel with Western Europe is made all the more striking by Crozier's statement that "a major turning point" in Europe came with the political turmoil that began in the late 1960s. This trans-Atlantic parallel is hardly surprising, since in the past hundred years the Southern Cone countries, which have been the most advanced in Latin America, have also had the strongest ties with Western Europe. But the parallel is not perfect, for some of Crozier's six causes apply to the Southern Cone in distinctly greater degree than others. The degree is perhaps highest in the cases of (2), the impact of economic growth, (4), the upsetting of the intellectual world, and (6), inflation; much lower for (1) and (3). For one thing, "collapse" is much too strong a term for what has happened to traditional institutions and hierarchical values in any of the Southern Cone countries, even Uruguay, where the process of social and cultural modernization has moved fastest. There has even been a revival of corporatism, especially in Chile and Argentina, which has no counterpart in Western Europe. With regard to the fifth cause, the Southern Cone has certainly had its full share of anomic rebellion and alienation, but if the media have been a major "source of disintegration of social control" here too, radio has probably contributed more to it than television, except in a few urban areas. Finally, Crozier's six causes do not seem to include certain factors that have been important in the crisis of democracy in Latin America, such as organized labor, economic dependency on foreign countries, and guerrilla violence much more formidable than any encountered in Western Europe in the 1960s and 1970s.

Still, when all exceptions have been taken, the similarities are more impressive than the differences between the Southern Cone and Western Europe as regards the social, economic, and cultural causes of the current crisis of democracy—a crisis which began to peak in both areas in the late 1960s. Here we have yet another reason for treating the Southern Cone countries as a group apart from the rest of Latin America. For it is doubtful whether such a comparison of any other group, or even any single country, in Latin America with Western Europe would yield nearly so close a similarity.

The events of 1973-1975, however, were a reminder that for all the resemblances between them, the Southern Cone was far from being a transplanted replica of Western Europe. By the close of

1975 almost all of Western Europe seemed to be weathering the crisis fairly well.* On the other hand, in the whole Southern Cone, as we shall see, almost everything went wrong and the crucial problem in the short run was political.

Argentina: The End of the Peronist Era

The belief that Juan Perón could have dominated the storm in Argentina had he lived is pure illusion. When the aging leader died on July 1, 1974, less than nine months after his inauguration, his regime had already provided a preview of the miseries which, in the next eighteen months, were to bring the administration of his widow and successor — and, in the opinion of many, the country itself — to the brink of ruin. Commonly referred to as María Estela by some and as Isabel by others, his widow lacked the magnetism of her predecessor Eva in the first Perón regime, whose remains were brought back from Spain and put on exhibition at this time for the edification of her ever-faithful followers. That was no help to the new president, who made matters much worse by her choice of an *éminence grise*. This was the same José López Rega, former policeman and publisher and still an astrologer, who had made himself as useful to the Peróns in both Spain and Argentina as they were to him. Secretary to the presidency under Perón and now a cabinet minister (social welfare), López Rega became Mrs. Perón's closest adviser and, some said, her Svengali. For the next twelve months his corruption and the regime's bias in favor of right-wing Peronism became more and more notorious, until in July 1975 she most reluctantly dismissed him, whereupon his son-in-law was ousted from the speakership of the Chamber of Deputies.

In dismissing López Rega, Mrs. Perón had yielded to heavy pressure from both the Peronist labor unions and the military. These two had been the main props of her shaky position, which they had supported for the same reason that Perón is said to have had for insisting that she be made vice-president and his successor: as a symbol of united Peronism, she offered the best chance of keeping the

---

*The chief exception was Portugal, which, along with Spain, was not included in this Trilateral Commission study except for general references to the "Latin countries." Portugal's long-established dictatorship was overthrown, but the country was then torn apart by increasingly violent strife over the kind of social, economic, and political regime to be set up in its place.

already fragmented party from flying completely apart and civilian rule from failing again. Now, labor leaders were furious because López Rega — who, they were sure, was lining his own pockets — had turned back large wage increases won by the unions, and military leaders were willing to go to great lengths to arrest the growing disorder before it forced them to take over the government again.

The high command seemed genuinely eager to avoid another such takeover — naturally enough, in view of the fiasco of their recent seven-year attempt to govern the country. But they, in turn, were under increasing pressure to intervene from junior officers convinced that this was the only means of saving the country from anarchy. The argument had all the familiarity of a worn phonograph record, but current circumstances gave it credibility and a strong appeal. The assorted and irrepressible guerrilla and terrorist groups were only the most flagrant example of a general lawlessness that was making the Argentine people seem ungovernable, as a president of Uruguay had said of that country's people in the late nineteenth century. Fear of provoking further disorders and reprisals at the polls deterred the imposition of austerity measures and thereby helped to accelerate the rise of inflation, which by mid-1975 was approaching 200 percent. Even the sobersided Alvaro Alsogaray, a former minister of economy, warned his fellow Argentines at this point that they were in imminent danger of falling into a spiral of "hyper-inflation" like those that had devastated Germany in the 1920s and Chile under Allende.

After her forced sacrifice of López Rega, Mrs. Perón made moves that aroused the suspicion that she was trying to build up a faction in the army for a military coup in her own behalf. That was blocked by the high command, which, since she gave signs of nearing a nervous breakdown, arranged for a sick leave at an isolated Air Force resort in the Córdoba hills. She was accompanied by the wives of three commanding generals, one of whom, Jorge Videla, was the leader of the reunified army and chairman of the joint chiefs of staff. In her absence a cabinet shake-up and general house-cleaning was started by the acting president. He had strong support from the trade unions, "who know that they will sink too if the government goes down," reported *The Economist* on September 20. "This is peronism's [sic] last chance," it predicted. "If the drift and disintegration continues, the army is bound to step in, though it does not want to be involved in the government just now."

To the great surprise of the many who assumed she would never return to the presidency, Mrs. Perón did so just in time to preside over the celebration on October 17 of the thirtieth anniversary of Juan Perón's likewise unexpected return to power. But he had returned to wild acclaim by descamisado masses that jammed the big Plaza de Mayo, whereas Isabel's hearers only half filled the plaza and their enthusiasm was not noticeable. And shortly before that, the Montoneros, left-wing Peronist guerrillas, as if to point out her weakness, had staged a sensational attack on a prison and military garrison at Formosa, the capital of the province of the same name in northern Argentina. The attack was financed by the ransom of $52 million that they had extorted by kidnapping two brothers of the wealthy Born family. The attack failed in its immediate objective to free several guerrillas from the Formosa prison, but it was a serious affair. Some 200 Montoneros took part in the attack; they were given "logistic support" by 500 more, and the death toll was more than 50. *La Nación's* comment was that the government seemed to be losing the war against the subversive organizations, which were responsible for 672 killings in the 15 months since Mrs. Perón became president.

Tardily, all-out war was now declared on these organizations. Legislation was tightened and control of the campaign was transferred from the police to the armed forces. Previously the armed forces had had charge of it only in the northern province of Tucumán, where a combination of rugged mountains and valleys covered with fields of sugar cane provided hospitable terrain for hit-and-run guerrilla operations. For all the brave words about "all-out war," however, the subversive organizations were not only still going strong at the end of the year in Argentina itself, but also were slipping men and weapons across the frontiers into Chile and Uruguay for a revival of the guerrilla movements in those countries.

Other acute problems clamored for attention. Nothing could check the inflation. Another "social contract" between labor and management for stabilizing prices and wages was concluded in late November, only to be broken again almost at once by the government itself, as happened in early 1974 under Juan Perón. This time it was broken in order to appease Mrs. Perón's trade union supporters by a substantial wage increase, in the hope, it was suspected, of warding off a threatened impeachment on grounds of incompetence and corruption. As reported by the *New York Times* in late October, strikes continued to multiply and increasing use was made of a new bargaining weapon: the threat to kill company executives if wages were not raised. A ban on Argentine beef by the European Common Market, overstocked by its own production, led to a sharp drop in the domestic price to the delight of consumers and the despair of cattlemen.

In the political realm plans for a revision of the constitution brought on a controversy over corporatism, which a majority of Peronists favored, while the Radical Party rejected it. The government disavowed censorship, but critical journals were threatened with expropriation. *La Prensa* was again, as in the early 1950s, high on the blacklist. Although it was not actually expropriated, an investigation by the Inter-American Press Association revealed that the government had tried to force it into line by economic pressure. Again TV and radio stations were taken over, as was the University of Buenos Aires, whose proper mission, the government advised, was to inculcate Peronist principles.

Though with far less success this time, nationalism was again exploited, as in Perón's palmiest days, to unify his heterogeneous following. In July 1974, for example, a new economic minister qualified his proclaimed dedication to free enterprise by expropriating all foreign-owned filling stations and a little later nationalized all foreign communications companies by purchase. The nationalist theme was also involved in efforts to play up Argentina's role in international affairs. Juan Perón even talked about making Argentina the leader of the Third World. After his death the same end was pursued by other means, as by renewing the old demand on Great Britain for the return of the Malvinas, the Falkland Islands, and redoubling Argentine activities in Antarctica. More practical benefits, too, were sought—in both cases, oil and other natural resources, and also, in Antarctica, a base for polar flights by Aerolíneas Argentinas (Argentine Airways) to Australia and Asia.

The government made modest gains in other sectors. In early 1974 it brought about a relaxation of the IDB's loan policy despite opposition from the United States. In a closely contested election in May 1975 an Argentine diplomat, Alejandro Orfila, was chosen to head the Organization of American States as secretary general. Nearer home, though, things did not go so well. In Bolivia, Argentina was already losing ground to its traditional and now more prosperous, stable, and influential rival, Brazil, when in February 1976

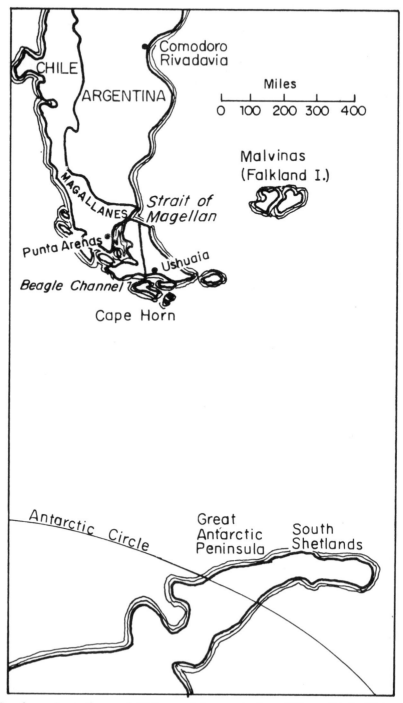

Southern Argentina and Chile, and Antarctic Area Where Their Claims
Conflict with Those of Great Britain

Secretary of State Kissinger, by singling out Brazil for recognition as a world power (see chapter XVII), dealt a severe blow to Argentine pride and the prestige of its Peronist government. Among the country's Southern Cone neighbors old rancors were compounded by fear of infection from the irrepressible terrorism in Argentina and from the Marxism that now pervaded a large part of the disintegrating Peronist movement.

By the close of 1975 the end of the 30-year-old Peronist era too seemed at hand. So did another military coup, which might be led by General Videla and result in the return to power of General Lanusse, who had shown considerable ability as president from 1971 to 1973, though he was constantly harassed by the Peronists. In 1973 he had cooperated in bringing them back to office, with the idea, according to a report from Buenos Aires by C. L. Sulzberger in the *New York Times* for November 22, 1975, of letting "Peronism destroy itself once and for all—which it now has done." This time, however, the military leaders would take over only if assured of active support and collaboration from strong civilian elements, such as Juan Perón had had when he inaugurated the era that bears his name.

The expected coup took place on March 23, 1976. It met with no resistance and General Videla's forces carried it off with "such precision, you might have thought they were Germans, not Argentines." So, reported the *New York Times* five days later, it was described by the upper-class porteño host at an all-night dinner party early the next week end. The military assured Mrs. Perón of her personal safety and packed her off to the Andean resort center of La Angostura in Neuquén province; from there, it was reported, she would probably be sent back to Spain rather than be brought back to face the charges of corruption and other offenses on which she had narrowly escaped impeachment earlier in the year.

Once again Argentina was ruled by a military dictatorship. Its organization followed the now familiar format of a junta composed of the three service chiefs—army, navy, air force—with the army chief, General Videla, as president and an all-military cabinet except for civilian ministers of Economy and Culture and Education. The junta set no time limit on its tenure, but it was not expected to restore civilian government in less than three years. Peronist personnel and policies were again purged as in 1955. Droves of office holders, high and low, were dismissed and a regime of austerity was planned in an effort to cope with the desperate state to which the economy had been reduced by inflation, slow-downs, strikes, corruption, and a breakdown of tax collections. As if to remind the junta of the scarcely less urgent problem of terrorism, guerrillas saluted its establishment with the murder of two Ford Company security guards and escaped unscathed. To deal with such cases the junta set up special military courts with the power to impose the death penalty for attacks on military personnel.

There was reason to doubt whether the new military dictatorship would be any more successful than its predecessors. Yet there were some factors in its favor. The most important was the discredit and disunity into which the Peronists, who were the largest opposition body, had fallen while in power. While no one could be certain that adversity would not reunite the warring Peronist factions, that seemed very unlikely. For after a return to power of nearly three years, their internecine rifts were so much deeper and the failure of their government so abject that it would be a wonder if the Peronist movement and its sustaining myth ever regained its former hold on the Argentine people. The military leaders' strategy of letting Peronism come to power and destroy itself had worked. Only time could tell whether they would receive the strong civilian support they were counting on. Here the chances favored them. With all its faults, their government from 1966 to 1973 had been far better than its Peronist successor, and memories of the only other civilian regimes since 1955 — those of Frondizi and Illia — did little to generate enthusiasm for that form of government in the situation Argentina now faced.

There were probably few Argentines, even among the military, who thought that dictatorship was a good thing; it was simply that protracted bitter experience had convinced many that it was the only thing in these circumstances. At any rate, for whatever reason, Argentina once more had the same form of government as the other Southern Cone countries. But that did not set them apart from the rest of the Latin American states, for eight of the ten in South America — all except Colombia and Venezuela — were now ruled by military dictatorships.

Chile under a Dictatorship

Death by violence is one way for a chief of state to achieve canonization, though it does not always work; to go no further than the history of the United States since the Civil War, compare the cases of Abraham Lincoln and John F. Kennedy with those of James A. Garfield and William McKinley. It did work in the case of Chilean President Salvador Allende, with the result that the military dictatorship set up by those who had overthrown him, which was sure to be vilified by the Communist world in any case, was handicapped from the start in the democratic West by a hostility that it could hardly have overcome in the next two years even if its performance had been perfect. David Holden, chief foreign correspondent of the *Sunday Times* of London, writing in the magazine *Encounter* for January 1975, obviously spoke for a minority when he denied the validity of Allende's canonization and of the "hysterical reaction" in his favor that took place instantaneously in most European countries (and the United States, he might have added). Holden's article sought with considerable success to expose the "myths" on which that reaction was based, but it also made clear the magnitude of the handicaps imposed on Chile's new rulers by the reaction. Allende's policies and his country "were shattered long before the end," but with death he became overnight "the most potent political cult-figure since his old friend, Che Guevara," among ordinary liberals and social democrats as well as extreme left-wingers. It followed, of course, that sympathy for Allende meant hostility against those who had ousted him.

As if to increase the handicap, the Chilean generals got their new government off to a bad start. *Economist* correspondent Robert Moss admitted as much in a "letter from Santiago" in *Encounter* for March 1974. His letter discussed their tasks and some of their mistakes. One of the latter, he said, was to fill most vacant positions, even university rectorships, with military men, thereby offending many civilian participants in the movement against Allende, including the anti-Marxist students, whose part in the movement had been a leading one. But, Moss added, the generals were "being reviled as much for imaginary crimes as for real ones," and most political leaders of the center as well as the right were glad to have the military stay in power and be held responsible for the austere measures economic reconstruction would require. This part of their task the generals had had the prudence to confide to civilians, trained economists, while retaining final decision on policy. (Though Moss did not say so, many of the economists had been trained by the University of Chicago and some were disciples of its distinguished and controversial Professor Milton Friedman.) What kind of political system might emerge, Moss did not predict, but he pointed out that it could hardly be a simple restoration of the former democratic system, since the generals had outlawed all the pro-Allende parties, which represented about 40 percent of the population (even more than the outlawed Peronists after Perón's overthrow in 1955). Moreover, he continued, among the high command and the jurists appointed to draft a new constitution for Chile were a number of corporatists — a minority, but an influential one — who were "fundamentally out of sympathy with the democratic system."

Through the remainder of that year and all the next, the generals, organized as a junta, made little headway. In some ways their performance went from bad to worse. To be sure, the conditions facing them also deteriorated. In some of its leading features, notably its heritage of hatred and economic wreckage from the Allende regime, the situation bore an ominous resemblance to the one that confronted the Argentine military when they overturned the first Perón regime. In addition, the establishment of the Chilean junta coincided almost exactly with the beginning of OPEC's squeeze on the price of oil, which Chile had to import in large volume. It was cold comfort to most Chileans that the rising cost of oil made Chile's government-owned nitrate industry profitable for the first time in ten years. In mid-1974 floods devastated large parts of the country, and a welcome rise early that year in the price of copper, still Chile's chief export item, was more than wiped out towards its close by a sharp drop in copper prices that continued into the next year.

Two other problems compounded the difficulties. One was the existence of terrorist and guerrilla organizations, notably MIR, remnants of which threatened to revive with foreign aid; the other, the increasing isolation of the Chilean military regime in the European-American world. Measures taken by the junta to solve the former problem aggravated the latter. All leaders of open resistance were jailed or exiled or fled abroad in a diaspora that spread from neighboring South American countries, principally Argentina, to Mexico and Western Europe from Italy to Sweden. MIR, already crippled in the coup of September 1973, lost more of its top leaders, among them a nephew of Salvador Allende, as well as secret arms caches and medical installations. Yet the junta was sufficiently worried about internal security to call up reserves in April 1974 and to close the frontiers not long after that; and MIR continued its underground activities. One of these was the issuance of proclamations against the junta to match those put forth by the exiles in Helsinki and other remote places.

The proclamations called for, among other things, an international boycott of Chile. By the close of 1975 the proposal no longer sounded completely fantastic. The junta's measures, taken in the name of national security, were credibly alleged to include regular use of torture, and the original "hysterical reaction" against the junta among left-wingers and liberals was broadened and reinforced by general condemnation of its refusal to permit the atrocity charges to be investigated on the spot by a committee of the United Nations Commission on Human Rights. No allowance seems to have been made in most quarters, even in Washington, either for the junta's countercharge that the committee was biased or for the fact that the junta had already permitted on-the-spot investigations by representatives of the OAS and other bodies.

Understandably, the generals felt they had few if any friends in the West and they knew they had only enemies in the Communist world. Accordingly, they turned to the Arab nations in the hope that by doing so they would be assured of moral support and plenty of oil. But the Arabs' price was Chile's vote in the UN General Assembly for a resolution linking Zionism with racism. Chile paid the price and thereby earned a sharp rebuke from a "high official at the American Mission to the United Nations," who, reported the *New York Times* of October 18, 1975, declared, "We are forced to assume that . . . Chile sold her vote to the Arabs." Unless the unidentified "high official" was the mission's head, Ambassador Patrick Moynihan, he would hardly have dared make such a charge without authorization from a still higher official in Washington.

Even Chile's fellow members of the Andean group turned against the junta because it adopted a liberal policy towards foreign private capital investments, contrary to a fundamental principle of the Andean Pact. By late 1975 the breakup of that once flourishing group seemed a serious possibility. There was even talk of war between Chile and another of its members, Peru, whose government, though also military, was left-wing. For obvious reasons, relations with Argentina were at best cool. So short of friends was the junta in this part of the world that Chilean authorities (among them the lady mayor of Santiago) were beginning to talk feelingly about the justice of Bolivia's demand for the restoration of its outlet to the sea — an outlet of which Bolivia had been deprived by Chile almost a century ago in the War of the Pacific.

The charge that Chile had sold her vote to the Arabs might have seemed to mark the end of the friendly support given by the United States in September 1973; but it probably was not. Since other Latin American states had likewise supported the resolution against Zionism, the United States could hardly afford to hold to a hard line on the matter with the junta. Developments in Chile suggested that a more productive and hence more likely course for Washington would be to shift its support, gradually and quietly, to the moderate and more democratic coalition that was said to be forming in Chile amidst mounting discontent with the junta's iron rule.

Some concessions had been made by the junta. As early as July 1974 the military government was given what was called a unique form, with a rotating headship, which, while maintaining the armed forces' monopoly of power, was supposed to make it more open and flexible. General Augusto Pinochet was confirmed as its first head, with the title of president. In April 1975 he took civilians into his cabinet. In October he announced an immediate relaxation of controls, including the state of siege, and the preparation of measures, to be announced in 1976, dealing with fundamental institutions, citizenship, and constitutional guarantees. Similarly, in 1975 workers were given a share in management, the traditional distinction between white-collar and blue-collar workers was abolished, and there was even tentative provision for the restoration of the right to strike, which had been prohibited since the coup of September 1973. Enterprise too was freed, with the denationalization of many companies (but not of the copper and other companies that had sold out, though under pressure, during Allende's administration) and the proclaimed establishment of a "pluralistic economy." Besides welcoming foreign private investments and obtaining loans for development and other purposes from the IMF, IDB, and World Bank, the government gave special encouragement to automobile manufacture and the search for oil and other natural resources (which gave special point to its celebration of Antarctic Week in September 1975), and happily reported the discovery of "huge" new deposits of coal in the far southern province of Magallanes.

Yet all the while discontent continued to grow. Inflation continued at a very high rate — 60 percent in the first quarter of 1974 and no lower a year later. Unemployment and underemployment rates, too, were very high and wages low. Controls, though relaxed, were still stringent and freedom of the press was for conformists. The presence of civilians in the cabinet was far from meaning freedom of action for the political parties, which remained outlawed if they had supported Allende, and "in suspense" even if they had opposed him, as Frei's majority Christian Democrats had done. The new labor laws smacked too much of paternalism like that of the Spain of Generalissimo Francisco Franco. Most businessmen, bankers, and their allied landowners applauded the junta for its maintenance of law and order, and yet there was a growing belief among them — especially among those interested in foreign trade and international affairs — that it should be possible to have law and order under a government less liable to be subjected to an international boycott or otherwise penalized. And although the full assembly of bishops of the Chilean Evangelical Church formally endorsed the junta in January 1975, the leaders of the far larger Roman Catholic Church were so deeply divided about it that the opposing factions tended to cancel each other out, as the clergy leaned to the left and the laity to the right. There was disunity even among the military leaders themselves. In *The Nation* for November 8, 1975, Peter Winn, an observer of Chile under Allende and a merciless critic of the junta, declared with obvious satisfaction but plausibly that its "days are numbered and the struggle for the succession has begun."

Just what group or coalition would supplant the junta, Winn was not sure, but he asserted without qualification that a shift to civilian rule was what was in the cards. Perhaps; but, although such a shift, from military to civilian, took place in Chile in the early 1930s, circumstances have changed so greatly since then that that precedent counts for little today. More weight might be accorded the Argentine precedents of the period since 1955 and they do not favor the civilian-return hypothesis, except in terms of a civilian-military shuttle movement. Chile has been so full of surprises in recent times that it may well have still another one in store. As the old Spanish saying has it, "Puede que sí, puede que no. Lo más probable es, ¿quien sabe?" (Perhaps yes, perhaps no. What is most likely is, who knows?)

Uruguay and the Southern Cone

Superficially, Uruguay's dictatorship differed widely from the all-military one in Chile. To mention only the most obvious differences, the Montevideo government was headed by a constitutionally elected civilian president, cattleman Juan María Bordaberry, and he was no puppet in the hands of his military collaborators. Yet in the next two years the performances of the two regimes were much alike in several very important respects. Socially and economically, both served entrenched upper- and middle-class interests, and with a single exception of great importance to those interests — the restoration of order and stability — neither government was able to make substantial progress towards solving the economic and social problems that had helped so powerfully to bring on the upheavals of 1973 in both countries. Politically, too, the trends in the two dictatorships converged in a determination not to re-establish the previously existing democratic system. Bordaberry was only somewhat slower than Chile's military rulers in reaching (or, at any rate, in announcing) that decision. At first he had given the ritual assurances that constitutional government would be restored once he had brought the country through its current crisis. By August 1975, however, he had completed the reversal of his position, and he now declared that Uruguay would never return to its pre-1973 constitutional system. At the same time he denounced "professional politicians" and outlawed all political parties. From now on he placed increasing stress on his anticommunist campaign. In November the campaign reached a kind of climax in the closing of the 30-year-old United Peoples Publishing House on the ground that it was a front for the outlawed Communist Party and served as the South American distribution center for propaganda from the Soviet Union and its satellites.

Bordaberry did not say what new system of government he had in mind, but according to the London weekly *Latin America* of September 5, 1975, what had "enabled" him to pronounce sentence of death on the pre-1973 constitution was the result of a recent opinion poll which showed that the Uruguayan people were far more exercised over the country's economic plight than over the loss of their political rights. This had been one of Mussolini's favorite talking points and it may be that, like conservatives in Argentina and Chile, Bordaberry was inclining towards some form of corporatism. At the close of the year, however, the question still remained open.

The conservatism of his economic policy was shown in several ways. To the disgust of many Uruguayans, his minister of economy followed a sound money policy. Though it held the inflation rate down to 100 percent—which was only half as high as the fantastic rates reached in Argentina and Chile in 1975—they denounced it for its "deadening" effect on the economy. Moreover, the policy was widely attributed to the influence of the IMF, *bête noire* of Latin American populist-nationalists. Bordaberry's measures to get the sluggish economy moving again characteristically included the abolition of income and inheritance taxes and the suspension of export taxes. By 1975 the hardest hit sector of the economy was its chief money maker, the cattle industry. In 1974, according to the issue of *Latin America* mentioned above, 68 percent of Uruguay's meat exports went to Brazil, Argentina, and Spain, but now all three countries were either looking for other sources of supply or tightening their belts. The great landowners and cattlemen looked to Bordaberry, one of their own, for relief. He gave them some, but was prevented by military opposition from giving them as much as both he and they would have liked. The question at issue was whether the National Meat Institute should favor the large ranchers or the small ones. The military in the government were split between liberal and conservative, but in this instance the liberals, populist-nationalists headed by General Gregorio Alvarez, were able to force the president to accept a compromise that salvaged something for the small fry.

The incident encouraged some wishful thinkers to conclude that Bordaberry was on his way out. On the contrary, soon after that he carried out, over strong military opposition, his economy minister's arrangement with a consortium of banks in the United States to raise a loan by pledging Uruguay's gold reserves in Switzerland as security. A meeting of Latin American military chiefs in Uruguay in October 1975 did nothing to weaken his position, and in the same month he easily survived another clash with his critics. This time it was with the Roman Catholic hierarchy. As reported in *La Nación* of Buenos Aires, the fifteen Catholic Bishops, acting as the Uruguayan Episcopal Conference, had prepared for circulation among the faithful a pastoral letter calling on the government to abandon its "philosophy of hatred and violence and the spirit of vengeance" and to declare as broad an amnesty as possible. The government's response was to prohibit the circulation of the pastoral letter, whereupon the bishops promptly complied and the church-state crisis expected by some did not develop.

Nevertheless, the military finally did oust him (June 12, 1976) as opposition to his now clear corporatist bias mounted and the state of the nation deteriorated. So bad were conditions that Uruguay's population problem was the reverse of most other Latin American countries': instead of an explosion, it was suffering a severe contraction. As *The Times of the Americas* suggested, Uruguay was running out of people because people were running out of it. One estimate in early 1975 placed the number of emigrants since 1970 at an appalling 600,000, or nearly one-fifth of the total. According to another estimate made the following June, the population had declined by 250,000 in only the last two years, from just over 3.0 million to 2.76 million. The reasons seemed clear enough. Chief among them were a decade or more of a sluggish economy and a declining standard of living, the Tupamaro era of violence on both sides, the dictatorship, the closing of careers to many talents, and the loss of faith in the country's future and the future of individual citizens. Another blow was the oil crisis, which hit Uruguay hardest of all the Southern American countries and coincided with a severe shortage of electric power.

Marxists blamed all the trouble on the dictatorship, but it began long before that. With better reason, non-Marxists laid much of the blame on the heavy cost of the welfare system and the swollen bureaucracy that administered it. The worst of that was that the massive emigration was draining the country of many of its best-trained people in their most productive years, while the welfare system and its administrators remained behind, so that it became more of a drag than ever on a crippled economy.

Almost as distressing tales of woe could be told by the other two countries of the Southern Cone at the end of the third quarter of the century, which had started out with high hopes in all three. To add to the gloom, the IDB report at mid-year on *Latin America in the World Economy* was bearish on the future price trend for this part of the area as well as the rest. The future was not, however, entirely bleak for the Southern Cone countries. Each had some means with which, given time, it could hope to meet the greatest economic challenge of all: the world oil crisis, which was serious for all three precisely because they were still among the most advanced in Latin America. One means was nuclear power. Argentina had nuclear reactors, uranium, and trained personnel; Uruguay had a nuclear reactor but no uranium, and Chile had neither. On the other hand, Uruguay had the prospect of an amply supply of hydroelectric power from plants in operation or under construction, some with aid from IDB and in cooperation with Argentina and Brazil. Chile had the potential to develop the same source in even greater abundance, along with its coal deposits, which were among the best in Latin America, and some petroleum, though much less than Argentina. Still better, those in power in all three countries were bestirring themselves to meet the challenge, and not waiting with folded arms for providence or the United States to bail them out. They were even doing something about their agrarian problems, though Juan Perón's widow and successor had not followed up his proposal—the most ambitious of all—to reform Argentina's agrarian system and give it once more top priority in national policy, and to take the lead in forming an international association of developing nations that would do for those producing foodstuffs for the world market what OPEC had done for the producers of oil. The new military government was more likely to favor the industrial than the agricultural sector, but that remained to be seen.

These and other economic and social problems could hardly even start on the way to solution until the peoples of the Southern Cone could learn to live together once more, in peace if not in harmony, under some kind of viable political system. To each of them, in its domestic as well as its foreign affairs, can be applied with equal force the admonition of Zbigniew Brzezinski in his introduction to *The Crisis of Democracy,* discussed above, in which he said that "the vitality of our political systems is a central precondition for the shaping of a stable international order and for the fashioning of more cooperative relations among our regions."

Part Four

United States Relations
with the Southern Cone

XVI Relations through World War II

Geographically remote, the Southern Cone countries were peripheral to the interests of the United States during most of the nineteenth century. They began to move closer to the center of its political interests soon after its war with Spain, and to the center of its economic interests just before and during World War I. Since the end of that war, one or another of those countries has played a conspicuous part in its foreign relations in some way—Argentina, for example, as a formidable competitor in agricultural exports and as a political affliction to secretaries and assistant secretaries of state on several occasions; Chile as the South American country under the most nearly complete domination in its private sector by U.S. capital and as the only Latin American country to come under a Socialist-Communist government by way of the ballot box; and Uruguay as the only Southern Cone country that followed a pro-United States policy most of the time. Uruguay was also the only one whose government was seriously threatened by the waves of guerrilla violence that swept over all three countries after 1960.

In its government-to-government relations with these distant countries, the United States did not develop a subregional policy like its Panama Canal policy for the Caribbean, though in the end it extended the dominant feature of that policy, interventionism, down to Cape Horn. On most occasions it followed its general Latin American policies in its relations with the Southern Cone. How they were applied and received there is the principal theme of this chapter and the next.

The Nineteenth Century

Rugged individuals from the United States established contacts with the people of the Southern Cone countries while they were still dominions of Spain, despite their remoteness and Spain's efforts (often relaxed in war time) to keep them closed to foreigners. Slavers from New England brought many shiploads of Africans to Montevideo from the opening of the trade there in 1793 to its closing some fifteen years later. Whalers, sealers, and assorted smugglers turned up frequently at Buenos Aires, Paysandú in Uruguay, and ports on the coast of Chile in those same years, during which Spain was involved in the wars of the French Revolution and Napoleon.

When the wars of independence began in Spanish America, the United States sent agents to various parts of it to cultivate commerce and the friendship of "our Spanish American neighbors" in "this hemisphere" — phrases that were in current use almost from the start. The first such agent in the Southern Cone, sent in June 1810, was Joel R. Poinsett, who was accredited to Argentina, Chile, and Peru. In a later age, Poinsett would have been called a Pan Americanist. Though that term did not make its appearance until the 1880s, he was an ardent one. In Chile, where he spent most of his time, he let his ardor get the better of him and not only violated the obligations of neutrality by aiding the patriots militarily, but took sides in their factional fighting among themselves. To make matters still worse, his was the losing faction, and since history is written by the victors, the heritage of dislike of the United States that he left behind when he quit Chile was lasting.

The new governments of Argentina and Chile likewise lost little time in sending agents to the United States to seek its aid. The results of these missions, too, were generally disappointing. They obtained some ships, arms, and ammunition, and much sympathy and moral support, but no direct military aid, no alliance, and, until 1822, no recognition of their independence. Some individual soldiers and sailors were recruited, but they were far fewer than the British legionnaires who fought on the patriot side in Northern South America. Moreover, when Poinsett, learning that British ships and cargoes were receiving preferential treatment from the patriots, complained of this to the new government of Buenos Aires, he was told quite frankly that it was given because British naval forces in the Plata estuary had prevented the royalists in Montevideo from blockading Buenos Aires. Poinsett's experiences were a fair sample of the course taken by relations between the United States and the new states throughout the long struggle for independence. This is not to deny that the United States had many friends, admirers, and even imitators in the Southern Cone countries. Yet it seems typical that one of the most enthusiastic of them, José Artigas of Uruguay, who began his country's liberation, was forced to take refuge in Paraguay midway in the struggle and never went home again.

Altogether, the situation was not very propitious for the reception of the Monroe Doctrine of December 1823 in this part of Spanish America. In Buenos Aires the American consul reported that "the men in power" received Monroe's message with "an unwelcome apathy," which, though it disgusted, did not surprise him in view of "the overweening partiality of the dominant party and of the highest classes of society for the English." "I can plainly foresee," he complained, "that all we have done for this people is poorly appreciated . . ." Montevideo was under Brazilian rule at this time. In Santiago the first official response to the doctrine was only too enthusiastic. It was the proposal of an alliance between Chile and the United States, to which the embarrassed American minister could only give the chilly reply that the United States reserved the right to "act as its own interest might hereafter require." But it would have done no good if he had been in a position to accept the Chilean overture. Only a few days later, those who made it were ousted and replaced by a regime represented by Diego Portales, who has been described as the founder of Chile's foreign policy and is still regarded by conservatives in that country as its greatest statesman; and Portales had no use for the Monroe Doctrine. The United States, he declared, planned to conquer all America, if not today, then surely tomorrow, and not by force of arms but by influence in every sphere.

At least in the Plata basin, Great Britain under George Canning's guidance found it easy to "counter the blow" struck by the Monroe Doctrine (as Charles Webster put it) and (in Canning's own words) "slip in between" the United States and the new states of Latin America. Britain's position in the Plata area, established in the first years of the struggle, was consolidated under a commercial treaty of 1825 that confirmed the preferential treatment it had been receiving. Three years later the long domination of Argentina by Juan Manuel de Rosas began, and Rosas had an "excessive friendship" for the English. Even when there was an undeclared war between Argentina and Britain, along with France, because the two European powers were blockading Buenos Aires and frustrating his siege of Montevideo, Rosas maintained secret ties and profitable business relations with the British. He also failed to press the question of title to the Falkland (Malvinas) Islands, to which Argentina had a valid claim, but which Britain seized and held. On the other hand, Rosas (and future generations of Argentines) blamed the United States for denying the aid requested by Argentina in the name of the Monroe Doctrine in this Falkland Islands case.

Most of the time, however, the United States played an inconspicuous role in the affairs of the Plata area until the twentieth century. It had no hand in the settlement that put an end to the war between Argentina and Brazil and gave independence to Uruguay in 1829. It did not even get around to recognizing the latter's independence until five years later. It did nothing of consequence to stop the repeated violations of the Monroe Doctrine by the frequent interventions of France in the Plata area, and occasionally by England, between 1838 and 1851. The United States was also a cipher in the diplomacy of the Paraguayan War of 1865-1870 between Paraguay and the triple alliance of Argentina, Brazil, and Uruguay. Occasionally, through its representatives or otherwise, it aided in the peaceful settlement of the many disputes between Argentina and its neighbors, especially Chile, in the latter part of the century. Not until the first Pan American Conference (Washington, 1889-1890) did the United States appear in a leading role in the foreign relations of the Plata countries, and even then it owed its prominence to Argentine delegate Roque Sáenz Peña's eloquent oratorical attack on Secretary of State James G. Blaine's proposal of a Pan American customs union.

The reasons for this state of affairs seem clear. First and foremost, the whole east coast of South America — Brazil as well as Argentina and Uruguay — was in effect a British sphere of influence from 1810 to the end of the century. Britain had the sea power, which was decisive, and was predominant in all three countries from the first in their foreign trade and, after the 1860s, in foreign investments as well. The United States, on the other hand, did not have a first-rate navy until the 1890s and did not make foreign private investments of any consequence, except in neighboring Mexico and Cuba, until the twentieth century. From the 1820s to the 1850s it had a brisk trade, built around the exchange of flour from Philadelphia for hides from Argentina and Uruguay. After the Civil War, however, with the decline of its merchant marine and the rise of foreign competition, the United States fell behind in trade with the Plata area and South America generally.

It was this situation that led Congress to send a commercial mission to South America in 1884 to investigate and report on the obstacles and opportunities in that quarter. The mission's report blamed the deterioration of "our position" there in the last twenty years on "our neglect to furnish the ways and means of commerce." It also pointed to opportunities for the United States in Chile, Uruguay, and Argentina, all of which "are booming like our Western Territories . . . but are almost *terra incognita* to us." The report helped to bring about the convocation of the Pan American Conference of 1889-1890, but the United States continued to play a very modest part in the economic as well as the diplomatic affairs of the Plata area for the remainder of the century.

In other important respects, however, its role was much more prominent. In Argentina, for example, the leaders of the post-Rosas generation, notably Juan Bautista Alberdi and Domingo Faustino Sarmiento, who were eager to modernize their country and develop its resources, regarded the United States as a model in its form of government, its liberal immigration and land policies, and its system of public education. Sarmiento, minister to Washington in the 1860s and then president of the republic for six years, urged Argentina to "North Americanize" itself. To forward the good work, he founded schools and teacher-training institutes along the lines laid down by his friend Horace Mann of Massachusetts and imported women school teachers from that state to make it work. When he established Argentina's first astronomical observatory, he induced Benjamin Apthorp Gould, also from Massachusetts, to become its director. Alberdi, principal planner of Argentina's long-lived Constitution of 1853, modeled it on the constitution of the United States more closely than Argentine historians like to admit — so closely, in fact, that for the next hundred years Argentina's Supreme Court buttressed its decisions with citations from those of the U.S. Supreme Court and leading commentaries on its constitution. Occasionally, enterprising individuals from the United States rose to prominence in Platine affairs. One such was William Wheelwright, whom President Urquiza engaged in the 1860s to build a railroad from Rosario to Córdoba. For the necessary funds, however, Wheelwright had to turn to Great Britain.

In Chile, too, an occasional Yankee entrepreneur such as rail-road-builder Henry Meiggs turned up, but otherwise the nineteenth-century roles of the United States in that country differed widely from its roles in Argentina and Uruguay. For its models, Chile looked not to the United States but to Europe. Its Constitution of 1833, likewise long-lived, was drafted by a single person, Mariano Egaña, who had lived in London several years and was convinced that the British system of king, lords, and commons had produced the proper balance between order and liberty and the resulting stability, which was just what his own country needed. So, while making the form suitable to Chile by changing king to strong president, the House of Lords to a conservative senate, and so on, he tried, with considerable success, to reproduce the essence of the British system in Chile's constitution. His view continued to prevail among the ruling classes for a century to come and after the civil war of 1890 a parliamentary system was established under the same constitution and lasted more than thirty years. Similarly, the intellectual life of Chile was confirmed in its European orientation by the great Andrés Bello, founder in 1842 of Chile's National University. By mid-century Chile had produced in Francisco Bilbao one of the first and most effective of a long line of Latin American purveyors of literary Yankeephobia.

There was another sharp contrast with the Plata area in Chile's international relations, for in these the United States played a very prominent role on several occasions, with unhappy results on most of them. In mid-century many Chileans joined in the gold rush to California. Among them were miners who contributed their skills to mining methods in California, and Chile gained a good market there for its food exports. After a few years, though, the market was lost and from the start the Chilean workers, regarded as foreign intruders, suffered more than most from the violence bred by the gold rush. They and their government were generally unable to obtain redress and the whole episode left a bad taste. Much more damaging was the favor shown Chile's enemy Peru by U.S. Secretary of State James G. Blaine during the War of the Pacific. The greater activity of the United States on the Pacific side of the Southern Cone was due in large part to an interest in Peru that had no counterpart on the Atlantic side, namely, the deposits of guano and natural nitrates which after about 1840 were shipped in large and increasing quantities to the United States, where the farming area and the use of fertilizers also were on the increase. Interest in Peru was also stimulated by the presence there of New Yorker Henry Meiggs, whom the government had brought there from Chile and who was building fantastic railroads over the Andes on an even larger scale. Sympathy with Peru, rivalry with Great Britain, personal interest, and perhaps a dozen other motives inspired Blaine and his associates to favor Peru over Chile when war broke out between them. What most concerns us here, however, is that the episode built up lasting resentment against the United States in Chile. A few years later it was exacerbated by, in rapid succession, the favor shown by Washington during Chile's civil war of 1890 to President Balmaceda, who lost, and, in the following year, the affair of the U.S. cruiser *Baltimore* at

Valparaíso. The trouble that began with a tavern brawl quickly escalated first into a riot and then into a dangerous dispute between the two governments. War was averted by Chile's backing down and the affair left its people so embittered that all classes sided with Spain against the United States when the two went to war in 1898.

On the heels of that war came the publication of Uruguayan Enrique Rodó's famous but much misunderstood essay *Ariel* (1900), which pictured the United States as the crude, materialistic Caliban and the Latin race of America and Europe as spiritual Ariel. As pointed out in chapter III, the essay was a warning not so much against the United States itself as against the readiness of Rodó's own fellow countrymen to accept Caliban's values in their lust for material progress. Yet, by a process that is easy to understand, Rodó's main point was soon conveniently forgotten and the beauty of his style helped to establish his essay in all Spanish America as a masterpiece in the growing library of literary Yankeephobia. And in the Southern Cone countries in those days most members of the ruling classes respected literature, and some even made a career of it.

From Drago to the Pan American Pact

Whether as a friend and admirer of the United States, or in an effort to tie its hands by an international agreement, the foreign minister of Argentina, Luis María Drago, proposed to the United States late in December 1902 the adoption of what he later described as an economic corollary to the Monroe Doctrine. At that time German and British naval forces had just begun blockading and shelling Venezuelan ports in an effort to collect long overdue debts from that country. Drago's proposal was that the American states adopt a rule banning the use of force by European powers in the collection of public debts in America, and ask the Europeans to agree to abide by it, as he believed they would do. This rule, he explained, would fill a gap left by the Monroe Doctrine, which barred European political intrusion in America, but not economic intrusion in the new form of debt collection that had developed since Monroe's day. Drago further explained that the new rule, like Monroe's original declaration, would not be international law but American policy. Perhaps with a view to underlining the multilateral intent of his proposal, Drago had tried to get Chile and Brazil to join with him in presenting it to the United States, but their support was not forthcoming immediately and he was unwilling to wait. Perhaps, again, his feeling of urgency was sharpened by news from London that at this very time the British government was under pressure from bondholders, with some support in Parliament, to help them collect on bonds of Argentine provinces and municipalities (not of the national government) that had been in default since 1891 or 1892.

When Drago's note was published in the United States, the press there gave it a favorable reception, which was gratifying to his fellow countrymen. On May 3, 1903, the leading Buenos Aires newspaper, *La Nación*, gave a sampling of the comment and observed: "It is highly significant that among thousands of articles that have appeared in the United States, there is not one that opposes the propositions contained in [Drago's] note." *La Nación's* observation in turn gratified the U.S. chargé in Buenos Aires, who, in reporting it to the State Department, remarked that it indicated the growth of a friendlier feeling towards the United States on the part of the general public in Argentina.

In Washington, however, Secretary of State John Hay gave Drago's proposal a cool, noncommittal reception. If he ever offered an adequate explanation of his attitude, it has not come to light. Probably one of his main reasons was the long-standing decision of his government to maintain the strictly unilateral character of the Monroe Doctrine, and not to share its interpretation or enforcement with any other government, as the acceptance of Drago's proposal would require it to do. It is significant that the United States then went on to bowdlerize the proposal. As a first stage, it induced the Pan American Conference of 1906 in Rio de Janeiro to refer the proposal to a general international conference, the Second Peace Conference at the Hague (1907). Then, at that conference the United States succeeded in getting a denatured version of the proposal adopted over the protest of Drago himself. This version, known as the Porter resolution, turned the proposal into international law (which Drago had said it was not intended to be and ought not to be) and made the ban on intervention for the collection of debts conditional (he had proposed to make it absolute). Drago later received some consolation in being made in 1910 a member of the Hague Tribunal — the first South American ever to serve on it — and in the Paris journal *Figaro's* tribute to him on that occasion as "a statesman of note and a kind of South American Monroe."

Far from driving a wedge between Argentina and the United States, this manhandling of the erstwhile foreign minister's proposal had the opposite result, for the plan had in effect been disavowed as incompatible with the thinking of his own government. Argentine policy makers quickly reverted to their country's traditional policy of opposing any form of American regionalism; whether the American customs union proposed by Secretary Blaine, or the concept of American international law advocated by the distinguished Chilean jurist Alejandro Alvarez, or the proposal of its own Luis María Drago. Washington's coolness towards Drago's proposal was therefore a relief to his successor as foreign minister, Carlos Rodríguez Larreta. On September 12, 1905, he countered a rising chorus of criticism of the Monroe Doctrine in the Buenos Aires press by assuring the Chamber of Deputies that he understood that doctrine "in no other way than as a doctrine of friendship between the republics of this continent and our great model to the north." Elihu Root, who succeeded Hay as secretary of state that same year, and who made a determined effort to cultivate friendly relations with the Latin American states, gave the Argentines further reassurance at the Pan American Conference of 1906. For one thing, he took the lead in having Drago's proposal referred by this regional American conference to the general conference at the Hague. For another, the main point of his notable speech at this conference was that the Pan American movement should be reduced to little more than a succession of good will meetings.

The United States took that position again at the fourth conference of the series, which met in 1910 in Buenos Aires itself. In that same year, *El Mercurio* of Valparaíso, a leading exponent of governing-class opinion in Chile, was still taking satisfaction in the thought that Secretary Root, in his memorable speech at the Rio conference in 1906, had "repudiated Blaine's imperialistic use of Pan Americanism." Apparently, events in the far-off Caribbean did not count.

Uruguayan leaders took a similar view. In 1904 President José Batlle, head of the Colorado Party, resenting the aid furnished the country's Blanco rebels by the Argentine government, twice asked Washington to remind the Buenos Aires authorities of their obligations to Uruguay as a good neighbor by making a naval demonstration in the Plata River. (This was not done. The nearest U.S. naval vessel was at the Cape of Good Hope on the other side of the Atlantic, and the Blanco uprising was soon put down.) Blanco leader Luis Alberto de Herrera had at least as much confidence in Washington at this time as did Batlle. He had been Uruguay's chargé d'affaires in Washington in 1902-1903, and he came away with a favorable opinion of the United States which was still intact in 1910. Writing in that year, he expressed the view that Argentina was a much greater threat to Uruguay than the United States would ever be, at any rate in the twentieth century. Argentina's border disputes with Brazil he described as "the best guarantee of our security" and he took anxious note of reports that negotiations were on foot for an alliance between these two "millstones" that could "grind us to dust." The United States, he believed, would continue to expand, but not south of Panama, and it would not intervene in South America "in this century," for "no urgent interest calls the Colossus here." Uruguay is tied to the United States, he continued, by many happy memories dating back to the time of Artigas, and the celebrated Monroe Doctrine, which liberated all these countries, especially the weak ones, is undergoing an extension that is no threat to us. Herrera described the friendship of the United States as exceptionally important to Uruguay because (and he recorded this comforting thought twice in three pages) a mere hint from "that great power" would be enough to "call our neighbors to order" and "restrain Argentina's pretensions in the Plata estuary."

In Chile, where memories of late nineteenth-century clashes with the United States still rankled, such agreeable reflections were seldom expressed at this time. A notable exception was the editorial comment with which, on May 15, 1910, *El Mercurio* of Valparaíso prefaced a summary of a recent article by former Secretary of State Elihu Root. After stating that Root's article showed how recent developments had changed the United States from a debtor nation to one seeking foreign fields for capital investments, the comment continued: "With this gigantic development of the United States have coincided the [achievement of] more secure tranquillity in South America and the incorporation of the republics of this continent into the commerce and industry of the world." In the 1920s comments of this kind became more frequent for a while, possibly because of the great increase that was taking place in U.S. capital investments and business enterprise in Chile. The increase laid up trouble for the future, but its short-term effect was to establish connections in influential Chilean circles that for a time gave the United States a better press.

More typical of the earlier years was Chilean Foreign Minister Luis Izquierdo's comment on the mediation of Argentina, Brazil, and Chile (the ABC block) between the United States and Mexico in 1914 at President Wilson's request. It would be a pernicious error, he warned, for "us" to limit ourselves to the United States in such affairs and, while friendly relations with the United States were all very well, they could not be lasting unless they rested on the firm foundation of mutual respect and equality, "at least the fictitious equality created by international law." In the touchy atmosphere of Santiago during an earlier stage of the negotiations leading to the establishment of the ABC entente, even Foreign Minister Carlos Rodríguez Larreta of Argentina gave it as his government's view that the clinching argument in favor of such an entente was the fact that it would be powerful enough to counterbalance the influence of the United States in southern South America.

In Argentina, as in Chile, the greatest burst of U.S. private investments was not to take place until the 1920s, but by 1909 they were already increasing at a rate and in a way that moved *La Prensa* of Buenos Aires to say: "Any other capitalists in the world could indicate their plans for doing business here without causing any disquiet, but the Americans possess the rare faculty of creating alarm by the mere suggestion of their approach."* This was written during the muckraking era in the United States, many reports of which reached the cities of southern South America with the assistance of its British and other competitors there.

Among the many evidences of Yankee enterprise in the area in those early years was the establishment in Argentina of General Electric in 1899, the United Shoe Company in 1903, the Singer Sewing Machine Company in 1905, and a Swift frigorífico in 1907. U.S. banking facilities, which were needed for successful competition, began to be established in the Southern Cone in 1914. First came a branch of the National City Bank, New York, in Buenos Aires, where it was soon followed by the First National Bank of Boston. In 1918 the United States finally succeeded in breaking the monopoly of the British-owned Western Telegraph Company in Argentina by obtaining permission from the government of that country to lay a cable to Montevideo, thus completing, reported the American embassy, "the last link in the chain of the Pan American cable from New York around South America."

*Quoted in Simon Hanson, *Argentine Meat and the British Market* (Stanford, California, 1938), 144.

There was no comparable expansion of American interests in Uruguay, where they encountered firmly entrenched European competitors, mostly British, and a strong nationalizing trend from 1904 onwards that had no counterpart at that time in the other two countries. Among its early casualties were foreign insurance firms, some of which were branches of companies in the United States. Undeterred by this trend, Swift built a frigorífico on such a scale that in its first full year of operation, 1913, it accounted for about half of all the cattle and sheep slaughtered in the whole country.

American interests made their most spectacular advance in Chile. It was spectacular partly because it was made in the face of stiff competition from two formidable sources: Great Britain, which held a seemingly impregnable position of dominance there through the 1890s, and Germany, which got its foot in the door in the late 1880s during the administration of the anti-English Balmaceda. By establishing the service of its steamship lines and branches of some of its principal banks and industrial firms, and by capitalizing on its ties with the German-trained Chilean army, Germany ncreased the value of its trade almost six-fold from 1895 to 1913 and rose to second place in Chile's total trade and first place as a source of its imports.

The rise of the United States in Chile was spectacular even in comparison with this German record because of its speed and the fact that it was accomplished entirely by economic means until 1914, after which the final stage, the achievement of dominance, was of course facilitated by Germany's heavy losses in World War I. The rapidity of the United States' rise is illustrated by the almost seven-fold increase in the value of its trade with Chile from $18.5 million in 1900 to $138 million in 1913, and the 40-to-1 increase in its direct investments in Chile from about $5 million in 1900 to $200 in 1920. Prominent among the pioneers were, from the 1880s, W. R. Grace and Co., a steamship line with varied interests, including nitrates; in 1900, the New York Life Insurance Company; in and after 1904, William Braden, who, in association with the Guggenheim group and others, developed El Teniente and other copper mines later sold to Kennecott and Anaconda; and from 1910 on, the Burrage Boston group that modernized production methods at the vast Chuquicamata copper mine. Other large American firms established in Chile by 1914 included DuPont, Bethlehem Steel and U.S. Steel, and American Smelting and Mining Co.

World War I gave a great stimulus to the trade and investments of the United States in all Latin America, but it also created tensions, particularly with Argentina and Chile and above all after xenophobe Yrigoyen became president of Argentina in 1916. After the United States entered the war in April 1917, questions arose about the continuing neutrality of the other two, which in Washington was mistaken for pro-Germanism, and about infringements of their rights as neutrals by the United States. Already associated in the ABC entente since 1915, Argentina and Chile were drawn closer together by this neutrality issue. Brazil, on the other hand, became a belligerent in October 1917, thereby in effect dissolving the entente, which, though never formally ratified by any of the three governments, had been maintained by their ministers of foreign affairs as a gentlemen's agreement.

When so small and compact a group as these three could not maintain even so loose an association as the ABC entente for more than two years, it is hardly surprising that President Woodrow Wilson was unable to carry out his plan for uniting the three of them and all the other Latin American states and the United States under his projected Pan American Pact of 1914-1916. Yet, although his effort failed, it was a noteworthy one because it broke with the past and foreshadowed the future in the development of Latin American policy of the United States. The pact is of special interest to us because the discussions of it provide a striking illustration of the political diversity of the Southern Cone countries. Throughout the negotiations, Uruguay argued for the pact and Chile against it, while Argentina took first one side and then the other.

Drafted in late 1914, taken up with several Latin American governments in early 1915, and referred to by President Wilson as almost an accomplished fact in his address a year later to a session of the Pan American Scientific Congress in Washington, the Pan American Pact consisted of four articles. They provided for the settlement of boundary disputes, control of the arms trade, suppression of revolutionary expeditions from one country against the government of another, and, most important, a "mutual guarantee of territorial integrity and of political independence under republican forms of government." This amounted to proposing the establishment of a regional security system in America, which would be a startlingly new departure in American foreign policy, since it would in effect multilateralize the enforcement of the Monroe Doctrine.

But it was not to be. Even if the U.S. Senate could have been induced to consent, which was most doubtful, Chile opposed the pact from the start, for fear that its adoption might somehow loosen her hold on her rich territorial gains from the War of the Pacific. Brazil held back out of deference to Chile, and Argentina, which gave the pact her support under a conservative administration, withdrew it when Yrigoyen and his Radicals came to power in 1916. In this situation the constancy of little Uruguay's support was wasted.

President Wilson himself had lost interest in the pact by May 1917 and soon graduated from regionalism to the universalism of the League of Nations. Nevertheless, his bold experiment in American regionalism was part of the heritage that was passed on to the Democratic administrations of Roosevelt in the 1930s and Kennedy in the 1960s. Both sought to avoid errors Wilson had made in his conduct of foreign relations, but neither president identified this as one of them.

From Paris to Pearl Harbor

Looking back to 1920 in an article on Latin America and the League of Nations, published nine years later, Chilean Agustín Edwards began by calling attention to the fact that Latin America had been enthusiastic about the League when it was set up by the Paris Peace Conference of 1919, but had cooled off so that in 1929 only 13 of the 20 Latin American states were members of it. These 13 comprised only one fourth of the population of the area, and Chile was the only large Latin American state that was still collaborating actively with the League. Why this decline of interest in it? Mainly, he answered, because the League had so far concerned itself largely with purely European questions. Another major reason, which Edwards only hinted at in this passage, was that the Latin Americans had also been disappointed in the expectation that the League would provide them with an alternative to Pan Americanism and protection against the United States. In 1924, for example, the Chilean government gave enthusiastic support to the Geneva Protocol, which would have required the League to apply sanctions to any non-member (such as the United States) that went to war with a League member. The United States, however, persuaded Britain to lead the opposition to the Protocol, and it was defeated. For a time, there was still hope in Chile of finding some way of using the League to curb the colossus, but by the end of the decade it was clear that the League was useless for that purpose.

To the many Latin Americans who saw the United States as a threat, the "Yankee peril" (*el peligro yanqui*) was even greater in 1929 than in 1920. One of the most obvious ways of estimating its growth was by appraising developments in American foreign policy. As Joseph Tulchin has pointed out, until 1925 the United States, in an attempt to profit by the lessons of the recent war, concentrated on ending its dependence on foreigners for fuel (such as oil) and means of communication (such as cables), which it equated with political dependency (as did Latin Americans, too). Accordingly, it sought to liquidate its protectorates, which had come to seem a liability and a drain. Then, however, in the most alarming development in years, President Coolidge asserted the right and duty of the United States government to intervene abroad for the protection of its citizens' property as well as their lives. The assertion could be construed as being even broader than the first Roosevelt's corollary to the Monroe Doctrine. To be sure, Coolidge made it with reference to a situation in Nicaragua, but by this time observers in the Southern Cone were no longer so confident that the United States would stop its southward expansion at the Isthmus of Panama. Its citizens had accumulated extensive properties in the Southern Cone since 1914 and its navy was now capable of dominating the adjacent seas. Its naval dominance in the whole Western hemisphere, in fact, had been recognized by all the world's principal naval powers in their establishment of a new, regional order of sea power at the Washington Conference on the Limitation of Arms in 1921-1922. Construction begun during the war had given the United States a "navy second to none" and Britain, to whose navy generations of Latin Americans, especially Argentines, had looked for protection, was no longer mistress of the seas.

The property interests of the United States, as measured by private capital investments, grew at a prodigious rate during and just after the war in the two largest countries of the Southern Cone: in Argentina, from $40 million in 1913 to $611 million in 1929; in Chile, from $200 million in 1920 to $400 million in 1928, by which time U.S. interests controlled both of Chile's two largest sources of national income, copper and nitrates. In Argentina the United States was still far behind Great Britain in investments and as a mar-

ket for that country's products, but it took first place as a source of
Argentine imports. As a result, Argentina ran a negative balance of
more than $200 million a year in its trade with the United States in
the 1920s. In Chile, too, the United States took first place by a wide
margin as a source of imports during this decade, but it also ranked
first or second as a market for Chilean products, though nearly half
of what it imported came from its own copper and nitrate mines in
Chile. There was no such rapid growth of either investments or
trade of the United States in Uruguay at this time. Its investments
there, like those of other countries, were restrained by Uruguay's
economic nationalism, and Uruguay's foreign trade, unlike Argentina's and Chile's, was not concentrated in one or two trading partners, but spread among several.

The rapid economic penetration of Argentina and Chile by the
United States during World War I and the ensuing decade provoked
a fresh outburst of anti-Americanism in both countries well before
the resentments of their people were exacerbated by the Great Depression. The outburst was by no means confined to the Marxist
circles that had flourished since the Russian revolution of 1917. A
Chilean conservative, Manuel Rivas Vicuña, writing in 1923 in the
conservative newspaper *El Mercurio*, declared flatly that the time
had come when his country and the rest of Latin America must fight
in defense of their economic independence against the United
States. Three years later his fellow countryman Ricardo Latcham, a
Catholic nationalist, took his stand with those in the Southern Cone
who no longer felt certain that the United States would stop its domination at the Caribbean. On the contrary, he warned, Chile faces
the danger that the United States will treat it as it did Colombia
(referring to the "rape of Panama") and the Dominican Republic
(referring to an intervention that began as only fiscal but in a few
years became total). Alejandro Alvarez, outstanding Chilean jurist,
redoubled the efforts he had been making since 1910 to alert his fellow countrymen to the dangers of foreign penetration. In the 1920s
his fire was concentrated on the United States, which he sought
somewhat unrealistically to curb by promoting the unity of the
Western hemisphere on the basis of, first, a special American international law, and second, a unified Latin America which the United
States would find an irresistible pressure group in the hemispheric
system.

A somewhat similar but less esoteric plea for Latin American union as a defense against the United States was pressed upon its peoples during these same years by an eloquent and peripatetic Argentine Yankeephobe, Manuel Ugarte. His campaign, like that of Chilean Alvarez, was launched in the patriotic fervor of the celebrations in 1910 of the centennial of independence, but was intensified in the 1920s. In *The Destiny of a Continent* and other works, Ugarte alternated between warnings against Yankee imperialism and exhortations to the Latin Americans to repel it by bringing all their countries back together in one united "Great Fatherland" (*Patria grande*, the title of one of his books). In the same spirit a Latin American Union (*Unión Latinoamericana*) was founded in Buenos Aires in 1925 by José Ingenieros, sociologist, philosopher, historian of ideas, and one of the most widely read of all writers in Spanish in that period.

To the list of literary Yankeephobes, which could be made much longer, should be added the name of Enrique Mosconi, soldier and engineer, who had early resolved to break the foreign petroleum trusts after an incident of shoddy treatment by one of them (see chapter V). Appointed head of the government's petroleum agency YPF in October 1922, he recounts, "I achieved my purpose in the next seven years." Mosconi's zeal for the cause did not diminish when he left YPF in 1930, and the United States continued to be his main target, as shown by his speeches in the years that followed. In one, for example, he stressed YPF's "nationalist spirit" as pointing the way to "our economic liberation," and in another, the need for the political and economic integration of Latin America as a counterpoise to the influence of "North America."

The Coolidge doctrine mentioned above was only one of several contributions that the United States made to the growth of Latin American antipathy against it in the 1920s. Some of these impinged directly on the Southern Cone countries. One was the brushoff it administered at the Fifth Pan American Conference, held at Santiago in 1923, to the well-intentioned proposal of an American league of nations made by President Baltasar Brum of Uruguay. Another, and probably the most galling although it was medically justified, was the sanitary embargo imposed in 1927 on uncooked and uncanned Argentine beef, because of the widespread infection of its cattle with the foot and mouth disease. When the head of the Argentine delegation to the Sixth Pan American Conference, held in Havana the next year, proposed that economic discrimination be

barred in a draft charter of the Pan American system then under
consideration, his proposal was defeated through the influence of
the United States, whereupon he refused to sign the charter and
walked out of the conference. His government overruled him, but it
never ratified the charter. At this same conference the United States
again took a position that was highly unwelcome to the Argentine
delegates. The issue in this case was intervention, which Argentine
statesmen—Carlos Calvo in the nineteenth century, Luis María
Drago in the early twentieth—had taken the lead in opposing. Although the United States was tiring of its protectorates, it was not
disposed to forswear the right to intervene under any circumstances.
Its chief delegate, Charles Evans Hughes, a jurist of great distinction, defended his country's position in a lawyerlike argument, the
essence of which was that what the United States practiced and was
not prepared to give up was not intervention but interposition. To
the Argentines and other Latin Americans, intervention by any
other name smelled just as bad.

Although in the 1920s the impulse to Latin American integration
came from so many and such varied sources—economic, political,
literary—nevertheless the United States did not need to follow a policy of divide and rule in dealing with the Latin Americans, for they
remained as divided as ever on national and other lines. Illustrations
abound. Although Chile and Argentina both distrusted the United
States, they could neither agree on a common policy about it nor
come together on other issues. At the Santiago Pan American Conference of 1923, for example, they clashed sharply over two problems. One was Chilean Alejandro Alvarez's project of making American international law the basis of the Pan American movement as
the only means of containing the United States, which could be
done through the two fundamental principles of that body of law:
nonintervention and the equality of states. Argentina objected
strenuously that there was no such thing as *American* international
law, but only universal international law, and that the term was
only another expression of the "America for the Americans" idea,
which it had combated at the Washington conference in 1890 and
ever since. In short, Argentina would have no truck with American
regionalism—a position which, incidentally, arrayed Argentina
against Uruguayan President Brum's proposal as well as against
Chile. The second clash with Chile was brought on by the conference's discussion of disarmament, Argentina charging the Chileans

with conspiring with Brazil and the United States to let Brazil out-strip Argentina in naval power.

Several other divisions among the Southern Cone countries developed or came to light in connection with the Chaco War of 1932-1935 between Bolivia and Paraguay and the peace conference in Buenos Aires that dragged on through the next three years. In 1932 Uruguay joined a block of would-be peace makers, led by the United States, which competed with another one that included Chile and Argentina. During the course of the war, however, the two took opposite sides, with Argentina facilitating the arms trade to Paraguay, and Chile doing likewise for Bolivia despite the bad blood between them over Bolivia's loss of its seacoast to Chile in the War of the Pacific. The split continued into the peace conference, in which the United States played a useful part through its representative, Spruille Braden. In this conference Uruguay sided for once with Argentina, apparently because, during the war, Uruguay, too, aided in the shipment of arms to Paraguay, by which it profited handsomely, as it had done by nurturing the arms trade to Paraguay's enemies in the war of 1865-1870.

By the end of the Chaco Peace Conference in January 1939, the Good Neighbor policy of the United States had taken shape. By that time, too, the Great Depression had nearly run its course. It had stimulated nationalism and statism in Latin America, as in many other parts of the world. A good example is Uruguay's creation in October 1939 of ANCAP, an "independent entity of the state," with a monopoly of the manufacture and sale of alcohol and of any petroleum deposits in Uruguay, and with varying powers of control and participation in the alcohol, fuel, and cement industries. Former President Brum a year later called ANCAP's establishment "a step to the economic independence of Uruguay." However, the further growth of what was becoming a chief product of Latin American nationalism, Yankeephobia, was checked, though not stopped, by the appearance of the Good Neighbor policy.

Built on some older ideas and a few precedents, the Good Neighbor policy of the Roosevelt period began by repudiating some of the past. The first step was to redress grievances, principally by commitments (with reservations at the Montevideo conference of 1933, unconditional and absolute at the Buenos Aires conference three years later) to the rule of nonintervention. In the next few years it evolved into a positive policy of cooperation for economic, political, cultural, and military purposes. Like all policies in international relations between equals (as the United States now emphatically described its relations with the Latin American states), it was based on the expectation of reciprocity. It was carried out by the United States both through the bilateral channels of its relations with individual states, and multilaterally through the Pan American (now rebaptized Inter-American) "system," which was in fact a highly unsystematic hodge-podge of accretions since the first Pan American conference in 1889-1890.

The Good Neighbor policy, formerly interpreted by most commentators in political terms, has been given an economic interpretation in two recent studies. The first is a moderate New Left account by David Green. After a brief bow to the good intentions that went into the formulation of the policy at the outset, Green pictures it as an essentially imperialistic design by the United States to effect "the containment of Latin America" (the title of his book), with a view to excluding all competitors and keeping the whole of the area as the United States' own permanently colonial domain. Perhaps "corral" would be a better term for this operation than "contain."

In the other study, "New Light on the Good Neighbor Policy: The United States and Argentina, 1933-1939" (unpublished), William Cooper maintains that "economic advantage was a central reason for the existence of the Good Neighbor policy" and takes issue with Bryce Wood's essentially political interpretation of it in *The Making of the Good Neighbor Policy*. In particular, he rejects the suggestion in Wood's analysis that economic interests were sacrificed to achieve the political aims of the policy, as they were in the Mexican oil expropriation of 1938. According to Cooper, Cordell Hull was the chief architect of the Good Neighbor policy, and his profound belief in trade as the principal force for peace in the world was his basic assumption in planning and executing the policy, which was closely related in his thinking to his worldwide program of reciprocal trade agreements. In Cooper's view, far from having imperialistic designs, Hull regarded the Good Neighbor policy as meeting the United States' moral obligation to lead the way to a liberalization of international trade, which would indeed help the United States but would not hurt others. Yet, whatever Hull's intentions, it seems that they might as well have been materialistic. He continued to think in nineteenth-century laissez-faire terms, and the Argentine and other Latin American economies were not strong enough to compete with the United States. Cooper himself recognizes in his conclusion that "Hull's plan, if implemented, would have meant the establishment of an economic order with the United States at its head." Latin American leaders reached the same conclusion, and in the changed atmosphere after the war Washington's insistence on giving effect to Hull's free enterprise ideas in inter-American affairs became a major source of dissension between the United States and Latin America.

All three Southern Cone countries played prominent parts in the first stage — the redress-of-grievances stage — of the Good Neighbor policy's development. It got off to a good start at the Inter-American Conference in Montevideo in December 1933. Uruguay was in the forefront there as the host country (though a reluctant host because of the depression, its own domestic tensions, and the nearby Chaco war). Chile was prominent as the country that had been foremost in advocating ideas of American regionalism that this conference began to carry out, and Argentina's chief delegate and minister of foreign affairs, Carlos Saavedra Lamas, played a leading role throughout the conference. Its outstanding event was the adoption of a ban on intervention with the support of the United States through its chief delegate, Secretary of State Hull. Hull attached a minor reservation regarding the United States' rights and obligations under international law and existing treaties, but intimated that it would be temporary, as indeed it proved to be. This major and unexpected concession by the United States, after long resistance, delighted the Latin Americans and made the conference seem a turning point and the beginning of an era of good feeling between the United States and Latin America.

Yet, in the next conference only three years later (Buenos Aires, 1936), it became clear that trouble was brewing again, despite the fact that the United States now completed the concession begun at Montevideo by joining the Latin Americans in making the ban on intervention absolute. The trouble arose over disagreements about economic relations and about how to meet the growing threat of another world war. On both subjects the prime trouble maker, from the point of view of the United States, was Argentina, and that was a serious matter, for at that time Argentina ranked first among the Latin American states in power, wealth, and prestige. In this conference it was at odds with the United States over plans presented by Washington for inter-American neutrality and consultation in the event of war; the disagreement only became sharper as the danger of war increased and after it broke out. Apparently the two governments could not agree where security questions were involved. In 1937, several months after the conference ended, Foreign Minister Saavedra Lamas heard that the United States was about to transfer several overage destroyers to Brazil, Argentina's traditional rival. He at once protested publicly that the transfer would upset the South American balance of power to Argentina's disadvantage, whereupon the United States canceled it. The incident added to the growing irritation between the two governments, but until the end of the decade even more constant source of contention was trade relations.

Each country was eager to obtain the removal of barriers to its products in the other's market. The United States objected to privileges Argentina had conceded to Great Britain in the Roca-Runciman-Pact of 1933, to the detriment of the substantial market the United States had built up in Argentina for its manufactures in recent years, whereas Argentina, very resentful of the ban on its beef, wanted the United States to remove that and open new markets to Argentine products. Hull and his State Department associates were favorably disposed but were balked by the Department of Agriculture and the farm block in Congress and unable to obtain the indispensable strong backing from President Roosevelt, who never gave the reciprocal trade agreements program high priority. As a result, Hull was unable to offer the Argentines the reciprocity promised by the name of his trade program. When it came to negotiating with them, Hull's aides, who argued for the superior merits of a multilateral system of international trade, met their match in an Argentine economic team committed to bilateral trade and led by the same skillful and persuasive Raúl Prebisch who, in the 1950s, was to rise to haunt the United States again as head of the Economic Commission for Latin America. After several years of inconclusive sparring, the negotiations were called off in January 1940 with a good deal of rancor on both sides.

In the meanwhile war had broken out in Europe and the American states had responded by holding a meeting of their foreign ministers in Panama in October 1939 to deal with the new situation. On the initiative of the United States an economic advisory committee was created to assist in adapting the American economies to the displacement caused by the war; a general declaration of neutrality was made, and a neutrality zone (laughingly described by reporters as a chastity belt) stretching far out into the Atlantic and the Pacific was drawn around the member states to keep the war away from America. All the Southern Cone states, including Argentina, as well as the rest of Latin America, approved these measures. Approval continued as one of two organs whose establishment was recommended by the conference got on with its work. This was the Inter-American Development Commission, in which Carlos Dávila of Chile played an important part and which gave a stimulus in Latin America to systematic economic development with government participation. There was much dissatisfaction in Latin America, however, over the failure to establish the other organ, an Inter-American Bank. Strong opposition to it came from private banks in the United States led by the National City Bank, New York, which had branches in Latin America to protect from such competition, and the project was not carried out until 1960.

War came closer to America, and unity of the all-American front began to crumble, particularly in the Southern Cone, when Germany defeated France in June 1940, thereby completing its conquest of continental Europe from Norway to the Pyrenees. Germany also acquired French Dakar on the west coast of Africa across the so-called "narrows" of the South Atlantic from Brazil. For the next two years, until British and American forces drove those of Germany and Italy out of North Africa, a German invasion of South America was widely feared. For a brief time the unity of the hemispheric front was maintained because the all-American neutrality declared the preceding year was not disturbed by the second meeting of American foreign ministers, which was held at Havana in July, just after the fall of France. The meeting strengthened defensive measures again, and again even Argentina supported them. In bilateral negotiations of the ensuing months, however, Argentina did not agree to the kind of military cooperation sought by the United States, and the rift soon widened. On the other hand, the United States obtained from Chile in October the defense facilities it desired, and from Uruguay in November sites for one or more air bases and naval stations, subject to continued Uruguayan sovereignty and control.

Other rifts were not long in opening up. To meet the new economic crisis, a plan for a giant Inter-American commodity cartel was drawn up in Washington, probably in the office of the Coordinator of Inter-American Affairs, Nelson Rockefeller. Exporting and shipping firms in the United States gave it warm support. Eugene Thomas, president of the National Foreign Trade Council, declared that the best way to ward off German influence in Latin America would be to tie the Latin American economies as closely as possible to the United States. The cartel plan was finally discarded. Hull found it incompatible with his liberal economic principles; Will Clayton, assistant secretary of state and cotton magnate, warned that only worldwide cartels would work; and the planners themselves decided that the economies of Argentina, Chile, and Uruguay would be particularly difficult to integrate into any such arrangement, since they competed with the economy of the United States.

That such integration would be extremely difficult was clear from the trade statistics for 1938,* the last full year before the outbreak of war in Europe. Although since the turn of the century the United States had built up substantial investments and a good market for its manufactures in these three countries, it still provided but a meagre market for their exports, which for the most part were absorbed by the United Kingdom and continental Europe. The share taken by the United States was largest in Chile and smallest in Uruguay. Yet even of Chile's copper and nitrates, which together made up two-thirds of its exports, the United States took only 18.4 percent of the former and 36.7 percent of the latter. At the other extreme, the United States took a mere 1.7 percent of Uruguay's wool, 8.3 percent of its meat, and 2.8 percent of its cattle hides. These were Uruguay's chief export items, and from 84 percent to 92 percent of each found its market in Europe or the United Kingdom. The United States did only slightly better by Argentina, accounting for 26.6 percent of its third largest export item, linseed, and 13.1 percent of the fifth largest, wool, but only 4.0 percent of its meat (by far the largest of all), none of its wheat (the second largest), and less than one percent of its corn (the fourth largest). More than 90 percent each of Argentina's meat and corn and three-fourths of its wool went to the United Kingdom or continental Europe.

If any other reason for dropping the cartel plan had been needed, it could have been found in the fact that the plan provoked opposition and alarm in the Southern Cone while it was still under consid-

---

*Those that follow are based on table 3, "South American Exports by Selected Countries and Commodities, 1938," in Percy W. Bidwell, *Economic Defense of Latin America* (Boston, 1941), 15.

eration in the United States. The Chilean newspaper *La Hora,* for example, warned Latin Americans against becoming dependent on Wall Street, and an Argentine Congress of Rural Societies declared that what its members wanted was not an agreement that would limit their freedom to sell where they chose, but one that would enable them to sell more to the United States.

Much more serious was the dissension aroused in Latin America by the United States' undeclared abandonment of neutrality, which began to become visible on the heels of the Havana meeting in July 1940. Opposition to Washington's new policy of aid to the enemies of the Axis powers, which split public opinion down the middle in the United States itself until the Japanese attacked Pearl Harbor in December 1941, was even stronger in Latin America, and probably strongest of all in Argentina and Chile. Its strength in these two countries was due to a number of factors. These included nationalism, devotion to neutrality (which was due in part to nationalism, in part to tradition), dislike of the United States, and particular resentment over its unilateral abandonment of a neutrality agreed upon by all the American states at the Panama meeting. Other factors were fear of being dragged into a war of giants which not a few Latin Americans regarded as one of rival imperialisms, local pro-Axis and fascist sympathies, and the conviction that Germany was going to win the war—a conviction that persisted in the politically important officer corps of the German-trained Argentine army even after the successful beginning of the Anglo-American invasion of Normandy in June 1944.

Another factor of special force in Argentina and Chile in 1941 was the belief, well established by mid-year, that the military planners of the United States had retreated from hemisphere to quarter-sphere defense, which would stop at the parallel of the bulge of Brazil, leaving the Southern Cone countries to shift for themselves. This and the other factors operated in Uruguay too, but there they were outweighed by a strong commitment to democracy among the majority of the people and the tradition, firmly established during World War I, of cooperation with the United States in international affairs.

World War II and the American Aftermath, 1942-1948

During World War II the Southern Cone countries were like the rest of Latin America, except Brazil and Mexico, in taking no part in the fighting, but their political and economic roles were important. From the point of view of the United States, Argentina's roles were sensational in both respects, Uruguay's were constructive, and Chile, politically uncertain at first, provided essential strategic materials throughout. In the three years after the war that were required to reach an American regional settlement, uncooperative Argentina overshadowed its two smaller neighbors in both respects, political and economic.

The Pearl Harbor attack, making the United States a belligerent, brought into effect inter-American defense agreements adopted since 1936 and led to a third meeting of American foreign ministers. This was held at Rio de Janeiro in January 1942 and highlighted by a controversy over a proposal made by the United States and supported by its client states of the Caribbean and Mexico to make a severance of diplomatic relations with the Axis powers obligatory for all the member states. Argentina and Chile objected so strenuously that Brazil counselled concession in order to save the conference. Finally, Undersecretary of State Sumner Welles, representing the United States, gave in for the sake of unanimity and joined in adopting a resolution which merely recommended the severance of relations. A personal clash by telephone with Secretary Hull in Washington resulted, for Welles had violated his instructions, but at least the conference held together and completed its work. Its other measures included the adoption of general rules for the severance of commercial and financial relations with the Axis and the establishment of an Inter-American Defense Board, to meet in Washington, and of a seven-member Emergency Advisory Committee for Political Defense (CPD), to meet in Montevideo. One of the CPD's members was designated by the United States.

This exceptionally active and useful committee turned out to be particularly significant for the Southern Cone countries. Three of its seven members were named by them; since its seat was in Montevideo, its chairman was an Uruguayan, Dr. Alberto Guani, foreign minister until his election; and two of the committee's earliest and most sensational publications exposed Axis activities in Chile and Argentina. Montevideo was an appropriate location for the CPD. The exposure in mid-1940, soon after the *Graf Spee* incident,* of a

---

*The German pocket battleship *Graf Spee* took refuge at Montevideo after a battle with three British cruisers. When forced to leave on the expiration of the legal period of grace, its captain sank his ship in the Plata estuary and shot himself.

Nazi plot in Uruguay to take over the country so alarmed Washington that it sent the cruiser *Indianapolis* to demonstrate at Montevideo as a sign that help was available if the Uruguayan government needed it. To the Uruguayans, however, outside aid in coping with the problem was superfluous. On the other hand, according to a study by Alton Frye, Argentina made only sporadic efforts to control German activities and until 1944 Buenos Aires served as the main base of Nazi efforts to "seduce the countries of Latin America."

The first of the CPD's two sensational publications was not its own work but a memorandum on Nazi activities in Chile that the United States had prepared and handed the government of that country. In November 1942 the CPD published the memorandum in accordance with its policy of giving pitiless publicity to all trustworthy evidence of subversive activities in the Americas. In Chile the CPD's action provoked much resentment against the committee, but even more against Germany, with the desired effect: on January 20, 1943, Chile severed relations with the Axis powers. Two days later the CPD published a similar report of its own on Argentina, but, although the German embassy in Buenos Aires was shown to be directly implicated, the Argentine government, still under the conservative Castillo, rebuffed the committee and continued maintaining relations with Germany. The CPD also had a hand in forcing the reluctant military dictatorship in Argentina to break with the Axis in February 1944, though that was mainly the work of Washington. The severance was so loosely enforced that the CPD continued to exert pressure on the Buenos Aires government, but this had no effect at all until, in September of that year, the committee adopted a resolution looking to the expulsion of its Argentine member. His government thereupon recalled him and his place was taken by a Peruvian—not a momentous achievement, but better than nothing. Much more important, and outstanding among the CPD's other activities, was its formulation of the Guani doctrine of recognition, already noted, in response to the Bolivian revolution of December 1943, in which Argentine and Nazi influence was suspected.

The United States gave the CPD conspicuous support; perhaps it even overplayed its hand. After the war, despite the excellent service the committee had rendered and Uruguay's eagerness to have it continued, most Latin Americans were happy to get rid of it in the inter-American reorganization under the OAS Charter of 1948. Apparently, their main reason for disliking it was their feeling that it had become, or at least would become, an instrument for extending the political influence of the United States among them. They were less successful in resisting the extension of its economic influence.

Argentina's political role, prominent from the beginning of the war, came to dominate inter-American relations much of the time from early 1944 to early 1946. It was the United States government's threat to publish proof of the implication of the Argentine regime in the Bolivian revolution of December 1943 and in other subversive activities, that induced the president, General Pedro Ramírez, to sever relations with the Axis. Shortly thereafter, he was forced out by the anti-rupturist military faction and replaced by General Edelmiro Farrell, under whom Colonel Juan Perón rose to second in command by mid-1944. From February of that year until November, when he resigned on account of ill health, Secretary of State Hull made Argentina front page news time and again in his effort to oust the recalcitrant Farrell-Perón regime by a combination of non-recognition, the blocking of funds, and a rhetorical campaign to which he persuaded President Roosevelt to contribute a denunciation of that regime as the citadel of Nazi-fascist influence in the Western hemisphere.

Hull's effort failed dismally for lack of the only element that could have enabled it to succeed, which was British cooperation in an embargo on trade with Argentina. The British market was indispensable to the Argentine economy. Argentina's total exports in 1944 amounted to $513 million, of which Britain accounted for $208 million, or 40 percent. Since the United States took an additional 20 percent, a joint embargo by the two would clearly have been economically crippling to Argentina. Unfortunately, it would also have severely hurt if not crippled the Allies. As Prime Minister Churchill objected when he was drawn into the controversy in the spring of 1944, cutting off British imports of Argentine beef would make it impossible to carry out military operations on the scale planned. The operation planned was, of course, the invasion of Normandy in June. Another consideration was frankly avowed by the liberal Manchester *Guardian:* "We [British] like the Argentine brand of Fascism as little as does Mr. Cordell Hull," it said, "but we also prefer Argentine beef to American pork."

Secretary Hull's resignation was followed by a lull in the controversy between the governments of the United States and Argentina. Under pressure from the other Latin American states and the approach of the first United Nations conference, a new assistant secretary of state, Nelson Rockefeller, arranged to heal the breach on terms publicly adopted by the Inter-American Conference at Chapultepec (Mexico City), February 22-March 8, 1945. The terms required Argentina to sign the conference's Final Act, enforce all inter-American measures against Axis nationals and interests in Argentina, and declare war on the Axis powers.

This last action was one required to qualify states for participation in the United Nations conference that was to begin in San Francisco on April 24 for the adoption of a charter. Chile and Uruguay made the necessary declarations in February, but the deadline had passed when Argentina did so on March 27. As a result, it could only be admitted by special action of the conference itself, and the Soviet Union's bitter opposition to admitting a state still under its "pro-Nazi" wartime government precipitated a fight in the conference that made Argentina an international sensation once more. Finally admitted, Argentina joined the other Latin American states that comprised nearly half (40 percent) of the conference's membership and functioned effectively as a block. Chile played an important part as a member of a small group that introduced a proposal to give autonomy to the inter-American security system. This proposal, along with others from non-Latin American sources, led to a major change in the original draft by the adoption of Article 51 on the right of individual and collective self-defense, which was invoked by the United States in the crisis of October 1962 over Soviet missiles in Cuba.

While the conference was still going on, the controversy between the United States and Argentina began again over the latter's failure to press on with its promised campaign against Axis national interests. In addition, a new U.S. ambassador, Spruille Braden, who arrived at his Buenos Aires post in May 1945, soon became identified with the opposition to the government. In late August, even conciliatory Nelson Rockefeller publicly branded Argentina "the black sheep of the Americas" the day before his resignation as assistant secretary of state was announced. Braden, who succeeded him, declared that his return to Washington would not change "my policy" towards the Argentine regime. We have already seen (in chapter X) how he proved it by getting the projected hemisphere defense meeting in Rio de Janeiro postponed rather than have the United States sit down at a conference table with the representatives of such a regime, and by following this up with the ill-timed "Blue Book on Argentina" just before the election of his main target, Perón, to the presidency. In June 1947 he resigned as a prelude to the postponed defense conference, in which Perón's government took part after all.

In this conference, held in Rio de Janeiro in August 1947, Argentina became again the chief trouble maker from the point of view of the United States by insisting upon limiting the defense arrangement to aggression coming from outside the hemisphere. The United States was just as determined that it should apply equally to aggression within the hemisphere, as had been provided in the preliminary defense agreement adopted at the Mexico City conference in 1945. The position of the United States has been interpreted by David Green as due to its desire to have "maximal freedom and leverage . . . to intervene, *if it so chose,* in intra-hemisphere disputes." Perhaps so, but he offers no proof of his assertion and it is implausible, since the treaty gave no warrant at all for "intervention" by that name. The only thing resembling intervention that it did authorize was multilateral enforcement action approved by two-thirds of the American states, and unilateral intervention was still absolutely prohibited by the convention adopted by the conference at Buenos Aires in 1936 and duly ratified by the United States Senate. Moreover, the U.S. position in question had strong Latin American support at the Rio defense conference, mainly because of fear of the Argentina of Perón, which had shown expansionist tendencies that seemed threatening in themselves and might prove contagious. Nowhere did the U.S. position find stronger support than in Uruguay, which, because of the situation in Argentina, launched the Rodríguez Larreta doctrine in late 1945 in an effort to protect human rights as well as national security from threats arising within the hemisphere. At any rate, in the end the United States prevailed at Rio and the Inter-American Treaty of Reciprocal Assistance adopted there provided for the maintenance of security in a way that proved generally acceptable to the Latin Americans as well as the United States for years to come.

It was quite otherwise in the field of economic relations and policy. Here there was great and growing antagonism between the two Americas that had roots in the period of the war. It was not that the Latin Americans had fared badly or been badly treated by the United States during the war. The Southern Cone people certainly had little or no ground for complaint. Of total lend-lease aid to Latin America from March 1941 to July 1945, which amounted to $263 million, nearly 60 percent went to strategically important Brazil, but of the remainder a substantial share went to the two Southern Cone countries that cooperated in the war effort. Chile's share, $20.7 million, was the largest except for Brazil's and the $21.1 million received by Guatemala, mainly for air defense of the Panama Canal. Little Uruguay's share, $5.8 million, was sixth largest among the eighteen countries in the list. Uncooperative Argentina received none. Before it was clear that she would not cooperate, the Argentine navy was put down for a tidy $20 million, which, of course, was subsequently canceled.

That loss was dwarfed by the huge reserve of gold and foreign exchange, amounting to $1,608 million, that Argentina built up during the war. Similar though smaller balances were built up in Uruguay and Chile. In fact, Uruguay's $252 million reserve was as large as Argentina's in proportion to population. Chile, with only $130 million, fell far behind the other two, but was consoled in September 1945 with two Export-Import Bank loans that would enable it to realize every development-minded Latin American's dream by constructing a modern iron and steel plant. Chile's, at Huachipato adjoining Concepción, would be the only steel plant in South America except for Brazil's still unfinished Volta Redonda plant, which was likewise being constructed with financial and technical aid from the United States.

In these circumstances it would have been easy for outsiders unfamiliar with the Latin American background to be surprised at the critical attitude towards the United States on economic grounds that prevailed in that area in the postwar period. The Southern Cone countries were no exception. In fact, Argentina under Perón was its chief exponent and that attitude was not confined to his followers; an anti-Peronist exile, Raúl Prebisch, was one of the most effective critics because of his moderation, expertise, and leadership in ECLA. As already noted, his differences with the United States over economic policy dated from the 1930s. That fact suggests one reason for the widespread Latin American opposition to the United States on economic grounds, namely, that the Great Depression stimulated the growth in Latin America of a vigorous economic nationalism which was fortified by the war and collided head-on with the doctrinaire economic liberalism-for-export propounded by the United States with equal vigor. And then there was the plain fact that the war had given the United States an overwhelming economic preponderance in Latin America and virtually eliminated its foreign competitors there. These competitors, too, had been targets of the xenophobia that was one facet of depression-bred nationalism. Now the United States was the only target left. Argentina illustrates the result, for the dominance of Anglophobia there in the 1930s was succeeded by Yankeephobia after the war.

Even before the war ended, the conflict between the two Americas over economic policy was clearly revealed and the main issues identified in early 1945 at the Inter-American Conference in Mexico City. There, as one Latin American observer comments, the delegates "found it easier to agree on the military, political, and social resolutions than on the economic." One of the most hotly contested issues was raised by the insistence of the United States upon a reduction of trade barriers, which the representatives from Chile and Uruguay, among other countries, declared must be kept high enough to protect their infant industries. Other leading issues arose over proposals by the United States, on the one hand, of blanket condemnation of "state enterprises for the conduct of trade," and on the other hand, of blanket protection of foreign private capital investments and free enterprise. Although most of the differences were papered over on this occasion, they remained to gather intensity in the years that followed, and still others were added.

Chief among the latter was the clamor for U.S. aid—a Latin American equivalent of the Marshall Plan for Europe. At the United Nations Conference on Trade and Employment held at Havana from November 1947 to March 1948, the representative of still prosperous Argentina, Diego Luis Molinari, tried to put the niggardly government of the United States to shame by announcing that his own government would provide five billion dollars to promote the economic development of Latin America. Molinari was critical of the Latin American policy of the United States on other grounds as well, particularly its effort, made at the Mexico City conference and repeated in this one, to obtain a commitment to a rapid reduction of trade barriers. This, he charged, was an economic imperialist's recipe for blocking the industrialization of the Latin American countries and keeping them in a permanent state of colonial servitude to the United States. No way of reconciling the interests of the developed countries with those of the underdeveloped countries was found at this conference, and neither the United States from one group nor Argentina from the other ratified the charter drawn up at it.

The futile Havana conference was followed immediately by the Inter-American Conference at Bogotá, Colombia, that rounded out the immediate postwar period in relations between the United States and Latin America. The Rio defense treaty of the preceding year had done that in the field of military security. Now, in March and April 1948, the Bogotá conference took similar action in other fields despite its near-disruption by a riot known as the *bogotazo*. Again Argentina was a major obstacle. Carrying on the Argentine tradition of opposition to multilateral security arrangements and to American regionalism, Perón disparaged this conference in public statements and sent an undistinguished delegation to it, whereas the United States' Secretary of State George Marshall and the president of the Export-Import Bank attended the conference and addressed it. Just as it was getting down to work, Perón underlined his disdain for it by saying publicly: "I believe the time is past for conferences, speeches, and foreign office dinners. That road leads nowhere . . . Our policy is to reach bilateral agreements with all the other Latin American countries." As if to prove he meant it, the only significant measure sponsored by his delegation was one inspired by Argentina's claim to the Falkland Islands: the creation of an American Committee on Dependent Territories. This new organ could have brought on a serious conflict with Great Britain and, in the matter of jurisdiction over such questions, with the United Nations, but actually its creation led only, after a considerable delay, to a noisy meeting in Havana that accomplished little except to discredit the new committee.

Of the principal agreements adopted by the Bogotá conference, the only one of lasting practical importance was the Charter of the Organization of American States—a new and colorless name on which Argentina insisted. A main feature of the charter was an article strengthening the ban on intervention.* Again, as at the

---

*This is Article 15. It reads: "No State or group of States has the right to intervene, directly or indirectly, in the internal or external affairs of any other State. The foregoing principle prohibits not only armed force but also any other form of interference or attempted threat against the personality of the State or against its political, economic and cultural elements." The charter was ratified by the U.S. Senate by an overwhelming majority and is still binding.

Mexico City conference of 1945, there was a rift between the United States and the Latin Americans over economic policy. It ended in the adoption of a so-called Economic Agreement, misnamed except that it consisted of innocuous generalities. This time the practical questions were referred to an economic conference to be held in Buenos Aires very shortly, but the United States succeeded in getting it postponed year after year until 1957.

XVII The Cold War Generation:
Hegemony or Leadership?

Since World War II the United States' preponderance of power in the Western hemisphere has been so overwhelming that, in discussions of its relationship to Latin America in this period, "imperialism" is the descriptive term most often used by its critics. Does the term fit, or is it, as is widely believed in the United States, only an opprobrious epithet? James Kurth, a political scientist, examines this question in a thoughtful essay* that is particularly valuable for having been written in the early 1970s. By that time the United States looked distinctly less imperial than ten or twenty years earlier. He concludes that "imperialism" does not quite fit and that a better term for the U.S. system is "neo-imperialism" or "hegemony."

Hegemonial Systems

Differentiating between hegemonial systems and the older suzeraintal or colonial types, Kurth offers a list of ten hegemonial systems, or close approximations thereto, covering the period from the Treaty of Westphalia (1648) to the present. He not only includes "The United States in Latin America (since 1945)" in the list, but declares that this is the one that "comes closest [of all ten] to being an ideal type." Such a system consists of a great power and its client states or protectorates and is characterized by six features, which are: resource inequality of at least 2 to 1 in GNP; formal treaties, such as those establishing the OAS and the Warsaw organization; military alliance, as in the Rio Treaty of 1947 and the Warsaw Treaty; economic dependency, as indicated by economic ratios of 20 percent or more in, for example, exports to the great power and its investments in the client state; intervention by the great power, or the expectation of it, if the client state transgresses certain limits; and stability and durability of the system.

The main purpose of Kurth's study is to determine the relation between U.S. foreign policy and military rule, which has been so common a feature of Latin American history since 1945 — not that it was unknown before then. After considering several countries, including those in the Southern Cone, he concludes "regretfully" that "a convincing case . . . has yet to be made" for the argument that

*"United States Foreign Policy and Latin American Military Rule," in Philippe C. Schmitter, ed., *Military Rule in Latin America* (Beverly Hills, 1973), 243-322.

U.S. foreign policies, in the strict sense of U.S. military interventions and military and economic aid, are a major explanation of the prevalence of military rule in Latin America. Similarly, he finds no "significant correlation" between U.S. economic aid to Latin America and "political outcomes" there. The argument may, however, become more convincing, he notes, if the private U.S. presence, especially in the form of direct investment, is considered; but he does not go into that question.

So much for the impact of U.S. policy, but what of its motivation? "Containment," answers Kurth, by which he means keeping competitors from gaining control over any client and exploiting its resources for their own benefit, strategic or economic. As already noted, historian Green, in his study of the Good Neighbor policy under Roosevelt and Truman, uses "containment" in the sense of excluding competitors, though he gives it not a strategic, but an entirely economic denotation. An example of his use of the concept is his assertion that the Inter-American System as completed under Truman "was intended to ratify United States supervision and control of Latin American economic development."

These broad generalizations cannot be analysed in the present brief account, which is focused on the Southern Cone. Their stimulating though not always convincing propositions should, however, be kept in mind while we review the high points in the postwar relations of the United States with Argentina, Chile, and Uruguay. Our starting point is 1947, when the cold war began in earnest and the assumptions and approaches of good neighborhood began to rust, except for the vitality of Hull's economic liberalism. In these three countries, as in the rest of Latin America, the outstanding feature of relations with the United States for the next dozen years was their deterioration; in the 1960s, it was the rise of Fidel Castro and Castroism (*fidelismo*) and the related rise and fall of the Alliance for Progress and the Latin American Common Market. In the early 1970s, at least in the Southern Cone, the most striking feature was the attitude of the United States towards the revolutionary upheavals that took place in all three countries, and above all towards the Allende regime in Chile and the military coup that destroyed it in September 1973.

During most of the quarter century covered in this chapter, Argentina continued to play a more prominent international role than its two neighbors. After the mid-sixties, however, it first shared the lead with Chile under Eduardo Frei and then lost it to Chile under Salvador Allende. Little Uruguay's role was becomingly modest as usual. When the Rodríguez Larreta doctrine fell flat in late 1945, Uruguay's wartime prominence ended. It was never regained more than momentarily, probably because the country was small and weak, distracted by mounting economic and political problems, and hampered from 1952 to 1966 by a collegial form of government that made effective leadership difficult if not impossible. Such prominence as the country did achieve was in most instances as a meeting place for international gatherings, as the object of designs attributed to its much stronger neighbors, or as the scene of a guerrilla movement that was for a time the most spectacularly successful of all the many such movements in Latin America.

The Southern Cone and the Cold War, to 1960

When the long-gestating cold war broke out in 1947, the United States was a superpower with the strongest economy in the world and with a monopoly of nuclear weapons that for a short time made it superior in military strength to the only other superpower, the Soviet Union. During and just after the hot war just ended, the United States had built up interests, taken on responsibilities, and developed ambitions on a worldwide scale. On that scale Latin America looked small indeed, far smaller than in the prewar years, when President-elect Hoover had taken time for a pre-inaugural good-will tour by sea around South America, stopping at all the principal ports to make friends and in Chile and Peru to (as he fancied) help settle their Tacna-Arica dispute, and when President Roosevelt had spent more than a month on a sea voyage to attend the Inter-American Conference of 1936 in Buenos Aires. After the war no president visited the Southern Cone again until President Eisenhower did so in the course of a Latin American tour designed to patch up relations after the fiasco of Vice-President Nixon's tour in 1958.

The same falling-off was apparent on the cabinet level. Secretary of State Hull spent weeks at a time at inter-American conferences in Montevideo and Buenos Aires, and when he had to miss others, his place was taken by Undersecretary Welles. After the war, on the other hand, Secretary Dulles attended a conference in South America (Caracas, 1954) only long enough to ram through it an anti-

Communist resolution, and neither he nor his predecessor, Dean Acheson, visited the Southern Cone or got further south than Rio de Janeiro, where they made brief stopovers on their way to or from Europe. Latin American affairs were left almost entirely to one of the assistant secretaries of state, who were becoming almost as numerous as the vice-presidents of a metropolitan bank. There may be some connection between the declining priority of Latin American relations, the consequent lessening of public exposure of the policy process, and the considerable influence on that process that the business community had acquired by the 1960s, as will appear below.

Protocolary visits may seem unimportant to others, but they did not seem so to Latin Americans at that time, and their rarity typifies the difference between Washington's appraisal of its Latin American connections in the pre- and postwar periods. The low priority given them for a dozen years after 1947 was officially justified on the ground that Latin America had suffered no destruction during the war and now lay outside the cold war area too (which meant that it was regarded as "safe," though that was not said publicly). Nevertheless, it was subordinated to the requirements of the cold war. Accordingly, the Latin American policy of the United States in this period was focused first on anti-Communism (as in the Caracas resolution of 1954, and in the covert intervention later that year, through the CIA, against the "communist-infected" government of Guatemala); second, on military defense of the Western hemisphere (in case the cold war should turn hot); and third, on inducing the Latin Americans to follow a liberal economic policy, which would be as different as possible from that of the Soviet Union and as favorable as possible to U.S. trade and private capital investment.

Among Latin Americans this period was characterized by resentment against the United States for what was called in official circles neglect. Outside those circles harsher terms, such as exploitation and imperialism, were applied to it. Resentment accumulated through the 1950s to produce in 1958 the demonstrations against Vice-President Nixon that began rather mildly in Montevideo but gained intensity as he moved north to the fracas in Lima and the explosion in Caracas.

In the Southern Cone the only government that took an open stand against the United States was Perón's in Argentina. His reversal of it shortly before his fall was one reason why he fell. Although he joined reluctantly in framing the Rio Defense Treaty of 1947, he did not ratify it until three years later. Even after doing so, he continued to insist that in his foreign policy he took a "Third Position" between the superpowers, independent of both and prepared to side with either or neither as Argentina's national interest dictated. Moreover, although economic necessity forced him into a rapprochement with the United States in 1953-1955, Argentina was the only state except Mexico that opposed to the end Secretary Dulles's anti-Communist resolution at Caracas. Uruguay tried to amend it, but gave up when that effort failed.

From 1951 to early 1953 Perón went so far as to attempt a revival of the ABC block, with encouragement from Getúlio Vargas, re-elected President of Brazil in 1951, and Carlos Ibáñez, re-elected President of Chile in 1952. Thomas Skidmore, writing from the Brazilian perspective, describes the block as designed to oppose the United States. Writing from the Chilean side, Alejandro Magnet, who saw some of the secret correspondence, seems to regard the effort as intended merely to carry out Perón's proposal, made in 1951 in one of his newspaper articles signed "Descartes," that the ABC "union" — first economic, then political — be revived with a view to filling an expected power gap after World War III, which Perón believed was coming soon. Whatever its purpose, the project moved ahead smoothly until Perón visited his good friend President Ibáñez in Santiago and the two signed a preliminary pact. Then, Vargas's foreign minister, who had been bypassed, got wind of the project and opposed it so strenuously that Vargas backed out. That finished it, for all practical purposes. Perón still tried to effect a union with Chile and Ibáñez reciprocated to the point of coming to Buenos Aires, where the two discussed the possibility of a military and political union and the establishment of a Peronist-style regime in Chile, but there was never a chance of its approval there.

By that time Chile and Uruguay had already, in 1952, signed military pacts with the United States, of the kind the latter was negotiating with most of the Latin American states. Perón was now isolated in southern South America. Ibáñez and Vargas were apparently still his friends, but Ibáñez was not Chile any more than Vargas was Brazil, and Uruguay, never friendly to Perón, now had its military tie with the United States. This turn of events on the diplomatic front, combined with hard times in Argentina, apparently pushed Perón into the waiting arms of the United States. There, what President Eisenhower called, at the close of his second term, the "military-industrial complex" had long since overcome the government's antipathy towards the Franco regime in Spain, and Perón's regime, which had never been found as offensive as Franco's, had always had good friends in Washington. So the two governments made up, and once that had been done, Washington remained Perón's friend to the day of his ouster in September 1955.

Under the Argentine governments that followed Perón's to the end of the decade, relations were neither very cordial nor seriously strained. The apprehension felt in Washington over the appointment of Raúl Prebisch as special consultant to the first post-Perón government turned out to be groundless. So too, in 1958, did Washington's even greater uneasiness over the election of Arturo Frondizi to the presidency. Frondizi had led his party's fight against the Rio Defense Treaty of 1947 and against Perón's contract with Standard Oil of California's subsidiary, had been tireless in his denunciation of U.S. monopolies (which seemed to mean all large business firms), was the author of a nationalistic book called *Petroleum and Politics,* and had harped on these and other disturbing themes during the presidential campaign. His inaugural address was not reassuring. Its only reference to the United States was the one implied in his warning that true continental unity could never be achieved so long as there continued to be such manifest inequality between the "progress and well-being" of "one part of America" (meaning the United States) and "the backwardness and misery" of millions of people in "the other part . . . our America" (meaning Latin America). Before the year was out, however, Frondizi had reversed his course and adopted a stabilization-and-development policy such as the United States government might have recommended, and one that the International Monetary Fund did recommend and support. Under it he even contracted with U.S. and other foreign oil companies to develop Argentina's petroleum resources. He held to this course for the brief remainder of the decade.

In Chile, at the beginning of our period in 1947, President González Videla ended his brief marriage of convenience with the local Communist Party and purged his cabinet of its three Communist members. Washington regarded this as a wholesome sign and relations between the United States and Chile ambled along without serious disturbance through the 1950s despite the return of the ever-doubtful Carlos Ibáñez to the Moneda for a second term in 1952. The conclusion of the military pact with the United States in that same year was hotly opposed by many Chileans, and in their demonstrations they were nearly a decade ahead of the Cubans of Fidel Castro's regime in chanting rhythmically as they marched through the streets of Santiago, "Chile, sí! Yanqui, no!" But Chile's Congress ratified the pact and that was what counted. Shortly thereafter, rumors transpired of Perón's secret negotiations with Ibáñez and Vargas, only to have time prove that Ibáñez could not carry the country with him in any harebrained foreign adventure. Still, it was a relief to Washington when, in 1958, he was succeeded by reliable, moderately conservative Jorge Alessandri. Washington promptly did what it could to make his administration a success by favoring Chile in the distribution of Latin American aid. It continued this practice through the next decade, at the end of which those who were competent to deal with such complex and arcane statistical problems said that in the past dozen years Chile had received more U.S. aid per capita than any other Latin American country.

Discussing the question why, from the early 1930s to the early 1960s, conservative rule in Chile was generally conducive to good relations with the United States although there was a strong strain of "anti-United Statesism" among Chilean conservatives, Fredrick Pike suggests two answers. One is that the actions of the United States generally aided in maintaining the established order, which was what the conservatives wanted done; the other, that they were rewarded for stifling their antipathy by the practical benefits they derived from letting U.S. capital hold a very important position in the Chilean economy.

Why relations between the two countries have often been amicable in the present century when the conservatives were not in control is another matter. One explanation is suggested by a speech delivered to the Chilean Senate in April 1954 by Eduardo Frei Montalva, a member of that body, Christian Democratic leader, and future president of the republic. His speech was in effect a report on the Inter-American Conference at Caracas, from which he had just returned. He was highly critical of the United States for ignoring Latin America's grave economic and social problems and seeking only a political triumph in the shape of Latin American support for the anti-Communist resolution demanded by Secretary of State Dulles. That was no way, Frei warned, to combat Communism, which was penetrating student, labor, and intellectual circles and the masses. Clearly (to paraphrase), said Frei, the United States has had to take on world leadership prematurely, was overburdened and impatient, and is trying to solve problems too hastily. And yet, he continued, Chileans ought to give the United States whatever help they can in building up a united continent, for if it fails to understand what its problem in Latin America is, tragedy will overtake its peoples and the world. Frei added that when he and Salvador Allende visited the United States, they found that its people were not imperialists and that it should be possible to find ways to use public opinion there in defense of Latin America. The United States can furnish many things: money, technical aid, political and military cooperation. Chileans must take care that the price is not too high, but, on the other hand, they must not expect the United States to aid them in maintaining democracy or driving out dictators. That is a job they must do alone, or it will not get done at all. In Chile's relations with the United States, the rule should be, "Neither surrender nor hatred" (*Ni entrega, ni odio*).

Many Chileans and other Latin Americans did not take Eduardo Frei's Olympian view of the problem. As the decade wore on, their resentment against the United States mounted. The central economic problem was aggravated as population growth gained speed and, in the Southern Cone, economic growth slowed down, sometimes to a halt. Yet, while the United States kept postponing action, even including the holding of an economic conference, its spokesmen kept on dinning into Latin American ears the same unwelcome words—"free enterprise," "private capital," "lower trade barriers," and the rest—that they had heard at Chapultepec (Mexico City) in 1945, at Rio de Janeiro in 1947, at Bogotá in 1948, and at Caracas in 1954. When Washington finally agreed at Caracas to hold an economic conference, the result was only a repetition of the old tiresome litany at a finance ministers' meeting in Rio de Janeiro at the end of 1954 and again at a full-fledged OAS economic conference at Buenos Aires in the late summer of 1957.

The barren results of the Buenos Aires conclave were particularly frustrating. By that time, the United States had had time to digest a report, prepared for the Rio meeting in 1954, that has been called a "precursor of the Alliance for Progress." Prepared at Prebisch's request by a high-level committee of Latin American experts under the chairmanship of Eduardo Frei, the report raised Latin American sights higher than ever. It called for commodity agreements to stabilize the prices of primary products, as well as increased aid for industrialization by Latin American entrepreneurs, national planning for development, the allocation of all investments, and the long-delayed establishment of an Inter-American Bank.

The report of the Frei group made as little impression on United States policy in 1957 as it had in 1954, which was none at all. Shortly before the Buenos Aires conference began, Secretary of State Dulles was still asserting that the Latin Americans "are now in the main able to meet their increased demands through private loans and Export-Import Bank loans." Just after the conference closed, the International Cooperation Administration announced in a press release on September 12, 1957: "It is a basic policy of the I.C.A. to employ U.S. assistance to aid-receiving countries in such a way as will encourage the development of the private sector."

It was also at the Buenos Aires conference of 1957 that the Latin American delegates had their first serious discussion of the idea of a regional economic association of their own. As will appear below, the idea found fruition of a kind three years later in the formation of the Latin American Free Trade Association (LAFTA). Until then, the United States remained cool, if not hostile, to any proposal for creating an exclusively Latin American economic association, the underlying assumption being that integration would make them harder to deal with. It made one very minor exception in favor of preferential arrangements between neighboring countries, and after 1958 it came around to acceptance of subregional groups of a small number of states. As late as 1959, however, it insisted that any common market in Latin America be subject to the conditions laid down in the General Agreement on Trade and Tariffs (GATT), of which only eight Latin American states (including Chile and Uruguay, but not Argentina) were members, and which was designed for the developed, not the developing, nations.

In other respects the United States had begun to show more flexibility since the anti-Nixon riots of May 1958 in Lima and Caracas. In the next few months it reversed a position it had maintained for nearly twenty years and agreed to take part in establishing an Inter-American Development Bank. It also provided easier credit terms through the Development Loan Fund and reversed its previous opposition to commodity price stabilization to the extent of reopening the discussion of an international coffee agreement. A little later it went on to increase the resources of the Export-Import Bank and initiate similar increases in the World Bank and the IMF. The favorable response in Latin America to the first of these measures encouraged President Eisenhower to make his good-will visit to the area in November 1959. Interestingly enough, he confined it to the three Southern Cone countries and Brazil and gave the chief trouble spots of 1958 a wide berth. Except for the student demonstration in Montevideo, the tour went off well.

Concessions by the United States seemed to end at this point. Fidel Castro brought his revolt in Cuba to a successful conclusion at the end of 1958, but when, at the meeting of the new Inter-American Committee of 21 in Buenos Aires in May 1959, he proposed that the United States provide $3 billion a year for the next ten years to finance Latin American development, the U.S. representatives rejected the proposal out of hand and it was tabled. In the next fifteen months, however, Castro's position in Cuba became so strong, his ties with the Soviet Union so close, his popularity in Latin America so great, and the threat of his regime to the United States so clear in the eyes of the decision makers in Washington, that the Eisenhower administration made one more concession, and a major one it was. At another meeting of the Committee of 21, this time in Bogotá in September 1960, it promised, through the U.S. representative, C. Douglas Dillon, to establish a $500 million Social Progress Trust Fund for various social projects not previously eligible for U.S. public loans under any of its programs. Here was another precedent for the Alliance for Progress.

A Stable of Trojan Horses: The Alliance for Progress Decade

The launching of LAFTA in 1960 was followed the next year by that of the Alliance for Progress. Both were undertaken with high hopes for the stimulus they would give the development of Latin America, both were of special interest to the economically sluggish Southern Cone countries, and both were failures.

Shortly after his election as president in November 1960, John F. Kennedy appointed a task force to prepare a confidential report on Latin American problems and policy. Presented to the president-elect early in January by chairman Adolf A. Berle, the report recommended the establishment of an "Alliance for Progress" under that name (which was already in use by Kennedy and his speech writers), and the recommendation was adopted. Berle personified the linkage between the Latin American policies of Franklin Roosevelt and Kennedy. A member of the New Deal "brain trust" and assistant secretary of state from 1933 to 1945, he had helped to develop and apply the Good Neighbor policy. Now, in 1961, he headed both the first task force on Latin America, which proposed the Alliance for Progress, and the second, which drew up the somewhat different and much more detailed definitive plan for it. The plan, adumbrated in an address by President Kennedy on March 13, was advocated by the U.S. delegation with considerable success in August in the Inter-American meeting at Punta del Este, Uruguay, that created the alliance and adopted its charter.

Two features of the administration's definitive plan for the alliance had special significance for the Southern Cone countries. These were its encouragement of thoroughgoing revolution in Latin America, on the assumption that this could be carried through peacefully, and its focus on Latin America's democratic left as the chosen instrument for bringing this about. Accordingly, though with considerable reluctance at the outset, Washington sought to make first Argentina under Frondizi, who had never overcome its distrust, and then Chile under Frei, whose Christian socialism kept it uneasy, "showcases" of the Alliance for Progress. This it did by concentrating its contribution to the alliance program successively on them. In both countries the effort failed because of domestic opposition, but this came from opposite directions: in Argentina, Frondizi was overthrown by the conservative right; in Chile, Frei was frustrated more by the radical left than the right.

As these experiences suggest, one of the reasons why the whole alliance effort was largely a failure in the Southern Cone countries was that it was essentially a middle-of-the-road undertaking in countries that were being torn apart by domestic strife between right and left along the whole political, social, and economic front. At the very start, in the closing session of the Punta del Este conference that adopted the alliance charter, Che Guevara of Cuba denounced it as an "instrument of economic imperialism." The charge was at once taken up, made an article of faith by parties of the left, and endlessly repeated throughout Latin America, with variations such as the description of the alliance by Uruguayan Vivián Trías as a "Trojan horse of Yankee imperialism." (Trojan horses were trotted out whenever the Yankees made a friendly gesture.) Conservatives

were hardly more tolerant of the alliance, but for the opposite reason. Its sponsors, including President Kennedy, insisted that it was
designed to bring about a political and social as well as an economic
revolution in Latin America — a peaceful one, to be sure, but a revolution at the conservatives' expense just the same. The conservatives
were warned that they must submit to this as the only alternative to
a violent, bloody revolution.

In addition, there were particular reasons for the alliance's failure
in each country of the Southern Cone. They can only be sketched
here. Argentina under Intransigent Radical Frondizi ruled out a
whole major reform area at the very start. In the Punta del Este
charter conference, the Argentine delegates watered down the article requiring agrarian reform by the insertion of the qualifying
phrase, "in accordance with the characteristics of each country,"
and their government then took the position that it was not a characteristic of Argentina for the government to concern itself with
land reform. Even before that, Frondizi had objected to Kennedy
that the latter's address of March 13 proposing the alliance had put
too much stress on social reform and too little on economic development. Or, as Frondizi expressed it in speaking to his fellow Argentines, they should make the pie bigger before they tried to decide
how it ought to be sliced. But he had been labeled a leader of the
democratic left, and in spite of these differences and his opposition
to the anti-Castro measures sponsored by the United States at the
Punta del Este meeting of American foreign ministers in January
1962, the Kennedy administration continued to favor him with its
aid almost up to the time of his ouster in March of that year.

For the next ten years the governments of Argentina were conservative, except for the rather ineffectual Illia administration
(1963-1966), which did lip service to the Alliance for Progress, but
neutralized any good effect this might have had on relations with
the United States by brusquely canceling the oil contracts Frondizi
had made with U.S. and other foreign firms. President Johnson
shifted in 1964 from Kennedy's so-called "ideological" policy of cultivating the democratic left in alliance affairs to one stressing economic development. Three years later, disturbed by mounting evidence that the alliance was failing, Johnson made another shift in
an effort to resuscitate it by tying it to a project for the economic
integration of Latin America with the support of the United States.
Now it was the turn of Latin American supporters of free enterprise

to brand the alliance a Trojan horse, for they feared that integration on these terms would only facilitate the economic conquest of Latin America by multinational corporations of the United States through their branches, subsidiaries, or affiliates in the area. Among the Southern Cone countries, this view probably had its strongest support in Argentina, where, as Mariano Grondona noted in his news magazine *Primera Plana* about this time, something very much like a military-industrial complex was taking shape; and nationalism was its prevailing spirit. If we accept Levinson and Onís's description of the alliance as characterized by ideology under Kennedy, by economics under Johnson to 1967, and after that by perplexity, Argentina should be recognized as a generous contributor to its perplexity.

Uruguay was the Southern Cone country least affected by the alliance, and Chile was its chief beneficiary. During the drafting of the charter, Uruguay led a revolt of the small countries against the requirement that, before receiving aid, they go through the same complex process of drawing up detailed development plans as the larger countries with their much greater technical and other resources. The small countries were given some satisfaction in the shape of emergency funds. Even so, the preparation of Uruguay's development plan was delayed, and although when completed it was a good one, the crippling collegial form of its executive until 1966 kept it from being carried out.

Chile, on the other hand, which was well supplied with technicians and applied early, received a lion's share of the aid. This began during the administration of Jorge Alessandri. Not even the blindest bureaucrat in Washington could have mistaken this estimable pillar of conservatism for a member of the democratic left. When, however, the alliance was launched midway in his administration, Alessandri was the only practical alternative in Chile to the head of the Socialist-Communist coalition, Salvador Allende, whom Alessandri had barely beaten in the election of 1958. Accordingly, his last, troubled years in office were brightened by an infusion of alliance funds—which only goes to show that even in its ideological phase, there was a strain of pragmatism in the alliance.

By the end of Alessandri's term in 1964 an even better alternative to Allende developed in Christian Democratic leader Eduardo Frei. In that year, aided by the conservatives, Frei defeated Allende for the presidency by a wide margin. The spectacular rise of the Christian Democrats in Chile seemed to mark them as the wave of the future in that country, and, it was hoped, in other Latin American countries. They had a regrettable attachment to such heresies as statism and expropriation, but their Christian socialism by now appeared relatively mild by the Latin American standards of the 1960s. If carefully nurtured, it seemed, they might become the most effective antidote to Communism, Castroism, and left-wing extremism in general. Washington accordingly proceeded to nurture them by providing Frei's administration with aid valued at some $400 million. As already noted, that turned out to be the highest per capita aid in the hemisphere.

The results were a keen disappointment to almost all concerned. An exception was Dr. Abraham Horwitz, a Chilean and director of the Pan American Sanitary Bureau. In October 1970 Dr. Horwitz declared that the alliance had been a "tremendous success" in improving health conditions in South and Middle America. On the other hand, Dr. Vicente Sánchez, professor of psychiatry at the University of Chile, complained a year later that the United States was causing severe psychiatric difficulties in that country. His conclusions were based on a three-year study of the impact made by eight "United-States-sponsored colleges" in Chile on youth and family life. The root of the trouble, it appeared, was the conflict between "the Protestant ethic, with its emphasis on doing and competition" and "our patriarchal system, which places family and political and intellectual realization ahead of material achievement." On a different plane, Senator Ernest Gruening in 1966 reached the gloomy conclusion in his "case study of U.S. foreign aid" that the United States was not getting its money's worth out of the alliance and that there was little to indicate that aid to Chile was having a "meaningful impact upon Chilean economic and social development." In order to make the alliance effective as "an alternative to Communist blandishments and revolutionary chaos," declared the senator, the United States must supervise the "end use" of aid funds, for Chilean agencies could not be depended upon to control them adequately.

Chilean left-wingers, too, were dissatisfied with the alliance's "impact upon Chilean economic and social development," but for very different reasons. As noted earlier, the Jacques Chonchol group of Christian Democrats broke with the party's majority, which was led by President Frei, and ultimately went over to Allende because they thought Frei had not made the reform revolutionary enough. The roster of the disillusioned was headed by Frei himself. In a *Foreign Affairs* article in 1967, he lamented that the Alliance for Progress had "lost its way" by abandoning its original emphasis on revolutionary social change for one on economic development. The result, he feared, would be to strengthen the forces of entrenched privilege and all other elements in Latin America opposed to desperately needed social reform.

A major source of Latin American disillusionment with the alliance was the way in which the United States handled its aid funds. How maddening this could become even for the most moderate and patient person is suggested by a Chilean case described in Levinson and Onís's excellent book, *The Alliance that Lost its Way.* In July 1967, it appears, a loan of $2 million to Chile was authorized for the purchase of tractors for its agrarian reform program. Tractors made in the United States had ceased to be competitive in Chile, where their share of the market had been reduced by European competition from 79 percent in 1951 to 9 percent in 1966, and even that 9 percent was accounted for by a single firm, John Deere Company, which sacrificed its profit on its tractors in Chile in order to hold the market for more profitable implements that were sold with them. The Chileans could have bought a larger number of European tractors with the $2 million, but since this was an Alliance for Progress loan, it was "tied"; that is, the tractors bought with it had to be of U.S. manufacture, and so did 90 percent of their components. An English subsidiary of Ford made the lowest bid, but this was conditioned on a reduction of the 90 percent requirement to 50 percent and was ultimately rejected for fear of Congressional wrath. In this stage and the ensuing duel between John Deere and International Harvester, which was won by the latter, several government departments in Washington and Santiago became involved and the issue even reached the presidential level. Not until 1969 did Chile at last get its tractors, and then they were the most expensive of the three entries in the contest, and larger than the Chilean agrarian reform administration wanted.

Chile played a leading part in formulating Latin American grievances on this and other grounds, and in presenting them to the United States government. From March to May 1969, Chile was host to the Latin American Special Coordinating Committee which met at Viña del Mar and discussed the whole broad range of trade and aid problems in Latin American relations with the United States.

The meeting produced a 6,000-word report, called "Consensus of Viña del Mar," which, without engaging in polemics, specified the Latin Americans' grievances and the remedies they desired.

In June, Chilean Foreign Minister Gabriel Valdés formally presented the "Consensus" to President Nixon. In the ensuing conversation Valdés tried to maintain the nonpolemical tone of the report, but that was not his style. According to the *New York Times* account, he stressed several complaints listed in it: that, for example, by "tying" aid (as in the case of the tractors for Chile) and by excluding Latin American exports produced under alliance programs, the United States made its aid seem designed to promote, not the development of Latin America, but the profits of U.S. businessmen. Another grievance was that U.S. firms in Latin America, instead of reinvesting at least a substantial part of their profits there, repatriated the great bulk of them—five-sixths in 1968. So, Valdés told the president bluntly, instead of the developed nations aiding Latin America, "it is the other way around." The Latin Americans, he added, "will not accept this indefinitely." In countless meetings and documents, everything had been said that could be said, he justly observed, and now "the time has come for action." In reply, President Nixon did not promise action, but "serious consideration."

The conviction that it was "the other way around" was by now widespread in the Southern Cone, as it probably was in the rest of Latin America. One of its side effects was keen irritation over the charge that came in one form or another from public and private sources in the United States that the Latin Americans were not doing enough to help themselves. They thought they had in fact done a good deal and that—it hardly mattered to them whether because of the war in Vietnam since 1964, the recurrent crises in the Middle East, or for some other reason—the United States had lost the spirit of the Alliance for Progress and was turning away from Latin America again, as it had done for more than a decade after World War II.

Their feeling that they had bestirred themselves while U.S. aid had been quite limited received statistical support in early 1970 from an address by Dr. Carlos Sanz de Santamaría, chairman since 1963 of the Inter-American Committee on the Alliance for Progress (CIAP), an organ of the OAS. "In the first eight years of the Alliance," he said, "the Latin American countries invested $120 billion —a sum that far exceeds the initial goal of $80 billion for its first decade . . . This self-help effort represents close to 90 percent of the total cost of development programs. U.S. official sources contributed 6.7 percent of the total investments." Then, in a passage italicized in the published text, he continued: "It is interesting to note that although the United States had disbursed $5.8 billion by the end of 1968, more than half of this sum had already been repaid by the Latin American countries in payment of principal and interest."

LAFTA, Multinational Corporations, and the Military

Another disappointment to the Latin Americans in the 1960s was the failure of their own trade organization, LAFTA, to come anywhere near fulfilling the expectations of promoting development with which it had been set up. This was a matter of particular concern to the Southern Cone countries, for they had taken a leading part in founding LAFTA. Although Latin American leaders had been for several years casting about for solutions to their multiplying economic problems, it was the establishment of the European Common Market by the Treaty of Rome in March 1957 that started them thinking seriously about making a similar arrangement among themselves. ECLA promptly began preparing a plan for a regional common market to embrace all Latin America, but before the plan was ready the Southern Cone countries and Brazil had drafted a treaty setting up their own less ambitious organization, a free trade association. These four countries accounted for more than half the total inter-Latin American trade at that time, and their association was open to any of the other countries of the area that wished to join, which may be why it prevailed over the competing common market plan. However, the framers of the Treaty of Montevideo (February 1960) establishing LAFTA contemplated its evolution into a common market that would lead eventually to the economic integration of Latin America.

The original membership of LAFTA was confined to the three Southern Cone countries, Brazil, Paraguay, Peru, and Mexico, but Colombia and Ecuador were soon added. Hopes for LAFTA's success in stimulating the economic development of Latin America were high. In 1959 a carefully controlled series of projections by ECLA indicated that by 1975 Latin America would be producing from 60 percent to 100 percent of its own consumption of industrial commodities ranging from machinery and equipment to steel, semimanufactured steel products, and chemicals and chemical products. There were, in fact, several favorable developments in the next few years, including a substantial increase in industrial capacity and a reversal of the recent downward trend in inter-Latin American trade. On the whole, though, the results were disappointing and the prime movers were partly responsible. At the very start, for example, Argentina raised a tariff wall to protect its steel industry from Chilean competition, and Chile retaliated by raising its duties on Argentine farm products, with the result that trade between the two countries dropped sharply.

A main obstacle to LAFTA's success was the right of each member state to veto any substantive measure. This not only obstructed the process of liberalization, which was supposed to be the heart of the whole arrangement, but in some cases actually helped make a bad situation worse, as in the excessive proliferation, mainly in Argentina and Brazil, of anti-economic automotive manufacturers. By the mid-1960s some forty of these were competing for a market no larger than a single European or U.S. producer could have supplied.

Disappointment with LAFTA was one of the reasons for the formation of its subgroup of smaller states, the Andean Common Market, in 1969. After an initial spurt that was very encouraging, the Andean group too bogged down, mainly, it would seem, because of clashing national interests.

Some of the fallout from these disappointments dropped on the United States. It was hardly to blame for them. In 1960 and 1961 it had first tempered and then reversed its opposition to exclusive Latin American associations for commercial and other economic purposes. The alliance's charter had designated LAFTA an "appropriate instrument" for attaining the objectives of the alliance. Yet fear and suspicion of the United States still remained so strong, that when President Johnson went one step further and not only endorsed the projected economic integration of Latin America but offered the support of the United States in bringing it about, the Latin Americans' ardor for integration turned to ice. Classicists enough to remember a tag from the Aeneid, they said they feared the Achaeans bringing gifts. In more modern terms, they feared the multinational corporations bringing more economic chains.

It was the big business firms of the United States, especially the multinationals, rather than its government, that alarmed them most. The new generation was as sure that the government in Washington was the creature of the multinationals as their fathers had been that it was run by Wall Street. For proof they pointed out how U.S. business had taken over the Alliance for Progress, as illustrated by the case of the tractors for Chile. Suspicions of this kind gained plausibility from two developments of that decade. One was the formation of the first effective organization of the principal U.S. business interests in Latin America — the Council for Latin America, already mentioned, which was expanded and renamed the Council of the Americas. The other was the first appearance of a considerable number of multinational corporations as, in the words of their left-wing critics, "new operational forms of . . . imperialist domination." More soberly described as constituting a "third economy" of worldwide scope, the multinationals grew most rapidly in the United States, whose direct private investments abroad increased from $32 billion in 1960 to $70 billion in 1968.

In Latin America most of this increase went into manufactures, rather than into extractive industries or public services, as formerly. By 1966, U.S. subsidiaries were producing 35 percent of Latin American exports and 41 percent of its manufactures. In the Southern Cone, Argentina conformed to this pattern, but in Chile extractive industry, led by copper, continued to predominate, although DuPont, Ford, and other firms established factories or processing or assembly plants. Uruguay remained a very minor field for U.S. investments, except peripherally, as through international-multinational ADELA (Atlantic Community Development Group for Latin America). Organized early in the decade and comprising 235 of the largest industrial firms and banks in the United States, Europe, Japan, and Latin America itself, ADELA by 1971 participated in some 100 enterprises, which were of widely different kinds, except that almost all of them were joint ventures with local capital. Joint enterprise was also the type favored by the Council of the Americas under the leadership of David Rockefeller. He urged his associates to cultivate "maximum international cooperation," political and social as well as economic, with the growing number of Latin Americans who took a "modernist" view of development.

This sophisticated approach might work but would take time. For early results it faced too many obstacles on both sides, North American no less than Latin American. On the U.S. side, a striking illustration was provided by the International Telephone and Telegraph

Company's effort to intervene in Chilean politics, which seemed more appropriate to 1907 than to 1970. Among Latin Americans, conservative as well as radical, the combined dislike and distrust of foreign, especially U.S. enterprise that had built up by this time would be hard to disarm. Little help in overcoming it could be expected any time soon from the local business groups, which, besides being relatively small, contained many economic nationalists. In this and other segments of society the government of the United States, rather than its multinationals, was cast in the role of chief villain. That was mainly due, in the Southern Cone countries, to the prominence of the military factor in American policy, beginning with the Rio Defense Treaty of 1947. In Argentina, that treaty was attacked with extraordinary bitterness by Arturo Frondizi and his Intransigent Radicals. In Chile and Uruguay the bilateral military pacts of 1952 encountered similar resistance; none was even proposed at that time in Argentina. The armed intervention of the United States in Vietnam in the 1960s and the destruction caused by its forces there were widely publicized, magnified, and condemned in the Southern Cone; the failure of this military effort only added to its discredit. The climax came when the results of Latin American training in U.S. counterinsurgency and police methods were brought home to these people by the slaughter of Che Guevara (an Argentine) and his band in neighboring Bolivia and by the crushing of the Tupamaros in Uruguay. Even the many who welcomed the elimination of terrorists and guerrillas resented foreign interposition in bringing it about.

How multinationals and military combined to bring left-wing xenophobia to a focus on the United States is illustrated by the fact that in Uruguay the first Tupamaro prisoner to be murdered was an Indiana police chief employed in counter-subversive training, and that in Argentina the victim of a kidnaping for a ransom that broke all records was an executive of the Ford Motor Company. In Chile, despite President Allende's efforts early in his term to avoid a confrontation with the United States, one could almost believe from the clamor of his followers about Yankee imperialism that he was not the chief of state of an independent republic but the leader of a provincial rebellion against its Yankee metropolis.

Allende's marksmen aimed their fire impartially at the government and the multinationals of the United States. The two were conveniently merged into a single target in 1972 by the beginning of a series of revelations that the Central Intelligence Agency and, in the first stage, the International Telephone and Telegraph Company, had tried to keep Allende from being elected, or, if elected, from taking office, or, if inaugurated, from remaining in office. During the Chilean presidential campaign of 1970, it was revealed, ITT had approached the CIA with an offer to provide up to one million dollars to "manipulate the results" of the election so that Allende would not become president. Apparently, the intention was to "manipulate" by bribing Chilean elections officials or members of Congress, or both. CIA did not accept the offer, but after Allende was elected it had second thoughts and came back to ITT with a similar but much broader proposal. By this time, though, ITT, too, had had second thoughts and consulted other large corporations before responding. When all of them declined to become involved, ITT did likewise. Even so, the U.S. Senate subcommittee that investigated this affair and related matters concluded in 1973 that ITT had "overstepped the line of acceptable corporate behavior." Another U.S. government organ, OPIC (Overseas Private Investment Corporation), set up in 1969 to insure U.S. private investments abroad against political and other risks, turned down ITT's later claim for compensation for Chile's seizure of its Chilean subsidiary on the ground that ITT's behavior had provoked the seizure. But the sharpest criticism of its behavior came from ITT's own legal department, which had been bypassed in the Chilean affair by the corporation's activists. One senior counsel, according to the *New York Times* of June 22, 1973, called their action "unbelievable" and another warned that actions of this kind would be "ideally calculated to support leftist assertions about American economic imperialism."

Faced with this caveat from its own legal counsel and the decision of other interested corporations to keep hands off, ITT dropped out, but CIA forged straight ahead. It was unhampered by the inhibitions and responsibilities of a private corporation and no doubt responded to prodding from higher up. All told, from 1970 to 1973 it poured $8 million into Chile in support of the efforts that were finally crowned with success by the coup that overthrew Allende and cost him his life.

Low Profile and High Policy

The CIA's activities in Chile were apparently conducted on orders from the highest government officials. Their policy towards Chile and the rest of Latin America at this juncture was a combination of "low profile" (their name for it) and *haute politique*. It was mainly the work of President Nixon, who prided himself on his expertise in foreign affairs, and of his special assistant for security affairs (later secretary of state) Henry Kissinger, who had first made a reputation by studies of Metternich and nuclear weapons. Both men gave top priority to problems of power politics, to which Latin America was usually peripheral. Kissinger is reported to have taken a close look at Latin America not long after his appointment and to have concluded that the back burner was the place for it. The president gave no indication that he did not concur. He had shown little love for Latin America since his harrowing experience there in 1958 and little interest in its affairs since recovering from that experience. There were, in fact, weighty problems in other parts of the world that clamored for attention. Even if they had not done so, the failure of the Alliance for Progress and Latin American recriminations on this and other grounds, as laid on the line for the president early in his administration by Chile's outspoken minister of foreign affairs, Gabriel Valdés, made it easier to think about other parts of the world for a while.

In these circumstances the Latin American policy of the low profile was conceived, gestated, and brought forth. The new policy signified an intention on the U.S. government's part to take a less prominent, and presumably a less active, part than formerly in affairs affecting the neighbors to the south. It was given very concrete expression in the economic aid policy of the United States. In May 1971, for example, at the annual meeting of the Board of Governors of the Inter-American Development Bank (IDB), the U.S. representative was a mere undersecretary of the treasury and he told the assembled Latin American ministers of finance that they would have to look elsewhere—to Europe, Japan, Canada, not to the United States—for help. He made it clear that the United States' "diminished position in world affairs" and its "serious social, economic and environmental problems" would make it necessary to curtail its foreign aid, and that its profile would be further lowered by the Nixon administration's new policy of funneling its aid through multilateral agencies such as the IDB and the World Bank, instead of through the direct bilateral channels formerly used for most of it.

The low profile also signified a political and military disengagement overseas that ran counter to the sharply rising curve of oversea expansion by the multinational corporations of the United States. Not unreasonably, a senior official of the Council of the Americas warned his fellow members that "as far as the protection of U.S. private investments in Latin America goes, we in the business community are on our own." One commentator on this statement* pointed out that the low profile stimulated the multinationals to search for a "substitute political capability" and that they acquired it in various ways, one of which was to defuse political hostility in Latin America by promoting joint business ventures of the kind discussed below.

At the same time that the Nixon administration lowered its profile, it pushed on with a carefully concealed multi-million dollar operation to subvert the government of Chile. It was an operation that did indeed call for maintaining that kind of profile, but hardly in the sense in which the catch-phrase was meant to be taken. Confidentiality was highly desirable, if only because such interference in the domestic affairs of Chile was a flagrant violation of the absolute nonintervention rule, to which the United States had solemnly committed itself and by which it was still bound. Why, then, was it done? One obvious answer was, to protect the substantial U.S. investments in Chile. The aggregate value of the three largest of these —Anaconda and Kennecott in copper, and ITT, mainly in a subsidiary telephone company—was about $960 million, which was one-thirteenth of all U.S. direct private investments in Latin America. This explanation seemed to be borne out by ITT's early effort to involve the U.S. government in precisely such an operation. Doubt was thrown on it by the fact that ITT found the government unresponsive and soon dropped out. Later, its credibility was restored when it came out that the government went ahead with the operation alone, without letting ITT or anyone else know, presumably in order to minimize the risk of detection (low profile again).

Still, it seems clear that the protection of U.S. economic interests in Chile was not the government's main purpose. When Operation Allende began in 1970,† it was not certain that expropriation, which the United States had acquiesced in ever since the Mexican expropriation of 1938, would be turned by Allende into virtual con-

---

*Luciano Martins, in Julio Cotler and Richard Fagen, eds., *Latin America and the United States: The Changing Political Realities* (Stanford, Calif., 1974), 379.

†The CIA had spent some $3 million in Chile in 1964 in helping Frei defeat Allende for the presidency, but that was no part of the operation of 1970-1973 under discussion here.

fiscation, which it rejected. In fact, Allende had not even won the popular election for the presidency, and the initial purpose of the operation was, in the simplest terms, to keep him from winning it. Both then and later, the purpose rose above the grubby realm of trade and investments to the highest level of high policy, the protection of the national security of the United States.

According to the fragmentary evidence now available, it all began on June 27, 1970, at a meeting of a select and ultra-secret group called the "40 Committee." The chairman of the committee was Presidential Assistant Henry Kissinger. Its name could be misleading. It consisted, not of 40 members, but—at that time—of only four besides the chairman. These were the chairman of the Joint Chiefs of Staff, undersecretaries of the departments of Defense and State, and CIA Director William E. Colby. The discussion that day focused on Chile's presidential campaign, which was still in progress. The campaign was beginning to heat up and the recent defection of left-wing Christian Democrats to Allende's Popular Unity coalition made his victory in the September election seem a real possibility. One statement attributed to Kissinger set the tone of this meeting and the three-year operation that grew out of it: "I don't see why we should have to stand by and let a country go communist due to the irresponsibility of its own people." Later, Kissinger said he could not recall making the statement, but he did not deny it and it was published on the authority of understandably anonymous "government intelligence sources."

At any rate, the statement represents substantially the same view of the situation in Chile as the one unquestionably presented by Kissinger in his background briefing of the press on September 16, 1970, which was brought to light in 1973 by the Senate investigation referred to above. The briefing was given just after Allende had won a plurality in the popular election, but before Congress made his election definitive, as it did in late October. In the course of the briefing Kissinger described Allende as "probably a communist" (in fact, he was and always had been a Socialist) and a "takeover" by him as presenting "massive problems for us." Clearly, Kissinger regarded a government headed by Allende as threatening U.S. security. It would be an even greater threat than Castro's Cuba, he implied, pointing out that Chile was "not an island off the coast which has not a traditional relationship and impact on Latin America, but . . . a major Latin American country." He went on to suggest the demonstration or domino effect that the establishment of a government under Allende could have on the already touch-and-go situation in neighboring countries, among which he specified Argentina, Peru, and Bolivia. There was also a military threat to our military security in the possible closing of the Strait of Magellan to all but Communist vessels.

In the face of repeated warnings emanating from no less a source than the intelligence division of CIA itself that any effort to tamper with the political process in Chile would most probably be counterproductive, Operation Allende was set in train. When fully developed, it was a combination of two main types of operation: first and most effective, the lavish expenditure of funds in Chile by the CIA; and second, what Allende, in a speech to the United Nations General Assembly in 1972, denounced as an "invisible financial and economic blockade." By this he meant the blocking of sales of Chilean copper and other commodities in Europe as well as the United States, and the reduction of foreign loans and credits to Chile by the United States and by the private and international institutions and foreign governments that it could induce to follow its lead. This second type of operation, as we shall see, was not pressed with great vigor, but it did not need to be. The Allende regime dug its own financial grave.

The United States and Allende's Overthrow

During the early months of President Allende's term, his administration and the one in Washington avoided public manifestations of their fundamental antipathy towards each other. Already in a vulnerable position as a minority president and facing a Congress controlled by the opposition parties, Allende had good reason not to become embroiled in a confrontation with Washington that would weaken him still further, and his coalition's left wing was not yet strong enough to push him into one. Washington reciprocated to the extent of adhering to its general Latin American policy of the low profile. It was restrained by the transient, but for the moment striking, success of the Allende administration's first few months in office, and waited to see whether he would live up to the assurances he had given at the outset that his government would not expropriate without compensation. Even when expropriation of Anaconda and Kennecott turned out to be virtual confiscation, Washington's public protest was confined to a warning from Secretary of State Rogers that this would lead to a cessation of aid.

Nevertheless, by the time of Allende's overthrow, leaks in Washington and charges by Allende in his address to the United Nations Assembly in 1972 had left no doubt that Nixon's administration was unremittingly hostile to Allende's. Consequently, the widely circulated allegation that the United States was responsible for overthrowing him was widely believed. It can be sustained, however, only if it can be shown that one or both of Washington's two kinds of anti-Allende measures described above contributed decisively to his fall. No other grounds for the charge have been advanced that merit serious consideration.

Oddly enough, even in non-Marxist circles in the United States the charge was justified largely, if not wholly, by invoking Allende's allegation of a "financial and economic blockade"—or, as others put it, of "economic strangulation"—of his country by the United States. This is odd because it was obvious that such blockade as existed was ineffectual and that the economic and financial woes of the Allende regime were largely of its own making. Convincing evidence on both points was presented by Paul Sigmund in *Foreign Affairs* for January 1974. As regards loans and credits, he shows in detail how reductions of these from the United States and sources influenced by it were "more than counterbalanced" in the Allende government's favor by a "considerable increase in alternative sources," which included Western Europe, Argentina, Mexico, Canada, and Australia as well as the Soviet Union, China, and Eastern Europe.

While admitting that the Nixon administration applied economic pressure to Chile, Sigmund maintains that its measures could have been "much more vigorous" and notes that in fact U.S. aid to Chile continued in some respects throughout Allende's administration: $800,000 a year in technical assistance, 26 to 50 Peace Corps workers, and Food for Peace shipments which rose in the last year, 1973, to 40 million pounds. Sigmund also properly stresses the Allende administration's own large contributions to Chile's economic distress, notably by reckless emissions of printing-press money. These increased the country's money supply by more than 1,000 percent in the less than three years of his administration and led to a runaway inflation that reached 320 percent in the year ending in July 1973, two months before his overthrow.

As additional evidence came to light, it seemed increasingly clear that whatever effect the Nixon-Kissinger campaign against Allende produced was due much more to the $8 million spent in Chile by the CIA than to the termination of new aid to Chile or any other feature of the so-called blockade. The CIA funds were spent to "destabilize" Chile, both politically and economically, in preparation for Allende's ouster, whether by the peaceful and relatively slow political process (as the State Department was said to prefer) or more quickly by force (which the same sources said was preferred by Kissinger, who did not become identified with the department as secretary of state until near the end of the affair). While details are not available, it appears that the CIA's funds were used mainly to support the political opposition's parties, leaders, and mass media. Not directly, but through anti-Allende organizations in Chile, part of the CIA's funds reached striking workers, truck drivers, shopkeepers, and professionals, particularly during the large-scale strikes of October 1972 and August 1973. Such indirect support of the second of these two strikes was probably the most effective of all the measures employed by the Nixon administration to unhorse Allende. By promoting economic chaos, this second strike brought on the decisive military coup of September 11, 1973.

Was the United States, then, really responsible for Allende's overthrow? If so, it might also be held responsible for defeating the Chilean people's struggle for social justice, as Richard Fagen (in *Foreign Affairs*, January 1975) and others have charged. The answer can only be provisional at this stage, since the evidence is far from complete, but on the basis of such evidence as we do have, it is negative —to the disappointment, no doubt, of the makers of U.S. policy towards Allende who flattered themselves on their success.

Obviously, the direct agent in toppling Allende was the Chilean armed forces and, for the reasons noted in chapter XIV, it is as certain as anything in human affairs can be that they would have ousted him and his left-wing team about when they did without the slightest encouragement from the United States. Even if it is assumed that a push from the United States was required, it still remains to be shown that this was administered. In 1970 the CIA tried but failed to promote a military coup, and there is no evidence that it was any more successful in its efforts, then and later, to bribe Chilean military and political leaders. Significance has been attached to the fact that, although the United States cut off additional aid to Chile in other respects, it continued to aid the Chilean armed forces. If this was done to woo them, the United States had a rival suitor, and a much more successful one, in President Allende himself. He courted the military with pay increases, money for arms, and personal flattery, and twice brought their highest officers into his cabinet, thereby stimulating their politicization. They responded by giving his regime indispensable support until the last few weeks of his administration of nearly three years, and no evidence has come to light that the United States had anything to do with the eleventh-hour reversal of their stand. Even the indirect influence of the training some of the higher officers had received in the United States can be given little weight in this connection. So far as the records show, such training seldom if ever had the political effect of making Chilean and other Latin American officers who received it follow the vagaries of foreign policy in Washington.

What may have been the chief contribution of the United States to Allende's fall was made indirectly and quite possibly unintentionally as a byproduct of its policy of detente with the Soviet Union. In December 1972, on the same trip that took him to New York for his speech to the UN General Assembly, Allende went hat in hand to Moscow in quest of sorely needed financial and moral aid. Though Chile lay almost at the other end of the world from Moscow, his regime was important to the Soviet leaders for the demonstration effect that would be produced by its success — the first in history — in "communizing" a country through the peaceful way (*vía pacífica*) of the political process, which Moscow was championing against the violent way preached by Peking. His regime would be important also for the stimulus its success might give the large Communist parties in Italy and France. In addition, Chile's relatively much better developed economy and more varied natural resources made it unlikely to be a protracted drain on the Soviet Union, as Castro's Cuba had been for a decade. Yet, in the face of all these considerations, Moscow disappointed Allende sorely by doling out limited commercial aid in "tied" credits and military aid that was an embarassment to him, given the touchy mood of the Chilean military about Communism.

Why the Soviet authorities passed up the chance offered by the Allende regime is a matter of guesswork, but the best guess, offered along with others by the London *Economist's* special correspondent in Chile and Uruguay, Robert Moss, is that the Russians "were probably not anxious to annoy President Nixon by interfering too blatantly in Chile," at a time when they were engaged in important negotiations with the United States on trade and security and had just been promised an "enormous American wheat shipment to tide them over a bad harvest." Whether the failure of Allende's widely heralded Russian trip to produce the extraordinary aid he needed was due to these or other considerations, it may have done him even more political than financial harm. In what was beginning to look like a rearguard action, he had been defending the Russians' "peaceful way" against strong pressure from left-wing extremists in his Popular Unity coalition to move on to violent revolution. Now, having failed in Moscow to obtain the extensive financial aid he needed and the moral support this would have signified, he was even more vulnerable to pressure from that quarter than if he had never made the trip. This made it quite impossible for him to comply with the insistent demands of the Chilean military leaders that he take vigorous measures to put a stop to his left-wing followers' revolutionary violence and their paramilitary build-up.

It can hardly be a mere coincidence that in the months following Allende's disappointment in Moscow, this left-wing violence and paramilitary build-up increased in intensity, to the finally intolerable exacerbation of the Chilean officer corps. His dependence on the latter likewise grew during this period, as shown by the fact that, over strong protests from his left-wing followers, he brought representatives of the armed forces into his cabinet from November 1972 to March 1973 and again in August of that year. But he was caught in the crossfire between his irrepressible left wing and the irresistible military, and if he had ever had a chance of escaping from that dilemma, it vanished with his cool reception in Moscow. For this, the administration in Washington should have been grateful, since Moscow's "stinginess" with Allende, as Moss calls it, quite possibly did more than the CIA's lavishness with the opposition to bring the Chilean leader's regime down.

From the Caribbean to the Strait of Magellan

In a sense, the United States by the 1970s had extended its Caribbean policy of intervention southward to the Southern Cone countries, but could its relations with them be described by the terms imperialism or neo-imperialism as defined earlier in this chapter?

Measuring by concrete criteria, the answer is no. Politically, the United States did not determine who should govern in these countries, or how. Even in Chile, where in 1973 it came closest to doing so, it only helped to determine who should not govern, and even in that case it only gave a push to a military coup that would have taken place anyway, after which it was quite unable to check the excesses of the new military government, though it deeply deplored them. As for Argentina, Washington's occasional efforts to interfere there were usually counterproductive. At the end, it reconciled itself to Perón's return only because the majority of the Argentine people insisted upon bringing him back. Nationalist Uruguay since World War II had cooperated with the United States in self-defense, but had never taken dictation from Washington. If, finally, mounting economic and political troubles brought Uruguay into any larger power's sphere of influence, it was that of Brazil, not the United States. Similarly, in the military field the United States was unable to control the arms supply of the Southern Cone, despite the Rio Defense Treaty and the bilateral military pacts. France and Britain were its most serious competitors there.

In the economic field, the United States had by the 1970s lost the dominant position it gained by World War II. Even in Chile, where its position was strongest, the government of that country already in 1967 owned 48.7 percent of the top 10 enterprises (43.2 percent of the top 30)* and its share rose to more than 70 percent under Allende. This left little room for maneuver for American enterprises. As measured by investments of private capital, the United States was already losing ground by 1970. After rising from $540 million in 1950 to $962 million in 1968, these investments declined to $748 million in 1970 and $721 million in 1971. In Chile's foreign trade the United States stood first by a wide margin as a source of imports, but as a market for Chilean exports it stood second to the Netherlands by a narrow margin and was closely followed by the United Kingdom, Japan, and West Germany, in that order.

In Argentina and Uruguay the situation was much the same in some respects and quite different in others. In both countries the proportion of enterprises owned or controlled by the state was high (upwards of 50 percent) and the United States was only one of sev-

---

*Arpad von Lazar and Robert R. Kaufman, eds., *Reform and Revolution: Readings in Latin American Politics* (Boston, 1969), 332, n. 16, citing Embassy of Chile, *Statistical Profile of Chile* (Washington, D.C., 1967), 59.

eral important trading partners. In Argentina it was far in the lead as a source of imports (followed by Brazil, West Germany, Italy, the United Kingdom, Japan, France, and Venezuela), but well down the list as a market for Argentine exports, in which Italy was well ahead, followed by the Netherlands, the United States, Brazil, the United Kingdom, Japan, West Germany, and France. As a source of Uruguay's imports, the United States stood second to Brazil and just ahead of Argentina, which was followed by West Germany, Kuwait (for petroleum), and the United Kingdom. As a market for Uruguay's products, however, the United States ranked near the bottom of the list, far behind West Germany, France, the United Kingdom, the Netherlands, Brazil, and even Greece. U.S. private investments in Uruguay were small and declining: $74 million in 1955 and $47 million in 1960, the last year for which the figures were available. In Argentina, on the other hand, they grew steadily from $414 million in 1950 to $1,840 in 1971, with an increasing concentration in manufactures ($133 million in 1950, $1,272 million in 1971).*

To what extent these changes reflect the influence of American foreign policy is a question we fortunately do not need to enter into. Our concern is with the character of that policy, which is easier to determine than its results. To begin with, the reader might be reminded that, after World War II as before, the United States generally followed the same policy towards the Southern Cone countries as towards the rest of Latin America. It did so during the dozen years after the war when its cold-war preoccupation with military and political defense of the hemisphere, accompanied by a veritable crusade for free enterprise, obscured its vision of the economic and social needs and desires of the erstwhile good neighbors, from the Rio Grande to Cape Horn. It did so again after 1960, when its general Latin American policy was marked by a shift of the focus of defense from external attack to internal subversion and by the gyrations of its Alliance for Progress policy until that noble experiment was lost to sight in the low profile fog or smoke-screen of the early 1970s.

During all these years the general policy was of course modified at times to meet particular situations. In the Southern Cone the most

*The data on investments in all three countries were taken from Kenneth F ddle and Kathleen Barrows, eds., *The Statistical Abstract for Latin America 1972* (Los Angeles, 1973), table 277, pp. 516-518; those on trade from *Statesman's Year-Book 1974-1975*, pp. 748, 811, 1459.

striking instances involved breaches of the inter-American nonintervention rule on security grounds and arose in connection with situations in Argentina at the beginning of the postwar period, and in Chile at its close. Uruguay, despite its strategic location, was too small and weak to be a security threat on its own account. When, late in the period, it showed signs of becoming one through the activity of Tupamaro terrorists, the United States, as already noted, merely provided it with counterinsurgency aid—which was a perfectly legitimate thing to do, though the Tupamaros did not think so.

Argentina, one of the principal powers of Latin America at the close of World War II, was an entirely different matter. In a continuation of a wartime effort that had some justification at that time in the Axis affiliations of the authorities in Buenos Aires, the U.S. government made an undeclared but obvious attempt to determine the outcome of a national election in Argentina. When that attempt failed, Washington did not repeat it. In the rest of our period, ending at the close of 1973, Argentina's importance, as seen from Washington, followed a fluctuating but generally downward course as, year after year, its economy moved by fits and starts while its political troubles never ceased. Even the return from exile in 1973 of Juan Perón, still the declared economic nationalist and once more anti-American, created only a passing flurry in Washington. The substantial U.S. business interests in Argentina were harassed by the unending wave of terrorism and its government seemed unable to protect them, but it apparently had its hands full protecting itself. Where the government could act effectively, its response was as negative as ever to initiatives from Washington. Nuclear energy, in the production of which by the early 1970s Argentina easily ranked first in Latin America, provided an example. The United States was a leading champion of the Non-Proliferation Treaty, but Argentina was one of the handful of states that refused to sign it. So was Brazil, which would hardly sign so long as Argentina held out, but on other grounds a close working relationship developed between the United States and the military dictatorship set up in Brazil (with U.S. aid, it was rumored) in 1964. All things considered, Argentina would have counted for little more with U.S. foreign policy makers at the end of our period than it had at the close of the nineteenth century, but for its nuclear capability and the rapid increase since 1960 of the Soviet navy and the strategic importance of the South Atlantic eastward to the Cape of Good Hope and south to Antarctica.

Chile, which had counted for enough with the United States in the 1890s to be the cause of a war scare, suffered a political eclipse between the two world wars. To Washington, however, it seemed by the 1960s more important than ever and by the early 1970s so potentially dangerous that the Nixon administration risked the veiled, low-profile intervention described in the preceding pages. Even if its purpose was achieved mainly through the efforts of others, its intervention still remains a serious matter for the future as well as the past. We can hardly agree with Richard Fagen's assertion in his *Foreign Affairs* article of January 1975 that "U.S. Chile policy marks" a transition to a new era in the sense that the "mix of overt and covert pressures put on the Allende government" was something new in U.S. operations. In fact, this mix had been employed before, notably against the Arbenz government of Guatemala in 1954. Nevertheless, whether or not one calls the era after 1973 new in this sense, Fagen has good grounds for warning that the era is "not likely to be much more congenial to the autonomy and interests of weak and marginal states than what existed before."

That prospect gained added credibility from the terms in which the Washington high command defended the intervention in Chile when it was exposed by a series of revelations from 1972 to 1975. Secretary of State Kissinger's defense was that the United States intervened to save democracy in Chile; President Ford's, that the United States acted in the Chilean people's own best interests. Both defenses showed a paternalistic attitude galling to Latin American pride. Moreover, so far as reported, neither official bothered to square the admitted intervention of the United States in Chile with the permanent treaty obligation, under Article 15 of the OAS charter (see chapter XVI), by which it is bound not to intervene in another American state in any form or on any pretext whatsoever. It was as if nothing had changed since President Theodore Roosevelt, in 1904 and 1905, proclaimed the United States' right of "protective" and "corrective" intervention in Latin America—nothing, that is, except the geographical range of the interventions carried out.

In the early decades of the century, these interventions were confined to the Caribbean and often related to the defense of the Panama Canal and its approaches. In 1910 this geographical limitation seemed so definitive that, as already noted, a leading statesman of Uruguay, Luis Alberto de Herrera, urged his fellow countrymen to form close ties with the United States, with the assurance that they had nothing to fear from it, since there was no danger of its extending its interventions to South America "in this century." He was wrong by thirty years. The 1970 intervention in southernmost South America was backed with the same old promise of protecting its people against foreign intrusion and the consequences of their own fallibility and of correcting situations of "chronic wrongdoing" and the "breakdown of orderly government." Except that in this case the Strait of Magellan replaced the Panama Canal as part of the justification, what was new about the Chile policy of the United States in the early 1970s? Whether the Latin Americans would find this era more congenial than its predecessors seemed doubtful at best, particularly where the most highly developed countries with the strongest anti-American movements—the Southern Cone countries—were involved.

XVIII Stabilizing
United States Policy

From Low Profile to New Dialogue

Secretary of State Henry Kissinger concluded an important address to an OAS meeting in Atlanta, Georgia, in April 1974 with a quotation from Uruguayan José Enrique Rodó's famous and much misunderstood essay *Ariel.* The passage referred to relations between "the two Americas," meaning Latin America and the United States. "To the extent that we can already distinguish a higher form of cooperation as the basis for a distant future," wrote Rodó, "we can see that it will come . . . through the reciprocal influence and skillful harmonization of those attributes which give our different peoples their glory."

This passage from a 74-year-old essay must have been chosen by some able Latin Americanist among the secretary's advisers, such as Luigi Einaudi or Assistant Secretary William D. Rogers, for it indicated a familiarity with the Latin American classics that Kissinger did not possess. At any rate, it was a happy choice for the climax of a speech describing a new "good partner" policy and aimed at promoting friendlier and more constructive relations between the two Americas through a "new dialogue." This was to replace the Nixon administration's previous policy of the low profile, which Rogers, a new recruit, dismissed with good reason as a "non-policy." Some such change was badly needed to repair the damage done to relations between the two during the low profile period, especially by revelations, made as early as 1972, of undercover political intervention by the United States against the Allende regime in Chile.

Unhappily for the secretary, his new dialogue had already begun to break down by the time he delivered his Atlanta address, and by the end of 1975 it was, to all appearances, dead. Some critics blamed him for its failure on various grounds — among others, for bypassing the OAS at the outset and attempting to conduct the dialogue separately with each government (the old divide-and-rule tactic, it was charged); for neglect, especially for postponing his scheduled visits to Latin America time after time; and for failing to use his influence in Congress to eliminate provisions in the General Trade Act of early 1975 that many Latin Americans resented as discriminatory against that area. In his defense it was said with perfect truth that he had been compelled to give precedence to one major crisis after another elsewhere in the world, especially in the Middle East, and that disagreement among the Latin Americans themselves as to what they wanted magnified the inherent difficulty of carrying on a multilateral dialogue with them.

Less publicity was given to another line of defense, which was that Kissinger's other difficulties were compounded by the strong, widespread, and growing anti-Americanism in Latin America. This found positive expression in two new forms of Pan Latin Americanism. One was ECLA's establishment of an all-Latin American commission on development and related matters, from which the United States was excluded. It was also excluded from the other and more ambitious form, a new organization called Latin American Economic System (SELA). The latter illustrated the clash of opinion among the Latin Americans themselves. Some of them wanted to pit the new organization against the United States, but others objected that this would be suicidal. When SELA was formally established, in October 1975, it was made nonpolitical.

The result of these opposing thrusts was a state of unstable equilibrium. In most respects relations between the United States and Latin America went on much the same after 1973 as before. The Southern Cone countries, particularly the two larger ones, played a prominent part in them, not least in frustrating the new dialogue. Argentina and Uruguay were conspicuous exceptions to the rule of the continued preponderance of the United States in the foreign trade of Latin America. On the other hand, according to *La Nación* (Buenos Aires) of October 6, 1975, Argentina and Chile were among the area's four chief customers of the United States in the surge of its arms sales to Latin America that followed President Nixon's lifting in 1969 of the restrictions on such sales that had helped France to become the area's principal "merchant of death" before that date. All three Cone countries shared in the increasing importance of the South Atlantic and Antarctica in world affairs.

Argentina's negative role in the new dialogue was played in many ways. A general air of anti-Americanism pervaded the government's foreign policy from Juan Perón's restoration on through the administration of his widow. This was shown on many occasions. A notable one occurred in March 1974, when the government muffled the new dialogue before it could be well started, by abruptly calling off an OAS meeting in Buenos Aires. U.S. citizens and business firms were the chief foreign targets of the organized violence whose depredations the government seemed unable either to check or to provide compensation for. The American embassy, both chancery and residence, had to be kept under heavy guard at all times.

Chile was an even greater impediment to the new dialogue. This was due in part to its military dictatorship's identification in the minds of many people in Latin America (as well as in other lands) with U.S. intervention against the Allende regime. There is irony in the fact that this dictatorship, for which the United States was in fact partly responsible, first became a heavy public relations liability to Washington in Latin America as elsewhere because of its alleged atrocities against human rights, and then also became so alienated from Washington that in late 1975 it voted with the Arabs against the United States in the UN General Assembly debate on the issue of Zionism as racism.

While relations between Washington and Chile's military junta cooled, congressional investigations continued to pile up evidence of political intervention by the United States against Allende. Such evidence, together with the friendly relationship between high state department officials and the Council of the Americas (formerly the Council for Latin America), gave the impression that the United States was on the side of the alliance between foreign capital and the Chilean "oligarchy" whose hold on Chile Allende had sought to break. The Council of the Americas, as already noted, represented principally the big business and financial interests of the United States in Latin America, and, reported *The Times of the Americas* (April 11, 1975), one of its members maintained that the multinationals were Latin America's best friends. The council seemed to have the inside track with the state department, which is hardly surprising since it was the strongest and best organized pressure group that represented a substantial interest, material or of any other kind, in Latin America. Though it had its headquarters in New York, it held important meetings in Washington. On one notable occasion, in June 1975, it held its meeting in the State Department's international conference room and had Secretary of State Kissinger as its principal speaker. The Chilean junta, which was kind to foreign investors as well as to the country's own economic upper crust, continued to enjoy the good will of the council and the state department until the human rights issue and the junta's defection to the Arabs made it seem a liability to them. When that became clear, attentive observers were prepared to hear that the United States was again intervening politically by shifting its support to Chilean elements less likely to go off the track and more likely to succeed at home and abroad.

The investigations by the U.S. Congress, which were still going on at the close of 1975, did not bring to light any evidence that military or other armed intervention by the United States had taken place in Chile. They did elicit testimony from Richard Helms that in a White House meeting with President Nixon, Henry Kissinger, and Attorney General John Mitchell on September 15, 1970, when Helms was director of the Central Intelligence Agency, he was ordered by the president to help organize a military coup to keep Allende from taking office. The evidence showed, however, that the nearest approach to carrying out the order was the CIA's involvement in a plot to kidnap top-ranking General René Schneider, who was loyal to Allende; but there was no evidence that the agency was responsible for turning the kidnapping into an assassination. As pointed out in chapter XIV, that crime in fact defeated the whole purpose of U.S. policy by provoking a strong reaction among Chileans in Allende's favor, thereby ensuring his inauguration as president. Likewise, no evidence was forthcoming to sustain the charge that the U.S. government had a hand in the military coup of September 1973 that overthrew Allende. For what it may be worth, we have a complete exoneration of the United States by the leader of the coup, General Augusto Pinochet, in an interview with C. L. Sulzberger reported in the *New York Times* of November 30, 1975. Indeed, he asserted he had avoided contact with the United States and had received no help, "not even good will," from it.

On the other hand, the staff report of the Senate Committee on Intelligence ("Covert Action in Chile, 1963-1973"), released a few days later (December 4), stated that, while it had found no evidence of direct CIA involvement in either the 1973 coup or the preceding truckers' strike, there was evidence of "intelligence contact" between the agency and unnamed Chilean officers who were participating in "coup plotting." The report confirmed the authenticity of Henry Kissinger's background briefing of the press on September 16, 1970, and buttressed earlier revelations that the CIA had then spent millions in Chile (mainly, the report said, in support of *El Mercurio* — a charge at once and indignantly denied by that journal) in an effort to undermine Allende's government politically. Although the report admitted that the "record on Chile" was mixed and incomplete, it showed once more that the policy of intervention was being extended from the Caribbean to Cape Horn. There was the difference that the intervention was now a political one spearheaded by CIA agents, instead of a military one by marines; but the OAS charter, to which the United States was a party, prohibited political and economic as well as armed intervention.

"If We Do Not Lead, There Will Be No Leadership"

Two notable events of February 1976 in the Latin American relations of the United States affected the Southern Cone countries adversely. One, which affected all three, was Secretary of State Kissinger's long delayed visit to South America. By confining it to Venezuela, Brazil, Peru, and Colombia,* he conferred on them a distinction denied their neighbors to the south. The other event, of special concern to Argentina, was his signing of a consultative accord between the United States and Brazil during his visit to Brasilia. The accord provided for semiannual consultations between the two governments "on the full range of foreign-policy matters." The United States had a similar agreement with Japan, but not with any other Latin American government. The accord implied the United States' recognition of Brazil as an emergent great power. Implication was made explicit by Secretary Kissinger when, at a dinner hosted by the Brazilian foreign minister, he spoke of Brazil as "a nation of greatness — a people taking their place in the front rank of nations."

As noted at the time by more than one observer, the accord and the secretary's accolade were bound to provoke jealousy and irritation among other leading Latin American nations. Nowhere were they more disturbing than in Argentina. The fact that the discrimination was obviously justified by the greater strength, stability, and promise of Brazil in the past decade did not make it more palatable to Argentine leaders. They had long been confident that their country would be the first in Latin America to achieve great-power status. Only a few years had passed since General Lanusse's warning to the military rulers of Brazil that Argentina would never settle for second place, and now that was just where Argentina found itself exposed in the limelight cast by Secretary Kissinger's tribute and his government's accord with Brazil. In view of these actions it seemed to many Latin Americans besides the Argentines that the traditional "special relationship" of the United States with Latin America had been converted into a special relationship with Brazil alone.

*The visit, which began on February 16 and lasted nine days, included Costa Rica in Central America. Kissinger stopped briefly in Guatemala, recently devastated by an earthquake.

Ill feeling on that score was mitigated early in 1976 as the United States and the great majority of Latin American governments came together in a common attitude towards the highly controversial military dictatorship in Chile. A thaw took place in the cold attitude assumed by the United States government in 1974. Its representative joined the Latin American majority in the decision of the Organization of American States to hold its next general assembly (June 1976) in Santiago. Secretary Kissinger let it be known that he intended to make an official visit to Chile — an announcement that required courage, for hostility to the Chilean regime was strong in Congress, as shown by the Senate's adoption early in the year of a resolution designed to cut off the sale of arms to Chile. About the same time there was a loosening of the purse strings for that country by the World Bank and the Inter-American Development Bank, in both of which the United States government had considerable influence, chiefly through its executive branch. It was the attitude of this branch that had its counterpart in Latin America. According to the *Times of the Americas,* March 31, 1976, all the Latin American nations except Cuba and Mexico now had normal relations with Chile and these relations seemed to be improving. The improvement was attributed partly to the liberality with which the regime permitted former supporters of Allende, even terrorists and their accomplices, to go into exile. Another factor, the report continued, was growing doubt about the truth of the atrocity stories and belief that the campaign against the Chilean regime in the United Nations and elsewhere was being orchestrated by the Soviet Union.

This thaw did not alter Washington's basic policy, and no change in that was even being considered, if we may judge from the transcript of an exceptionally interesting interview of Secretary Kissinger by William F. Buckley, Jr., of "Firing Line," published by the State Department on September 13, 1975. Buckley raised the Chilean question several times. First, with reference to the violent fluctuations of public opinion in the United States, he remarked that Kissinger's critics "started to give you hell when they found out that you tried to 'destabilize' the coming to power of Allende in Chile," and added, "I don't think they would have given you hell for trying to do that in an age, which was not so long ago, when it was understood that . . . we certainly were going to do everything that we could to help people stay free." Without mentioning Chile by name, the secretary replied that "the nature of our domestic debate on foreign policy has been severely affected by the upheavals of the 1960s, . . . by Vietnam, by Watergate," and that the conduct of foreign policy was "a much more complicated task than the one that existed in the 1950's"—at which point Dean Acheson would surely have raised an eyebrow. Kissinger went on to explain that "what we have attempted to do is . . . to find a policy that is geared to our national interest and to our basic values and that can be sustained over a period of time," from which one might conclude that the Allende government was destabilized in the interest of stabilizing U.S. foreign policy.

Buckley brought Chile up again in connection with the current clash between pro- and anti-communists in Portugal. If, he said, Kissinger "had elected to go to the help of Portugal," his critics would "haul you up and ask if you were up to your old Chilean tricks again." Once more the secretary replied in terms which, while relevant and important, such as the need for "educating the public in the United States," did not apply specifically to Chile. Not to be denied, Buckley tried once more: "Well, if I understand you correctly, if an Allende were to come to power tomorrow, you would not feel that you could recommend such action as you thought appropriate in 1970 . . ." This time, Kissinger obliged. "No, I am not saying that," he replied, and added a little later that "in the case of Chile — a case that has been wildly oversimplified in much of the discussion — I think our perception of the problem would not be radically different from what it was in 1970."

Historians of American foreign relations can find much food for thought in the second of the two grounds on which the secretary proceeded to differentiate the case of Portugal from that of Chile. The first was that "the realities of the domestic evolution [in the United States] required a rather deliberate approach" to the Portuguese problem, and the second, that this was required "particularly because Portugal is more a West European than a U.S. problem." This second reason echoes not only Secretary Cordell Hull's main justification of the United States' acquiescence in the farce of nonintervention in the Spanish Civil War, but also the original Monroe Doctrine of the "two spheres," the New World and Old World or the American and European spheres, and the underlying Western Hemisphere idea. In accordance with these notions, the United States had the right and duty to act as it saw fit in the case of Chile, but not of Portugal, although Chile is 6,000 miles away and Portugal only 3,000.* Moreover, Kissinger's reasoning, together with his actions, was also reminiscent of the Roosevelt Corollary of 1904-1905, which, if not hegemonic, was surely paternalistic. How his reasoning brought these threads together in the case of Chile is suggested by his statement in the course of this interview that the "general public" in the United States, "despite all the shocks," is "basically healthier, basically more vital than in any other Western country. *And therefore, fundamentally, we are the hope of the non-Communist world. If we do not lead, there will be no leadership.*" (Italics mine.) The Cold War, it seemed, was still going on, despite detente.

This conception of the world role of the United States has a special significance for its relations with Latin America and not least, in the years just ahead, for the exceptionally troubled and tumultuous countries of the Southern Cone, which are Latin America's most "Western" countries. It is a conception so flattering to American pride, and so seductive to anyone who holds the helm of foreign policy, that, as the bicentennial celebration of the independence of the United States takes place, it seems likely to survive changes of administration and personnel for years to come, barring some cataclysm not now in sight.

---

*I discuss these matters more fully in the Spring 1976 issue of *Orbis, a Journal of World Affairs*.

Appendix

Table A-1. Area in square miles

Argentina	1,072,163
Chile	292,256
Uruguay	72,172
Bolivia	424,165
Brazil	3,286,488

Source: *New York Times Encyclopedic Almanac, 1971*.

Table A-2. Total population, 1850-1970 (in thousands)

Country	1850	1900	1930	1940	1950	1960	1970
Argentina	1,100	4,743	11,896	14,169	17,083	20,850	24,352
Chile	1,287	2,904	4,424	5,147	6,058	7,683	9,717
Uruguay	132	915	1,704	1,947	2,198	2,542	2,889
Bolivia	1,374	1,696	2,153	2,508	3,013	3,696	4,658
Brazil	7,205	17,318	33,568	41,233	52,321	70,327	93,245

Source: Nicholás Sánchez-Albornoz, *The Population of Latin America* (Berkeley: University of California Press, 1974), 169, 184. Reprinted by permission of the University of California Press.

Table A-3. Estimates of mid-year population, 1964-1973 (in millions)

Country	1964	1967	1970	1973
Argentina[a]	21.17	22.16	23.21	24.29
Chile[b]	8.50	9.14	9.72	10.23
Uruguay[a]	2.68	2.78	2.89	2.99
Brazil	78.73	83.84[c]	93.39	101.71

Source: United Nations, *Monthly Bulletin of Statistics*, Dec. 1974, 1-4, table 1.

[a]Estimates of questionable reliability, but probably not far wrong.
[b]Includes adjustment for underenumeration in 1960 and 1970 censuses.
[c]1966.

Table A-4. Life expectancy at birth, 1965-1970 (both sexes)

Uruguay	69.2
Argentina	67.4
Chile	60.9
Brazil	60.6
Bolivia	45.3

Source: Sánchez-Albornoz, *The Population of Latin America*, 193.

Table A-5. Proportion of foreign-born in total populations in the Southern Cone (percent)

Year	Argentina	Chile	Uruguay
1860			35.0
1869	12.1		
1895	25.4		
1907		4.2	
1908			17.4
1914	29.9		
1960	13.0		

Sources: Zulma L. Recchini de Lattes and Alfredo de Lattes, *Migraciones en la Argentina* (Buenos Aires: Centro de Investigaciones Sociales, Instituto Torcuato di Tella [1969]), 80, and Sánchez-Albornoz, *The Population of Latin America,* 154.

Table A-6. Nationality of foreigners in Argentina and Chile (percent): the six largest groups in each by country of origin

	Argentina (1914)[a]	Chile (1907)[b]
Total foreign-born	2,357,052	134,521
Italy	39.43	9.68
Spain	35.19	13.94
Russia[c]	4.10	
Uruguay	3.66	
France	3.37	7.28
Ottoman Empire[d]	2.73	
Germany		7.97
Great Britain		7.32
Argentina		5.17

Source: Carl Solberg, *Immigration and Nationalism, Argentina and Chile* (Austin: University of Texas Press, 1970. For the Institute of Latin American Studies), 38.

[a]Not ranked: Great Britain, 1.17, Germany 1.14, Chile 1.43.
[b]Omitting Peru and Bolivia because of Tacna-Arica and Tarapacá, respectively.
[c]Including Poland.
[d]Mostly Syrians and Lebanese, called "Turcos."

Table A-7. Gross domestic product (annual percentage growth rate)

	1950-60	1959-64	1965-69
Latin America	5.1	5.4	5.3
Argentina	3.1	3.4	4.5
Chile	6.0	5.3	4.0
Uruguay	2.1	1.4	0.8

Source: ECLA, *Economic Survey of Latin America 1970,* 40, table 9.

Table A-8. Armed forces, 1973

	Argentina	Chile	Uruguay
Total armed forces	135,000	60,000	21,000
Estimated GNP, 1973	$71.8 billion[a]	$18.3 billion	$2.7 billion
Defense budget, 1974	$1,286 million	$213 million	$68 million
Army	85,000	32,000	16,000
Reserves	250,000	160,000	100,000
Navy	33,000	18,000	3,000
Naval Air Force	3,000		
Marines	4,800		
Air Force	17,000	10,000	2,000
Paramilitary Forces	19,000	30,000	22,000

Source: The International Institute for Strategic Studies, *The Military Balance 1974-1975* (London, 1975), 63-68. By permission of the International Institute for Strategic Studies.

[a]Large increase in GNP attributed to high inflation unmatched by exchange rate movements.

Table A-9. U.S. direct investment in Argentina, Chile, Uruguay (book value in millions of U.S. dollars)

Year	Argentina	Chile	Uruguay
1950	356	540	55
1960	472a	738	47
1965	992	829	
1970	1,281	748c	
1971	1,350	721	

Source: Kenneth Ruddle and Kathleen Barrows, *The Statistical Abstract of Latin America, 1972* (Latin American Center, University of California, Los Angeles, 1974), 516-518.

aBook value adjusted downward by $42 million in 1958-1959 to reflect declining exchange rate.

bProvisional estimated data.

cBook value dropped in 1969 owing to sales of majority interests in two U.S. mining enterprises to the Chilean government.

Bibliographical Notes

These notes are intended as an aid to further reading on topics discussed in this book. In view of its broad scope in space, time, and subject matter, the notes are necessarily selective. A comprehensive list of relevant materials would fill hundreds of pages and be more likely to confuse and repel than help the reader. To keep this list as brief as possible, it has been confined almost entirely to the writings that were found most useful in preparing this book and, among those writings, to books, except for a very few articles of exceptional value. As in the text, attention here is also confined to the national period and largely to the twentieth century. Preference is given to works in English, although many in Spanish and a few in French are included, and to works published since 1950.

The arrangement of the following notes is by sections, first on general works, then on each of the Southern Cone countries in alphabetical order, followed by a section on relations with the United States, and ending with a few suggestions for those who wish to look further and keep up with current publications.

General Works

This section includes all works that deal with more than one of the three Southern Cone countries. Since they are studied as a group only in approximations such as Fernando Márquez Miranda's pre-Columbian *Región meridional de América del Sur* (Mexico, D.F., 1954), which include more than the area of these three, and are only occasionally studied in pairs (Argentina-Chile, Argentina-Uruguay, Chile-Uruguay), most of these general works are broad in a geographical as well as a topical sense. The broadest have the merit of providing background, perspective, and bases for comparison. One of the most stimulating of this kind is Jacques Lambert, *Latin America, Social Structures and Political Institutions* (Berkeley, 1967), translated from the French by Helen Katel. Lambert, along with Pierre Monbeig and other specialists, took part in the interesting round-table discussion reported in *L'Europe et l'Amérique Latine* (Strasbourg, 1965, Centre Universitaire des Hautes Etudes Européennes). Another notable example of comparisons is Peter Ranis, *Five Latin American Nations: A Comparative Political Study* (New York, 1971). Spanish-born Victor Alba's *The Latin Americans* (New York, 1969) and Peter Calvert's *Latin America: Internal Conflict and International Peace* (New York, 1969) are even broader than the foregoing. Leadership problems in various sectors of society are discussed in Seymour Lipset and Aldo Solari, eds., *Elites in Latin America* (New York, 1966). Milton I. Vanger, "Politics and Class in Twentieth-Century Latin America," *Hispanic American Historical Review*, XLIX, 1 (Feb. 1969), 80-93, contains acute observations on this subject. John J. Johnson's concept of middle-class leadership has lost much of its original impact, but his *Political Change in Latin America: The Emergence of the Middle Sectors* (Stanford, 1958) is still required reading. Richard P. Schaedel, ed., *Social Change in Latin America* (Austin, 1967), includes "Main Stages of Modernization," by Gino Germani, whose *Política y sociedad en una época de transición* (Buenos Aires, 1962), though it stresses Argentina, has much wider projections, and "Political Aspects of Social Change," by Kalman H. Silvert, whose *The Conflict Society* (New Orleans, 1961, rev. ed. 1966) is particularly valuable for Argentina and Chile, though likewise of broader scope. Another aspect is presented by J. Gregory Oswald, compiler and translator, *Soviet Image of Contemporary Latin America: A Documentary History, 1960-1968* (Austin, 1970). For a historical survey full of suggestive comparisons, see *Historia contemporánea de América Latina* (Madrid, 1972), by a leading Argentine historian, Tulio Halperín Donghi.

Another broad study that is unusually stimulating is Juan F. Marsal's *The Image of a Changing Latin America: A Sociological Criticism of Some Current American and Latin American Models* (Princeton, 1965), published in Spanish as *Cambio social en América Latina: Crítica . . .* (Buenos Aires, 1967). More action-oriented is *América Latina y desarrollo social,* by Roger Vekemans et al. (Barcelona, 1966, 2 vols.). James Petras and Maurice Zeitlin, *Latin America: Reform or Revolution? A Reader* (New York, 1968), is balanced by *Obstacles to Change in Latin America,* ed. Claudie Veliz (London, 1966), which is especially valuable for the account its distinguished contributors (all Latin Americans) give of the obstacles to political as well as economic change in Latin America from Mexico to Cape Horn. A positive approach to the same problem is John Mander's *The Unrevolutionary Society. The Power of Latin American Conservatism in a Changing World* (New York, 1969). One aspect of change and the obstacles to it is delineated in *Female and Male in Latin America,* Ann Pescatello, ed. (Pittsburgh, 1973). A phenomenon that is sometimes a help and sometimes a hindrance to change is discussed in *Dictatorship in Spanish America,* Hugh M. Hamill, Jr., ed. (New York, 1965). For the literature on the urban guerrilla movement, see Charles A. Russell et al., "The Urban Guerrilla in Latin America: A Select Bibliography," *Latin American Research Review,* IX, 1 (Spring 1974), 37-39, and James Kohn and John Litt, *Urban Guerrilla Warfare in Latin America* (Cambridge, Mass., 1974), which features Argentina, Uruguay, and Brazil, but not Chile.

A most useful book for both horizontal and vertical comparisons is *The Population of Latin America: A History,* by Nicolás Sánchez-Albernoz, tr. W. A. Richardson (Berkeley, 1974). The subject is discussed in global terms by Marcel R. Reinhard, et al., in *Histoire générale de la population mondiale* (Paris, 1968), which, like the preceding work, is generously equipped with statistics and graphs.

Among general works on politics that deal directly, though not exclusively, with the Southern Cone are Robert J. Alexander, *Prophets of the Revolution* (New York, 1962), containing essays on Batlle, Arturo Alessandri, Perón, and eight others; Martin C. Needler, *Political Development in Latin America* (New York, 1968); *Models of Political Change in Latin America,* ed. Paul E. Sigmund (New York, 1970); *The Politics of Violence: Revolution in the Modern World,* Carl Leiden and Karl M. Schmitt, eds. (Englewood Cliffs, 1968); and *Marxism in Latin America,* ed. Luis E. Aguilar (New York, 1968). Particular political aspects are covered in Rollie W. Peppino, *International Communism in Latin America* (New York, 1964); Edward J. Williams, *Latin American Christian Democratic Parties* (Knoxville, 1967); Arpad von Lazar and Robert C. Kaufman, eds., *Reform and Revolution: Readings in Latin American Politics* (Boston, 1969); Richard C. Fagen and Wayne A. Cornelius, eds., *Political Power in Latin America: Seven Confrontations* (Englewood Cliffs, 1970); Weston H. Agor, ed., *Latin American Legislatures . . .* (New York, 1971); T. Lynn Smith, ed., *Agrarian Reform in Latin America* (New York, 1965); Gustave Correa, "El nacionalismo cultural en la literatura hispanoamericana," *Sobretiro de Cuadernos Americanos* (Mexico, D.F., 1958);

Arthur P. Whitaker and David C. Jordan, *Nationalism in Contemporary Latin America* (New York, 1966); Samuel L. Baily, ed., *Nationalism in Latin America* (New York, 1971); and Carl Solberg, *Immigration and Nationalism: Argentina and Chile* (Austin, 1970). A. James Gregor, *The Fascist Persuasion in Radical Politics* (Princeton, 1974), deals in part with Latin America.

Edwin F. Lieuwen, *Arms and Politics in Latin America* (New York, 1961) has been followed by many other studies in that field. Those of a general character include John J. Johnson, *The Military and Society in Latin America* (Stanford, 1964); Liisa North, *Civil-Military Relations in Argentina, Chile, and Peru* (Berkeley, n.d. (1966?)); Philippe C. Schmitter, ed., *Military Rule in Latin America* (Beverly Hills, 1973); and John R. Redick, *Military Potential of Latin American Nuclear Energy Programs* (Beverly Hills, 1972). Current data on the armed forces of Latin America are included in The International Institute of Strategic Studies, *The Military Balance 1974-1975* (London, 1974), an annual survey.

In the economic field, older general works that are still very useful for historical background and other reasons include Dudley M. Phelps, *Migration of Industry to South America* (New York, 1936); Percy W. Bidwell, *Economic Defense of Latin America* (Boston, 1941); J. Fred Rippy, *Latin America and the Industrial Age* (New York, 1947); George Wythe, *Industry in Latin America* (New York, 1949, 2nd ed.); Wendell C. Gordon, *The Economy of Latin America* (New York, 1950); and Simon G. Hanson, *Economic Development in Latin America* (Washington, 1951). W. S. Woytinsky, *The U.S. and Latin America's Economy* (New York, n.d.) is most useful for the 1950s; the author and his wife wrote *World Population and Production*. Robert Mayer, "The Origins of the American Banking Empire in Latin America: Frank A. Vanderlip and the National City Bank," in *Journal of Inter-American Studies and World Affairs*, 15, 1 (Feb. 1973), 60-76, and Mira Wilkins, *The Maturing of Multinational Enterprise: American Business Abroad from 1914 to 1970* (Cambridge, Mass., 1974), go against the tendency of recent studies on concentrate on development.

Outstanding among the latter are William P. Glade, *The Latin American Economies: A Study of Their Institutional Evolution* (New York, 1969), and several works by Albert O. Hirschman, a fair sample of which is *A Bias for Hope: Essays on Development in Latin America* (New Haven, 1971). André Gunder Frank reflects a very different and quite left-wing Latin American view of the subject in his *Capitalism and Underdevelopment in Latin America: Historical Studies of Chile and Brazil* (New York, 1969). More orthodox views are provided by Keith Griffin, *Underdevelopment in Spanish America* (Cambridge, Mass., 1970), and *Latin American Integration: Experiences and Prospects*, ed. Miguel S. Wionczek (New York, 1966). See also Oswaldo Sunkel, "Big Business and 'Dependencia': A Latin American View," *Foreign Affairs*, 50, 3 (April 1972), 517-531. The obstacle to such integration interposed by nationalism is the subject of *Nacionalismo latinoamericano* (Santiago, Chile, 1967), by Felipe Herrera, a leading integrationist and head of the Inter-American Development Bank. Other aspects of the problem are discussed in Raymond F. Mikesell, et al., *Foreign Investment in the Petroleum and Mineral Industries: Case Studies of Investor-Host Relations* (Baltimore, 1971), which devotes most of its case studies to Latin American countries, including Argentina and Chile; *The Flow of Capital from the European Economic Commu-*

nity to Latin America, by the Department of Economic Affairs, Pan American Union (Washington, 1963); *Income Distribution in Latin America,* by the Economic Commission for Latin America (ECLA) of the United Nations (New York, 1971); and two articles by Edward S. Milenky, both in *Inter-American Economic Affairs:* "From Integration to Developmental Nationalism: The Andean Group, 1965-1971," XXV, 3 (1971), 77-91, and XXVI, 4 (1973), 49-68. Changing conditions in labor relations are reflected in three books by Robert J. Alexander: *Labor Movements in Latin America* (London, 1947), *Labor Relations in Argentina, Brazil, and Chile* (New York, 1962), and *Today's Latin America* (New York, 1968).

Nationalism and development are linked with ideology in Kalman H. Silvert, "The Costs of Anti-Nationalism: Argentina," in *Expectant Peoples* (New York, 1963), edited by him, and in Fredrick B. Pike and Thomas Stritch, eds., *The New Corporatism, Social-Political Structures in the Iberian World* (Notre Dame, 1974). Ronald C. Newton, "On 'Functional Groups,' 'Fragmentation,' and 'Pluralism' in Spanish American Political Societies," *Hispanic American Historical Review,* L, 1 (Feb. 1970), 1-29, is tangential to that theme, but important.

The changing role of the Roman Catholic Church since the early nineteenth century is brought out by three books: Fredrick B. Pike, ed., *The Conflict between Church and State in Latin America* (New York, 1964); Henry A. Landsberger, *The Church and Social Change in Latin America* (Notre Dame, 1970); and Karl M. Schmitt, ed., *The Roman Catholic Church in Latin America* (New York, 1972). As Schmitt says, the study of church-state relations in the national period should begin with the revised edition of J. Lloyd Mecham's *Church and State in Latin America* (Chapel Hill, 1966).

W. Rex Crawford, *A Century of Latin American Thought* (Cambridge, Mass., 1961, rev. ed.) is still outstanding in its field, as is Enrique Anderson-Imbert's *Spanish-American Literature: A History,* tr. John V. Falconieri (Detroit, 1963). Particular aspects are developed by Harold E. Davis in *Latin American Social Thought* (Washington, 1961) and, as compiler, in the report on *Conference on Developing Teaching Materials on Latin American Thought for College Level Courses* (Washington, 1972); by the Council on Higher Education in the American Republics, *Student Activism and Higher Education: An Inter-American Dialogue* (New York, 1970); by Samuel Shapiro, ed., *Cultural Factors in Inter-American Relations* (Notre Dame, Ind., 1968); by Julio César Chaves, *Unamuno y América* (Madrid, 1970); by Fredrick B. Pike, *Hispanismo, 1898-1936* (Notre Dame, 1971); by the Pan American Union's series *Pensamiento de América;* and by Los *"fundadores" en la filosofía de América Latina,* Secretaría General, OAS (Washington, 1970).

Most of the works on the Southern Cone's external relations are among those listed either above, or in the section on the foreign relations of each country, or in the section on U.S. relations with the Southern Cone. Exceptions on topics of special interest are Harold E. Davis, et al., *Latin American Foreign Policies* (Baltimore, 1975); Alton Frye, *Nazi Germany and the American Hemisphere, 1933-1941* (New Haven, 1967); Robert E. Wilson, "National Interests and Claims in the Antarctic," *Arctic,* 17, 1 (March 1964), 15-31, which deals extensively with Argentina and Chile, active claimants since early in the century; and Walter F. Hahn, "Nuclear Proliferation," *Strategic Review* (Winter 1975), 16-24, about a process in which Argentina has figured with considerable success, Chile with almost none, and Uruguay with none at all. In this connection, see John R. Redick, *Military Potential of Latin American Nuclear Energy Programs,* cited above.

Argentina

The extensive guide to the literature on Argentina in James R. Scobie, *Argentina, A City and a Nation* (New York, 1971, 2nd ed.) will meet the needs of most readers. The titles that follow are suggested for some special reason, such as their importance in the preparation of the present work or because they were published so recently or stray so far from the beaten path that they are not likely to have become widely known. Among general histories of Argentina is the two-volume work on the nineteenth and twentieth centuries by Jorge Abelardo Ramos under the main title *Revolución y contrarevolución en la Argentina* (Buenos Aires, 1965), which is well worth reading, although most readers in the United States would probably be put off by its unrelenting left-wing bias. The same can be said of his *Crisis y resurrección de la literatura argentina* (Buenos Aires, 1961, 2nd ed.). More conventional and notable for the author's skill in creating an illusion of actuality is Gustavo Gabriel Levene, *Historia argentina* (Buenos Aires, 1964, 3 vols.). Thomas F. McGann's perceptive essay, *Argentina: The Divided Land* (Princeton, 1966) is the best brief interpretation.

Among special works to be noted are two on caudillos and gauchos: Héctor Domingo Arias et al., *Encuesta sobre el caudillo* (La Plata, 1965), and Félix Luna, *Los caudillos* (Buenos Aires, 1967). Others are Yderla G. Anzoátegui, *La mujer y la política* (Buenos Aires, 1950); Darío Canton, *El parlamento argentino en épocas de cambio: 1890, 1916 y 1946* (Buenos Aires, 1966); José Luis de Imaz, *Los que mandan* (Buenos Aires, 1964; English tr., same main title, Berkeley, 1969); Alberto Ciria et al., *La década infame* (Buenos Aires, 1969); Alberto Ciria, *Parties and Power in Modern Argentina, 1930-1946,* tr. Carlos A. Astiz with Mary McCarthy (Albany, 1974); David Rock, *Politics in Argentina, 1890-1930* (Cambridge, 1975); John J. Kennedy, *Catholicism, Nationalism, and Democracy in Argentina* (Notre Dame, 1958); Federico Ibarguren, *Orígenes del nacionalismo argentino, 1927-1937* (Buenos Aires, 1970); Tulio Halperín Donghi and Torcuato S. di Tella, eds., *Los fragmentos del poder* (Buenos Aires, 1970). The outstanding work on a theme of increasing interest is Robert A. Potash, *The Army and Politics in Argentina, 1928-1945* (Stanford, 1969); also important are Marvin Goldwert, *Democracy, Militarism, and Nationalism in Argentina, 1930-1966* (Austin, 1972), and relevant items listed above under General Works.

On the Perón regime, three works in English were published while it was in progress: Robert J. Alexander, *The Perón Era* (New York, 1951), Geore I. Blanksten, *Perón's Argentina* (Chicago, 1953), and a large part of *The United States and Argentina* by Arthur P. Whitaker (Cambridge, Mass., 1954). Chilean Alejandro Magnet's *Nuestros vecinos justicialistas* and *Nuestros vecinos argentinos* (Santiago, 1952 and 1956) are contemporary eyewitness accounts and much the best by any journalist. All these books are now outdated to some extent and, though many of the subsequent works on Perón and Peronism have important merits, all fail to satisfy, mainly because of a widespread obsession with the rather futile debate over whether or not they should be tickĕted as "fascist." Publications since Perón's overthrow in 1955 include Joseph R. Barager, ed., *Why Perón Came to Power* (New York, 1968); Mark Falcoff and Donald H. Dolkart, *Prologue to Perón* (Berkeley and Los Angeles, 1975); Pierre Lux-Wurm, *Le Péronisme* (Paris, 1965); Carlos S. Faytt, *La naturaleza del peronismo* (Buenos Aires, 1967); Hugo Gambini, *El 17 de Octubre de 1945* (Buenos Aires, 1969); Félix Luna, *El 45* (Buenos Aires, 1969); Kalman H. Silvert, ed., "Peronism in Argentina: A Rightist Reaction to the Social Problem in Latin America," in Fredrick B. Pike, ed., *Latin American History: Select Problems* (New York, 1969); Jeane Kirkpatrick, *Leader and Vanguard in Mass Society: A Study of Peronist Argentina* (Cambridge, Mass., 1971); Martin S. Stabb, "Argentine Letters and the Peronato: An Overview," *Journal of Inter-American Studies and World Affairs*, XIII (1971), 434-455; and *Coloquios con Perón* (Madrid, 1973). Perón wrote several books, including *La hora de los pueblos* (Buenos Aires, 1968). Peter H. Smith, *Argentina and the Failure of Democracy: Conflict among Political Elites, 1904-1955* (Madison, Wis., 1974), closes with the first Perón regime.

The murky politics of Argentina in the 1960s and early 1970s are illuminated by Darío Canton in " 'Revolución Argentina' de 1966 y proyecto nacional," *Revista Latinoamericana de Sociología*, V, 3 (Nov. 1969), 520-543, and by David C. Jordan in two articles: "Argentina's Bureaucratic Oligarchies," *Current History* (Feb. 1972), 70-75 and 113-115, and "Perón's Return, Allende's Fall, and Communism in Latin America," *Orbis*, XVII, 3 (Fall 1973), 1025-1052. "Urban Guerrillas in Argentina: A Select Bibliography," by Charles A. Russell et al., *Latin American Research Review*, IX, 3 (Fall 1974), cites publications into 1974.

José Luis Romero, *A History of Argentine Political Thought*, tr. Thomas F. McGann (Stanford, 1963; reprint, with epilogue added, 1968), remains standard. One question it raised, that of Argentine national character or "basic personality," is addressed directly in Arne Clausen, *Una imagen del hombre Argentino* (Cuernavaca, Mexico, 1969), and by implication in Guillermo Ara et al., *Qué es la Argentina?* (Buenos Aires, 1970). H. Ernest Lewald, ed., *Argentina, análisis y autoanálisis* (Buenos Aires, 1969), consists of excerpts from writings by Spaniards as well as Argentines. Juan Carlos Torcha Estrada, *La filosofía en la Argentina* (Washington, 1961) is in the Pan American Union's very useful *Pensamiento de América* series. Diego Abad de Santillán, *Historia institucional argentina* (Buenos Aires, 1966), updated that subject.

Gino Germani's exceptionally important pioneer studies of society are represented by his *Estructura social de la Argentina* (Buenos Aires, 1955) and *Política y sociedad*, cited under General Works. A notable contribution in that field was made by Zulma L. Recchini de Lattes and Alfredo E. Lattes in their *Migraciones en la Argentina* (Buenos Aires, 1969) which covers both "internal and international migrations," 1869-1960. José Luis Romero linked the history of ideas with social and cultural history in *El desarollo de las ideas en la sociedad argentina del siglo XX* (Mexico D. F., and Buenos Aires, 1965). Juan F. Marsal, *Hacer la América* (Buenos Aires, 1969) and *Cambio social* (cited under General Works) are noteworthy. Juan José Sebreli created a porteño sensation with his *Buenos Aires, vida cotidiana y alienación* (Buenos Aires, 1964) and provided a lively sketch of social life over several decades at a once fashionable seaside resort in *Mar del Plata, el ocio represivo* (Buenos Aires, 1970).

The Argentine Economy, by Aldo Ferrer, tr. Marjory M. Urquidi (Berkeley, 1967), combines a compact history of the subject with an analysis of major postwar problems to the early 1960s. Carlos F. Díaz-Alejandro, *Essays on the Economic History of the Argentine Republic* (New Haven, 1970), throws new light on several old problems. Adolfo Dorfman, *Historia de la industria argentina* (Buenos Aires, 1970) updates and substantially expands the original 1942 edition. The sectors of the economy indicated are freshly examined in Peter H. Smith, *Politics and Beef in Argentina: Patterns of Conflict and Change* (New York, 1969); James R. Scobie, *Revolution on the Pampas: A Social History of Argentine Wheat* (Austin, 1964); ECLA, *Economic Development and Income Distribution in Argentina* (New York, 1969); and Clarence Zuvekas, Jr., "Economic Growth and Income Distribution in Postwar Argentina," *Inter-American Economic Affairs*, 20, 3 (Winter 1966), 19-38. Within the limits indicated by its title, Winthrop R. Wright, *British-owned Railways in Argentina: Their Effect on Economic Nationalism, 1854-1948* (Austin, 1974), meets the need for a scholarly history of railways in Argentina. The labor movement to 1955 is traced and a guide to the Argentine literature on the subject provided by Samuel L. Baily, *Labor, Nationalism, and Politics in Argentina* (New Brunswick, 1967). Eduardo I. Rumbo, *Petróleo y vasallaje: Carne de vaca y carnero contra carbón más petróleo* (Buenos Aires, 1957), is better balanced and more informative than one might expect from its Peronist author's choice of a title. *El petróleo argentino* by Adolfo Silenzi de Stagni has passed through several editions. Arturo Frondizi, *Petróleo y política* (Buenos Aires, 1954), is strong on politics. Arturo Sabato, *Economía y política del petróleo argentino (1939-1956)* (Buenos Aires, 1957) is more economic. Raúl Larra, *Mosconi, general del petróleo* (Buenos Aires, 1957), is about a leader in the Argentine "battle over petroleum" and the first director of YPF, Enrique Mosconi, who is also represented by his own *Dichos y hechos, 1904-1938* (Buenos Aires, 1938) and *La Batalla del petróleo*, and by *YPF y las empresas extranjeras* (Buenos Aires, 1957), which contains selections from his speeches and writings. Britain's major influence on the Argentine economy is documented in *Britain and Argentina in the Nineteenth Century* (Oxford, 1960), by H. S. Ferns, who made excellent use of British sources; there is no similar work on the twentieth century. For foreign investment in petroleum and mining, see Mikesell et al., under General Works. Francis Masson and James Theberge discuss the investment-development problem in broader terms in "External Capital Requirements and Economic Development: The Case of Argentina," *The Journal of the Royal Statistical Society*, Series A (General), 130, 3 (1967), 378-407.

The broad problem of economic development is laid out in detail in ECLA, *El desarrollo económico de la Argentina* (Mexico, D.F., 1959, 3 vols.). The important role of entrepreneurs in Argentina is examined in a single case in Thomas F. Cochran and Rubén Reina's pioneering *Entrepreneurship in Argentine Culture: Torcuato di Tella and S.I.A.M.* (Philadelphia, 1962). Entrepreneurs as a "class" or group are studied in Dardo Cúneo, *Comportimiento y crisis de la clase empresaria* (Buenos Aires, 1967) and their influence is stressed by Torcuato S. di Tella in "Stalemate or Coexistence in Argentina," in *Latin America: Reform or Revolution?*, eds. Petras and Zeitlin, cited in General Works. Eldon Kenworthy, "Argentina: The Politics of Late Industrialization," *Foreign Affairs*, 45, 3 (April 1967), 463-476, is referred to in the text.

For works on Argentina's relations with the United States, see below, section on U.S. Relations with the Southern Cone. Other postwar works on Argentine foreign relations in general are Isidoro Ruiz Moreno, *Historia de las relaciones exteriores argentinas (1810-1955)* (Buenos Aires, 1961); Sergio Bagú, *Argentina en el mundo* (Buenos Aires, 1961); Carlos A. Florit, *Política exterior nacional* (Buenos Aires, 1960); Lucio Manuel Moreno Quintana, *Elementos de política internacional* (Buenos Aires, 1955); and Alberto A. Conil Paz and Gustavo E. Ferrari, *Argentina's Foreign Policy, 1930-1962,* tr. John J. Kennedy (Notre Dame, 1963). Sir David Victor Kelly's *Ruling Few, or The Human Background to Diplomacy* (London, 1953) stands out among its kind both because of the author's lively comments on people and politics in Argentina while he was Britain's ambassador there and because the Argentine part of his memoirs was promptly put to political use by the publication of a Spanish translation of it by Armando Cascella under the title *La traición de la oligarquía . . .* (Buenos Aires, 1953).

Chile

For the considerable period it covers, Fredrick B. Pike's *Chile and the United States, 1880-1962* (Notre Dame, 1963) renders much the same kind of bibliographical service for Chile as James Scobie's book for Argentina. The main difference is that Pike's references are not gathered together in a bibliography, but scattered through the notes. They are so numerous, however, that not much that was relevant could have been omitted and many are accompanied by descriptive or critical comments. Accordingly, in this case too, the present bibliographical note will be confined mainly to works useful in the making of the present one and published since about 1950.

Among general and largely historical works, a good one to start with is *Fisionomía histórica de Chile*, by Jaime Eyzaguirre (Mexico D.F., 1948), which has lost none of its freshness or cogency with the passage of time. The two most recent works in English, Kalman H. Silvert, *Chile Yesterday and Today* (New York, 1965) and Jay Kinsbruner, *Chile: A Historical Interpretation* (New York, 1973) are compact, informative, and stimulating, and Kinsbruner updates Pike's bibliography on several topics. Julio César Jobet examines a large sweep of the history of Chile with sweeping disapproval in *Tres ensayos históricos* (Santiago, 1950) and *Ensayo crítico del desarrollo económico-social de Chile* (Santiago, 1955). Hernán Ramírez Necochea does likewise in his *Historia del imperialismo en Chile* (Santiago, 1960), which records the rise first of British, then German, and finally U.S. imperialism in Chile, and ends with the triumph of the last-named during World War I. For immigration in Chile and the local reaction, see Carl Solberg, *Immigration and Nationalism: Argentina and Chile,* cited under General Works. A recent work of capital importance on the Germans in Chile is *Les allemands au Chili (1816-1945)*, by Jean-Pierre Blancpain (Cologne, 1974).

Alberto Edwards Vives produced a classic of Chilean political history in *La fronda aristocrática* (Santiago, 1945), and he and Eduardo Frei Montalva did their best to enliven a dull, though important, subject in *Historia de los partidos políti-*

cos chilenos (Santiago, 1949), which is still standard. James Petras brought fresh ideas to bear on Chilean history in his *Politics and Social Forces in Chilean Development* (Berkeley, 1970). Ricardo Donoso, *Las ideas políticas en Chile* (Santiago, 1967, 2nd ed.) is indispensable for the nineteenth century, but stops with 1891. Donoso's *Alessandri, agitador y demoledor: Cincuenta años de historia política* (Mexico D.F., 1952) created a sensation but did not demolish Alessandri. The verdict is not in on his attack on Chile's most prestigious but somewhat overrated historian in *Francisco A. Encina, simulador* (Santiago, 1970, 2 vols.). Much valuable information, historical and of other kinds, is contained in *Area Handbook for Chile* (Washington, 1969), prepared at American University.

A few items on the nineteenth-century history of Chile should be noted. Mateo Martinic Beros, *Presencia de Chile en la Patagonia Austral, 1843-1879* (Santiago, 1971), discusses the internal history of Chilean activity in Patagonia, whereas previous accounts dealt with the area only from the point of view of Chile's diplomatic relations with Argentina. Peter J. Sehlinger, "Cien años de influencia de la obra de Agustín Letelier," *Revista Chilena de Historia y Geografía*, 139 (año 1971), 72-85, sheds more light on the career of this intellectual and political Chilean leader of French Basque extraction. Julio Heise González, "Balmaceda y el parlamentarismo criollo," *ibid.*, 138-140, gives new life to the old controversy over Balmaceda and the revolution of 1891, which it describes as a civil war between two sectors of the bourgeoisie.

"The Social Determinants of Political Democracy in Chile," by Maurice Zeitlin, in Petras and Zeitlin, eds., *Latin America: Reform or Revolution?*, cited, offers seven hypotheses about those determinants. Federico Gil, *The Political System of Chile* (Boston, 1966), is excellent for the system and its operation in the pre-Allende period. Weston H. Agor, *The Chilean Senate* (Austin, 1971) describes that body as exercising "real influence" in Chile and contributing to its political stability. North, *Civil-Military Relations in Argentina, Chile, and Peru*, cited in General Works, notes that the military have been isolated from politics only in Chile, where the middle and upper classes have been largely united. Robert R. Kaufman breaks new ground in *The Chilean Political Right and Agrarian Reform* (Washington, 1967) and *The Politics of Land Reform in Chile, 1950-1970* (Cambridge, Mass., 1972). Two works about the Chilean Communist Party appeared in 1965: Ernst Halperin, *Nationalism and Communism in Chile* (Cambridge, Mass.) and Hernán Ramírez Necochea, *Origen y formación del partido comunista de Chile* (Santiago). This and other parties and groups and their functioning in recent years are described in Ben G. Burnett, *Political Groups in Chile* (Austin, 1970). One postwar development that merits special note is described in Donald Bray, "Peronism in Chile," *Hispanic American Historical Review*, XLVII, 1 (Feb. 1967) 38-49. One of the most valuable works on the blurred border between politics and economics is *Politics and the Labour Movement in Chile,* by Alan Angell (London, 1972).

On the Chilean economy, the first item to be mentioned is *Geografía económica de Chile* (Santiago, 1962 and rev. ed., 1965, 3 vols.) prepared by the Corporación de Fomento de la Producción (CORFO). Studies of the economy since 1950 abound. Some of the best are by Aníbal Pinto Santa Cruz. They include his *Hacia nuestra independencia económica* (Santiago, 1953), *Chile: Un caso de desarrollo frustrado* (Santiago, 1962), and *Chile: Una economía difícil* (Mexico D. F., 1964).

Most authors concentrate on particular aspects: Bruce H. Herrick, *Urban Migration and Economic Development* (Cambridge, Mass., 1965); Markos Mamalakis and Clark W. Reynolds, *Essays on the Chilean Economy* (Homewood, 1965), especially useful for its treatment of the copper industry; William C. Thiesenhausen, *Chile's Experiments in Agrarian Reform* (Madison, 1966); Martin Zañartu and John J. Kennedy, eds., *The Overall Development of Chile* (Notre Dame, 1968), which treats political and social as well as economic development; Ricardo Lagos E., *La concentración del poder económico—su teoría, realidad chilena* (Santiago, 1965, 5th ed.); Donald W. Pearson, "Does Chilean Social Security Fulfill Its Potential for Contributing to Economic Development?," *Inter-American Economic Affairs*, XXV, 1 (1971), 65-83, answers no to this often-asked question; Mario F. Rothschild, "Regional Development and Sectoral Specialization: The Chilean Case" (Ph.D. thesis, Cornell University, 1973); José Cademartori, *La economía chilena, un enfoque marxista* (Santiago, 1971, 2nd ed.), not an unusual *enfoque* (focus); and J. Ann Zammit, ed., *The Chilean Road to Socialism* (Austin, 1973).

Contrary to the impression the foregoing might give, not everyone studies problems of Chile's development in the twentieth century. Arnold J. Bauer, "Chilean Rural Labor in the Nineteenth Century," *American Historical Review*, LXXVI, 4 (Oct. 1971), 1059-1083, strikes nonspecialists and specialists alike as an original work of high quality. See also the same author's *Chilean Rural Society from the Spanish Conquest to 1930* (New York, 1975).

Robert Mosa, *Chile's Marxist Experiment* (New York, 1974), the work of a first-rate British journalist, is useful in correcting the distortion of Chile's domestic history under the Allende regime through excessive concentration on the reported role of multinationals and the U.S. government in bringing about the overthrow of the regime. The domestic history of the Allende period, for the present, has to be written very largely from accounts in newspapers and periodicals. Little reliance can be placed on most of the books on the subject that are worth notice. One of the rare exceptions is Ariel Peralta Pizarro, *El mito de Chile* (Santiago, 1971), which is useful for its analysis of the upper class and the managerial sector. Another is Peter S. Cleaves, *Bureaucratic Politics and Administration in Chile* (Berkeley, 1974), which includes the administrations of both Frei and Allende. Still another is *Chile: A Critical Survey*, by Pablo Baraona Ursúa et al. First published in Santiago in April 1972, the book is frankly anti-Allende, but it contains some substantial articles by well-qualified authorities, such as one on foreign relations by Francisco Orrego Vicuña; one on the church in Chile by the corporatist leader Jaime Guzmán; and one on scientific development in Chile by Igor Saavedra. On the other hand, *Fuerzas armadas y seguridad nacional*, published just after Allende's overthrow, tells little about the armed forces and a great deal about threats to national security coming from Allende's supporters and concludes its justification of the military coup with citations from St. Paul's epistles to the Romans and the Summa Theologica of St. Thomas Aquinas. Almost all materials contain some grist for mills equipped to handle them, but until the works on the Allende period are much more abundant and of better quality than at the present writing, any historical account of it should be regarded as only an interim report.

Chile's foreign relations to 1938 are examined by Mario Barros, a professional diplomat, with patriotic zeal, acumen, and a prologue by veteran historian Jaime Eyzaguirre, in *Historia diplomática de Chile, 1541-1938* (Santiago, 1970). Interest in this aspect of history has not been intense among Chileans since mid-century, if one may judge from the volume of the output. Alejandro Magnet's *Neustros vecinos argentinos* (1956, cited above), contains some information about the attempt by President Ibáñez to involve Chile in a dubious arrangement with Perón's Argentina. The same incident is discussed in an Argentine book by Ginna Maggi Blanco, *Patria y traición (confabulación Ibáñez-Perón)* (Buenos Aires, 1957). Juan José Fernández, *La República de Chile y el Imperio del Brasil, historia de sus relaciones diplomáticas* (Santiago, 1959), brings out an early phase of a familiar theme in Chilean foreign policy. Robert N. Burr, *By Reason or Force: Chile and the Balancing of Power in South America, 1830-1905* (Berkeley, 1965), makes an original and well-documented application of the balance-of-power pattern to South America. Guillermo Lagos Carmona, *Las fronteras de Chile* (Santiago, 1966), is mainly about relations with Argentina. Robert Talbott, *A History of Chilean Boundaries* (Ames, Iowa, 1975), appeared too late to be consulted, but is described by the publisher as the first book to discuss not only the familiar disputes with Argentina, but also all other Chilean boundary disputes from colonial times to the present. Sergio Teitelboim V., *Chile y la soberanía en el mar* (Santiago, 1966), is addressed to an issue of increasing international as well as national significance—the extension of the limit of territorial waters from the once conventional three-mile and then twelve-mile limit to 200 miles or more—an issue that involves fishing rights first of all, but probably much more besides. On the Allende period, items of special interest are Herbert Goldhammer, "The Nonhemispheric Powers in Latin America," in Rand Corporation, *Latin America in the 1970s* (Santa Monica, 1972); James D. Theberge, *Soviet Relations with Allende's Chile and Velasco's Peru* (Washington, n.d.); Régis Debray, *Conversations with Allende* (London, 1971); and Fidel Castro, *Fidel in Chile: Selected Speeches* (New York, 1972).

Uruguay

Although there are many works of broad scope and high quality on Uruguay, none of them provides the same kind of extensive and recent bibliographical coverage for that country that lightened the present bibliographical task in the sections on Argentina and Chile. On the other hand, in the case of Uruguay the task is much lighter to begin with. Partly because it is so much smaller than the other two, Uruguay has produced fewer writers, and for the same reason and others besides, it has attracted much less attention from foreign scholars, journalists, and other writers. As a result, the bibliographical task is of the same order of magnitude and the main difference is that more frequent reference to works published before 1950 will be needed.

Among general histories of Uruguay, first place belongs to the comprehensive and scholarly *Historia de la República Oriental del Uruguay, 1830-1930*, by Juan E. Pivel Devoto and Alcira Ranieri de Pivel Devoto (Montevideo, 1945). A close second is Alberto Zum Felde's stimulating *Proceso histórico del Uruguay* (Montevideo, 1967, 5th ed.), first published in 1920. Luis C. Benevenuto, *Breve historia del Uruguay* (Buenos Aires, 1967), is clear as well as brief and brings the narrative through the 1950s. A work of fine scholarship is Juan Antonio Oddone, *La formación del Uruguay moderno: La inmigración y el desarrollo económico-social* (Buenos Aires, 1966). Unfortunately, none of these has been translated into English.

The best broad but scholarly introductory work in English is George Pendle's admirably compact *Uruguay,* but it is outdated even in its most recent edition (London, 1957, 2nd ed.), particularly in its statement that since 1911, constitutional reform has been the main issue in Uruguayan politics. Russell H. Fitzgibbon's *Uruguay, Portrait of a Democracy* (New Brunswick, 1954), might have served the purpose for a while and still has merit, but within five years he was already questioning his book's central proposition that Uruguay was a "great exemplar of democracy": see his essay on Uruguay in Fredrick B. Pike, ed., *Freedom and Reform in Latin America* (Notre Dame, 1959), 231-255. Similarly, Simon G. Hanson, *Utopia in Uruguay* (New York, 1938) sounds utopian indeed in the 1970s, although many of its detailed findings are still valid. In this situation, the very good *Area Handbook for Uruguay,* by Thomas Weil *et al.* (Washington, 1971), becomes doubly important to readers of English only. Martin Weinstein's topically comprehensive *Uruguay: The Politics of Failure* (Westport, 1975) covers the last two decades.

Contributions to a better understanding of Uruguay's development in its first century of independence include Edmundo M. Narancio, ed., *Artigas. Estudios publicados . . . en el centenario de su muerte, 1850-1950* (Montevideo, 1951), which shows, among other things, how the African slave trade stimulated the growth of Montevideo; John Street, *Artigas and the Emancipation of Uruguay* (Cambridge, England, 1959), is the best book on that liberator; Luis Alberto de Herrera, *Los orígenes de la Guerra Grande* (Montevideo, 1941, 2 vols.), contains a wealth of information about a war that was really great in the history of the Plata area; Carlos M. Rama, *Garibaldi en el Uruguay* (Montevideo, 1968), shows how the Italian "hero of both worlds" aided Uruguay not only by his martial exploits, but also by stimulating Italian immigration; Juan Antonio Oddone, *El principismo del setenta* (Montevideo, 1956), stresses the 1870s in tracing that important movement in favor of establishing civilian control; Arturo Ardao, *Rodó: su americanismo* (Montevideo, 1970), and Hugo Torrano, *Rodó—Acción y libertad: Restauración de su imagen* (Montevideo, 1973). Milton I. Vanger, *José Batlle y Ordóñez of Uruguay: The Creator of His Times, 1902-1907* (Cambridge, Mass., 1963), an excellent first volume, has not yet been followed by the intended second, but Vanger made important supplementary observations about Batlle and his successor in the presidency in his "Politics and Class," cited under General Works.

An excellent introduction to the political system and politics of Uruguay, Philip B. Taylor, Jr.'s *Government and Politics of Uruguay* (New Orleans, 1960), was outdated in part by the adoption in 1967 of a new constitution replacing the collegial with a presidential system, and still more by the establishment of a dictatorship. Nevertheless, much that he wrote is still valid, partly because he took heed of the warning signs that appeared in Uruguay's public life from the mid-1950s onwards. Ronald H. McDonald added greatly to an understanding of the political system by two articles: "Legislative Politics in Uruguay. A Preliminary Statement," in Weston H. Agor, ed., *Latin American Legislatures,* cited under General Works, 113-135, and "Electoral Politics and Uruguayan Political Decay," *Inter-American Economic Affairs,* XXVI, 1 (Summer 1972), 25-45. That Uruguayans had been well aware of this "political decay" for some time is shown by Carlos Real de Azúa's *El impulso y su freno; tres décadas de Batllismo y las raíces de la crisis uruguaya* (Montevideo,

1964), and by Juan José Ayala, *Las críticas de un "amargado." (Corrupción pública y privada de nuestra sociedad)* (Montevideo, n. d.). See also Carlos M. Rama, "El Uruguay indócil," *Cuadernos Americanos,* No. 6 (July 1972), which described the Catholic clergy in Uruguay as the most democratic in Latin America, but warned that a military dictatorship "is now possible" and blamed the U.S. aid program for promoting the militarization of Uruguay. A valuable commentary on the Constitution of 1967 is provided by Julio María Sanguinetti and Alvaro Pacheco in *La nueva constitución. Ensayo* (Montevideo, 1967).

A recent account of the armed forces, formerly trained by France, is found in Gabriel Ramírez, *Las fuerzas armadas uruguayas en la crisis continental* (Montevideo, 1971). They were brought to the fore by the organized violence that welled up in Uruguay, as in the other Southern Cone countries, after the early 1960s. The urban Tupamaros, by far the most important guerrilla group in Uruguay, rate a 10-page section in John Gerassi's international roundup of such groups, *Towards Revolution* (London, 1971, 2 vols), and have had several books written about them. A fair sample is *The Tupamaro Guerrillas,* by María Esther Gilio, tr. Anne Edmondson, introduction by Robert J. Alexander (New York, 1972). The British ambassador to Uruguay, Sir Geoffrey Jackson, who was kidnapped and held prisoner for eight months by the Tupamaros, wrote a book about his experience, *People's Prison* (London, 1973); in the New York edition, 1974, the title was expanded to *Surviving the Long Night: An Autobiographical Account of a Political Kidnapping.* Up-to-date data about the numbers and equipment of the armed forces and the police are provided in *The Military Balance, 1974-1975,* cited under General Works.

Social problems are examined critically in Carlos Rama, *Las clases sociales en el Uruguay* (Montevideo, 1960), and in Aldo Solari, *El desarrollo social del Uruguay en la postguerra: Ensayo* (Montevideo, 1967), and through rose-colored glasses in Isaac Ganón, *Estructura social del Uruguay* (Montevideo, 1966). A previously neglected area is covered in Ildefonso Pereda Valdés, *El negro en el Uruguay* (Montevideo, 1965). Rosanna Segni and Adela Pelegrino, eds., *Bosquejos e impresiones de Montevideo: Selección de viajeros, 1850-1914* (Paysandú, n.d.), contains brief excerpts from the writings of 17 foreign travellers including French statesman Georges Clemenceau. Two of the most interesting excerpts are from A. F. de Fontpertuis, *Etudes sur l'Amérique Latine* (Paris, 1881), and Theodore Child, *Les Républiques sudaméricaines* (Paris, 1891), the last-named recording his visit to Uruguay during the economic crisis of 1890.

The scarcity of thorough economic studies of Uruguay is explained by the statement of the Instituto de Economía in its *Uruguay: Estadísticas básicas* (Montevideo, 1969) that the statistics it gathered for this work and its separately published *El proceso económico del Uruguay* were hard to get and incomplete because, for one thing, there had been only two general censuses in this century and, for another, only recently had sample surveys begun to be made for the purpose of gathering data on occupation, unemployment, distribution of income, and other aspects of the economy. Aldo Solari, et al., *Uruguay en cifras* (Montevideo, 1966), is a conveniently compact assemblage of statistics. Major economic problems are discussed in Abraham Guillén Arapey, *Uruguay: País en crisis* (Montevideo, n.d.), collected newspaper articles, the latest published in 1965. In Albert O. Hirschman,

Development Projects Observed (Washington, 1967), one project that he observed without pleasure was aimed at the improvement of livestock and pastures in Uruguay on the basis of a joint mission report of the World Bank and the Food and Agriculture Organization. Russell H. Bannon, *The Agricultural Development of Uruguay* (New York, 1968), blames the *latifundistas* for the failure to invest in technological improvements. Hanson's *Utopia in Uruguay,* cited above, fully justifies its subtitle, *Chapters in the Economic History of Uruguay.*

Culture is perhaps even more closely bound up with politics in Uruguay than in the other two Southern Cone countries. Nowhere is their union brought out more clearly than in the works of that country's leading intellectual historian, Arturo Ardao. It stands out most of all in his *Racionalismo y liberalismo en el Uruguay* (Montevideo, 1962), which concludes with the close of the nineteenth century and sets the stage for José Enrique Rodó and *Ariel.* Juan Zorilla de San Martín, *Detalles de historia* (Montevideo, 1930), reports the current opinion of "not a few Hispanic Americans" that it would be a good thing to send Ariel packing and acclimate Caliban. How this attitude developed in the next generation into the absorption of many intellectuals with public affairs, is shown by Carlos Real de Azúa in his two-volume *Antología del ensayo urugayo* (Montevideo, 1964).

Although Uruguay owed its independence to international action and had important foreign interests from the start, its government's international role was, nevertheless, rather negative until the country's time of troubles ended (for almost half a century) in 1904. Two years later, Luis Alberto de Herrera, a leader in public life for the next four decades, published an attack on the Argentine Drago Doctrine for what he took to be its bias against the United States. In 1912 he followed this up with *El Uruguay internacional* (Paris, 1912), which was full of foreign policy prescriptions. During the world war that broke out two years later, Uruguay did in fact begin to play the positive (and generally pro-United States and pro-Pan American) role that it was to maintain for the next third of a century, as illustrated by Oscar Abadie-Aicardie in his *El Uruguay, los Estados Unidos y la Unión Pan-americana (1916-1918)* (Montevideo, 1969); Telmo Manacorda, *Itinerario y espíritu de Jacobo Varela* (Montevideo, 1950); Alberto Guani, *Motivos internacionales: Algunos discursos . . .* (Montevideo, 1943); and Eduardo Victor Haedo, *En defensa de la soberanía; discursos . . . 1942-1946* (Montevideo, 1946). For a contemporary account of the Rodríguez Larreta Doctrine of 1945, in which this phase culminated, see *Inter-American Affairs: An Annual Survey,* ed. Arthur P. Whitaker, No. 5 (New York, 1946), 30-36. Left-wing pressure for a radical change in foreign policy is illustrated by Vivián Trías, *El plan Kennedy y la revolución latinoamericana* (Montevideo, 1961) and *Imperialismo y petróleo en el Uruguay* (Montevideo, n.d. [1963?]). In this connection, see Aldo Solari's *El tercerismo en el Uruguay: Ensayo* (Montevideo, 1965), in which he shows that something like "third-worldism" and not very different from Perón's Third Position of the late 1940s was espoused in Uruguay as early as the 1930s. Juan Antonio Oddone opened a new mine of source materials with his *Una perspectiva europea del Uruguay: Los informes diplomáticos y consulares italianos, 1862-1914* (Montevideo, 1965).

U.S. Relations with the Southern Cone

To an even greater extent than in the foregoing categories, the reader who wishes to follow up developments in this one is dependent on works dealing with Latin America in general. The scanty literature on U.S. relations with individual countries of the Southern Cone consists mainly of widely scattered articles in periodicals. The only recent books on any of the three that cover a substantial period of history are Harold F. Peterson, *Argentina and the United States, 1810-1960* (New York, 1964) and Fredrick B. Pike, *Chile and the United States, 1880-1962,* cited above, which is mainly about Chile. There is no such book on Uruguay, though R. H. Fitzgibbon and P. B. Taylor do something to fill the gap in the twentieth century. There are a few books of more limited scope on U.S. relations with each of the three countries, such as Ariosto Fernández, *Primeras relaciones políticas y sociales entre la República Oriental del Uruguay y los Estados Unidos de América* (Montevideo, 1958); Alberto Conil Paz, *La Argentina y los Estados Unidos en la sexta conferencia panamericana (La Habana, 1928)* (Buenos Aires, 1965); Clarence H. Haring, *Argentina and the United States* (Boston, 1941); and James Petras, *The United States and Chile: Imperialism and the Overthrow of the Allende Government* (New York, 1975). Articles are numerous; some are cited below.

Previously published books and articles are cited and some are evaluated in Peterson, Pike, and the general histories of relations, among which are Samuel Flagg Bemis, *The Latin American Policy of the United States* (New York, 1943); Dexter Perkins, *A History of the Monroe Doctrine* (1963); and J. Lloyd Mecham, *The United States and Inter-American Security, 1889-1960* (Austin, 1961). Bibliographical aid is provided in more circumscribed but still broad fields by James W. Gantenbein, ed., *The Evolution of Our Latin American Policy, a Documentary Record* (New York, 1950); Arthur P. Whitaker, *The Western Hemisphere Idea: Its Rise and Decline* (Ithaca, 1954); J. Fred Rippy, *British Investments in Latin America* (Chicago, 1959); Joseph S. Tulchin, *The Aftermath of War: World War I and U.S. Policy toward Latin America* (New York, 1971); Richard B. Gray, ed., *Latin America and the United States* (Itasca, 1971), a collection of articles, most of them written in the 1960s; Martin C. Needler, *The United States and the Latin American Revolution* (Boston, 1972); and James R. Kurth, "United States Foreign Policy and Latin American Military Rule," in P. C. Schmitter, ed., *Military Rule in Latin America* (cited under General Works), 243-322. In many cases, however, the reader will have to refer to the usual guides.

Times have changed since Bemis, in the work just cited, found the record of the United States in its dealings with Latin America ever since independence all but spotless. Even he called our Caribbean policy imperialism, though he qualified it as benevolent and protective. Imperialist action, however, was generally agreed, by attackers and advocates alike, to be restricted to the unstable and backward Caribbean area and to have ceased in the 1930s with the adoption of Roosevelt's Good Neighbor policy. Now, in the 1970s, the record is being re-examined as the old Caribbean policy is being extended to the Southern Cone of South America and fidelity to the nonintervention rule is giving way to the doctrine of inevitable intervention. Critics of U.S. Latin American policy in this country flourished again in the 1960s and 1970s. They were appearing in somewhat delayed response to the influence of the New Left revisionists who were descended from Charles A. Beard and led by William Appleman Williams, and who were mainly concerned with debunking the role of the United States in World War II and the Cold War and took little interest in Latin America.

A leading revisionist work of this kind is *The Roots of American Foreign Policy,* by Gabriel Kolko (Boston, 1969), which in the more limited Latin American field has a milder companion piece in *Latin America and the United States: The Changing Political Realities,* Julio Cotler and Richard Fagen, eds. (Stanford, 1974). Both are polemical in part, but in both there are important points that rest on a firm foundation and are unmarred by what Kolko calls "debilitating ideological differences." An example from his book that is as significant for U.S. relations with Latin America as with any other area is his conclusion that from 1944 to 1960 the "top foreign-policy decision makers [in Washington] were . . . intimately connected with dominant business circles and their law firms"; and his conclusion is based on a Brookings Institution study, *Men Who Govern,* by Daniel T. Stanley et al. (Washington, 1967), as well as on his own investigation. The same point is illustrated by several of the wide-ranging essays in Cottler and Fagen's book, but best of all by Ernest R. May's elegant case study of United States-Argentine relations, 1942-1947, under the main title "The Bureaucratic Politics Approach."

The impact of the revisionist approach was barely perceptible or nonexistent in most U.S. works on Latin American relations even in the 1960s — in, for example, *The Framework of Hemisphere Defense,* by Stetson Conn and Bryan Fairchild (Washington, 1960); Bryce Wood's *The Making of the Good Neighbor Policy* (New York, 1961) and *The United States and Latin American Wars, 1932-1942* (New York, 1966); Willard F. Barber and C. Neal Ronning, *Internal Security and Military Power: Counterinsurgency and Civic Action in Latin America* (Columbus, 1966); and Leslie B. Rout, Jr., *Politics of the Chaco Peace Conference, 1935-1939* (Austin, 1970).

The New Left influence was clear, though moderately expressed, in *The Containment of Latin America: A History of the Myths and Realities of the Good Neighbor Policy,* by David Green (Chicago, 1971). Green, who stresses the relations of the United States with Argentina, concedes that the policy was benevolent in intention, but maintains that in practice it became a protracted effort to "contain" Latin America. Since his text shows that by contain he means dominate, monopolize, and exploit, "corral" might have been more accurate. The principal works on the Good Neighbor Policy are cited by Green, and Wood's political interpretation of it is challenged by William G. Cooper with an economic one in "New Light on the Good Neighbor Policy" (Ph.D. thesis, University of Pennsylvania, 1972). See also Dick Steward, *Trade and Hemisphere: The Good Neighbor Policy and Reciprocal Trade* (Columbia, 1975).

A good starting point for reading on political relations between the United States and Latin America during World War II and the aftermath is Mecham's *The United States and Inter-American Security,* cited above. Since its publication a valuable addition to the literature has been made by the publication of *Diplomats and Demagogues: The Memoirs of Spruille Braden* (New Rochelle, 1971). Braden played an important part in the Chaco Peace Conference in Buenos Aires, 1935-1939, and in U.S. relations with the Southern Cone countries, especially Argentina, from 1945 to 1947; and in addition he had personal ties, beginning much earlier, with Chile. The postwar years are discussed in Pike, *Chile and the United States;* Arthur P. Whitaker, *The United States and Argentina,* and Peterson, *Argentina and the United States,* all cited above.

The Alliance That Lost Its Way: A Critical Report on the Alliance for Progress, by Jerome Levinson and Juan de Onís (Chicago, 1970), is the most useful book on that subject. The work of a former alliance official and a journalist familiar with Latin America, it provides an account of the background in the 1950s and of the adoption and operation of the alliance in the 1960s, and its footnotes contain abundant references to the sources and secondary works. Chile was a chief recipient of alliance aid and one of the four Latin American countries on whose experiences the authors drew most heavily. Argentina, along with Mexico, they note, had only a "marginal relationship to the alliance in domestic terms," and they make only a few references to Uruguay. The best account of the alliance from early 1961 to late 1963, as viewed from the White House, is in Arthur M. Schlesinger, Jr., *A Thousand Days* (Boston, 1965). Adolf A. Berle, who played a major part in getting the alliance started, is not very informative about its start in his otherwise very good, though too brief, *Latin America—Diplomacy and Reality* (New York, 1962); much more about it will be found in his published correspondence and papers.

Disappointment with the alliance helped promote the search for better ways of aiding developing countries that is reflected in *American Aid for Development* (New York, 1972), by Paul G. Clark, which is global but makes several references to Latin America and proposes its continuation there as elsewhere. Also global, but hostile to aid as practiced so far, is *The Trojan Horse: A Radical Look at Foreign Aid* (San Francisco, 1974), by Steve Weissman et al. It is cited here as another example of revisionist writing about U.S. relations with Latin America.

The spread of revisionism in academic as well as nonacademic circles was stimulated by current events, not only in Southeast Asia and the Middle East, but in all three Southern Cone countries as well, and above all by Allende's overthrow. Prime examples are James Petras, *The United States and Chile,* cited above, and Richard Fagen, "The United States and Chile: Roots and Branches," *Foreign Affairs* (January 1975), 297-313. See Fagen's epistolary clash with Paul Sigmund in the same issue, 375-377; the latter's better balanced and more persuasive account of U.S. policy, " 'The Invisible Blockade' and the Overthrow of Allende," in the January 1974 issue of the same journal, 322-340; and the revelations in *Multinational Corporations and United States Foreign Policy.* Hearings before the Sub-Committee on Inter-American Affairs of the Senate Committee on Foreign Relations, Parts 1 and 2 (Washington, 1973). The charge of U.S. intervention was pressed by Armando Uribe, a former member of the Allende government, in *The Black Book of American Intervention in Chile* (Boston, 1974). The thesis that Allende fell for other reasons was sustained by two British writers in *Encounter:* David Holden, "Allende and the Myth Makers. Political Realism and Revolutionary Romance," XLII, 1 (January 1974), 12-24, and Robert Moss, "Chile's Coup and After. Letter from Santiago," XLII, 3 (March 1974), 72-80.

For U.S. relations with the Southern Cone countries in or through international organizations, see particularly John A. Houston, *Latin America and the United Nations* (New York, 1956) and Jerome Slater, *The OAS and United States Foreign Policy* (Columbus, 1967). Divergent views of the Organization of American States are expressed in *The Organization of American States and the Hemisphere Crisis* (New York, 1962), by John Dreier, an old State Department hand, and *The Inter-American System* (London, 1966) and the broader *The United States and Latin*

America: An Historical Analysis . . . (New York, 1974), both by Gordon Connell-Smith, a British scholar. For a French view, with historical background, see *L'Amérique latine, la Doctrine Monroe et le Panaméricanisme: Le conditionnement historique du Tiers-Monde latino-américain* (Paris, 1969), by Pierre Quenille, a former member of the French delegation to the UN Assembly.

Further Reading

Readers who wish to look further will find many suggestions, sometimes formal bibliographies, in the works listed above. They should also consult the annual *Handbook of Latin American Studies* and the appropriate journals listed in it, especially those in economics, international relations, government, history, literature, and sociology. Charles C. Griffin, ed., *Latin America: A Guide to the Historical Literature* (Austin, 1971), is selective and includes few items published after 1966. The most useful government publications in the United States are likely to be the State Department's series, *Foreign Relations of the United States,* and its *Bulletin,* and the Commerce Department's *Survey of Current Business.* Statistics will be found in various ECLA publications, most regularly in its annual *Economic Survey of Latin America;* the annual *Statistical Abstract* of Latin America, prepared at the University of California, Los Angeles; the UN *Statistical Yearbook* and other publications; and the *Statesman's Yearbook.* For voracious readers, there are periodic reports by major New York and Boston banks that have (or until recently, had) branches in the Southern Cone and by governmental or private organizations active in that area, such as the IMF, the World Bank, FAO, IDB, and ADELA. For current news, convenient regular sources are *The Times of the Americas* (Washington, D.C., biweekly) and *Latin America: A Weekly Political Report* (London). Irregular but sometimes more detailed reporting is provided by the *New York Times, The Times* (London), *Le Monde* (Paris), and other newspapers, and by *The Economist* and other magazines. Censorship in recent years has made it prudent to handle with care news reports emanating from all three Southern Cone countries.

Index